CAMELOT'S HONOUR

Sarah Zettel was born in California in 1966. She is the author of the acclaimed *Isavalta Trilogy* (*A Sorcerer's Treason*, *The Usurper's Crown* and *The Firebird's Vengeance*), a romantic fantasy based on the folklores of Russia, China and India, as well as *Camelot's Shadow*, her first Arthurian romance. She has also written several science fiction novels and many short stories in various genres. Sarah Zettel lives in Michigan with her husband and their son.

By Sarah Zettel

A Sorcerer's Treason
The Usurper's Crown
The Firebird's Vengeance

Camelot's Shadow
Camelot's Honour

SARAH ZETTEL

Camelot's Honour

HarperCollins*Publishers*

This novel is entirely a work of fiction.
The names, characters and incidents portrayed in it are
the work of the author's imagination. Any resemblance to
actual persons, living or dead, events or localities is
entirely coincidental.

HarperCollins*Publishers*
77-85 Fulham Palace Road,
Hammersmith, London W6 8JB

www.harpercollins.co.uk

Published by HarperCollins*Publishers* 2005
1

A catalogue record for this book
is available from the British Library

ISBN 0 00 715869 6

Typeset in Meridien by Palimpsest Book Production,
Polmont, Stirlingshire

Printed and bound in Great Britain by
Clays Limited, St Ives plc

This book is dedicated to Susan Cooper,
with thanks, from a grateful reader.

ACKNOWLEDGEMENTS

I had a great deal of help on the details for this one. I'd like to thank Lisa Spangenberg for her help with the Welsh Language and insight into the story of Geraint and Elen, Mercedes Lackey for her help with the habits of hawks, Susan Shwartz and Jane Yolen and the women of SF-FFWs for their advice and insight on the Matter of Britain.

All mistakes, accidental or intentional, are my own.

As ever, I'd like to thank the patient Untitled Writers Group, my editors and agents, and my loving husband and son.

WELSH PRONUNCIATION

Many of the names in this story, both for people and places, are in Welsh. The following are some general guidelines for pronouncing some of the less familiar Welsh spellings.

CH   Has the hard sound as in 'Bach' or 'loch'.

DD   Pronounced 'th' as in 'thin' or 'this'.

F   Pronounced 'v' as in 'villain' or the 'f' of 'of'.

FF   Pronounced 'f' as in 'fox'.

LL   Can be pronounced 'thl'.

RH   Pronounced as if the 'h' came before the 'r'.

U   Can either have the short sound, as in 'run' or a long 'ee'.

W   Pronounced 'oo' as in 'pool'.

Y   Generally pronounced as the long 'ee' when at the end of a word, or as the short 'u' when at the beginning or in the middle.

I only desire ... that this game shall no longer exist here, nor the hedge of mist, nor magic, nor enchantment ... Cause, then, the mist to disappear from this place.

From 'Geraint the Son of Erbin', translated by Lady Charlotte Guest.

PROLOGUE

The West Lands, Midsummer's Eve, Anno Domini 350.

Maius the Smith sat beside the river, where the shadow of the bridge would fall come the morning. He kept a solitary vigil as the evening star rose up from the horizon. His cloak was thick, but the night was warm, and he had it slung back over his broad shoulders. The wind blew softly across his tattooed arms and shaved scalp, bringing with it the sweet smoke of the bonfires that burned on top of the hill. The rest of his folk were feasting themselves nearly sick on pig's flesh and strong beer. Later, they would dance and drink and cheer the long days, and make sacrifice of love and life to bring god and goddess down to walk among the grain.

Maius himself had not participated in the bonfire rites since he took the iron hammer from his father. He had a different watch to keep.

The bridge beside him was made of great stone slabs. Some said they were kin to the healing stones of the plain henges which were won from the *scoti* witches on the green isle. The Roman lords who forced their road beside the river looked at them and shook their heads, talking in their odd, flat tongue of levers and rollers, ropes and weights. They did not believe what Maius told them, but neither did they laugh. They lived in strange cities far from the good earth, but they knew well there were other worlds that were none of men's making. They knew that those who dwelt there must have their roads, even as men must.

Twice a year, midsummer and midwinter, the crossing was open. Twice a year, one would come from that other world, tall and beautiful, or small and brown. They would have a thing to mend – a cup or a jewelled brooch, a wheel or a sword. Their kind could not work metals, but they used them, all save iron which was man's secret alone. Maius would take the thing and mend it and bring it back for the morning. That must be done or those others would be angry, and the great bridge would be taken away, and far more than that.

There was safety to be had dwelling beside the bridge, for there were things that would never come here, hauntings and bad luck and famine, but there was danger too. The anger of these neighbours would be terrible if it ever fell. They accepted that. The chief stood surety for all of them, and Maius paid tribute by the loan of his skill when it was asked for, as his son would after him.

Hoofbeats sounded against the stone, and Maius surged to his feet. No man with wit about him stood unafraid before those that crossed from the twilight road, but Maius's iron hammer hung from his belt. No elfshot could touch him, no glamour overtake him, not with iron his protector.

All the same, he whispered a prayer to Rhiannon and Mother Don as the shadow took shape on the bridge, crossing from the eastern side.

The horse drew near enough for Maius to see the rider, and the bulky smith felt his jaw drop. This was not one of the tall white steeds favoured by the Fair Ones. This was only . . . a horse. A good horse such that a Roman might not sneer at, but just a brown horse. And the man in the saddle was no more than a man wearing a belted tunic of good cloth with a golden torque flashing around his throat and gold rings on his arms. He carried a long spear, the shaft of which was carved with runes so strange that Maius, who knew the mysteries of his craft and more besides, could make nothing of them.

The rider reined his horse to a halt at the edge of the steps, and beast and man looked down on Maius, standing there gaping like a boy in his surprise at seeing a mortal man on this night.

The stranger smiled. 'The gods be with you. Are you the one they call Maius the Smith?'

Maius gripped the cool iron of his hammer and gathered his wits together. 'I am. Who are you that comes unafraid by such a road tonight?'

The question seemed to amuse the rider. 'I am the king of the Little Country, Maius Smith, the ruler of the hidden lands and the secret way.' He chuckled at his own riddles.

For all that he wore gold, he was just a man, and Maius's astonishment turned fast to anger. 'Well, Little King, I tell you, you should not be abroad, but should take shelter with other men.'

'But, Maius, I have come to make your fortune.'

Maius's brow furrowed. This stank. It stank like iron gone rotten with rust. What was this riddling man? 'How's that?' he asked.

'I have need of a smith who knows the deeper mysteries, whose hands know how to work more than earthly gold. I have come a long way at a dangerous time to invite you to my service.' His hand reached beneath his cloak, and he tossed something small and dark at Maius's feet. 'Come willingly and this toy is the least reward you shall have.'

Maius did not take his eyes from the stranger, but he did

bend down and feel through the grass until he found what
had been thrown down. A great jewel lay heavy and cold in
his palm, winking in the light of the rising moon. He could
not tell its colour, but in the moonlight it was so dark as to
be almost black, and its facets were so sharp and so tiny he
could not count them all.

Involuntarily, Maius thought of what he could do with
such a gem. With gold enough he could work it into a ring
that could grace the arm of the Governor's wife, or the
Governor himself. It was cattle, this gem, it was dowry for
his daughters, goods for his house and pride for his wife,
perhaps it was even a second wife to grace him. And more
where this came from.

He looked up at the rider, and the man had a serious
demeanour.

'I need you, Maius Smith,' he said, his words as weighty
as the rich stone in Maius's hands. 'I need a man who is not
afraid to touch the great workings, who can bend his craft
to the arts invisible. No common man can aid me in my
kingdom. You are the only one.' He stretched his hand out.
'Come with me and I swear you will learn mysteries beyond
the telling and craft such as no smith has worked since the
god Vulcan walked on the earth.'

The stranger's words went straight to Maius's pride, and
from there to his heart. He looked at the outstretched hand
and all the promises overcame sober wisdom. Not even the
shining ones, the *tylwyth teg*, had offered him the secrets of
the things he mended, much less such wealth. With these
thoughts filling him, Maius grasped the hand the rider held
out to him, and in that oldest gesture, he sealed the bargain.

Before Maius could pull his hand from that strong grasp,
the rider swiftly touched the smith's shoulder with the tip
of his spear. The night shivered around them, split and folded
in on itself, and smith and rider were swallowed whole.

The hammer which should have protected the life and soul of Maius Smith lay alone beneath the stars, waiting to be found with the morning.

ONE

Pont Cymryd, Anno Domini 521

'So, your mother welcomes the men from Camelot?'

A shadow fell across Elen where she knelt beneath the trees. She did not turn. She recognized the booming voice well. Elen sighed towards the morning's treasure: an oaken stump that had yielded a magnificent and unexpected crop of crooked-capped mushrooms. Reluctantly, she stood, carefully brushing off the skirt of her dress, then her hands, tossing her black braids over her shoulders before smoothing down her green cloak.

It was only then she turned to face Urien, whose followers styled him *y Tarw* 'the Bull'. He certainly looked the part. He was a bluff and rugged man with thick red-brown hair and arms like a smith's that were banded with blue tattoos and silver rings. He rode a shaggy, black beast of a horse. His iron knife and nail-studded club hung in plain view on his leather belt. His broad shoulders were only partly hidden by the green-and-brown striped cloak that was clasped with a silver brooch in the shape of three cranes. Behind him, on uncombed ponies, rode two of his men. Both were hulking creatures with thick shoulders and strong hands. The one on Urien's right had a round face with a toad's goggling eyes. The other was a starved wolf, his brown hair and beard equally tangled. He kept looking down the path as if he expected enemies to leap through the trees.

Elen wanted to ask him what he feared so, but she made herself pay attention to Urien. 'Arthur's ambassadors came with all signs of respect and asked for the hospitality of our house,' she said, keeping her tone carefully bland. Whatever she thought of him, Urien was the chief of the cantrev Eufaen, their neighbour immediately to the west. As such, he must be given at least the show of respect. 'Is it your counsel, Sir, that my mother should have turned them away?'

Urien's face clouded. *Not that it was not dark enough to begin with,* Elen thought sourly to herself.

'It is known that since your father died your mother looks east.' Urien's black horse stamped impatiently.

Elen's jaw clenched. Father had thought well enough of the High King at Camelot, and mother had concurred, but it would accomplish nothing to remind this man of her father's feelings. It was the shade of her father that kept him at bay, and that shade was stretched very thin these days.

'My mother has not yet shared her thoughts with me on this matter.'

'I don't believe you.' Urien leaned over his mount's neck to peer more closely at her. 'In this cantrev, the women rule.'

Elen picked up her basket, although it was only half full and she had not yet picked the stump clean of its treasures. The earthy scent of mushrooms rose invitingly, making her stomach growl. 'Do you wish to speak of this with my mother? You will find her in our house.' Elen did not have the patience for the verbal dance. She had work to do.

'Perhaps I will, at that.' Urien took up his reins again. 'As her daughter seems to know so little of what happens in her family's house.'

Elen held her peace, but only with difficulty. Overhead, the wind whispered to the trees and their branches swayed back and forth. A crow cawed three times. An omen, surely, but of what? Elen shook her head.

'You are a bright spark,' Urien went on. 'You look suspiciously on this embassy of Camelot's, and I'll wager your brother does too. He's no fool either.'

Elen opened her mouth, but did not know what to say. It was no help at all that she was worried by the arrival of these men. Urien had a darkness in him, but at least it was a darkness she knew, like the storms in summer. What came from Camelot was utterly strange, and to her shame, that strangeness frightened her. But she would not give voice to any such thoughts before Urien.

The sound of footsteps on the path saved her from having to answer. Carys, her brother's betrothed, picked her way down the crooked path, a pale basket resting on one ample hip.

Carys saw Urien and pulled up short. 'My lord Urien,' she said, bowing her head respectfully. 'I had not thought to find you here. I was coming to my sister, who has not yet broken her fast.' She rummaged beneath the white cloth that covered the basket's contents and pulled out a fresh loaf of bread. Elen could smell its enticing warmth from where she stood. 'Will you stay and eat with us, my lord?' Carys had an easy way with courtesy that Elen envied. She would make Yestin an excellent wife and do honour to their house.

Elen felt a rush of relief as Urien shook his head. 'I thank you, but I must continue to the house. I have words to speak with *Arglwyddes* Adara. Think on what has passed here, Elen,' he added before he sent his shaggy horse trotting down the path.

Once Urien was well out of earshot, Carys asked, 'And what is it you're to remember?'

'To fear the east, I think.' *As if we needed reminding.* She took a deep breath and with difficulty turned her thoughts from Urien. 'Have you been to the bridge yet?'

Carys shook her head. 'I've the milk with me. Your mother said we should go together.'

Elen took up her own basket. 'That should be done before we eat. Come.'

They took the path, heading in the opposite direction from the way Urien had gone. It sloped downwards through the thick trees, meandering as it went, in the way of a track that had been made by passing feet rather than by careful plan. Soon, it joined up with a broader way suitable for a cart, a herd of cows, or even a group of men on horseback. The birds called all around them, saluting the morning and each other. The sun slipped through the trees, making patches of warmth on cheeks and shoulders as they passed beneath the leaves. A beautiful summer morning. Were it not for the shadow of Urien, Elen would be enjoying herself.

They did not have far to go before the greenwood opened onto the grassy riverbank. The River Usk sparkled gold and silver in the morning sun. A pair of boats floated on it, with their men setting out lines to fish the waters as they flowed beneath the bridge. On the other side, beyond the rushes, rolled green meadowland cut by the old Roman road that led all the way to the coast. Beyond that, rose the ranks of the Black Mountains, dark green and brooding, fencing in their valley and guarding their own.

Their cantrev was Pont Cymryd – the Taken Bridge – and the bridge that gave their land its name was an ancient thing. No graceful Roman arch, it was a pair of grey stone slabs lain end-to-end, each wide enough for two men to ride abreast. Six pillars that had been sunk into the river bed supported the great stones a bare yard above the water. More than once, Elen had seen the spring floods wash over the bridge. The shallow steps had hollows worn in them from generations of feet. There was no rail or wall to keep the unwary from falling from one of the edges, only the wide water below.

There were those who said no one knew who had built the strange bridge. There were others who said it was known all too well. Mother was inclined to keep certain observances and customs in regard to it. Elen had never found cause to fault this, whatever the travelling priests might have to say. One of them swore he would show the cantrev that all the old tales were nonsense, and on midsummer's night he rode his horse over the bridge, brandishing his cross and singing loudly. Priest and horse vanished into the darkness, and neither was ever seen again. They did find the cross, though, or so old Trent told her, on the near side of the river, floating forlornly among the rushes.

Then there was the even older story of Maius the Smith whose daughters were the founding of her own line. He had withheld what belonged to those whose lands lay across the bridge, and for punishment was taken away and never seen again. Only his iron hammer was found. Aeddan still kept its head wrapped in white linen at his forge.

She and Carys were not the first to visit the bridge this morning. Bouquets of flowers, little heaps of grain and even a few late strawberries, had been placed beside the worn steps. Most other days, there would be men at the bridge, taking the toll from any bringing goods or cattle across. Not today. Today, all could pass freely, until sunset. When dark came, no one would set foot on the bridge. Tonight, the bridge belonged to those who placed it there. In other cantrevs and other lands, folk would light fires, dance and feast and celebrate the summer and the long, bright days.

The folk of Pont Cymryd would close themselves up in their houses and their hall and leave the night to itself.

Carys set her basket down, removing the cloth to reveal a clay jar of milk and four small white flour cakes alongside the bread. Elen took these offerings out and set them beside the others.

Her encounter with Urien still rested heavily on her mind. 'Abide, abide.' She whispered the ritual words fervently as she set milk and white cakes on the soft clover. 'And let no trouble come to our house this year.'

The River Usk flowed past wide, silver, and calm, but the wind blew hard, whipping her cloak out behind her and carrying the smell of rain from the hazy horizon. Elen set her jaw and turned away towards the woods. The future would bring what it might. Until then, there was work to be done. Carys saw Elen's mood and did not attempt to talk. She just rummaged in her basket for the bread. The scent rose in a delicious cloud as Carys tore it open. She handed Elen a goodly portion so they could eat while they walked. It truly was a beautiful morning with summer stretching brightly before them. The people of the cantrev were waking to their tasks, and the road became crowded with beasts and their keepers heading down to the riverside to drink or graze, or to make their own offerings. Pleasant greetings and snatches of gossip and song, along with the good bread in her stomach, lightened Elen's mood as they turned up the gentle hill towards home.

The dwellings of the cantrev's people clustered around the high house like pebbles scattered around a boulder. Smoke rose from the holes in the thatched roofs. The clatter of voices, both human and animal, competed with the noise of the thousand tasks of living. Sheep bleated, cattle lowed, pigs squealed and grunted. A sharp tang on the wind and a metallic clanging said Aeddan was at his forge. The west was one great carpet of green with the new grain almost knee

high. Men and women were out with their hoes, chopping
out the weeds, inspecting the stalks and new-formed heads
to see that they were strong and there were no early blights.
Mali stood in her doorway, sweeping dust vigorously back
out across the threshold. A noisy flock of grey and black
geese waddled fussily past followed close by Nia with her
willow-wand switch. Her belly was huge with her first child
nestled safe within. She smiled and called out to Elen who
stopped and laid her hand on her rounded stomach. Elen
was the cantrev's midwife, having taken over the duties her
mother could no longer perform.

The babe stirred at her touch and kicked once. 'We'll be
seeing each other before another seven days have passed,'
Elen predicted. 'That one's anxious to be out.'

Nia patted her belly proudly. 'It's a boy, mother said. She
can tell by the way he's lying.'

Elen eyed the wool-clothed mound critically. 'I hope she
remembered to tell the babe!'

They all three shared a laugh at that, and continued on
their separate ways, Nia to the river and Elen and Carys up
to the hall.

The great house of Pont Cymryd stood within a ring of
earthworks and deep ditches. The men on watch hailed Elen
and Carys as they passed. The house was a long, low hall
with grey stone walls and a timber roof. The yard was as
busy as the surrounding village with everyone scurrying back
and forth to take care of the work of the day, as well as the
extra work of preparing for the welcoming feast. The breeze
was warm with the smell of baking bread and little Ana
hurried by with a basket of eggs clutched tightly in both
arms. Before the great iron-banded doors waited Urien's
shaggy, black horse. His two men, the toad and the wolf,
lounged beside their ponies. Not one of the hall's men had
come to make conversation with them.

Urien would be in there with mother. Elen thought for a moment about circling around to the ovens to deliver her basket of mushrooms. She did not want to trade more barbs with Urien. But stronger than the desire for peace was the desire to know what Urien was saying to mother, and what reply she made to him.

'Carys, take the mushrooms around to Siani.' She handed her basket to her sister-to-be. 'Make sure she knows these are to stew with the onions. Say I'll be with you shortly.'

Carys gave her a knowing glance, but took the basket under her arm without comment and started on her way. Elen schooled the frown from her face and walked through the great door into her house. Urien's men eyed her as she passed, but both bowed respectfully all the same.

Inside, the world was dim, smoky and cool. The beds and sleeping pallets had already been cleared away. Women tended the black kettles of porridge that hung over the hall's three fire pits. Boys set up trestle tables and benches for those who had the leisure to come and eat beside their warmth. Children raced to and fro as if constant motion could keep the scolding grandmothers from identifying them and giving them their chores. A cluster of women, young and old, sat in the corner at work on the eternal tasks of carding and spinning.

Mother sat in the great, carved chair that had once belonged to Elen's father, Ioan. Urien stood before her. A bright blaze of colour caught Elen's eye. As a courtesy to their guests, Arthur's saffron and scarlet banner hung above mother's seat beside father's shield emblazoned with his blue boar. Urien could not like standing beneath that bright red dragon.

Adara, Lady of Pont Cymryd, widow of *Penaig* Ioan, was tall and straight despite her years. Her hair fell in a grey cloud past her shoulders, held in place by a circlet of bronze. Her face was lined with wisdom and laughter, especially around her dark eyes. The only sign that the years might weigh on her was her hands. Once strong and clever, her fingers were now bright red and chapped, with joints so swollen they lacked the strength to pick up anything heavier than a wooden spoon. The pain in them was harsh, Elen knew, but mother never complained of it. She still carried herself with the dignity and grace of a woman in the prime of her years.

Where's Yestin? Elen wondered to herself. The answer came to her a heartbeat later. *Keeping our guests occupied so they do not hear what is said at this moment.*

Urien had a warrior's senses, and he turned as Elen approached, although he could not possibly have heard her over the other noises ringing through the hall. He frowned deeply.

'I see your daughter would have words with you, Adara. Shall we speak more of this later?'

'What do you have to say that my daughter may not hear, Urien?' mother asked pleasantly, extending one of her swollen hands. Elen took the sign and stepped up to mother's side. Mother, it seemed was not in the mood to make things easy on her neighbour.

For a moment, Urien looked as though he could spit on the floor, but he evidently decided having his say with Adara was more important than whether or not Elen heard it. She could see the preparation in his face. He meant to shoot his bolt now, and aim it true.

'Adara, we are of the oldest blood, you and I,' said Urien, holding up his right hand to show the tattoos there. The raven, the pig, the mare, all the old signs of luck and fortune were embedded in Urien's skin. 'You have knowledge and skill that stretches back to the druids and further. You know the voices and the names of the oldest gods. You could bend those powers to help keep the usurper from our lands.' Now he pointed at her, as if he brought the accusations of the gods with him. 'But even you must be prepared. Should

Arthur come suddenly, all your learning will be as nothing to protect you.'

Elen felt the tension thrumming through her mother. She wished she had deflected Urien when she still had the chance. Mother had enough to worry her. She wished she could speak now, but it would not be proper.

'It is not Arthur who has made threats against our land,' said Adara.

That surprised Urien, or it seemed to. 'You think I threaten you? I would leave us all free as we have ever been.'

'Free, so long as we agree to abide by your word.'

'A house must have a master.' His tone said this was obvious to all who had any sense. 'It is only when we work together as one house that the border cantrevs have a chance to stand against Arthur.'

Adara was not dissuaded, or softened. 'Again I ask, Urien, what threat has Arthur made against you or I?'

'He himself is the threat. His dominion increases every year. Such power feeds on itself, lusting to grow ever greater. You know that. We have both seen it.'

For the first time, mother's gaze wavered. 'Yes.'

'Even the men of the north have been forced to bend their knees and call Arthur king. To the south of us, Mark has sworn his allegiance. Arthur knows our land breeds kings. Why should he leave us alone till one of ours rises to challenge him?'

'Those who know of Arthur speak of his honour and the fairness of all his dealings with them.' Mother spoke steadily, but the certainty of her words was not absolute. Elen remembered her own fears of the strangers and the power that rose behind them. Urien took note of all, and he went down on one knee, leaning close and whispering urgently.

'You know as well as I the tales of how Arthur came to his power. The bones of innocents lie beneath the foundations of Camelot.' Adara looked away. 'Yes, I will speak of it. Can you depend on the wolf in his soul remaining leashed and muzzled?'

'Too much power will blight the soul of any man,' said Adara, but without looking at him.

Urien nodded soberly. 'This is truth.'

The hall door opened again. Elen recognized her brother's silhouette black against the bright morning light. Behind him followed three men, each tall and well-shaped. Arthur's men. Elen could make no move to warn him, but Yestin had quick eyes, and stopped in his tracks before their guests could approach Adara, turning swiftly. Elen watched him gesturing them towards the trestle tables being set up by the fire, inviting them to break their fast out of earshot of Urien.

Mother's mouth formed a thin, tight line as she reached her decision. 'Very well, Urien. Join us at board tonight. Speak with the men of Camelot and let us see what they have to say to you.'

What! It was all Elen could do to keep the word from bursting out of her. Mother was going to let Urien confront Arthur's men? What was she thinking? There'd be blood on the stones. She thought again of the crow cawing in the woods. Was it death it foretold?

Urien rose to his feet and bowed, his face calm and serious, completely without the smirk Elen expected to be there. 'Thank you, *Chwaer*.' Sister. The old title of respect between equals. 'That is all that I want.'

'Is it?' murmured mother, although at the same time she nodded her head to Urien.

She said nothing more as Urien walked past the table where Yestin was ensuring that the men from Camelot were served warm food and small beer in the good crockery mugs.

'Wait here, Elen,' said mother as she got to her own feet. Elen opened her mouth, but mother waved her to silence. 'I would speak with you and your brother.'

Adara walked down the hall to where her son and their guests waited. Elen seethed in frustration at having to keep her place. Arthur's men had arrived the previous day on their tall, beautiful horses, their bright pennants snapping in the breeze, with Arthur's scarlet dragon flying over all. That last was brave of them, for in the border cantrevs there were as many who would lop off their heads for the showing of that pennant as there were who would bow before it.

They'd been given the hospitality of the hall, but Elen had still not had a close look at them. They'd kept themselves and their men out of the way all the previous evening. Some thought that was haughtiness. Others thought it was because they were determined not to be too much of a burden to the house. Elen could not tell which was truth, yet. She wanted to see these men. She wanted to hear whether their voices rang true or false, to watch the way they watched the world around them. As it was, all she could see was that as mother approached, the men rose, and the guests bowed to their hostess. She stood before them, probably making some inquiry about their comfort and whether all was as they would have it. Adara touched her son's arm, and said something which made the others laugh. Mother beckoned women over with more bread and pitchers of beer, then she returned to her chair, Yestin following behind her.

Adara did not elect to stay in the great hall. Instead, she walked through the small rear door and down the narrow, dark corridor between the stores and extra sleeping quarters that opened on either side. Mother wore a single iron key on her girdle. She used it now to open the lock of an oaken door. On the other side was the treasury.

It was filled with sacks and chests, bolts of good cloth, wooden casks, and graceful clay jars and plates that came from as far away as Rome. In the centre was a long table of age-darkened oak with only several balances and their weights to clutter its surface. This room sheltered the wealth of the cantrev, and was one of the few places they could speak without being interrupted or overheard.

Yestin closed the door without being told. He was not tall, her brother, but he was broadening to become stocky and strong as their father had been. His beard was dark to match his hair. He dressed simply, in a plain tunic, breeches and sandals, but his wrists were clasped with silver rings to show his rank and honour, though his bearing, if Elen was honest with herself, was becoming such that he did not need such outward show for one to mark that.

Mother sat down on a folding stool. Elen could not help but see how tired she looked. Her swollen hands lay in her lap, useless.

'You may speak now, Elen.' Mother's tone held no anger, only acknowledgement.

'Why did you do it?' The words burst out of her like water from a broken barrel. 'Why invite Urien to the feast?'

'What!' cried Yestin, looking from Elen to Adara.

Adara met her children's disbelieving gazes calmly. 'Because I want to see how Arthur's men react to him, and he to them. We are in the middle of this game, my children. It is best to see how those to either side will play.'

Yestin swallowed, nervousness showing plain on his face. 'You are not truly thinking you'll side with Urien?'

Mother rubbed her temple, trying to stave off a coming ache, Elen was sure. 'I do not want to, but it may be that we have to. We are small here, and we are weak. We cannot ever forget that. If Arthur will not lend us protection, then we must not stand in Urien's way.'

Elen moved closer to her brother. In this they'd present a united front. 'It's like we're choosing which knife to have pointed at our throats. Why does this come to us?'

But she knew why. They all did. The wealth of Pont

Cymryd lay not in the number of its kine or the extent of its fields, but in the placement of their land. If you came from the east, it was the last gentle land before the mountains, and the best crossing of the river from the Roman road for miles in either direction. If you came out of the mountains from the west, it was the best way to the enemy, and the river and its bridge would give guard to any retreat.

Mother looked into the distance. Did she see the past, or the future? Adara's eyes had looked on both before. 'Since the Romans left us, we have had no overlord. It was to the benefit of all that the bridge was a free passage, and we were careful to deny use of it to no one. But now, overlords are rising from among our own, and that time is gone. We must choose a side, or sword and fire will choose it for us.'

Cold settled in Elen's heart, but it was Yestin who spoke first this time, leaning across the table, planting both hands firmly on its surface. 'Mother, what have you seen?'

Adara shook her head. 'Nothing beyond what some understanding of the world's ways has shown me, Yestin, I promise. Should I resort to other means, you will know.

'This is the truth, my children. Arthur is four days' ride away in good weather and does not care to pick a fight. Urien is over the next hill and chafes to break the peace of the countryside. We need to care very deeply what he thinks of us.' She sighed again. 'Come next spring, Yestin, you will be married and my place will be yours. That will make some things easier, but I do not know that we can hold off making an alliance until that time comes.'

Yestin straightened up, pulling himself back, ordering his thoughts. A memory struck Elen, of her brother toddling behind her when she was a tiny girl herself, holding onto her skirts to keep upright. It was still startling to her sometimes to see him as the grown man he was, especially since he had come to look so much like their father.

'Winter puts a halt to all matters,' Yestin said. 'There are ways to delay while we take good measure of our choices. When the men from Camelot are gone, let us send Seith and Teilo to Urien with gifts and soft words. Let them see what can be learned from him and his men. Some in that house have loose tongues. While they are gone, let me go to Caerleon and see this Arthur Pendragon. Let him make his offers in his own house with his own words. By the time we all return, it will be too late in the autumn for any matter of treaty or arms to begin. We will know better which way to turn when the spring comes again.'

Mother nodded, and Elen thought she saw relief in Adara's eyes. What had Urien said to her that Elen had not heard? What else was happening that remained unseen? 'There is much sense in what you say, Yestin. What do you say, Elen? You know in any such agreement . . .'

'I know, mother. My betrothal will likely be made with this treaty.' The words left her throat dry, but it was as it must be. 'Better the future of our house be made by marriage than by the spear.' Her marriage day had been long delayed, and now she thought she knew why. Mother had known the stakes in that game would rise, and she was waiting to see how high they would go before she made the bargain. 'Against all expectation, my brother is proving to be a man of sense.' Yestin scowled at her, an expression Elen had known for years, and she smiled back at him. 'Let us see them together tonight and then separately over the summer.' She bit her lip. She would marry for the good of her land and her people. She knew that. She was prepared. But still . . . 'W . . . would it be Urien himself?'

'No,' said mother firmly. 'It need not to come to that, thankfully. Urien has another lady.'

'I have never seen any.'

'No. Urien has secrets, and he keeps them close. The name

of his lady love is but one.' She got to her feet. 'So, let us learn what we may of them, as my son so wisely suggests, and then we will see.' She pulled on her public face, all distance and dignity. 'Now, to your work, my children. We must not disgrace ourselves this night.'

Elen and Yestin stood aside, letting their mother pass through the door before them. Elen glanced at her brother.

Are Arthur's men steady? she tried to ask him. *Are they true men?*

Yestin gave the barest hint of a nod. Elen had hoped to find relief, but instead her worry deepened. Honest offers from the High King might only tempt Urien to desperate measures. She thought of his men, the wolf and the toad, and wondered if Urien's honour could be counted on to hold them and their fellows back.

Fortunately, preparations for that evening's formal welcome of their guests left Elen little time to dwell on her fears. The good cloths had to be brought from the treasury, shaken, brushed and aired. Fresh rush lights had to be prepared and placed. The stock of precious tallow candles had to be assessed and those lights set behind the high table. Their hall had no dais. The high table was wherever the great chair stood. Mother's old chair was brought out for the first among the guests to sit in.

This was only the beginning. There were the mountains of food to be gathered, cleaned, and prepared. Those who tended the outdoor ovens watched the sky anxiously as the clouds gathered, and prayed to the ones who watched the making of bread that the rain would hold off until the feast was safely laid. Barrels of beer had to be brought up from storage and tapped. What wine there was had to be tasted and watered. Cider jugs put in the river to cool had to be retrieved. All the good serving dishes had to be brought out from the treasury. The boys and girls who would be serving with those dishes had to be washed, combed and dressed, inspected and, finally, fed so they would not grow faint during what would be a long, slow meal.

After all this, Elen barely had time to dress herself, but it was not something she could neglect. Her appearance was also part of the honour of house and cantrev. She had the unmarried women's quarters to herself as she put on her good dress of white wool trimmed with deep blue ribbons embroidered with a complex pattern of waves and knots. She belted the dress with a girdle that was similarly embroidered and tipped with two hollow silver balls that rang pleasantly when she moved. She took her black hair from its customary braids and combed it down until it flowed freely across her shoulders and settled a bronze circlet chased with images of birds on her brow.

Lastly, she clasped her cuffs about her wrists. These were part of the wealth of the family. Ioan had brought them into the house when he married Adara, and Elen would take them with her when she went to her husband's house. They were cunningly worked into a chain of silver dancing women holding a knotted ribbon of gold. Garnets flashed in the women's flowing hair and topaz made their eyes.

They were beautiful things and Elen always enjoyed the chance to wear them, but today she felt as if she were a warrior girding herself for battle. She hoped she looked well. She felt that she did. They would show these strangers a rich and honourable house. They would show Urien they were not to be intimidated or overwhelmed.

The door flew open and slender Dicra, also in her best woollen dress, hurried in.

'My lady Adara bids you come. It is time.'

Elen drew her shoulders back and picked up her hems so they would not drag in the dirt of the floor. It was time to welcome the guests, to welcome the future and all it held.

The long hall was full to the brim by the time Elen arrived.

All three fires were lit, as well as the rush lights and stout candles. The head men and women of the cantrev stood before the tables and benches along the walls. Their ornaments of bronze and silver glistened in the bright light. They all contrived to look stern and dignified, even ancient Daere who bent almost double over her walking stick. Mother sat at the high table clad in a dress of brilliant green embroidered with yellow knotwork with sleeves that almost covered her ravaged hands. Golden rings flashed on her fingers where they showed beneath the cloth. A cloak of beaver fur hung from her shoulders and a band of woven silver studded with garnets the size of Elen's thumbnail circled her throat. Another silver band held back the braid of her grey hair. She looked entirely the mistress of house and land and ready to turn back the spring flood with the merest glance.

Urien waited at the foot of the table, combed, washed, cloaked, and looking stern, but not overly so. He appeared ready to allow the welcome to proceed without interference. Still, his presence unnerved Elen, and she was torn between the desire to look away, and the desire to watch him closely for any sign of mischief.

Elen took her place to her mother's left, and glanced to Carys. Her sister-to-be looked fine in her gown of rich blue. She stepped up at once and passed Elen the carved tray that held three of the silver wine cups. The fourth waited before mother. Adara watched Elen with a keen but cheerful eye. Over her head, Yestin gave Elen a quick and sardonic smile, and Elen found herself returning a smile of her own. Yestin, his young man's beard combed and clean, was all in blue for this ceremony, with a cloak of black bear's skin covering his shoulders, pinned with a gold brooch in the shape of a running mare. A belt of bronze and silver circled his waist, but it supported no sword. The only sword in the hall for such a feast was now hanging beside her father's shield, and it was a great, gilded weapon suitable for carrying in sacred ceremonies, for treaties and weddings. Should a formal agreement come between their people and Arthur, Yestin would carry that sword to the table where the bargain would be struck. Now, it was just one more reminder of their history and honour. Elen felt the strength of her pride supporting her. Her family were with her, their people surrounded them. Together they could face anything that might come.

Mother inclined her head. At the far end of the hall, square-built Rob pulled open the great door, and the three messengers from Camelot entered, followed by their train of men and boys. These stayed at the rear of the hall while the messengers approached the high table with long, martial strides. They were dressed in leather jerkins covered over with silver rings. Madder-red cloaks hung from their shoulders and were clasped with gold at their throats. In perfect time with one another, they knelt before Adara, bowing their heads in formal greeting. Mother nodded again, and Elen, moving carefully so as not to spill the wine, circled the table to bring them the guest cups.

'Let me bid you welcome, my lords,' said her mother as Elen reached them. 'Please, do you rise and accept the hospitality of this house.'

Finally, Elen was able to satisfy her burning curiosity and look closely on these men.

The senior among them was called Bedivere. Some adventure or accident had taken his right hand above the wrist, but he accepted the cup neatly with the one that remained to him. While his hair and beard had gone winter-grey, his brown eyes were still keen, taking in every detail of their hall. His back and shoulders were both broad and straight. He was said to be one of Arthur's ten champions, who were his high council. Their cantrev might be small, it might even be weak, but the High King was not treating it as such. That alone made Elen incline towards hearing well what these men had to say.

She offered the next cup to the man on Bedivere's right. He was Kynon, and was brown-skinned, hawk-nosed and brown-haired. Gossip said he came from Dinas Pwyl. She had heard him in the yard as she'd rushed to and fro, swapping jokes with the men, speaking flawlessly with no trace of eastern accent to his words.

'Many thanks, my lady,' he said now as he took the cup.

The man to Bedivere's left was the youngest. He was Geraint, one of Arthur's four nephews. He was a lean, tall man, with a knight's strong hands and arms. His black hair waved back from a high brow and deep blue eyes. His skin was fair beneath the tanning wind and sun had laid on. He said nothing as he took the remaining cup, but he bowed his head to show his thanks.

Probably he does not speak our tongue. Elen found herself a little sad at this, and wondered what his voice would sound like if he did speak.

Remember yourself. As much as she enjoyed the jests and boasts of a flirtation, now was not the time, and this was most certainly not the man. Not while the chance that she and hers might soon be at war with these men was as great as the chance she might become a sworn vassal to their lord.

Eyes discreetly lowered, Elen returned to her place beside her mother's chair. This did not keep her from catching a glance from Yestin, who lifted one quizzical brow and quirked his mouth as much to say *liked that one, did you?* She wished mightily she could cuff him on the ear.

Sir Bedivere raised his cup in salute to Adara, but it was Sir Kynon who spoke. 'My captain, Sir Bedivere, bids me render our thanks for this plentiful hospitality, Lady Adara.' Bedivere drank deeply and the other two did the same. There were mutters of approval from around the hall. Sir Kynon

let them die away before he spoke again. 'Sir Bedivere bids
me say that we bring the Lady Adara of the cantrev Pont
Cymryd the greetings of our lord Arthur Pendragon, High
King of the Britons. He wishes you and yours joy, prosperity
and deep friendship. As tokens of this, he asks you to receive
these gifts of him.'

Bedivere beckoned with his cup to the men and boys of
the knight's train. These came forward, bearing two heavily
carved and banded chests between them, which would have
been gift enough. Now came Yestin's turn, and her brother
walked down to stand before the chests as they were opened.
The first revealed red clay jars sealed with white wax and
packed carefully in straw.

'Vintage wine,' proclaimed Kynon. 'And white salt for the
savour of life.'

The men opened the second, smaller chest.

'For the Lady Adara, the High King sends this belt of silver.'
The men lifted the ornament out, and it flashed in the firelight. It was long enough to wrap twice around mother's
waist, and each link was worked into the shape of a hunting
cat with peridots for eyes. 'For the Lord Yestin, the High King
sends this sword.' The men lifted out a scabbard and Bedivere
handed his cup to Geraint so that he might draw the sword
and hold it up. This was a princely gift. Even Elen could see
the edge was keen and the weapon light and well balanced.
The hilt was inlaid with gold and garnets. Elen thought she
saw Yestin's hands twitch, itching to take hold of the weapon
and gauge its worth.

'For the Lady Elen, the High King sends this necklace.'

It was a heavy and beautiful thing he held up, bronze and
silver worked together into the shape of a flowering vine
setting off pearls, amethysts and garnets. But even with that
rich present sparkling in the light of the fire and torches,
Elen found her gaze slipped sideways to rest on the blue-

eyed knight. A warm shiver went through her as she saw
he was indeed looking steadily back at her.

Take care, Elen, she cautioned herself. *Take great care.*

The necklace was returned to the chest, and the ambassadors and their men bowed.

'Most heartily do we thank Arthur Pendragon for these
gifts and the friendship they betoken,' said Yestin. He looked
a great deal like father as he stood there, one hand on his
hip with his head held high, and Elen felt herself smile. 'It
is the honour and pleasure of this house to accept both.'
Kynon murmured into Bedivere's ear, translating Yestin's
words for him.

Yestin raised his hand and four of their own men stepped
forward to bear away the chests to the treasury. 'Most glad-
dened are we by the presence of such friends. It is in peace
and honour we greet you and welcome you thrice more to
this house. Now, Sirs, it is our lady's will that you and your
men do come sit with us, that we might take meat and bread
as well as counsel and conversation.'

It was a pretty little speech and Yestin had been working
on it for several days. Words were not what he was best at,
but he knew that, and he laboured at them with a will.

Little brother, you make a fine man.

Sir Bedivere bowed. 'Our thanks to the lady of the house.'
The words fell awkwardly from his unaccustomed tongue,
but there was unmistakable dignity in his speech. 'We accept
with honour and great pleasure.'

Yestin stood aside, and let the knights circle the table to
take their places at the board with Sir Bedivere at mother's
right hand. Elen wished she could sit with them too, and
hear what was said, but her work was a long way from done.
Women and boys spread out through the hall with pitchers
of cider and beer. The wine was reserved for the high table
and Elen and Carys served there themselves. Old Beven sat

before the nearest fire with his harp and played sweetly, singing light and gentle airs.

Once the drink was served, the food was brought in successive processions. First came her mushrooms stewed with onions and served with plenty of good brown bread. Then came silver trout from the river, cooked in their own broth and served on long wooden platters with fresh herbs sprinkled over them. Then came roasted wood pigeons stuffed with more herbs and the very last of the previous year's chestnuts and covered with peppery gravy. They'd traded six head of cattle for that pepper, but the way the men of Camelot exclaimed over it made Elen believe her mother had been right to acquire it.

Last came two swine, roasted whole and shimmering in their glaze of broth, thyme and honey, filling the entire hall with their luscious scent. Their arrival, each borne in at shoulder height by two boys in white tunics, sent a cheer through the hall. The men of Camelot raised their wine cups to their hostess, and even Urien smiled and clapped his hands in appreciation as the great dish was set on the high table.

The evening passed in enjoyment and fellowship. Urien kept his manners and spoke only to the men on his left and right, although he watched the men from Camelot most carefully. But so too did every other man in the hall.

Slowly, the swine were picked down to the bones. Beven at last began running short of songs and was bringing out his most ancient jokes. Elen's feet ached from running back and forth, and her hands were weary from hefting the jugs of cider and jars of wine, but she was proud and happy. They had shown their house to be a proper one, worthy of respect.

As if to prove her thought, Sir Bedivere rose to his feet. Beven laid his hands against his strings, stilling them.

In the silence, Bedivere bowed towards Adara. 'If my lady permits . . . ?' Mother nodded her assent. Sir Bedivere gestured to Kynon who also stood and bowed. He spoke, pitching his voice to carry to all assembled. 'My captain, Sir Bedivere bids me speak in praise of this high house, and all within, but first and foremost Lady Adara who has given three outlanders such brave and honourable welcome.'

A cheer went up at these words, and cups were raised. Elen felt herself smiling. She also found her gaze drifting to the silent knight with the blue eyes. He was watching Sir Bedivere and Sir Kynon with all signs of attention. Did he understand the man? She still had not heard him speak once during the entire feast. He only watched.

What do you see? she wondered. *And what do you make of it?*

'True friendship between men is a rich treasure,' Kynon went on. 'It is a glory to go in quest of it, and one of the rewards of Heaven to find it.' The speech was beginning to sound rehearsed, but it was pretty and proud nonetheless. 'How much more so, then, is the friendship between great chiefs and kings? For when there is friendship between kings, there is peace and prosperity between their lands, and all of Heaven and Earth must smile upon them and shower them with plenty for as long as their friendship shall last.'

More cheers went up at this, and more toasts were drunk in praise of it. But not by Urien. He too sat in silence, and watched Bedivere like a fox watching a hen, waiting for his moment to strike.

Elen tensed. Urien would only bluster a little, she told herself, nothing more. Then they would see how Bedivere and his men answered, as mother had planned. Urien could make no greater upset. Not here, not at the board in another chieftain's house.

He wouldn't dare.

'This is the friendship Arthur Pendragon extends to the Lady Adara,' Sir Kynon was saying. 'He has heard much of her great wisdom, of her honour and courage. He has heard

what a true man is her son, Yestin, and how fair and proud
is her daughter, Elen. It will increase the honour and worship
of both our peoples when hands are joined and goodwill
flows freely between them. Should the lady be willing to
bestow this honour upon him, High King Arthur swears in
return that all her enemies shall be enemies of the High King
and the Round Table, and that all her friends shall likewise
be his friends. No trouble of our friends shall go neglected
nor any plea unanswered where a neighbour may
honourably hear and help.'

There were no cheers now, but there were thoughtful
rumbles, of approval, perhaps, and definitely of consideration. This was not a thing to be decided here at board, but
was the talk of many days, of months, even, if Yestin's plan
played itself out. The knights Bedivere and Kynon bowed
again, to mother and to the room, and reclaimed their seats.

Urien decided this was his time. 'A question, if I may,
Chwaer Adara.' He laid his emphasis on the honorific, to
remind her that they were of the same blood and these men
were strangers.

Mother frowned. So did Yestin. Elen itched to move closer
to them, but held her place. This was what they had all
wanted, after all. This was where the men of Camelot would
stand the test of courtesy. It would be barbs only, nothing
more.

'What question, Urien?' asked mother mildly.

Urien rose, ponderously, like the bull he was said to be.
His eyes glinted in the firelight. His face was slick with grease
and red with wine. Or was it more than wine?

'I would ask the *marchog* Bedivere, what became of the
men of the *llawer buchod* when they accepted Arthur's friendship?' *Llawer Buchod,* they were a clan of wanderers, drifting
about the Black Mountains, driving their cows before them.
From time to time they lent their hands to this little war or

that. What had they to do with Arthur? Urien spoke casually, using *marchog*, the title of respect, for the knight. Despite this, his eyes were narrowed and glittering.

So were the blue eyes of the silent knight.

Kynon bent close to Bedivere, translating the question. Bedivere's face went stern as he came to understand what was said. He kept his seat, though. 'You speak of Fyrsil Longshanks?' he asked quietly.

Urien nodded, relaxed and easy, as if they discussed the health of cattle or the likelihood of rain. 'Fyrsil who lies dead with thirty of his men after accepting the hand Arthur said he extended in friendship.'

Again Kynon and Bedivere conferred. This time it was Kynon who answered. '*Penaig* Urien, I speak with respect. It is true Fyrsil is dead, slain by knights owing their allegiance to Arthur, but their tale makes sad and distasteful telling. Arthur sent messengers among them, and Fyrsil invited them to sit and eat and be heard. Fyrsil and his men concealed weapons about them, and after the food was served they rose up to slay all Arthur's deputation. Those men who remained were forced to fight for their lives or be slain as well.'

'Truly, a false and bloody deed,' said Adara, looking hard at Urien. 'It is shameful that the laws of hospitality should be so violated.'

But Urien kept his feet. 'Such may be the tale they tell at Camelot, but the tale they tell in the Black Mountains is far different. There they say it was the men of Camelot who invited Fyrsil to sit with them. It was they who took their knives and slit the throats of men who had come in peace and honour, so that they might not have to face the men of the west in pitched battle in these hills that are our bones.'

Kynon rose to his feet, slowly, as Urien had done. If Urien

was a bull, this man was a greyhound, lean, quick and sharp. Bedivere spoke a question and Kynon answered. Elen bit her lip. She had some understanding of their eastern tongue, but they were too far away and spoke too softly and quickly for her to follow their words. She could only see how Bedivere's face went red, and how he laid his one hand on Kynon's arm, speaking his soft reply.

Every man in the hall had put down his cup. All watched Adara. Yestin's hands were under the table, and Elen knew they were knotted tight. He could not move, though, until mother gave the word.

Mother kept peace in her voice. 'The dead tell us many tales, and those tales may be woven to please the hearer. We all know too that there are men of the west who are friend more to the snake than to the mare, and love stealth more than honour.'

Urien smiled, and the smile was as sharp as a knife. 'Who says I heard this from the dead? It was one of my own who witnessed the deed.' He extended his hand, pointing down the hall. At the gesture, the toad-faced man stood up from his place, his head bowed humbly.

Despite this, all heard him when he spoke. 'It is true. I was there. It was Arthur's men who invited Fyrsil to eat with them. It was in Arthur's name he was slain by stealth.'

The hall erupted. Men leapt to their feet. Benches toppled over, thudding hard against the floor. A hundred questions were shouted, fingers pointing, fists shaking. Kynon's hands had curled to fists, their knuckles white, and he was speaking to Bedivere, who grew more pale with each word. Sir Geraint pushed his chair away from the table, his attention no longer on Urien's face, but on his huge hands.

Urien stood stock still in the midst of this chaos, smiling.

'*Silence!*' The single word thundered through the hall, and the men froze in their places.

Mother did not have to stand to command attention. Everyone's gaze was on her where she sat, cold and straight as any queen.

'*Penaig* Urien, how *dare* you bring this claim to my board, and in such a fashion?' Her voice was low and hard. It seemed to Elen it could crack the stone walls around them. 'This is a matter for the council table. You will offer apology to my guests.'

No one moved. Elen's heart thumped madly in her chest. Urien's eyes slid from Adara to Kynon and Bedivere.

'No,' he said. 'I offer no apology. What I say is truth.'

Muttering voices rose in the air, and they were dark now, and ugly. The retinue of Camelot moved more closely together. The men of the cantrev straightened themselves. Elen could hold her place no longer and hurried to stand by her mother and Yestin.

Kynon spoke again, and his voice was quiet and deadly. 'Do you say the High King is a false man?'

Urien did not flinch, much less relent. 'I do, and I will say more. I say his aim is conquest, by the flattery of women where that can be done, and by the slaughter of true men where it cannot.'

'Urien!' shouted Adara. 'You will be silent or you will leave this house!'

Urien showed no sign of doing either, instead he spoke to the whole of the hall. 'It is known that Arthur lusts to be as the old Roman emperors. He apes their ways and their laws, and their hunger for the conquest of our lands. He works hand in glove with sorcerers and cunning men, and,' here he turned his hard eyes back to Adara, 'women in other ways wise who would turn witch and poisoner for the prizes he gives.'

Which was at last too much for Yestin who was now on his feet. 'Do you speak this way of my mother in her house?'

'I speak truth,' said Urien again, and again he was smiling as if this were another small triumph for him.

Yestin flushed red. Elen could tell he wished for his knife, or better, the new sword waiting in its chest. 'You came here to bring this quarrel. You are no man.'

Urien snorted, folding his smith's arms. 'This from a boy peeping out from behind his mother's skirts.'

Too much. Yestin raised his hand. Sir Kynon and Sir Bedivere fell back a little. Sir Geraint tensed, ready to move. *Yestin's going to strike Urien. He's going to fight him*, thought Elen wildly.

He's going to die.

'Yestin,' said mother, firmly, quietly. 'Hold.'

Yestin bridled, then obeyed, lowering his hand, and then, when mother's gaze did not leave him, he resumed his seat. Sir Bedivere nodded to Sir Kynon and they too sat down. Sir Geraint alone did not move, nor did he take his eyes from Urien's hands.

Mother rose, standing before Urien, white-faced in her anger. 'Urien, you have brought a quarrel to my house. You have broken hospitality and faith. You will go at once from here, or my son and his men have leave to do as they must to make you go.'

For a moment, Urien stayed where he was. Something flickered behind his eyes, but Elen could not say what it meant. 'Your ears are not so long as they once were, Adara. You had best think twice about what I say.'

Mother's hands shook with the effort of her self-restraint. 'Had I ears long enough to reach to the sea's shore, I still would not hear you,' she barely spoke above a whisper, but Elen knew Urien understood each word. 'Leave this house.'

Urien held his place one heartbeat longer, then he nodded, as if in acknowledgement, or satisfaction. He turned on his heel and strode down the centre of the hall, his cloak billowing out in his wake. His two men fell in behind him.

As they strode through the door, Rob leapt forward and slammed it shut.

As the crash reverberated through the hall, Adara turned to the men from Camelot.

'Honoured guests, I beg of you, accept my apology. It was by my doing that Urien was here, and I am deeply ashamed at his actions.' She bowed her head, and Elen saw the way her hands still trembled.

It's not your fault, Elen wanted to say. *This was Urien's doing from the beginning.* But to speak, to lessen mother's apology, would be to add to the shame. She could only bow her head despite the anger burning in her, as Yestin did.

Sir Kynon spoke to Sir Bedivere, and Bedivere murmured a reply. 'My Lady Adara,' Sir Kynon said for his captain. 'Sir Bedivere is sorry he has not the words to speak thus much for himself, but he bids me say this is no reflection on your house. You have shown us nothing but respect and fair treatment here, and we are grateful. The High King has many who speak against him in these lands, but, we learn by breaking bread with you that he also has many friends who show courtesy in all their ways.'

Bedivere took up his wine cup in his one hand and drank.

That act broke the tension in the hall. Beven struck up his harp again. Benches were righted. Carys had the presence of mind to send the women scurrying around with more beer and cider. Elen caught up the wine jar again to refill her family's cups, and those of the men of Camelot.

She caught Yestin's eye. *Well done,* she tried to say with her glance.

Yestin's shrug said, *But what have we done?* and Elen found she could not help but look towards the great door, closed fast against Urien's return.

What have we done?

Outside, the rain began.

TWO

Elen dreamed.

She dreamed a hawk soared free in the wild blue sky. She stood high on a green hill, watching the bird's flight, marvelling at its beauty. But then, the hawk wheeled on its wingtip and dived towards her, its hooked beak open, the curving knives of its talons extended. Elen could not move, could not even struggle, as the hawk plunged its talons into her flesh. She felt skin, bone and sinew tear and screamed aloud. The hawk soared up again, Elen's blood pouring as red rain from its wings.

Elen stood mute and stunned in her pain, her fresh blood staining her dress and cloak. The thunder of hoofbeats shook the ground and the shimmering air. A rider appeared over the crest of the hill, his cloak flapping behind him. A spear was in his hand and he hurled it impossibly high into the blinding blue sky. It pierced the hawk like an arrow and the blood-stained bird dropped to the earth at Elen's feet. It clutched her heart in its talons and the horseman's spear had split her heart and the bird's in two.

Elen looked at the horseman, and saw under his helm he had eyes the colour of the evening sky. She spread her hands, now covered with her own blood.

'You have slain me,' said Elen, and she fell into darkness. Thunder boomed.

Elen shot upright. Sweat drenched her and her heart pounded frantically against her ribs. A draught curled damp and heavy around her throat, and she shivered hard. All about her, sleeping women snored, sighed, and muttered to themselves, turning and reshuffling beneath their blankets, pulling closer together for warmth, but none woke.

Elen wrapped her arms around herself, trying to stop her shudders. She could still see the blood raining from the hawk's feathers, and the eyes of the rider who looked at her so steadily.

What does it mean? Elen shivered again and outside the wind whistled under the eaves, calling out the souls of the sleepers to come and play.

Elen tossed her blankets aside and found her shoes and woollen over-dress by touch. Shuffling her feet, she threaded her way carefully through the maze of beds and pallets, earning a grunt and a sleepy curse here and there as her toes prodded backs and hands. At last, her hand found the threshold and the door and Elen made her way into the great hall.

In the centre of the hall, a few embers had been uncovered in the central fire pit. In their orange glow, Elen saw her mother sitting on her stool wrapped in her grey, fur-lined cloak. She looked up as Elen came forward.

'So. You feel it too, my daughter?' She looked towards the doors as the rain knocked hard against them. 'There is more than wind and thunder out there tonight. I fear your brother will be drowned, but he insisted on going out to the sentries, to make sure none of Urien's men come back to try more mischief.'

Elen knelt at her mother's feet, huddling between the woman and the fire for her warmth. Adara lifted her chapped and swollen hand and stroked her daughter's hair in a gesture Elen had known since she was a child. 'I dreamed, mother,' she said.

Adara nodded, as if she already knew. 'Tell me your dream.'

Elen told her of the hawk and the blood, the horseman and the spear.

'Mother, I think it was Geraint, Arthur's man.'

'Are you certain?'

Elen thought carefully, searching her feelings. 'No, but it was very like him.'

Adara blew out a sigh. 'Bad to worse. Very well, daughter.'

Elen bit her lip to silence a curse, against Urien, against Camelot, against prophecy and dreams. Why could they not be left in peace? It was all their father had wanted, all their whole family had ever wanted. 'What do we do?'

'Tonight, nothing. Tomorrow . . . it may be we must call on a tie of blood to settle the truth of these things.'

'Blood?' The word sat Elen up straight.

Mother nodded. 'You know of Arthur's cunning man, Merlin?'

Elen frowned. 'The one they call No Man's Son?'

'Yes.' Mother's gaze grew distant, watching memories much more than the glowing coals before her. 'He may have no father, but he had a mother, and she and my grandmother were kin.'

There were as many tales of Merlin as there were of Arthur, and as with Arthur, not all those tales told of honour and triumph. 'That is a weak tie, mother,' Elen said uncertainly

'But better than none.' Mother's hands fell back into her lap. She looked at them, and scowled at their weakness. 'There are other reasons I might trust him more than his master, but I did not want to have to call on that trust until

I had to. Now I think I must.' She raised her eyes, staring at the stout stone walls of their home, but not seeing them. 'Unless we want our men to question any alliance we might make, we need proof of Urien's lies.'

Elen heard those words, but in her mind she also heard them spoken differently. In her mind she heard, *we must have proof* that *Urien lies.*

Elen shifted herself until she was on her knees. Gently, she took Adara's hands in hers. They were ice cold. 'Mother . . .'

Let me help. Teach me what to do next. Yestin's out there in the rain and the dark with that shiny new sword . . . let me also be of use to our family.

Before she could speak her thoughts, a mad pounding sounded against the door, as if someone were trying to batter it down with bare fists alone.

'By all the gods, what is this now?' Mother got to her feet and strode to the door.

'Mother . . .' Elen scrambled to follow. *Don't,* something inside her tried to say. *It's a bad night. Leave whatever, whoever, that is outside. Don't . . .*

'Help me with this, Elen.' Mother laid a hand on the bar.

Elen bit back her fear and obeyed. What if it was Yestin? What if something had happened? She wrestled the bar aside and grasped the iron ring and pulled the door open.

There in the rain crouched three people. Their sodden cloaks seemed to weigh them down. One of them carried a pierced lantern. The rain hissed and spat as it fell against the hot sides. They all looked pinched and starved and their eyes were too large for their faces. Elen thought they were all three men, but she found she could not be certain.

'We seek Adara,' said one.

'Our lady's time has come and it goes hard with her,' said the second.

'She must have a midwife,' said the third.

They had small voices, like frightened birds. They huddled together in a tight knot, shaking, from cold, from effort, or from fear. Perhaps from all three at once.

Elen thought mother would invite them in, but she made no move. She only stared at the three strangers huddled there

'I cannot come,' Adara said quietly. 'I cannot midwife any more.' She held up her misshapen hands.

'Our lady's time has come and it goes hard with her,' said the second.

'She must have a midwife,' said the third.

The wind blew, whipping a curtain of rain through the door. The strangers shivered and drew closer together, and still mother did not invite them in. Elen wondered how they had come past the sentries, and past Yestin.

'I'm most truly sorry,' said Mother. 'It is beyond my power to aid your lady in this.'

But they still did not move, and the third one only said doggedly, 'She must have a midwife.'

All at once, Elen knew. She knew who she was seeing, and why they were so small and so brown, and why they came this night, of all nights, and her heart went cold and still inside her.

Mother nodded. 'Very well.'

Elen drew her mother aside at once, out of the light of the tin lantern and the glow of the fire. 'Mother! You cannot!'

'No, I cannot.' Adara laid her hand over Elen's. 'But you can.'

Elen's heart thumped once. 'No, mother, I have not the skill.'

'You do,' said Adara steadily. 'You have all the skill you need. It will be as any other birth. You know the ways in

which you must take care. Be especially certain not to eat
or drink anything until you return to our lands again.'

'But . . . this could take . . . days.' *Don't think of the other
chance. Don't think it.* 'How can I leave you and Yestin now?'

*Don't think how those such as stand at the door take men under-
hill for seven times seven years, or longer.*

Adara looked deeply into her daughter's eyes. 'They have
come to us for help and we cannot turn such a plea away,
daughter. No matter who they are.'

Elen swallowed, and tried to pull herself together, to stand
as tall and proud as her mother did. 'Of course. Forgive me.
Let me get my cloak.'

This time Elen did not bother with caution as she waded
through the women's quarters. Curses rose in the darkness,
as did worried queries.

'Baby's coming,' was all that Elen answered, pulling on
her cloak and boots. Everyone would think it was Nia.

Her hands shook. It took her four attempts to fasten her
cloak pin. It was as well it was dark. She didn't think she
could see clearly anyway.

Once, when she was very small, mother went to midwife
a birth and she returned at twilight the next day. There was
nothing strange about this, save that when mother returned
she was usually full of stories; of the family, of the birth and
how it went, of the child and how well it was likely to
thrive. This time, she said only, 'The babe lives and it is
strong.'

The next morning, there was a new sow in the pen. None
of the swineherds could say how it came to be there. She
was milk white and she bore litter after litter of strong,
healthy piglets, all as white as their mother. She never
savaged them as other sows might, and they never took
sick no matter how cold the winter or how scarce the feed.
Their pigs became famous throughout the cantrevs, and

were much prized at markets and for any trade they might make.

When the sow finally died, mother forbade its flesh to be eaten. Instead, she ordered it buried by the bridge.

Everyone knew that sow had been her midwife's fee for the birth she never spoke of. What everyone did not know was what Elen overheard mother say to father in the darkness and quiet.

'They wanted me to stay with them. It was only the thought of my children that brought me home.'

It was only the thought of my children. Elen had no such anchor. If the Fair Ones wanted her to stay, would she be able to say no?

Elen gritted her teeth tightly together and hurried back to the hall. The scene there was as it had been. The rain, the flickering light of lantern and fire, the small brown folk cringing beneath their sodden cloaks. They looked so miserable, Elen could not help but feel pity for them.

Mother took Elen's hand and held it as tightly as she was able. She looked directly into Elen's eyes, trying, Elen thought, to impart some of her strength and calm. 'Our good neighbours here promise you will be returned to your family, safe and whole, when your work is finished.'

The three little people looked up at her, blinking their sunken, over-large eyes. Elen's throat was as dry as dust, but she managed to say. 'Very well. I am ready.'

Mother released her hand and stepped back. 'You do our house proud, my daughter.'

Elen drew her hood over her head and stepped out into the rain. She did not look back as the door to her house closed behind her.

The rain was cold as winter and relentless as fury. The little men (were they men? By the flickering lantern light she was even less sure than she had been in the hall) clustered silently around her, herding more than leading her to a little cart. It was a rickety thing with a pair of soaked and dispirited donkeys in its harness. Silently, the one with the lantern held it high so she could step into the cart and find a place to sit among sodden straw. All three of her . . . guides climbed onto the seat and the cart lurched forward. Elen wrapped her cloak more closely around her to fend off the rain, and tried not to feel like a calf being delivered to market. *Or to slaughter.* Elen closed her eyes against that thought. *Home safe. They promised I would come home safe.*

The cart bounced, creaked and jolted. The donkeys' hooves squelched in the mud. The rain pounded down until she was soaked through her cloak and her hands fell numb. The little men said nothing, nothing at all.

Then, the cart lurched to a halt. Two of the three little men scrambled off it and came around behind. Elen peered ahead as far as rain as lantern light allowed. She could see nothing but shadow, but she could hear the river. The cart moved, creaked and tilted. The donkeys' hooves clopped on stone. The little men behind shoved hard, and Elen had to grab the cart's slats to keep from tumbling over. She bit her tongue until the blood came to keep from crying out.

The bridge. It was midsummer's eve and they were crossing the bridge.

The cross found floating in the rushes . . . Maius Smith withheld what was theirs and was never seen again . . . Only the thought of my children brought me home . . . neither priest nor horse ever seen again . . . abide, abide and bring no trouble to this house . . . The cart lurched up the steps and evened out again. *Where are you taking me?* she wanted to scream. *What are you doing?*

Safe back with my family. They promised. Safe home.

The cart's driver waited while his companions returned to their places. Then, he touched the donkeys with his switch. The beasts' hooves clopped hollowly against stone. Elen heard the familiar swirl and splash of the River Usk as it flowed around the pillars. The rain began to lessen. She peeked out from under her cloak's hood. The lantern light showed only darkness, and a slight haze.

Fog?

Fog it was, and it grew thicker even as the rain slowed, and stopped. It was as if all the raindrops diffused and became mist. Elen could barely see the little men who accompanied her. They were shadows beneath a silver shroud. She could scarcely even see the slats of the cart that held her, and the donkeys were completely invisible. All that remained was the steady clip-clip of their hooves.

We must come to the end soon, she thought, a little dizzily. *It takes but moments to cross.*

But they did not. The hooves clopped against stone, and they picked up speed. The cart rattled and swayed, a loose assembly of wood and wicker driven by shadows through mist. *How can the animals see? How can the driver? We're going to fall. We're going to hit the stairs and crash and be lost . . .*

The clatter of hooves that sounded so far away in the mist picked up the word. *Lost, lost, lost, lost . . .*

Then, the moon came out.

The silver light poured down thick and heavy as the mist. Elen lifted her head, feeling strange and sudden awe at the sight of the pure white sphere overhead

Sphere?

This moon was flawlessly full. It should not have been. It should have been waxing towards half-full. Elen pressed her hand hard against her mouth to stop her scream.

Then she noticed that the sound of hooves on stone had turned to the sound of hooves thudding against dirt. She no longer felt the wet straw beneath her.

Then she noticed she no longer rode in a wicker cart pulled by a pair of donkeys.

The floor beneath her was smooth and dry. The speed that pulled at her was dizzying. Solid sides, like those of a boat, curved around her, and behind, in the light of the strange moon, she could see a straight, flat, white road rushing away.

A chariot. This was a chariot, one of the great conveyances such as carried men in triumphant procession.

Up front, two white horses with fair manes streaming out behind them galloped steadily, not straining or snorting. Their reins gleamed in the moonlight, as if they were silver, or gold, and the driver . . .

The driver was a tall young man, well-muscled and proud. His hair was as pale as the horses' manes and streamed out in the wind of their passage. A deeply coloured cloak fell from his shoulders. His companions were both matches for him, with their long, pale hair and their skin white as milk. Gold and gems flashed on their arms.

One of them, the one on the left, turned towards Elen, and smiled. Elen felt his beauty like a blow to her heart. His eyes were still too large for his perfect face, but even with nothing but moonlight, she could see they were as green as all of summer. She could lose herself in those eyes, and she knew she would go willingly into that beauty, that mystery, that wondrous perfection . . .

It was the hardest thing Elen had ever done to drop her gaze. Laughter pealed overhead like golden bells. Elen felt her heart shrivel within her. Then, a second voice growled, dangerous as a wolf and as incomprehensible, and the laughter ceased. Elen realized she was panting hard.

Breathe, she told herself. *Breathe. You must keep your wits.* Her hands knotted together. *You are the daughter of Adara. You are midwife and healer. You know the names of the gods and the ways of the other world. You are Elen of Pont Cymryd and you will uphold the honour of your house.*

Pride strengthened her spine and calmed breath and heart.

Eventually – Elen had lost all sense of time – the driver pulled on the shining reins and the chariot slowed, and stopped. The man to the driver's left turned and gestured that Elen should climb out. Beneath her feet, the road shone white and flawless. Around her, she saw the shadows of a forest. She smelled the sweet scents of herbs, and the sharpness of pine. There was no wind. The air was still and strangely heavy. It brushed against her skin like fine cloth as she stepped aside to make way for her companions. The driver led them onward, and Elen had no choice but to follow him. The other two fell in behind her. Elen's shoes made no sound on the strange road. She peered ahead, trying to see where they had come to, but despite the moonlight, which should have made all as clear as day, she could see nothing beyond the chariot but vague shadows.

They passed the milk-white horses and Elen thought she was beginning to see the outlines of a dwelling. She had an impression of solidity to the shadows, of great size. Here and there, something glinted in the moonlight.

Then she was passing underneath a threshold that curved high overhead and the whole world swam as if her eyes were blinded by tears. She blinked hard, and her vision cleared.

She was in a great hall. The walls around her shimmered whitely as if they were made of pearl. The roof soared overhead impossibly high, held in place by pillars of gold made in the shape of branching trees so lifelike Elen would not have been surprised to see them bearing fruit. The perfectly smooth floor was white marble shot through with veins of gold, which made it seem as if the roots of the golden roof trees ran through chalk soil. The light was brilliant and pure, and yet she saw no candles nor any hearth.

Now she could see that her companions were dressed all in shades of green – bright emerald, sombre olive, the green of the sea and the green of the wood. Their belts and their

arm rings were indeed of gold both red and white. They gave
her no time to marvel at these sights, but led her swiftly
down the length of the shining, empty hall. At the end waited
a white door carved with the image of an apple tree bearing
both fruits and blossoms. The one who had driven the chariot
pushed the door open, and stood aside, waiting for Elen to
enter.

She felt shabby. She felt ugly, dirty and unworthy. How
could she go yet further into this pristine and golden place?

They came to you, she reminded herself. *They need you.*

Elen laid her hand on the white door. It was cool and
perfectly smooth, without the grain of wood or stone. It
swung open at her touch and she made herself walk through.

The room on the other side was much smaller, almost on
a human scale. The walls were covered in tapestries that
stirred and shimmered with each movement, tricking the eye
into thinking the images of fabulous birds and beasts truly
lived. At least, Elen thought it must be a trick of light and
eye. She did not have the courage to believe otherwise.

A cluster of green-clad women ringed a huge bed piled
with white pillows and coverlets. All of them had silver hair
and milk-white skin. Four posts held up a golden canopy
over the labouring woman who lay there, clutching her belly,
her head thrown back and her face tight with her terrible
strain. The white hair that streamed over her shoulders and
breasts was darkened with sweat. A man, pale as the woman,
stood by the head of the bed and looked up as Elen entered.
She saw fear plainly in the way the skin of his face stretched
tight over his bones. This being was husband and father. On
the bed lay the wife and mother and she was in pain. Elen
was the one to offer succour to them and the babe that was
trying so hard to be born.

That understanding broke her paralysis. Elen strode to the
bedside. The waiting ladies parted silently for her. The woman

on the bed panted, and looked towards Elen, but Elen doubted she saw her clearly. She was too lost in her own pain. Elen laid her hands on the woman's exposed belly. The skin was hot as fever and slick with sweat. The woman screamed as if Elen's touch burned her. The ladies behind closed their ranks, and Elen felt their eyes boring into her shoulders and heard their mutters. She closed her eyes to focus on her hands, to feel the babe within. The shape of the belly was wrong somehow. The woman screamed again, and her muscles pushed and strained, and Elen bit her lip and reached within her, keeping one hand on the belly. She touched only slick warmth and she knew why the woman strained and strained and yet no babe came.

Oh, Mother Rhiannon. It's laid wrong. With the babe like this, she could labour till she died, and she would take the babe with her.

What do I do? Elen wiped her hands nervously on her cloak. *What do I do . . . the babe must be turned, but can't be turned while she's straining, she'll crush it with the straining . . .*

'Wine,' she barked out. 'We need wine and mistletoe, mint and rosemary.' She did not bother to ask if they had any of these things. 'And grease from a pig or goose, and any locks in this place, they must be thrown open. Now!' she barked the final word.

Whoever they were, whatever they may have been, they began to move. Three of the women ran out the door. Knotted cords held the bed curtains back. Elen undid the first. One of the women began on the others. Elen unknotted her own belt and unclasped her pin, letting the cloak slide to the floor. Open, open, everything must be open . . .

The woman in the bed screamed, loud, high and hysterical. She clutched at her belly.

'Someone must hold her hands,' ordered Elen. 'What am I to call her?'

'Lady,' said the white-faced man. 'You may call her Lady.' He took her hands, holding them back above the woman's head. Her eyes looked at his, full of fear, full of pain.

'Lady.' One of the women reappeared with a cup of wine so red it might have been blood, and a bundle of herbs. Elen tore them to pieces and rolled the leaves between her hands before she dropped them into the wine. Their scent filled the air, even over the odours of sweat and birth.

She carried the cup to the bed and leaned close to the woman's ear. 'Lady, listen to me!' she shouted. She must get past the pain, past the panic. 'You must drink what you are given. Drink it all. We must turn the babe inside you. This will help. You must drink!'

The woman nodded and parted her lips, just a little. The woman who'd brought the cup lifted the Lady's head. Elen poured the wine into her mouth. She coughed, and sputtered. The man – the Lord? – tightened his grip on her wrists. She swallowed. Little by little, Elen tipped in more wine, and the lady drank between her screams. The cup was deeper than it seemed, and it took a long time to empty. But the straining and spasms eased, a little.

Please let it be enough.

One of the other women had returned with a white oak bowl filled with snowy grease. Elen scooped out a great handful and slathered it onto the Lady's belly, and began to rub it in.

She worked hard, as if she were kneading dough for bread. She squeezed and rubbed and worked and squeezed again, working against muscle, against instinct and nature. The woman screamed, she whimpered, she cried and she wailed. She strained and kicked until the Lord shouted out and two of her women went to hold her ankles down. Sweat poured down Elen's face. Her hands grew weak, went numb, and still she worked. Sometimes she thought she felt the child move, only to have it slip back into place.

The Lady fainted, and Elen wished she could do the same. Her hands were nothing but pain. Her arms were lead and stone hanging from her shoulders. Her feet and knees screamed to be allowed to buckle, to fall. Her lips were raw from being chewed in her efforts, and her mouth was full of the tastes of blood and bile.

The babe turned.

She felt it. She felt it slide into place, and settle, and stay. She thrust her arm where she must, and her fingertips brushed the wet, warm crown.

'Wake her!' she croaked, the only noise she could make. 'Wake her! She must push now!'

She expected the Lord to call out, or slap her, but instead he began to sing. It was the sound of summer. It was the sound of beloved heart calling to beloved heart. Elen felt her own exhausted heart strain against her breast, longing to follow where that song led.

The Lady's eyelids fluttered, and opened. She looked up at the Lord, and the birth pain took her again and she screamed.

'Push!' bellowed Elen. 'Hold your breath and push!'

The Lady pushed, and Elen screamed, and the blood poured and the Lord sang, and all was noise and confusion and salt wet and red . . .

The baby fell into Elen's arms. It was pale beneath its coat of blood. It's hair was shocking white. It lay limp and still in Elen's numb hands for three frantic heartbeats, but then its arms flailed, and its mouth opened and it cried. It cried for pain and hunger and cold and life. Oh, it cried so hard for life.

Elen was so dazed, she barely realized what she was doing as she bound and cut the cord. Someone handed her towels. A basin of water came from somewhere and she washed and swaddled the babe – a girl with regular limbs and strong lungs – and laid it where it longed to be, on its mother's breast.

Hands led her away. Other hands washed her arms and face clean of blood and sweat in water that smelled of thyme and rosemary and something else she couldn't name. She couldn't see straight. She could barely think. Her throat burned with thirst and she ached all the way to her bones.

A soft white towel was handed to her then and she dried herself. Footsteps approached. The hands removed the basin. Someone stood before her.

I must collect myself. I must. Elen rubbed her eyes with her freshly cleaned hands.

The Lord stood before her in all his glory. Elen had just enough presence of mind to remember to look past him rather than into his deep and wild eyes.

'You have my gratitude,' he said. His voice was like music. Just the sound of it made her sway on her feet. It was as well she had been severely distracted when he had sung for his lady. 'The Lady asks you to stay. She asks you to be nurse to our child. Say yes, daughter of Adara, and you will have a life such as you could never dream of.'

Those words had not faded in her hearing before she saw it all in her mind's eye, as clear as a dream to a sleeper. The feasts, the hunts, the music and laughter, the riches and casual wonders. Love and lovers if she so pleased, and life without death, without sorrow, or trifling care.

The dream was so bright and glorious that Elen's heart yearned towards it with physical force. It promised meat and drink and she was starved. It promised rest and warmth and she was cold and exhausted. She thought of the little, pale babe she had helped bring into the world, and how wondrous it would be to see it grow . . .

But to never see mother or Yestin again? They seemed so far away, and they would have each other, and Carys. But could she leave them with so much trouble creeping towards the walls? With the men of Camelot inside and Urien without? And what of her other dream of the hawk and the spear?

If she said yes, she would never have to find the answer for the dream or know the bloody resolution of its riddle. She could live in bliss and peace and never know fear again.

Without mother, without Yestin, without knowing the riddle of the horseman with the blue eyes.

She shook her head. 'No, Lord,' she said, the words grating against her parched throat. No one offered her anything to drink and even in her exhaustion she remembered not to ask. 'I regret I cannot accept what you offer.'

The Lord remained silent for what seemed like an eternity, but Elen said nothing more. She wanted to lie down on the gold-veined stone and sleep. She wanted to drink the whole of the River Usk as it flowed beneath the bridge.

She wanted to go home.

'Very well,' said the Lord. 'You shall be returned to your mother, safe and whole, as was promised. You will be taken to the bridge, and you may cross. When you reach the other side, you will come safely to your family.'

There was something in his words that made Elen shiver, some hint in them of things unsaid and unseen, but her weary mind could not riddle out what it might be. The Lord gestured with his fine, white hand, and the three who had brought her here came to stand before her again. This time these three beautiful and noble creatures bowed with deep respect. One of them held the cloak she had let fall, and she took it from him with trembling hands. Then, with one before and two behind, they led her from the gold and marble hall to the waiting chariot and horses.

The moon had not moved at all.

That should have made her feel afraid, or left her to

wonder, but she was too tired. Her guides helped her into
the chariot. This time she stood, holding on to the sides with
what strength remained in her hands. The horses galloped
along the straight, white road without balking or tiring. The
wind whipped back her hair, and the world passed in shadow
beneath the motionless moon. A day passed, an hour, no
time at all. At last, Elen saw the grey stone steps of the bridge,
the one solid and familiar thing in this strange, moonlit world.

One of her guides unfastened the gate at the rear of the
chariot and Elen stumbled towards the bridge. She remembered herself long enough to turn, and to curtsey to the three
white-faced, green-eyed men who bowed solemnly in return.
Then she turned her back on them, and mounted the steps.

They felt strange underfoot after walking the moonlit halls.
Their roughness made her stagger, and they felt oddly warm.
The memory of sunlight? The memory of life itself? As she
walked, it was as if she left the bright moonlight behind her
and she staggered forward into darkness. She couldn't hear
the river, but she thought she could smell the clean, cold
water on the wind that stirred as she moved forward. Was
the darkness beginning to lift? Her tired eyes could not tell
for certain.

No, the darkness was lifting, pulling back and away,
making room for the silver mists to rise and envelop her.
She would have been afraid, but the mist did not obscure
the stone. She saw the solid, graceless way in front of her.
The way home, to earth and hearth and kin, and she followed
it eagerly and paid no heed to anything else.

Gradually, the mist thinned, and vanished, and now lovely
moonlight came back filtered through a haze of clouds. The
rain had thankfully spent itself. She descended the steps and
her shoes touched the honest earth of home. The living wind
blew hard now, bringing the scents of smoke. It was cool,
but not cold. Elen swayed on her feet. She could go no

further. Not even to get home. Although the moon was high, there was still not light enough to see clearly by, even if she had strength to make the journey.

Beneath the bridge, the bank sloped gently away. The grass there was sparse, but dry of dew. Elen took shelter beneath the stones of the Taken Bridge and wrapped her cloak around herself. Tomorrow would bring her safe home. She had been promised.

The memory of the unspoken hint in the Lord's voice was washed away by the whisper of the river, and she fell asleep where no other sound could reach her.

THREE

Elen woke with the dawn, stiff with cold and soaked with dew. Her hunger had subsided to a leaden ache, but the sound of the river in her ears woke the burning thirst in her throat. She emerged from under the bridge, blinking in the early sunlight. The morning was still; not even the birds called to each other.

Bleary-eyed and muzzy-headed, she made her way down the bank and scooped up great draughts of river water, drenching her sleeves and cloak further in her haste to drink. It didn't matter. She was home and safe, and everything else would be taken care of in its time.

Once she had eased her thirst, she picked her way back to the path and started up the way towards home. The sky was clear blue and the day warmed quickly. No sign of the previous night's rain remained.

Was it only the night before? That gave Elen pause. There had been no way to tell how much time had passed in that other country. It could have been two days, or even longer. She was certainly tired enough. The fae were known for the games they played with time. How long *had* she been gone?

Elen picked up her pace. *It cannot have been too long*, she told herself. *The promise they gave mother saw to that. I was to be returned safe and to her. They could not have kept me seven years, or a hundred . . .*

She was running now, her feet drumming against the dry and rutted road, her heart pounding in her throat and her breath coming in gasps.

It's all right. It's all right. Any moment now I'll see Taf with his cows coming to the river, or Dai with the pigs, or Carys with the buckets. They'll tell me I left last night . . . It'll be all right . . .

But no one came. She had the forest track to herself. The birds still did not sing. Elen's panic deepened. The sun was well up. The way to the bridge should have been busy.

Where are they all?

There should have been watchmen on the bridge, and there were not.

What's happened?

Then, the breeze sharpened, and she smelled smoke. Not gentle hearth smoke; this was thick and acrid, the iron and ash taste of it filling her mouth. This was the smell of disaster.

Elen grabbed her skirt in both hands and raced up the hill, finding the shortest way by instinct rather than sight. She crashed through the encroaching bracken, swatting aside thorns and branches, never heeding how they tore her skin.

Hands yanked her off her feet, dropping her onto her back so hard her head spun and all the air left her lungs in a single rush. A filthy palm clamped itself over her mouth and another gripped her wrists. She kicked out desperately and bared her teeth, trying to bite down.

'Elen! Stop, stop, you're safe!' hissed a raw voice.

Yestin.

His head and shoulders blocked the sky as he leaned over

her and all she saw for a moment was a blur of darkness. Then, the darkness resolved itself, and she stared into her brother's face. He was smeared with blood and mud and his eyes were wide with fear and fury.

He removed his hand and let her sit up. 'What!' she cried, but she got no further before he crushed her to him in a smothering embrace.

'All the gods be praised,' he whispered hoarsely. 'I thought you were dead!'

Elen pushed herself away and stared at him. 'What's happened?' Her voice was high and tight and the words came out almost as a squeak.

He stared back at her, disbelief dropping his jaw. Ash caught in the tangle of his hair. His chin was covered in stubble and sprinkled with yet more ash, as if he had rolled in a fire.

'You . . . you don't know?' he croaked.

'I only returned with the dawn. Yestin, what's *happened?*'

Stark disbelief bled away, replaced by sorrow. Tears welled up in the corners of her brother's eyes. 'Oh, Elen,' he whispered. 'It . . . I . . . While you were gone . . . Urien came back.'

The scent of smoke, the sight of blood, the sorrow on her brother's face, all these piled on top of each other in Elen's mind.

'Mother?' she said, high and lost like a child.

Yestin's face hardened instantly. 'They left her where she fell.'

The tears came at once, a great, blinding flood. She pressed her hand over her mouth to silence her own screams.

No! No! No! howled her mind. *It cannot be! It CANNOT! They said I'd come home safe to her! They promised I'd come home safe . . .*

And she was safe, safe with her family, which was all she

had been promised. She had been gone just long enough to
ensure that she remained safe while Urien . . .

'They said . . .' Yestin's voice broke as he said the words.
'Oh, gods, Elen, they said they'd show all the West Lands
the price for defying Urien.'

The world snapped into sudden, knife-edged clarity. Elen
gripped both Yestin's wrists hard. 'What are you doing here?'
she demanded. 'They must be searching . . .'

Yestin's face was grim. 'I will not leave her. Urien has said
he'll take her head.'

Anger and outrage tore through Elen. To take an enemy's
head was to trap their spirit, lest they rise to take revenge
on their killer. There were arts that could make that head
speak, to advise the murderer. Even if such arts were beyond
Urien, even if he could not make Adara serve him in death
as she had refused to serve in life, even then, he still meant
the ultimate desecration and he meant for Adara to be
trapped for eternity.

'Madyn and Til are drawing the sentries off,' said Yestin.

Mother, mother dead. Dead at Urien's hand. Dead while
Elen stood in a hall of gold and dreamed of casting off her
world and her family . . . guilt and shame burned with the
rage in her blood.

Elen surged to her feet. Yestin reached for her, trying to
find some comfort to give. 'No, Elen, you're . . .'

'No.' She slapped his hand away. 'I'm going home.'

'You can't. This is my . . .'

She rounded on him, her fury as reasonless as it was
strong. 'I was promised I would be returned safe to my home
and family! I will *not* be safe home while my mother is
defiled!'

Her tears had frozen inside her and her vision was perfectly
clear. She strode ahead into the woods and let her brother
follow, or not, as he chose. She could hear nothing but a

strange ringing in her ears. Her face felt hot, as if she stood too near a great fire, but her hands were cold as ice. She was only distantly aware of her own motion. The trees seemed to pass by of their own volition, reaching out and touching her arms and shoulders gently, uselessly.

The woods opened before her, letting the cleared lands spread out. Where there should have been green rows of grain, there was black and trampled earth. She heard shouts, but they were distant, broken by the rumble of hooves, and the clash of metal. Bracken rustled and broke. Urien's sentries were beating the bushes for Madyn and Til and whoever else followed them. Elen barely thought of this. Instead, she began again to run. Yestin snatched at her arm, but she tore herself free and ran without looking back. She stumbled over the clods of torn earth but she kept going. She realized some marauders would still be prowling the edges of the village, that if they knew she was not among the dead they would be looking for her as well. They would surely kill Yestin as soon as they caught him. None of these thoughts slowed her down at all. Yestin swore and she heard the rasp as he drew his sword, not his gilded gift from the High King, but the keen and seasoned sword that had belonged to their father, and he ran behind her.

Shouts, clashes. Names shouted to the wind. Nothing mattered. Nothing mattered but getting home. Home to mother. Mother waiting for them to mutilate her body and enslave her soul. No. No. No.

Fire had taken the village. It had clawed at walls and torn away roofs. Pens that had been filled with fat animals were broken and empty, and here and there among the ruin her unwilling eye caught sight of the fallen. Familiar faces contorted by death, familiar hands covered in blood and dirt, reaching for help that never came. She did not let herself stop. She had to get to the house. She had to find her family.

Finally, her headstrong blindness was too much. Her foot caught some unseen piece of wreckage. She sprawled full-length in the mud and ash. She hauled herself to her knees, shaking her head to clear it, and she saw yet another hand stretched out, as if to snatch at her, and she could not help but look for the man.

Beven. Beven, their harper, lay curled over his instrument like a mother over a child. The harp too was broken and dead, its strings draped across the musician's bloody hands as they lay together in the bright morning light.

They'd killed the harper. They'd broken the harp. They did not care for even that. Bile rose in her throat and she stared at her brother, mute in her fear of it. But Yestin was staring down the hill, towards the shouts and the clashes.

Forgive me, forgive me. Elen left Beven as he lay, scrambled to her feet and ran again, only dimly aware that Yestin still followed.

At last, the great house was before her, whole despite the ruin around it. The hinges that had once held the great door hung loose and twisted from the lintel. The remains of the door lay on the floor so Elen had to step over them to enter her broken home.

She could smell blood here, and all the stench of death. The pitiless sun shone in through the doorway behind her, casting its bright beams into the ruined hall, lighting up the scattered ashes, the smashed and shattered benches, the torn cloth, and the bodies. There had been a last stand here, and she could count all the dead and give them their names.

She found Carys just beyond the door. Her sister-to-be huddled on the stones, eyes open and staring. Her head had been all but torn from her neck. Her blood was smeared and trampled into the floor by the boots that had run past her to get to the treasury.

The wealth of Elen's family lay in a heap in the middle

of their hall, the gold, the jewellery, the silver, and the fine pottery and plate. The bright sword brought by Arthur's messengers for Yestin stuck out of the pile, flaring like a torch in the sunlight.

Mother lay on her belly next to the plunder, her hair spreading out across her face and shoulders to trail in her own half-dried blood.

Utterly spent, Elen dropped to the ground by her mother's corpse. She reached out and took Adara's bloody hand. It was cold. The flesh was soft and slack. The blood was sticky against her palm. She did not cry, she only held her mother's hand and stared stupidly into her dead eyes, blinking now and again.

'Elen, we need to go. Now.'

She barely heard him. Her head was too full of other sounds. It should have been quiet in this house, but it was not. She heard the echoes of the shouts, the screams, the laughter of neighbours turned marauders. They emanated from the stones. They reverberated in the scent of blood and death that was everywhere. She inhaled them with every breath. They filled mouth, throat and lungs. She absorbed them through her skin. They would never leave her, any more than the sight of her dead would. She knew that with dreadful certainty, because they were all calling out for her.

Where were you? the dead wailed. They screamed, they pleaded, they cursed and they cried. *Where were you when we needed you?*

Their voices were so loud, she barely heard the scrape of bootsoles against the floor.

'There you are, Elen. I wondered when you would return to us.'

Rage burned hard in her veins. Elen laid her mother's hand gently down, and she stood, turning slowly to see Urien standing behind her, his sword held casually in his fist.

Nor was he alone. Three of his men had come with him to see the bloodied children steal back into their ruined home. Yestin, white with fury, watched those three, wondering, Elen knew, how many he could kill before he died himself.

'Get out, Elen!' cried Yestin, but Elen could not make herself move.

'I would have spared you this sight.' Urien spread his hands in a dreadful parody of an apology. 'But your mother left me no choice. She would not say where you had gone, and your brother . . .' he grinned in mockery at Yestin. 'Well, I would have said he was too clever to be caught, but he too has come back, hasn't he?'

A trap. They'd threatened desecration as a trap, so Yestin would come back, and so, if all went well, would she. They meant to end the line of Pont Cymryd, here in the house it had built.

Elen's mouth was dry and filled with the taste of blood and ash. Her mind was too full of red rage to think clearly. 'Why?' she croaked. 'Why?'

'I could not let Adara bring the invaders into our lands,' he said flatly. 'I could not stand by while she betrayed her own for the outlanders and opened the way for them to take the rest of us.'

Elen felt her jaw go slack. The bridge. Her family had been destroyed for the bridge.

'Come now, girl.' Urien held out his hand.

To her dismay, Elen laughed, a high, bubbling hysterical noise. 'You think I'd go willingly with the one who murdered my mother?'

Urien shook his head. 'Your mother taught you to be sensible. This place is mine now. *You're* mine now and there're uses for you alive yet.' He took a step towards her, his hand still held out.

Elen drew herself up tall. She stood in the home of her

ancestors, anointed with the blood of the fae and of her family. What made him think he could touch her here?

'What do you know of my mother's teaching?' she asked, coldly. 'Her curse is on you as her blood is on my hands!' Elen lifted her hands, spreading her fingers, letting him see what he had done, what he called down. 'Thunder and lightning take you Urien! Earth open where you stand! Night itself hunt you down and swallow you whole!'

She felt each word she spoke resonate in her bones and echo down into the earth. The air grew thick and heavy with her words. The smoke grew dense and pulled close, blocking the sun, bringing down the night to cloak the daytime sky. Before her, Urien grew pale. The hand that held his short sword that had drunk so deeply of her family's blood trembled. His men backed away uneasily. Elen felt her power swell, felt her words become stone, become truth. She felt eyes on her, watching, measuring, judging. What did they see, those eyes? The thought was gone almost as it formed. It didn't matter. Nothing mattered but Urien before her now and the truth of the curse she levelled. The dark drew closer, grew thicker, thick as blood, thick as hate.

Then Urien threw back his head and laughed, and the power of Elen's words crumbled away.

'Very good, little Elen. Very brave. But I too have my friends and protectors. You may not touch me by such means.'

Elen's chest heaved with the force of her breath. The unspent curse surged through her blood, causing her hands and knees to tremble with its force. How could he have turned her words here and now? What protection did he have? What friend had he who could do so much?

'Now, come here, girl, before I grow angry.'

Yestin stepped between them. 'You will not have her.'

Urien sighed. 'It's time you remembered you were a man,

Yestin.' He jerked his chin to the man on his left. He was broad faced and broad shouldered and carried a knife and a club, and grinned as he came forward.

Yestin did not wait for him. He screamed and charged, the sheer fury of him knocking the man's defence aside to plunge his sword up to its hilt in the other's breast. But the dead man's companions seized Yestin by the shoulders, cursing, wrestling him off, even as he spun to face them, blade dripping gore.

Elen ran too. She ran for the treasure heap. Urien's foot shot out and caught her ankle, sending her sprawling across the floor, skidding obscenely in the fresh blood. He lunged for her, but she rolled and kicked, and he missed her. He lunged once more, but she wrapped her hands around the hilt of the gift sword. She could barely lift it, her hands were so weakened by hunger and failure, but she raised its tip to Urien's belly.

Urien threw back his head and laughed at the sight of her, trembling and pitiful with the bright sword in her shaking hands.

He should not have. Elen dived, almost fell, but the long sword was sharp enough to do the work. Its weight drove the blade into his side, through his leather jerkin and into his gut.

Urien screamed, his back arched like a bow and he fell, blood oozing from the wound. Before Elen could raise the sword again, Yestin grabbed her by the wrist, causing her to drop the sword.

'Get her out of here!' he screamed.

The wider world came back in a rush of sound – shouts, screams, clashing metal – men and women rushed to fill the hall, some of them allies, others Urien's men, riding straight in on their foaming, snorting ponies. Elen collided with Madyn, big, grizzled, a wound on his bald scalp pouring blood down his face. He grabbed her arm and hauled her away from the surge and storm of the battle.

She wanted to pull away, to scream at him that she would have Urien's head. She would parade it before his men and hang it from what was left of the walls of her home. But at least one of Urien's men ran behind them, and she saw more of them charging up the hill, two on horseback and at least four more afoot, knives and axes out. They came to their chieftain's cries, coming to cut down her and Yestin, and all their own.

And Elen found she was not so ready to die as she had thought.

Madyn was running, heading for the rear of the hall and the ovens. Elen followed at his heels, every muscle straining, her lungs gulping down air. Madyn was shouting, but she could not make out the words. The hoofbeats were getting closer, mingling with the pounding of her heart. They would have to turn, have to face them or be ridden down. She would make sure they let out their blood as the price for hers. She would strike that much of a blow . . .

Another crowd of men surged forward, and women too, coming from behind the ovens and the ruined storehouses. They screamed as they ran, holding up picks and hammers and improvised pikes as well as knives and clubs. Elen knew them, every one. They ran past her, and the two horsemen were at once surrounded. They flailed out, but the defenders of Pont Cymryd were too many for them, and they were toppled from their saddles. It came to Elen that Yestin had planned this. Her little brother had thought Urien might be waiting for them. Yestin had allowed for the chance of escape.

Elen heard the sick crunch of breaking bones and in the pit of her heart she wanted both to cheer and to be violently sick.

Madyn grabbed her wrist again, pulling her into a run

behind him. Her feet stumbled. Her body had gone too long without food. Her heart had been torn in two. Her strength was all but spent. She could not see clearly. A fog descended over her mind as thick as the one she had been driven through, how long ago? An hour? A lifetime? She didn't know.

They headed up the hills into the deep woods. Bracken dragged at her hems and branches slapped her face and shoulders. Madyn laboured to hoist her up the rough slopes. She tried to help him, she truly did, but she had no help left. It was momentum alone that kept her upright. If they stopped, she would fall. She knew that, but she no longer had the strength to care.

At last, they did stop. She heard the trickle of water, saw the play of light and shadow before her that told her they were in the old heart of the wood. The ground sloped away from her feet, and as she had known would happen, her knees buckled and she fell onto the sweet smelling loam. Hands touched her, rolling her over, checking to see if she had taken any hurt to her body. A cloak was laid across her, and Elen closed her eyes, and slept.

She was surprised when she woke. Her dreams had all been of death and darkness. Her sleeping soul had not believed there could be an end to them, let alone one that brought the slanting yellow sun of afternoon and the scents of earth and herbs. She found she could sit up, and while her limbs were weak, they were under her control. Her throat burned with thirst. Her hunger was a dull, persistent ache below her heart.

A bowl of broth was put into her hands. She looked up to see Corsen, Cate's daughter. Corsen was dishevelled and dirty, and she gave Elen a smile as she straightened up. The steam rising from the broth smelled of meat and sorrel. Elen drank down the broth, although it was hot enough to scald her throat, and ate the shreds of quail and wood pigeon with her fingers, barely remembering to be careful of the bones.

Corsen took the bowl and refilled it from the iron kettle that hung over the small fire, then handed it to Aeddan so the blacksmith could eat his share. For a moment, Elen felt ashamed. She should have made sure everyone else had eaten before she took her portion. That was what mother would have done. She pushed that thought aside. She needed food. She needed strength. She needed to be able to see and understand so she could think what to do. She was alive and she must stay that way, for her people, for her revenge.

There were about a dozen survivors huddled around that fire, each one dirty and weary, their torn and mud-spattered clothes hanging limply from their bodies. Saffi was giving her baby suck. Little Tev was leaning against his father's bruised knee. Col and Tori were sitting so close together it looked as if they hoped to meld into one being. Shadows between the tree trunks told Elen there were more of their people standing watch against what pursuit might come. She looked more closely at those shadows, and she saw, to her joy, one of them was Yestin.

Yestin, with a gash on his head, and another down the length of his arm, was standing on the far side of the fire, whispering with Madyn. He looked up and saw her watching him. He put his hand on Madyn's shoulder, and Madyn vanished into the trees. Yestin came around the fire to sit beside her.

'You are well, Elen?' he asked, and there was fear in his voice.

Elen nodded, hoping that would be enough to reassure him. She did not trust herself to speak just yet.

'You did us great service, Elen,' he said, a grim smile on his face. 'With a sword cut to the belly, Urien might not last long. If we can hold for a few days, we'll be able to . . .'

Slowly, regretfully, Elen shook her head. 'He's not dead.'

That pronouncement startled Yestin. 'He will be,' her brother said carefully. 'I saw it. That was no small hurt he took.'

'Nonetheless, he lives and he'll stay alive. I know it.' She did know. The fact of Urien's life itched beneath her skin. Yestin peered closely at her. He cursed softly, but he did not deny her word. She realized he was treating her pronouncement as he would have one of their mother's, and that new truth settled heavily on her.

'Tell me how . . .' she began.

Yestin sighed and shook his head. He had aged while she had been gone. His eyes had sunk into his head, pushed back by what he had seen. 'The men from Camelot stayed two more days. Everyone asked after you, Elen. We were worried, but mother was calm. She said you'd be back when your task was done. She listened fair to Arthur's men. She liked what she heard, and I know they liked what they heard in turn. We gave no firm answer, though, as we had planned . . .' he faltered. 'Just sent them away with polite words and promises to exchange more.'

She could picture them doing just that, mother sitting in her great chair, Yestin standing at her right hand, Arthur's men ranged in a half-circle before them, speaking earnestly.

'It seems that even this was too much for Urien.' Yestin's voice hardened. 'He came back. He . . . he stood before our mother in her own house and he ordered her to reject the hand of friendship Arthur offered. She tried to put him off, saying it was too soon to make any such decision, that there must be careful and deliberate thought. But again, he ordered her. She told him to take himself away.

'And he told her she had sealed her own doom, and he left.'

This too Elen could see. Urien swelling with rage until

even his hair stood on end. Mother calm as stone, and just as unmoveable. She could hear his final words falling from him, one by one, like pebbles cast in the river, and see him turn on his heel, his cloak spreading out like a crow's wings behind him.

'We were all afraid at that. We . . . I rallied the men, and we rode out to watch the borders. Mother and . . . Carys were to get everyone into the hall. We knew, you see, he'd try something. We were determined to be ready.'

Carys. Bright, blithe Carys, who was meant to be her sister come spring . . .

'We didn't know he had his men already in the woods. We didn't . . .' Yestin faltered. 'They came before we could even harness the horses. They cut us down like straw. I tried to hold him back from the house . . . I swear before all the gods I tried, Elen . . .' It was finally too much for him and she saw the tears beginning in his eyes. He could not break, not now. They needed to be strong. She took his hands, holding them tightly.

She could see him, running through the night, father's sword in his hand, shouting. Her brother, her little brother, covered in blood, death on his hands and in his heart.

'I should have died with them, but mother ordered I should get our people away.'

Elen swallowed the fear and bile that bubbled up in her as she looked around at the tiny crowd of weary friends.

'Are these . . . all?'

'No,' answered Yestin quickly. 'Urien's taken many as slaves, and he's already marched them away. Those of us who have managed to stay free were scattered. Ellis and Win are out in search of the others. We hope to meet up with as many as we can at Olwen's well.'

Olwen's well was a pool in a valley deep in the hills. It had no visible stream to feed it, and yet it was never dry. It

was a place all knew. It had few easy approaches, so it could
be held by a handful of men, and however long they had to
wait there, at least there would be water.

'So we abandon our home?' she whispered.

Yestin looked at her as if she accused him of nothing short
of betrayal. 'He holds the house, Elen. You saw . . . we
couldn't even . . .' he bit back his anger.

Could not even save mother's body from him. She would have
seen her by now if Yestin had been successful. She would
be lying here beneath her shroud, waiting for her daughter
to do the rites for her. But the living were here alone.

Yestin turned his face away to hide his shame and defeat.
'Without help, we can do nothing.'

'I'm sorry, Yestin,' Elen whispered. She pushed both
hands through her hair, trying to put her mind in order.
The others were watching them. With mother . . . dead . . .
Yestin was chief now, and she was . . . She was her mother's
daughter, and she was beginning to understand what that
meant. She was keenly aware that the others watched her.
No, it was more than that. They were looking to her for
guidance, as they had looked to her mother, and before
her, to father, as their families had looked to hers down
the generations. Their people needed them to be strong, to
set all in order.

Oh, mother, help us. What do we do?

'How hard is he likely to be looking for us?'

'Harder now that his trap has failed,' said Yestin heavily.
'He'll want me dead so our people are without a . . .' he
stumbled. 'Chief. You he'll want, dead or married off to one
of his men.' He spat. The thought left Elen feeling more dirty
than did the blood on her hands.

'I've been talking with Madyn and Aeddan.' Yestin
huddled in on himself, needing comfort, but trying desperately not to show it. 'They . . . we . . . think the best thing is

to head up the river. Tuder ap Howel is an honourable man. He'll not want Urien lording it over his borders or the bridge.'

And his cantrev is even smaller than ours. Will he be able to raise enough men? And what if we can't . . . what if we've lost our home . . . no. No. I won't believe that.

'There's someone else,' she said, lifting her head and turning her face, not west, but east. 'Arthur is holding his summer court at Caerleon on the Usk, is he not?'

'So his men said.' Yestin sounded almost wary.

'This High King promised our enemies would be his.' Elen's voice was stone. 'Now we will see how he keeps his word.'

'We thought of that Elen, but Caerleon is four days away.'

'Then you must keep our people together and alive until I can return with men and arms.' She stood. 'Does Urien think we are defeated? We will teach him better.' Around her voices muttered their agreement. Here and there, a fist clenched, imagining a weapon in its clutch.

'Elen.' Yestin gripped her elbow. 'This may be what he wants. He may have done this to lure Arthur into a fight. Would you be used by him?'

That gave her pause. Could Urien have designed so brutal a plan?

Oh, yes.

'Nonetheless, I will go. It is all we can do. We cannot slink into the hills and be forgotten while our people's bones are left for the ravens.'

'She was my mother too, Elen,' said Yestin sternly. 'I saw them ride Carys down as she fled. My Carys. You think I do not burn for vengeance?' Even now his hand had gone to his sword. 'But we cannot abandon our people.'

'We will not. I will ride out and you will take our own to whatever safety there is, and set free the captives.' Her jaw ground back and forth. 'What else can we do, Yestin? We *cannot* leave Urien unchallenged.'

Yestin sat silently for a long moment. 'It will be dangerous.'

'No more so than fleeing while he follows. It is you who can make the stand while our people escape.'

She saw the loneliness in him, saw that he was at least as tired as she was. He'd been living this nightmare for days now, and had no time to grieve, not for their mother, not for lost Carys. He was too young for this, and she was leaving him alone with the burden of it all.

But at last, he rallied himself. 'It is too late for you to begin today. And,' he said stonily, 'you cannot go alone.'

She did not want to agree, but she knew him to be right. The fire of her thwarted curse had all gone out, leaving behind nothing but a weakness where heart and bone should be.

Yestin touched her shoulder. 'I must go see to the watch.'

Elen nodded, and wrapped her cloak more tightly around her. The day was rapidly dimming. She heard the movement of the camp, heard the murmurs as the others spoke with Yestin. She heard concern in their soft words, but not doubt. He was their chief now, and she their lady. These men and women they had grown up among would do as they said.

She could not fail them. Elen pushed aside her weakness and stood. With clear eyes and steady hands, she went down to the others, to do what she could, and to keep her mind from what the morning must bring.

Pain. Pain and blood and the draining weakness that came with blood's loss, and someone calling his name. All these things filled Urien's mind as it rose from darkness. He was lying on his side, and his shirt had been stripped off. The air was cold against his skin and seemed to make the pain worse by its touch.

By an effort of will, he opened his eyes and saw Wyx's broad and ugly face leaning over him.

'Master Urien!'

Urien licked his dry lips. 'How bad?' He'd been a fool, underestimating the blood rage in the girl, and for this he paid.

Wyx's face scrunched up and seemed to blur, which gave Urien his answer before his man could speak. 'Bad. It's deep, master, and you've lost a lot of blood. I can't stop it.'

Urien grunted. 'Where's . . . my cloak?'

Wyx pulled back, obviously concerned his master was growing delirious. But he moved quickly out of Urien's sight and returned with his woollen cloak. The brooch with the three cranes was still pinned to the cloth. Good.

Urien tried to move his hand, but the effort was too great. Gods, he was close to the night. 'Take some of my blood. Smear it on the brooch,' he whispered.

Again, Wyx hesitated. 'Do it, curse you!' croaked Urien. *Curse you. The girl tried to lay her curse on me. Maybe she did. Maybe this is the end here.*

No. Not yet. She will learn the price of her blood's treason.

Wyx dipped his finger in the dark earth where Urien's blood had puddled and rubbed it against the brooch, smearing the cranes' beaks and bodies. Good.

'Leave me,' Urien said. 'Find Adara's cublings. Kill the boy and bring me back the girl. If you cannot bring her alive, bring her dead.'

'But . . .' began Wyx, but he closed his frog mouth around whatever words he thought to speak. He did not know much, but he knew enough not to question Urien on such a matter. Not even now.

Wyx left. Urien heard his boots on the hard dirt as he hurried away. He let his head drop onto the pillow of his arm. He hurt. He thought he had hurt worse in his time, but could not remember when. His throat ached with thirst. He should have had Wyx bring him water, but he could not raise his voice to shout now. He would have to bear it. All he had to do was live, was breathe, for just a little longer.

But each breath was fire, and each was harder than the last.

The world around him was growing dark, and a cold began to creep across him. He had lost all sense of time and could not tell whether night had come or whether it was his death drawing ever closer.

Visions passed before his eyes. He saw the dim past. He saw his grandfather as a boy labouring for his Roman masters in their iron mine, until his mother was able to steal him away and hide in the Black Mountains. He saw his father, cut down in battle against Uther's men as they fled back across the Usk. He had not been there, but he saw it now – Uther's bright sword, his father's blood, the pain on his face, how he fell into the mud while his men fled around him.

He saw the future. He saw Arthur, Uther's son, the city man, the Roman man, coming into the mountains. He saw his people slaughtered, scattered, enslaved. He saw their death because he died now, because he had not been strong enough to carry the burdens the gods placed upon him.

A roaring noise filled his ears, as if the river itself were rising up to claim him. Fear sent a tremor through his heart, and the pain of his wound seemed to laugh in return.

'Oh, Urien.'

He had closed his eyes at some point. He opened them now. They were crusted with sand and dirt, and perhaps with the salt of his tears. Ah, gods, but he hurt. He would have given all for a drink of water, even from dead Adara's hands.

He tried to open his mouth, to make his tongue move, to ask for water, blessed water. His whole body trembled with the effort. Warm hands touched his brow.

'Lie still, my beloved.' Her very words caused the pain to ebb. Her touch was a stronger balm than a river of water could have been. It calmed all fear, brought warmth and strength where before there had been only weakness and the cold of fear. 'Close your eyes.'

He obeyed willingly and let himself sink into the blessed warmth she brought him. Distantly, he felt her long fingers touch the wound on his naked belly, probing its size. Then, he felt her stretch full length beside him, felt every curve of her body pressing against him. Her mouth touched his, kissing him hungrily. His body began to respond to her, lust and need rising impossibly but irresistibly. He should have been surprised, but he was beyond surprise in this dark warmth that she brought him, and he kissed her in return, letting his body do as it would.

She wrapped her arms around him and drew him close. Her kisses grew hungry, even greedy, and Urien heard himself groan. She straddled him and he welcomed her heat. He was dying. How could he feel such pleasure, even distantly?

Pain. Red and black and burning like all the fires of Hell. A scream ripped itself from his throat as he arched his back, and the motion he could not control only made the pain worse. All the time, she held him, pressing herself against him. Bright stars exploded in his skull, and every fibre of his being seemed to tear itself apart.

'Yes!' She laughed. 'Yes, my love!'

And it was over. Utterly spent, Urien collapsed panting onto the earthen floor. It was a long time before he realized what was missing from him. All the pain had been taken away. He was weak, but nothing more. Even his thirst had left him.

He lifted his head, and looked up into his lover's black and shining eyes.

'Morgaine.'

She only smiled and extended her hands. He took them both, and stood when she did. His body was strong and whole, as if he had just woken from a pleasant night's sleep. Now it was he who took her in his arms and kissed her, long and lingeringly. His skin itched where his blood had dried, and he was no doubt filthy in other ways, but she answered his embrace without hesitation.

When at last he released her, she stepped back from him, looking him up and down.

'Admiring your handiwork, my lady?' he inquired.

'And so much more.' But her smile quickly faded. 'Who did this, Urien? What happened here?' She looked down at Adara's corpse with distaste.

'I was a fool,' he admitted, and he told her what had occurred.

Morgaine frowned. 'You were lucky, Urien. The girl could have laid waste to all our plans with her words.'

'Well I know it.' Urien retrieved his cloak from the floor and slung it around his shoulders. 'It is fortunate she is not so strong as she believes.'

'I think none of us know how strong she is. Her weakness is that her teaching is incomplete.'

Her words left him uneasy. He looked again at the dead woman on the floor. Perhaps he should take her head after all, keep her ghost prisoner, lest it walk to warn her child. 'My men are out in the hills.' Urien refastened his brooch. The blood on it had completely dried, smearing the fine silver with dark swirls. 'They'll find her.'

Morgaine's eyes narrowed. 'But perhaps not soon enough. No. I do not like this. She has powerful blood, this girl. I think we should not leave her to the likes of Wyx.'

Urien bowed. 'I trust your judgement in these matters, my lady.'

'Good. Then leave the girl to me. I will bring her back to you before she can do any more damage. You and your men secure what you have won, and let your new neighbours know that rather than honouring their promises, Arthur's men ran away like rats when the fight came to them.'

It did not matter that this was not true. What mattered was that such words spread among the men of the west. Urien felt himself smile. 'I'll take pleasure in that message, you may be sure, Morgaine.'

She too smiled, a smile for triumph and the future, love and hatred all together. It was at such times that he could see why men called her Morgaine the Goddess. Her power fairly shone from her, radiant and deadly, like a knife in the darkness.

He bowed to her then, he who bowed to no man, and when he straightened himself, she kissed him once more, and once more she stepped away, into the deepening shadows of the treacherous house they together had brought down, and she was gone.

Still smiling, Urien turned on his heels and strode out to find his men and issue their new orders.

FOUR

In the end it was decided Madyn would go with Elen. Yestin wanted two men for her escort, but only two ponies had been rescued from the sack of Pont Cymryd, and only one of those had proper harness and a blanket for a riding pad. Madyn was a grey-headed, grizzled and stolid man. He'd travelled with their father and knew the way to Caerleon.

In peaceful times, it was not a hard way. The Roman road lay just across the bridge and it could be followed all along the Usk down to the fortress that Arthur claimed for his summer court. A coracle could float down the river and be there faster than a horse could, even with the portages that had to be made.

But Urien held the bridge, and if he didn't have men on the road before, he surely had them there now. They'd have to make their way through the hills, following the meandering river valley for a day at least before it was safe to come down and seek the ferry at Llangyadyn, or someone who might trade them a boat for their ponies. Even then, if Urien got wind of what they meant to do, his men might take the river route and be waiting in Llangyadyn for them.

Everyone sacrificed something to the journey: one of the three water skins; the only whole loaf of bread; the cold, cooked remains of the quail fished from the pot and wrapped in oak leaves; a pouch to carry their meagre supplies in.

'Keep safe, sister,' said Yestin as he handed her the pony's reins. 'May all the gods watch your road.'

She nodded. Her mouth was dry. Fear made her heart beat fast, but they could not linger. Dawn was brightening all around them, and Urien's men would be on the move. If she spoke, her voice would shake, and the tears she was holding back might break forth. She could not take her leave like that. Instead, she embraced her brother, trying to draw strength from his hard arms as he returned the gesture.

Then, she turned her back on all who stood watching and nodded to Madyn. In single file, they led their ponies up the slope into the trees.

It was hard going at first, and Elen was glad of it. The effort kept her from having to think. Madyn picked a careful way for them and their ponies up the hills, holding the branches away so they would not slap the animals' eyes and make them skittish. Although they needed to hurry, they still stopped frequently; to listen for the sounds of men, to check their directions against the sun whenever the trees cleared enough, to give their ponies a drink from a spring.

All this time, she heard nothing untoward. The birds sang undisturbed by any passage but theirs. The thousand sounds of the forest – the digging, shuffling, rustling, yipping and scuffling – were as they should be. At first, this cheered her. Then, it began to worry her. If Urien's men were not following her, what were they doing? Were they combing the hills for Yestin and the other survivors? They were barely armed. They could do nothing but flee, and even in the woods, if Urien's

men were on horseback . . . Elen clenched her jaw and struggled up the slope, hauling the baulky pony behind her. Madyn
eyed her, but did not question. He just clucked more urgently
to his beast, prodding its sides with the switch he'd cut.

Despite all this, they covered a good bit of ground. Once
they reached the ridge, the land was fairly level, save for the
sharp gullies cut by the streams that fed the Usk below. These
they had to coax the ponies down, sometimes having to go
far out of their way to find a slope that the beasts could
handle. Elen more than once questioned the wisdom of
bringing the creatures, and Madyn always patiently explained
that they might not find a boat when they came down. If
they had to take to the road, they'd need the ponies.

The day wore on. Woods gave way to meadows which
turned back to woods again, all passing far too slowly. Even
when they struck an old track and were able to ride for a
while, they were too slow. Memories whirled through Elen's
mind like autumn leaves – of chasing Yestin through the
village, of listening to mother lecture on the nature and properties of herbs, of Yestin's face when Carys came to the house,
of the first birth she ever attended, how she had laid the
infant on its mother's breast, and how her own mother had
whispered 'well done'.

After each memory came the sight of mother dead on the
floor of their home. Her tears flowed repeatedly, but could
not slake her grief or damp down the anger burning in her.
She should not have let Yestin pull her away. She should be
taking Urien's head to Caerleon to throw at Arthur's feet.

'Have to find us a place to stop soon,' said Madyn, jerking
Elen out of her bloody thoughts.

She blinked and looked about her. She had been so far
gone in memory and the lust for vengeance that daylight
had begun to give way to twilight without her noticing. Soon,
it would be too dark to see.

'I don't like the idea of spending the night in the open,' she said, surveying the deepening woods that surrounded them.

'Nor I,' replied Madyn gruffly. He sat hunched on his pony's bare back. He was almost ready to fall asleep where he was, for all he struggled to hide it. Had he stood watch last night? She tried to remember, but could not. 'But there's no' much choice, if we stay up here.'

He was right. The moon might give enough light to see the way by once it rose, but even so, the ponies must have a rest. It would do no good to drive the beasts to exhaustion. Impatience and anger jabbed at her and she felt a sudden desire to curse the sun for not standing still in the sky for her need.

'We should head back down for the river,' Madyn went on. 'If I'm right, we're almost to Llangyadyn. Might be some house where we can shelter, and hear the news.'

Elen nodded her agreement. Then, she heard a strange and unexpected sound. A high-pitched bleating, familiar as daylight, but strange to hear in this greenwood. It was a goat. A thrashing and crackling in the underbrush told Elen where the creature was, and its voice told her it was afraid.

Madyn heard it too. 'There.' He pointed towards a clutch of ferns that waved and churned in a rhythm that had nothing to do with the wind.

It didn't take long to find the creature. A raven-black kid with bright yellow eyes had caught its hind leg in a snare set for birds. The little creature danced about comically, trying to get hold of the thong to gnaw itself free.

Elen laughed once, and knelt, catching the kid expertly around the neck. It bawled pathetically at its plight, but Elen paid no heed. There was just enough light left to see the slip knot. The kid kicked in its impatience while Madyn picked it loose. Two more kicks and the black kid was free, and pawing at Elen's lap with its cloven hooves, trying frantically to get down.

'Hold it tight, Elen,' said Madyn. 'That's payment for the ferryman or a boat when we get to the river.'

But Elen shook her head. 'It's a croft to spend the night in if we let him lead us to his home.'

She released the struggling animal and the kid galloped immediately for the track they'd been following. Elen scrambled to her feet. She and Madyn snatched up their ponies' reins and followed the kid as it danced down the path, kicking up its heels in its joy at being free. For a moment thoughts of the *puka*, the shapeshifter, flashed through Elen's mind, but pukas were always pure white, or so the stories went. This kid was black as midnight, which was coming closer with each breath. They had no choice but to follow.

An owl hooted overhead. The kid plunged off the track. Madyn swore. Elen pushed her way into the trees after it, down the steep slope heading for the river valley. She could no longer clearly see the ground beneath her feet. Roots and holes tripped her and made her pony stumble. That would be the end of everything, if one of the ponies went lame, or worse, broke its ankle in some creature's burrow.

Then, over all the crashing and thrashing of their passage, Elen heard the sound of running water. The kid splashed through a narrow beck, pausing to take a drink and then shake the clear drops from its muzzle and beard. Ahead, the trees thinned, and Elen saw the unmistakable spark of a fire.

The kid saw it too. It gave a delighted hop and charged forward through the bracken, leaving the humans and lesser beasts to struggle on as best they could. But, at last, they broke free of the forest into a meadow of knee-high grass. In the distance, Elen could just see the dark surface of the Usk. The nightingales and nightjars sang and chugged and finally took off in an indignant huff at their clumsy approach.

Ahead, Elen could just see a low house with a round roof. Madyn pointed. Beside the dwelling hunched a human figure holding a torch up high.

Elen stopped where she was. 'Hail the house!' she called out. 'We're two travellers seeking shelter!'

The figure raised its free hand, and beckoned, waving them forward with a sweeping gesture. Grateful, Elen went ahead as quickly as she was able. The grass was filled with brambles and nettles that snagged her hems, dragging on her with every step. The ponies whickered and stamped as the unkind plants scrabbled at their hides.

The croft was a wattle-and-daub house with curving walls and a thatch roof. Loose wicker fences surrounded a collection of ramshackle outbuildings and lean-tos. The human figure resolved itself into an old woman, the weight of her years bending her back nearly double. Her hair was snow-white and tumbled freely across her shoulders. Beside her, a black nanny goat nuzzled the kid they had rescued, which in turn was butting his head at both mother and mistress, its little tail waggling its whole backside as it tried to wedge itself between the two females to reach the nanny's udder.

As Elen's lieutenant, Madyn spoke for them. 'Good luck on this house, mistress,' he said. 'We were glad to be able to return your goat. We are on a long journey, my lady and myself, and need to find shelter for the night. '

The old woman nodded, her sunken lips pursed. 'His mother is a wise one.' The old woman laid her hand on the head of the nanny goat. 'She knew he would return, but she did not tell me he would bring guests.' She thrust her head forward, peering up, first at Elen, then at Madyn. Elen saw that the woman's eyes were so dark they were almost black, and they looked surprisingly young and sharp in such an ancient face. 'See to your animals and then come inside.'

Without further ceremony, the crone turned around and hobbled towards the house.

Elen let out a long sigh of relief. That the woman spoke to her goats did not trouble her. Probably the family put her out here in the summers to look after the herd as it grazed. Ada spoke regularly to the pigs, and swore they foretold the weather.

But then, those were the white pigs, and they just might have.

'I'll see to the ponies,' said Madyn, taking the reins from Elen. His eyes were bleary and he blinked too much. 'You go speak fair to our hostess.'

Elen nodded and touched his arm in thanks. Gods all grant they'd be able to get him to a bed soon.

With the night following close behind her, Elen walked into the dark, windowless house.

The torch had been extinguished. What light there was came from a low fire burning in a central hollow. A tripod had been erected over it and an iron pot hung on a chain. The scent of porridge, onions and sage filled the close and smoky air. Elen's stomach cramped and growled as she breathed it in. The old woman stirred the kettle with a long-handled spoon. She lifted it to her mouth and slurped the porridge noisily, smacking her lips in satisfaction.

The place had little in the way of furnishings. The flickering fire showed up a plank table and bench that looked hastily pegged together, and near the fire was a pallet bed that was little more than a frame of sticks and a lumpy bag for a mattress. But the place shut out the sound of wolves, and the warmth of the fire was like a blessing.

The old woman cocked her head towards Elen. 'Come in! Come in!' She waved the spoon. 'It's not often I have a chance to talk. Come, talk and eat!' She picked a bowl up off the earthen floor and began spooning porridge into it.

She added a lump of brown bread and handed it to Elen. There was no spoon.

'I thank you, grandmother,' said Elen, mustering her courtesies. 'Could you please tell me whose hospitality I am accepting?'

'Whose?' The woman smiled, showing all the gaps in her teeth, and her bright eyes sparkled. 'Well now, let's see . . .' she tapped her pointed chin. 'You can call me Mother Morwith. And who accepts her hospitality, eh?' She said it as if she asked a riddle, or told a joke.

All at once, Elen remembered the faces of the ones who had come to take her away, with their big eyes and their brown, pinched faces, impatient and frightened in the dark. Her throat was dry. Her stomach cried out for the food that steamed in the bowl in front of her, but her mind was suddenly afraid. 'I am Elen,' she said.

Mother Morwith pointed the spoon at her. 'Elen daughter of Adara, you mean to say.'

Elen stared, her tongue frozen to the roof of her mouth, but Mother Morwith only laughed and picked up her own bowl. 'Look at the girl! She goggles like a sheep. Eat, eat! Like Mother Morwith!' She tipped the bowl up to her mouth, supping the hot porridge. She lifted her head and sighed in satisfaction. 'Ah!'

But Elen could not make herself move. It seemed as if the shadows had taken on weight and held her in place.

'I . . . I'd best see what's taking Madyn so long.' The words sounded weak. The old woman cackled as she set the bowl down, and she cackled again as Elen hurried out into the yard, drawing in great lungfuls of the fresh, chilly air.

Maybe we should dare the wolves after all. I do not like this place.

Behind the house waited a little lean-to with some dry hay in it. Inside stood the two ponies, unsaddled and unbridled, munching the fodder. They looked up briefly at her approach, then went back to grazing carefully around Madyn, who was stretched out in the hay, fast asleep and snoring gently.

Elen covered her mouth to stifle a laugh. A bony finger tapped her shoulder. Mother Morwith had come up behind her. She grinned and clucked her tongue at the sleeping man, then jerked her thumb towards the house. Eased in her heart, although she could not truly have said why, Elen followed her back.

'Now eat!' cried the old woman when they reached the table again. 'I swear you will take no hurt from my food, girl. Eat!'

It was the oath that made up Elen's mind. She sat herself at the bench and sopped the lump of bread in the stew of oats and lentils. She was more hungry than she had realized and the first bite almost overwhelmed her, it was so delicious. Abandoning caution and manners, she wolfed down the rest, able to think of nothing but filling herself with food.

'There! That's better!' Mother Morwith cackled with satisfaction. She shuffled into the shadows and returned with a crockery jug and a wooden cup. She pulled up the stopper and released the scent of strong beer. She poured a good measure into the cup and handed it to Elen.

'Drink that now. After such a time as you have had it will do you a great world of good.'

No longer famished, Elen was able to sip the beer slowly. It was indeed strong, but it was not so stale as she had thought it might be. Someone kept this woman well supplied. 'Mother,' she began cautiously. 'How is it you know of my name and my trouble?'

'Ah!' sighed the old woman again. She lowered herself onto the bench in front of Elen. 'Now how could I not know? Anyone with eyes could know. You hide nothing of yourself, my girl. Your heart and your hatred shine free for anyone who can look to see.'

'Mother . . .' How to ask? It might be better just to let it be, but she couldn't. They had to spend the night here. She needed to know where she was, and with whom. 'Mother, are you a seer?'

'Mother Morwith is many things.' The old woman grinned her leering, gap-toothed grin. 'As are you, I think, my girl.'

Elen looked into the depths of her cup. The liquid was black, with only the barest reflection of the firelight flickering across its surface. 'More than I would be if I had my way.'

'And you think it is the High King who can bring you relief from all these troubles, hmmm, my girl?'

Elen found she was completely prepared to hear Mother Morwith speak of her destination. Prophecy was all around her, and magic. She smelled it in the smoke and felt it in the touch of the shadows. 'It was his embassy that brought this catastrophe down. It is his duty to avenge the wrong done.'

'Are you sure? Are you sure there is no one closer at hand?'

Elen paused. Her insides felt cold and hard, as if her bones had turned to iron. She dared look in the woman's eyes, her black, deep, youthful eyes. She knew if she chose, she could see many things in those eyes. It would be like scrying in a forest pool. They reached for her, compelling her to come close. But Elen did not move. She was stone, she was iron. She would not be called or culled so easily.

'Do you say there is such a one?' Elen asked quietly.

Mother Morwith nodded once, not in answer, it seemed, but in satisfaction that Elen remained unmoved. 'Perhaps. It would depend.'

Careful, careful, Elen's heart warned her. *This is a place where words can bind. This woman could be anyone, any of the gods, any of the spirits. She might even be one of the dead. Be very, very careful.*

Elen set her cup aside. The click of wood against wood sounded very loud.

'Upon what would it depend, grandmother?' She suddenly felt no desire to speak the woman's name, nor to call her 'mother'. It was a false name, a disguise. She would not give it any more substance than it already had.

'On many things,' said her hostess archly. 'On loyalty, on price, on promises.'

'Whose loyalty?' shot back Elen. 'What price and which promises?'

'Oh, that too depends, my girl.' The crone smiled. 'That depends very much indeed.'

Elen felt her head begin to ache. She was fast becoming tired. Her reserves of strength were still very low, and she wanted nothing more than to stretch out on this dirt floor with only her cloak for blanket and pillow and fall into blessed sleep.

'Grandmother,' she said, pulling her cloak more tightly around herself, as if the thick wool could fend off the touch of the shadows. 'If you offer me help, I thank you, deeply and from the bottom of my heart. But I cannot make any promises until my journey is complete.'

The old woman shook her head slowly. 'Arthur will not hear you.'

'I will make him hear,' answered Elen evenly.

'He will not hear you,' Mother Morwith said again. 'For you, his hall is as far away as the stars. Your voice will not reach his ears.'

Elen swallowed. *How can you know? How can you even believe you know such a thing? What are you?* 'Do you speak prophecy to me, grandmother?'

'I speak truth, daughter, and you know that I do.'

'Then tell me, grandmother, what would you have me do?' Elen threw her arms out wide. 'My mother's blood stains my skin even now. I have no strong friends to whom I can take my feud. What am I to do but go to the enemies of my enemy?'

At this, Mother Morwith only smiled. 'You do have friends,' she said softly, certainly. 'Old friends, strong friends. Friends of well and hill, twilight and moonrise. You know them. You could turn to them.'

The darkness wrapped around her. Elen felt it at her back, reaching around her throat. It would bind her tight if she did not move soon. She bowed her head, trying to make herself smaller. 'My curses are weak as ashes.'

'No.' She spoke the word mildly, perhaps a bit reprovingly. 'Urien has powerful protection, that is all. But there are ways around it. You could learn.'

Elen lifted her head and felt her mouth tighten into a mirthless smile. 'Who would teach me? You?'

But the old woman with her young, black eyes smiled back more kindly, and more wisely. 'Perhaps.'

She meant it. Elen could feel that with every heartbeat. 'Would you teach me the death of Urien? Would you teach me the rebuilding of my home?'

'I would teach you power, and the use of it,' the woman answered. 'I would teach you the rightful destiny of yourself, your land and the people of your land.'

Elen stared into those young, black eyes in the old, old face. Real power, such as she saw in her mother a few times in her life, such as she knew lay asleep in her blood, waiting for knowledge and for need. There was a name for the power which she saw, and perhaps she could even find it if she looked hard. But could she grasp its hand? Could she accept what this woman promised and bide her time for her revenge?

Could she abandon Yestin to his own fate? Yestin and all the others who survived in the cold hills, or in the fetters of slavery?

No. 'Grandmother, I do not want destiny. I do not want truth or power or hidden friends. I want Urien to die and I want to reclaim my home and bury my family.'

Mother Morwith drew back. The shadows gathered about her, blurring the lines of her body. 'Beware, Elen, Adara's daughter. You are walking on the edge of the precipice. Put your foot wrong now and you will plummet from that height, and it is your death you will be taught.'

Elen stood. 'Grandmother, I thank you for your offer. But I am young, and my hate burns hot. I will go to Arthur. I will make him hear me. Perhaps you are right, perhaps he will not listen. If he turns his back on me, then will I come back to you, and learn all you have to teach so that I can tear down Camelot and use its stones to make Urien's cairn.' She spoke without anger, only with deadly certainty.

'There are doors that cannot be entered twice, Elen. You should know this. Turn away this hospitality, and you turn away the days that might have been yours.'

The air thickened as the woman spoke, growing close and hard to breathe. Fear took hold of Elen's heart, damping down the fire of anger. The black eyes watched her, waiting. They were filled with power, those eyes, and promises yet ungiven.

The next thing I do will be the true thing, thought Elen over the pounding of her heart. *If I do not relent, I will be lost.*

So be it. 'Grandmother, I thank you for your words of caution, for the food and shelter you have offered me, but I will go.'

'No,' said the old woman. 'You will not.'

She straightened and the shawl slid from her shoulders. As it slithered to the floor, the disguise fell away, and the shrunken old woman grew tall. Her white hair turned black. Her face grew round and fresh, not young, but not so old either. Only her eyes did not change.

Elen's throat closed shut around her breath. She stumbled backward, raising her hand automatically, making the old sign to avert ill-will.

The woman smiled. 'Oh, Elen, I would have taught you far better than that.'

Her eyes glittered and she stretched out her hand. Elen could retreat no further. It was as if her back pressed against a stone wall.

The woman crooked her fingers. 'Come here.'

Elen moved, without thought or hesitation. She stood before the woman, her heart pounding with fear, the blood roaring in her veins, and she was unable to move, unable even to scream.

'Now, then.' She looked Elen up and down, measuring her as if she were fitting a garment. 'What shall we do with one who will not listen to those who are wiser than she?'

Who are you? The question battered at Elen's frantic mind. *What are you?*

This younger woman tapped her chin just as the old woman had done, making a great show of considering. Elen pushed at the boundaries of her own mind, trying to force her will to her limbs, to her throat. *Who are you?*

A memory flickered through the storm of her thoughts. Mother sitting by the fire, Elen at her side. Beven was playing the harp softly, singing, no reciting . . .

'And Morgaine the black-eyed goddess spoke, and she said "My curse be on him then, and he shall be brought low at my word . . ."'

Morgaine? Was this she? Morgan the Fae? But she dwelt far in the mountains to the north, up past the Beautiful Lake. What would bring her down here?

Arthur, and the threat of Arthur coming, crossing the bridge Pont Cymryd held.

'I think you must be taught obedience, Elen.'

Desperate in her fear and her anger, Elen dug deep into her mind for the formulas her mother had taught her. *Morgaine. Morgaine. I deny you. Morgaine, your eye shall no more light on me. Morgaine, your will shall no more hold onto me.*

Elen felt her tongue loosen. She had it. This was Morgaine before her and her name had power. Elen gathered her will and wits, and put all the force of her fear into her words.

Morgaine opened her mouth and lifted her hand.

'Morgaine!' Elen whispered. 'I avert your will! I break your word. By the white mare and the raven, I defy you, Morgaine!'

She could move. She could think. She could run and she did. She fled into the night, away from Morgaine's black eyes and the power of her voice.

'Madyn! Madyn!' she screamed.

But Madyn did not come.

There was just enough moonlight to show her the gate in the rickety fence. Elen grabbed up her skirt in one hand and ran, heart pounding, ears singing. She had to get away, get beyond the circle of the fence. It marked a boundary of power, she was sure. She had to get to Madyn and the ponies. His knife was steel, it would cut through the boundary . . .

A wall of blackness reared up in front of her. Elen fell back, throwing her hands up. The wall became a man who swept his foot forward and kicked her legs out from under her. Elen fell to the ground, rolled and scrambled frantically to get out of the way, but moonlight flashed on steel. The man had drawn a sword, and he circled her easily, daring her to try to run past him.

Then she saw his face and her breath froze in her lungs.
Urien.

Urien, whole and unharmed, stood before her, his teeth bared, flashing like the blade of his sword as he laughed. 'Why are you so surprised to see me, Elen? I was expecting you,' he said mildly as he lifted his arm to sheathe the sword. Moonlight flashed on gold, and Elen's heart clenched tight.

That was Yestin's sword he held. Not the bright gift, but the older blade. Their father's blade. The one he had been wearing when she left him, that he would never give up unless . . .

'Ah, so you've taken care of the cubling then, my lord.'

Lord? Shaking, Elen got to her feet. Morgaine glided across the yard to stand at Urien's side. Oh, by all the gods! Urien's unknown lady was *Morgaine*? Elen's mind reeled. Taken care of the cubling . . . he carried Yestin's sword . . .

'Did you truly think I would let you leave here?' Morgaine asked coldly. Elen could not clearly see her face. The sorceress was a shadow that spoke like a queen. 'After you offered to give a foothold in these my lands to my enemies? After you struck my lover down?'

Elen's heart hammered against her ribs. Her mind screamed her brother's name. It occurred to her, distantly, that Madyn must be dead as well. He'd come to protect her, and she'd brought him to his death. Her eyes darted left then right, searching for some route of escape, but there was none. Morgaine's house was at her back. Urien and his stolen sword were before her. All she had were her bare hands, and she could barely see which way to go.

'You betrayed me,' she whispered hoarsely to the sorceress. 'I was your guest. I ate your bread and salt, and you deliver me to my enemy.'

Morgaine's face hardened, and she made no answer, but neither did she make any move.

Elen swallowed and tried to slow her heartbeat. It was but a moment to come, after all. Only a crossing. 'Kill me then,' she said, and her voice was harsh. 'Let my life's blood flow and know I will curse you both with my dying breath for the murder you've done.' *Murder of my mother, murder of my brother. Oh, Yestin!*

'No, little girl,' said Morgaine smoothly. 'I have said you will learn obedience, and it shall be so.'

Morgaine held out her hand to Urien, and Urien drew Yestin's sword, handing its hilt to the sorceress. She raised the blade high. Elen staggered backward, lifting her own hand to ward off whatever blow was to come. Morgaine was before her in a single stride. The sorceress knocked her feeble gesture aside and tapped Elen's forehead with the sword hilt. Elen collapsed to the ground as if she had been struck a mighty blow. She huddled, dazed, on the cold earth while Morgaine and Urien towered over her. Morgaine began to sing. Her voice was high and eerie in the moonlight, calling out across the whole of the land in some language Elen could not understand. Despite that, the words cut straight through her, pinning her to the ground, robbing her blood and heart of all strength, leaving only water and dust and fear inside her.

A high, keening cry sounded over Morgaine's song and the sorceress lifted her wrist. A merlin hawk, a bird that should not have flown at all in night's darkness, lighted easily on her naked wrist, fluffing its feathers, waiting her word.

Morgaine's song grew low and crooning. She set the bird on her shoulder. Its talons must have pierced her skin, but if there was pain, she gave no sign. The bird sat on its living perch, still and patient.

Morgaine raised the silver blade. Swiftly, she stabbed downward.

The sword plunged into Elen's breast, and pain cut through the whole of her soul. Elen screamed, for fear, for pain, for death, for the blood pouring hot and red from her riven body she screamed.

'Hush, child,' Morgaine bent over her, laying the gory sword aside. 'It is but the work of a moment.'

She laid her long fingers against Elen's mouth and Elen could scream no more. Throat and breath were frozen. She could feel only the burning pain, the pouring blood. She could only watch as Morgaine took that same hand and reached into the gaping wound, and pulled Elen's heart free.

She held it up to the moonlight for a moment, red and beating in her hand. Elen's mind swirled and tried to swoon, but Morgaine's workings denied her even that release. There was only the pain and the horror. Her heart beat in the sorceress's hands. She did not die, she should die, she could not live, it was too much, too much pain, too much fear . . .

With a word, Morgaine coaxed the hawk from her shoulder. Gently, lovingly, she pressed Elen's heart against its feathered breast, and the bird's body absorbed Elen's heart into itself, and left not even a trace of blood to show what had been done.

At that same moment, Elen felt her own wound close, her flesh and bone reforming, melding back into their proper configuration. The pain ebbed away, leaving only a hollow-ness in the centre of her chest and a weak, dry feeling, as if she were waking from a long illness.

'Sit up,' said Morgaine.

Elen sat up. She did it without thinking.

'Kneel.'

Elen knelt, again without thinking. The words went to the hollow place where her heart used to be, and from there to blood and sinew, to will and soul. It was imperative that she kneel. The touch of the hard ground was a blessing, for it was the place she must be. Her hands must be crossed just so. Each finger had to lay exactly in her lap.

'I am giving you this hawk, my lord,' said Morgaine over her head. 'As you have seen, it holds the little girl's heart. Whosoever is its master, is hers. She will do whatever he bids her do.'

To hear her doom spoken so clearly sent a fresh shaft of fear through Elen's distracted mind. Her head lifted itself, and for a moment she was afraid she might begin to plead with them.

Urien held the hawk now on his naked hand. As Elen looked at it, it seemed to her she could hear the sound of its heart, her heart, beating in its breast. It beat fast and light, like the sound of a drum played for dancing. It called for her. She wanted to reach for it, but that would be wrong. She must kneel. She must reach for her heart. The twin needs clutched her so tightly it felt as if she would be torn in two.

Urien stroked the hawk's neck. The bird's ruffled feathers settled, and Elen felt the tension in her own shoulders ease. She had not thought there could be any new horror to this, but now the ache of it overtook her, for Urien's touch soothed the hawk, and it soothed her as well.

Her mouth moved. 'Let me die,' she heard herself whisper. 'I will die silent. There will be no curse. Let me die.'

Urien sighed. 'Believe what you will, but I am sorry things must come to this. Yours was a proud house and I would have taken your mother willingly as friend and ally. Alas, it was not to be and I could not permit her to endanger us all. Perhaps in time you will come to understand this.

'In the meantime, however, you are of use to me. Marriage to you is a good for barter I cannot waste. But I agree with my lady, first you must learn to obey.

'Wait.'

With that word, Elen's eyes were drawn to the earth. She saw that the silvered grass was fascinating in its perfection, each blade limned with moonlight, sheltering the bare patches of earth that could be seen as pure darkness, turning the whole into a vast and complex puzzle to fill the mind. The hawk had dropped a small feather and it lay over the grass, white and black in the darkness. What colour would it be when morning came? She must wait to see. She must wait forever. It was right. It was good.

She heard the footsteps as Morgaine and Urien left her. She heard the hawk creel softly and a wail escaped her own throat, but she did not move. To move would be anathema. How could she move away from the perfection of the grass in front of her? The way this blade slanted, and that blade had been kinked. There was a message there, for her alone, and she must understand it. If she could only understand the runes written in the grass, then all things would become clear. She must wait and understand.

The chill of the night began to seep into her skin. The hard earth bit into her knees. But she did not move. She could not even struggle. She knew she would wait here until she died of thirst and hunger and she would not move, because Urien had ordered it. Her heart did not beat inside her. The lack of it made each breath wrong. Her lungs moved to take in the air, but there was only emptiness at her centre, and although she could feel the sick fear of what had happened, she could raise no strength to fight it. The fear was nothing compared to the compulsion to wait.

It was so cold. Her skin prickled and shivered. She was thirsty. Tears began to stream down her cheeks, making lines of warmth, and then cold. Her joints ached. Her dress was obscenely torn and her blood had dried against her skin. Her cloak flapped uselessly in the night wind. Her breath came fast and hard, and she began to sob, hoarsely, uncontrollably. And still she could not move.

Oh, mother. Mother, come take me. Let me die. Don't leave me here.

Elen's eyes were crusted with sand and salt from her tears. The moon tracked its path overhead and the stars wheeled around it. The dew settled on her, and she shivered. She could not feel her legs or her feet any more. Her back screamed in pain. Her mouth was completely parched. Her head fell forward because she lacked the strength to hold it upright any more.

She might have fainted, then, she was no longer sure. The grass and the fallen feather were so beautiful and filled her mind so completely that she could not truly tell whether she dreamed it or saw what was truly before her.

Elen.

The sound of her name lifted Elen's head again, even though the movement was painful. Mother knelt before her. Her skin was white and her hands were long and strong and without blemish. Even mother waited here. It was right to wait. It was perfection.

Elen, your blood is your salvation. Your blood is your escape.

Blood. There had been so much blood when Morgaine took her heart, and now she must wait. She must wait. Mother was so beautiful. She shone in the moonlight, even though the moon had set. Maybe mother would take her away. She didn't understand why she hurt so much. She was waiting and it was the right thing to do.

Blood calls to blood, Elen. Blood must hear.

'Blood,' murmured Elen, her mind so fogged she scarce understood the word.

She felt lips brush her cheek, cool and soft as the night's breeze. *I can give you so little now, daughter. I can tell you before you find your freedom you will ride into a far country where you will breach the wall and you will take death and return life. You will be allowed to bestow three gifts by the power of your blood. Three only in the name of the mothers who are birth and death. Use them wisely, daughter. Use them in blessing.*

And mother was gone, and there was only the grass and the pain and the stillness of her blood.

The power of blood . . . Blood. Mother. Mother had told her something. Something she must remember now. Remember beyond the perfection of the grass, beyond the touch of the shade, beyond the need to wait. It was there, beneath it all.

Blood calls to blood. Blood must hear.

There was blood all over her dress. Her heart's own blood that Morgaine had spilled. More blood stained her cloak. Her mother's blood from her corpse. The fae blood from the birthing she'd attended.

I must wait. I must wait.

There was blood still in her veins.

Wait. Wait. Wait.

Blood in her veins. Her family's blood. It flowed out from her slaughtered kin.

Merlin is kin to me.

Memory jolted through Elen. Merlin, Arthur's cunning-man, his sorcerer. Merlin was kin to Adara.

Merlin was kin to Elen.

They shared blood, he and she. Blood called to blood, and blood must hear.

But I must wait. I cannot leave. I must wait. It is wrong to want this. Wrong. I cannot. I must wait. Her mind crawled and cringed at the idea of moving. Only waiting was right. Only stillness was good.

But I do not have to move. The thought was delicious, like the thought of a young man lying in the darkness, waiting just for her. It was wrong, it was forbidden, but so tempting. *My blood is already free. I can call and still wait. It can be done.*

Wait. Wait. Wait. The word pounded in her as her heart had once done. It surged through her still blood. It disordered her thoughts. *Wait. Wait. Wait.*

I will wait. I will. I will just tell him I am waiting. I will just tell him I am waiting, and why.

That eased the revulsion that curdled her mind, and made

it a little easier to move her hand. It was so cold. She reached out and claimed the fallen feather from the hawk.

Where is it? Where has it gone? I must wait until it comes back. I must wait to hear my heart again.

She raised her hand to her mouth, and she spat. Her mouth was so dry, there was almost nothing there, but she managed. She curled her aching fingers around the torn and bloody cloth of her dress and the humours of her body mingled with the gesture and rubbed themselves into the feather. She closed her eyes.

I will just tell him I am waiting. He needs to know I am waiting.

Her mind was so dazed with all that had happened, it was easy to slide into the dreamlike state that allowed one to conjure visions. She thought of the feather curled tight in her hand. She thought of its shape, its colour, the lightness of it. She thought how it bore the hawk high and free on the summer winds.

As feather bears hawk, so shall mind be born. As blood gives power to body, so shall blood give power to the feather and the feather shall bear my thoughts to Merlin.

Wait. Wait. Wait.

With a force that made her body shudder to the bone, Elen forced the word down and away. She thought of the feather. She pictured the hawk soaring free. She willed herself to feel the winds. It was only her thoughts, only her spirit that would fly. She would wait here, but her mind would fly free. She would soar and see as the birds of the air saw.

All at once, her spirit lifted itself free from the chains of its body, and the wind snatched it up. She rushed through the darkness, flying free and fast. It was glorious. It was terrible. It was all she could do to hang on to the name of the one she must find, and she must hang on to it tight, or be lost forever in the dark winds.

Merlin. Merlin. Blood calls to blood, and blood must hear.

She saw light before her, bright and golden like a star in the darkness. The winds grew still and she moved no more. The light changed, it stretched, it grew, until it was a man with a long beard standing before her holding his white staff like a bar to her way.

'Who calls Merlin?' The voice filled the whole of Elen. She could not have held back her answer if she wanted to.

'Elen, Adara's daughter.'

There was silence for a moment, and then the voice asked, 'What would you of Merlin?'

Her mind cramped and constricted. This was wrong, *wrong*! Unless it was for the waiting. All she must do was continue to wait.

'I would tell him I am waiting.'

There was a pause. All her body strained. She knew this was wrong, it was worse than any other thing she had ever done, but yet it was not forbidden. It was hard though, oh, so hard and, she was so tired.

'For what do you wait?' the question came at last.

I can tell him this much. I can. 'For Urien who is my master.'

'Why do you wait?'

This much more. It is only a little more. I can tell him why I must wait. 'Because Morgaine has made it so.'

Again there was a long pause. Elen swayed on her knees. She did not think she could stay upright much longer. She longed to let herself fall into the grass. The closer she was to the earth, the more sure would be her waiting.

'Why does Morgaine concern herself with you?'

This was harder. Her mind rebelled. It was as if a wind swirled around her, buffeting and distracting her. 'Because my mother would have allowed Arthur across the bridge.'

Silence again, and in that silence her will and vision at last began to waver. The old man who stood so still before her became nothing but a blur of light again.

'Please, please, I can't . . . I must . . .' *I must wait, I must wait. This is wrong. I must wait.* The darkness folded around her vision.

'You have been heard, daughter.' His voice was barely a whisper and fading until it was no more than the echo of a thought. 'I have heard you. Believe that.'

She woke then, and she was as she had been, kneeling on the grass with the stars overhead. Pain throbbed in every joint, and yet she was once again completely obedient. The relief that swept through her was so great the pain of her waking felt like a blessing.

You have been heard, daughter. The words echoed through memory. *I have heard you.*

They meant more than was said, those words. They meant her will was not entirely gone. They meant she could fight this curse. There was room still for her to bite the hand that held her so tightly.

Elen took that knowledge and drew it down deep into the hollow place inside where her heart had once been. She closed herself around that precious secret, and alone in the darkness, she waited.

FIVE

Someone was shaking Geraint's shoulder. A haze of light penetrated the warm darkness of sleep. *What in Heaven?*

'My lord Geraint. My lord, wake up.' Donal's voice reached him. Geraint opened his eyes. His squire stood beside the bed holding a lantern. His fair hair was still tousled from his own interrupted sleep.

'My lord, the High King summons you.'

Geraint swung his feet out from under the blankets. Around him, men shifted in their sleep, snored or muttered curses as they rolled over trying to get away from the light. Geraint had moved back into the barracks after Gawain's marriage. Unlike Agravain, he did not have enough possessions that he required the extra space. Added to that, a room to himself felt lonely, and a little presumptuous.

Donal set the lantern down and scurried to the chest beside the bed for a robe while Geraint got his feet into his sandals. He felt it must be near morning, but not near enough. He rubbed his face to try to clear the last of the sleep's fog from him.

Donal held up a burgundy robe lined with fur. Geraint pulled it over his head. His squire was still a few inches too short to easily drape a cloak around the shoulders of a tall man. Another summer would cure that.

Geraint nodded his readiness as he tied the robe's belt and Donal picked up the lantern and hurried before him to light the way out of the barracks and across the yard to Caerleon's main hall. The summer night was warm and dry, but the wind was chilly with dew. The hall was silent enough that his sandals and Donal's sounded overly loud as they slapped against the stones. No light welcomed them until they reached the king's private chamber. There, a fire burned in the roomy hearth and its light gleamed on the mosaic floor, the rich tapestries and dark wooden furnishings. It filled the room with warmth and the smells of wood smoke. Arthur stood beside the hearth, his back and folded hands to the flames. Merlin stood to his left, clad as always in his simple, black robes and holding the white staff Geraint had never seen him without. Both men looked tired and strained, but Geraint chiefly watched the king, even as he knelt. Arthur's face was drawn, and his steady hands smoothed down the sleeve of his bright blue robe needlessly.

'Rise, Geraint,' said Arthur. 'Your brothers will be joining us in a moment.'

My brothers? Geraint did as he was bid, his mouth suddenly dry. *Is it come then? Has our father died?* He looked to Merlin, and the sorcerer's wise eyes read his thought. Merlin shook his head. *But what else would call us all here?*

The page opened the door, and Agravain and Gawain entered, accompanied by their squires. They were both in green robes trimmed with grey fur, and both were uncombed and unshaven. But where Gawain looked alert and concerned, Agravain simply looked annoyed. There was comfort in such a familiar sight.

Geraint's elder brothers knelt before the king and were raised up. Their boys joined Donal standing with their backs to the far wall, waiting until they were called. Arthur looked to them. 'You may go,' he said. Then to the page. 'You as well.'

The boys looked to one another, uneasy at this strange command, even as their elders did. But they bowed and then filed out to the corridor, though not without many a backward glance at their masters.

When the door was closed again, Gawain was the first to speak.

'What's the matter, Majesty?'

'That is yet uncertain, Gawain.' Arthur's voice was heavy, but Geraint could not tell what weighed it down so. It was far more than lack of sleep. 'Adara of Pont Cymryd, she had a daughter named Elen, did she not?'

Had? The Lady Elen? What has happened? Geraint saw before him the graceful maid with her merry, searching eyes. He'd done no more than share a few glances with her, and yet, days later he could recall each one of them, along with every line of her face and form.

'She did, Majesty,' he made himself answer calmly. 'Has there been news?'

The king looked to Merlin, who gave the answer. 'Elen is captive, of Urien, and of Morgaine.'

Geraint felt the fibres of his body harden into stillness at those words.

'Which is why I wanted you all here with me,' Arthur was saying. Geraint barely heard him. He saw Elen again, the quiet smile, the grace, the eyes that spoke of a wise and perceptive woman waiting within the dutiful maiden. He thought of the hall that was so much like their home had been in better days. He saw Urien on his feet, making his sly insinuations and blatant slanders.

'Morgaine?' Agravain was frowning hard. 'What means she to us?'

'She is your mother's sister,' said the king, looking at the fire as he said it. 'And mine. She concerns us.' He did not look up. He would speak to them of Morgaine, but would not meet their eyes. It was a strange thing. It discomfited Geraint and he was not alone. Gawain was shifting his weight from one foot to the other. Geraint also noticed that Gareth was not here. The king spoke of blood and family, and yet left him out. Well, he was still mostly a boy, and had been barely walking when their mother, Morgause, had left them to try to set matters right with her sister Morgaine. It would be natural enough for their uncle to assume he knew nothing of these matters. Now was not the time to correct him.

A long-necked wine jar waited on a table beside the hearth with some small cups. Gawain, upon receiving a nod of permission from their uncle, poured a drink for himself. He downed most of it before he spoke. 'I thought Morgaine died years ago,' he said to the dregs of his cup.

'No. Not dead,' answered Merlin. 'Confined only.'

Agravain folded his arms. 'You are very certain of this.'

The sorcerer nodded.

Anger darkened Agravain's face. 'If you know so much of the matter then why do you bring us here? We were only boys when our mother left us and she never spoke of her sister. You clearly know much more than we.'

But it was Gawain who had the answer, and he gave it to the king. 'Because, uncle, you believe this is much more than a conflict over a bridge and a small cantrev in Wales.'

Arthur nodded. 'It could soon become that.'

Gawain set the cup down. This was more familiar territory, and Geraint could see the urge for action grow warm within his oldest brother. 'Does Morgaine rally against you, Sir?'

'Yes.' Still the king watched the fire. What did he see in

the flames? It seemed to Geraint some heavy memory waited there for him and that he could not turn away.

'Has she strength?' Gawain wanted to know. Of course he did. 'Or only shadows?'

Merlin's answer was quiet, but quick. 'Gawain, you of all men know better than to dismiss shadows such as these.'

For a moment, Geraint thought Gawain was going to blush. 'Forgive me,' he said with a small bow. 'I spoke my hope, not my mind.'

'So men may in the darkness,' said Merlin evenly, but his hands still gripped his white staff tightly. 'Does she herself have martial strength? I do not know. We do know, however, that Urien does have strength of this kind.'

It was Geraint's turn to nod.

'And that is what we must deal with first of all,' said Arthur, turning around at last. 'This other . . . this other you needed to know.' Geraint thought he wanted to say more, but in the end, he lost that struggle, and kept it to himself. 'Let Bedivere come in,' he said.

Which would end all talk of Morgaine. There were perhaps half-a-dozen living souls who knew of her relationship to the king, and all but the queen and Gareth were in this room.

The door was duly opened, and Sir Bedivere, followed by the train of squires and pages, came in to kneel before Arthur, and be raised up. The boys immediately set to their duties, bringing chairs and wine for their masters and retreating to wait by the walls until they were needed. Curiosity burned bright in them, but they would have to learn to accustom themselves to it. Bedivere most certainly also wondered at what council had been taken that excluded him, but he said nothing and gave no sign of impatience. It was enough for him to know that the High King had wished him to wait.

'Tell us, Bedivere,' said Arthur as he sipped his wine, 'how urgently does Urien strive against us?'

'Most urgently,' Bedivere replied, looking to Geraint, who nodded his confirmation. 'Or so the men of Pont Cymryd believe. They say he has been riding amongst his kinsmen and fellow chieftains, making loud orations against the High King, and they have been opening their ears. Pont Cymryd was only one of the houses he visited.'

Arthur frowned into his cup. 'Since my father's time, trouble has come on us from the west. It was where cursed Vortiger chose to hide himself while he gathered his own strength. I had hoped the embassies would be in time to stem this latest, but it seems we were too slow.' He drank a long swallow of the warm, watered wine. 'Has Urien had time to do any more than talk?'

Bedivere shrugged. 'Some said yes, some said no.' The stump of his arm tapped restlessly against his thigh. 'His anger and defamation in Adara's house was real enough. I don't believe he is a man to offer insults where he is not ready to back them with steel.'

The men nodded and murmured their agreement with the logic of this assessment, and fell silent, waiting for the king to speak.

'We need to know more of this Urien and his plans, but we also need to ready our men.' Arthur's voice changed as he spoke, becoming sure and strong once more. To Geraint, it seemed Arthur was setting aside some old and painful part of himself, with gratitude. Could even the thought of Morgaine make a man such as he grateful for talk of war? 'The Lady Adara looked with favour on our offers. We must be ready at once to defend her. If her daughter is already captive . . . we may be too late, but if we cannot offer rescue to the parent, we can offer vengeance and succour for the children. My lord Bedivere, who can we best send who can see and not be seen?'

Bedivere paused, considering, and Geraint knew he could not wait for his answer.

'I will go,' he said.

All the men turned to look at him, and he had to work to hold himself still beneath their varying gazes. Bedivere looked surprised. Scorn was fast filling Agravain's eyes. Gawain looked cautious. But the king, who was the only one who mattered in this, looked thoughtful.

Only Merlin looked as if he had expected these words.

'You're known there, Geraint,' said Bedivere. 'We cannot risk Urien catching word that our men are abroad at this time.'

Geraint had his answer ready. 'The man from Camelot is known there, clean shaven, in mail and a madder cloak. No one's seen the wandering fighter peddling rough wares.' His smile was tight. 'The men of the west and we *scoti* are not so different in our home lands.' He wondered if his brothers would take exception to that, but neither spoke up.

Not that Agravain intended to remain silent. Of course. 'Geraint,' he said sternly. 'This is not for you.'

Geraint faced his brother. 'Why not?'

Agravain gave out a strangled sigh of impatience at having to explain the obvious. 'It is for someone who knows the country and the man. You would be of no use there.' Agravain looked to Bedivere for confirmation, but that captain kept his counsel behind his own eyes.

Geraint himself turned towards his king. 'Sir, I ask you to let me go.'

Arthur looked closely at Geraint for a moment, and then glanced at Merlin. The old cunning man also watched Geraint. His gaze was heavy, like the air before a thunderstorm, but what he saw with that gaze, Geraint could not say.

Then, Merlin inclined his head. 'Let him go.'

'Sir!' Agravain started to his feet, remembered whose company he was in, and sat down again. 'This is nonsense,' he said, gritting his teeth in an attempt to control himself.

'The ones who go may need to hold congress and conversation with Urien to ascertain his plans. Geraint will be known as soon as he opens his mouth. Then there will be one more hostage for Urien to bargain with, if indeed this Elen is still more than cold clay.'

Merlin did not rise to those words. He only pushed the tip of his staff back and forth across the floor tiles, but anger, sharp and unfamiliar flashed through Geraint. 'Do you say this is beyond my skills, Agravain?' he asked softly.

Agravain was never one for gentle speech. His words were easily as hard as his hands. 'I think you have spent too much time listening to Gawain expounding on the need for heroics.'

'Perhaps you have not spent enough.'

Gawain opened his mouth to say something consoling, but Agravain spoke first. 'I will remember those words, brother, when Urien has cut off your head and hoisted it on his pike. Then they will give me great comfort. If his Majesty will give me leave to depart, I will see you in the morning.' Agravain knelt before his chair, his head unbowed and his face absolutely uncompromising.

In the face of this, Arthur, to Geraint's surprise, spoke most mildly. 'His Majesty does not give you leave, Agravain, for you will accompany your brother.'

'Sir?'

Agravain's shock made both Bedivere and Gawain grin, but Arthur remained quite serious. 'This task calls for prudence more than gallantry, for a sharp mind as well as sharp eyes. If the battle is already joined, it will call for skill with the map as well as with men. Were he not so well known, I would send Kai, but instead you will go.'

Slowly, and not without a struggle against himself, Agravain closed his mouth and bowed his head in acceptance. What other answer could he make? The king's words were a compliment, and an order. He could not argue them without defaming himself, and as brutal as he might be with others, Agravain felt his own worth keenly.

Something we all have in common, we brothers. Geraint looked across to Gawain. He too seemed to be enjoying the king's decision, but there was still a troubled mind behind his eyes. Geraint could well understand that.

'They should leave as soon as they can make ready,' said Bedivere briskly. 'We do not want rumour to fly ahead of them.'

'I agree.' Arthur got to his feet and all the others followed suit. 'If the weather holds, you will leave today and make what start you can. In the meantime, Bedivere, Gawain, we will see what men we may quickly gather for this fight and send out word if we must call up the levies.' He turned to his two younger nephews. His heart was in his eyes at that moment, reminding them of the hidden danger, the one he would not speak of before other men. 'God speed you, Geraint, Agravain.'

'Thank you, Majesty,' said Geraint fervently as he bowed. Outside, dawn was just beginning to brighten the horizon. It was the coldest part of the morning and the wind felt harsh against Geraint's skin. It smelled dry though. If there was to be rain, it would not be until later in the day. They could start out soon, as Bedivere recommended. Beside him, Donal was all but dancing in his impatience to talk about what had been said and what was to come, but the boy knew enough to hold his tongue.

Despite the urgency of the task ahead, Geraint faced his brothers and waited. If Agravain was going to rail against Geraint, it would come now.

Bedivere also guessed what was about to happen. 'I will see you before you leave, Geraint. Agravain.' He gestured to his boy and together they strode across the courtyard.

Agravain did not turn to acknowledge Bedivere's departure. His jaw was working back and forth and he held his mouth so tightly, Geraint thought he was trying not to spit even more than he was trying not to speak.

'Will you meet me at noon, at the stables, Agravain?' asked Geraint. 'It will give us half the day to make good our start.'

'Yes.' Agravain turned on his heel and marched from the yard, anger billowing behind him like the sleeves of his robe.

Geraint looked to Gawain, his brows arched, but Gawain did not meet his eyes. He just wrapped his robe a little more tightly around himself and looked up at the brightening sky. 'I'll go back to my room. Rhian will be wondering what's happened.'

They nodded to each other, and Gawain headed after Agravain. Geraint turned himself towards the barracks, with Donal hurrying to catch up.

'Is it to be war then, my lord?' the boy asked breathlessly. 'Will we go to fight the Welshmen?'

'That's as it may be,' said Geraint. 'But you'll have to wait awhile to find out. I'll be travelling rough on this one, lad. I fear you'll only call attention to us.' The boy's face fell. 'Don't worry. I'll see that Sir Gawain takes you under his wing while I'm gone.' Donal lit up at once. 'Remember that smile, lad,' Geraint said grimly. 'Once my brother puts you to work, it may not come again so easy.'

He laughed at the sudden consternation in Donal's expression, and that cheered them both a little.

Back in the barracks, men were climbing from their beds, yawning, scratching and swearing, running hands through their hair and across their chins. The air smelled heavily of unwashed bodies. Some called out to Geraint with mocking curses for being up so early. Geraint waved back to them in passing salute as he returned to his own cot. There, he sent Donal running for wash water and a towel.

Two carved, flat-lidded chests stood beside Geraint's bed. He contemplated them for a moment before he opened the

smaller one. Beneath the plain shirts and breeches waited a
cloak, in a simple weave of grey and dark blue. There was
an enamelled brooch on it in the shape of a falcon with a
bead of blue glass for its eye. Beneath that was a stout leather
belt and a sheathed knife. Beneath these, waited a sword.

Geraint lifted the sword. It was a dark, heavy thing, scarred
from generations of use, but its balance was surprisingly good,
and the hilt fitted well in his hand. Its cool touch brought a
flood of memories to him: of summer on the hills below Din
Eityn, of his father in the good times, teaching his big son
to swing this blade, of the chill winters and of running
through snow up to his knees, trying to catch up with long-
legged Gawain.

Of his mother. Of his sister.

'You kept it then,' said Gawain's voice behind him. 'I threw
mine into the river when I was made squire.'

Geraint turned, not really surprised to see his oldest
brother standing there. 'I don't know why.' He slid the blade
back into its sheath of unworked leather and stood. 'But it
will be useful for this errand.'

'If anything will.'

Ah. Geraint sighed and tried to remember patience, but it
seemed far away this morning. 'Why have you come, Gawain?'

'Because I think Agravain might be right.'

'Well, it is a day for miracles.'

'Geraint . . .'

Over Gawain's shoulder, Geraint saw Donal approach with
the basin of water, and waved him away. This much he did
not want the boy to hear. 'Brother, you think I cannot do
this,' he said, keeping his voice low, but letting all that he
felt fill it nonetheless. 'You, and Agravain and probably
Gareth and the whole of the Round Table with you. It is no
longer your decision, if ever it was. The king has spoken and
the rest of you will have to be content with his word.'

Gawain shook his head, and tried again. 'Geraint, no one doubts your skills . . .'

'Don't they?' *This once I will speak of it, brother, and this once you will listen.* 'You think I do not know why I have my place at the Round Table? Is it because of my great feats of arms? Or because like Agravain and Kai I am a great thinker? No. It is because I am brother to Sir Gawain and nephew to the king. I know it, you know it, and all the Table and their people know it, and I am tired of it, brother. This one thing, small and foolish as it is, is mine to do and I will do it.'

Geraint met Gawain's gaze without flinching for a long moment. His hands clenched at his sides and his breath came too fast. Gawain's mouth twitched. Geraint was not certain whether his brother was trying to refrain from frowning, or smiling.

'Go then, brother, and God's blessing go with you.' Gawain did smile and laid a hand on Geraint's shoulder. 'And mind you bring Agravain back with you. I don't know what we'd do without him.'

Geraint found he could unclench his fists, and answer his brother's smile with one of his own. 'The cooks would all be needing a new source for vinegar, that's certain.'

They shared a laugh at that, for all it was an old jest. Gawain turned to go, but there was something else that needed to be said.

'Will you tell Gareth?' asked Geraint.

'What?' Gawain did not turn to look at him, which told Geraint he knew exactly what was meant.

I don't wish to acknowledge it either, brother, but Gareth is one of us. 'Of . . . our mother and her sister. He should hear it from one of us before the rumours fly.'

'Yes, I suppose you are right.' Gawain sighed and rubbed his eyes. He spoke in so low a whisper that Geraint could barely hear him over the noise of the barracks. 'I had thought this all behind us, Geraint. Truly.'

'You hoped. As did I.'

'None of it can be truly over while our father lives, can it?'

'Brother, none of it can be truly over while we ourselves live.'

Gawain tilted his head back, looking to the ceiling, to Heaven, hoping God could hear his pleading whisper and bring an answer. 'And what of our sons?'

Perhaps God had an answer, but Geraint did not. He could only lay his arm over his brother's shoulders and stand beside him. They stayed like that for awhile. Then Gawain patted his arm and they parted, Gawain heading back to his wife and their youngest brother, Geraint turning towards the weaponry he had not worn for seven years at least. Donal, seeing Gawain's departure, hurried forward with the basin. Geraint took his time with his washing. With Donal's help, he donned a pair of brown breeches, a simple white tunic and brown belt and his well-worn boots.

'I'll go to meat,' he told his squire. *Be the man of Camelot for another hour.* 'See those blades are cleaned and ready for use.'

'Yes, Sir.' Donal sounded a bit puzzled. Probably the boy was picking up on Geraint's own reluctance to return to the trappings of his past. That was all right. Geraint was a little puzzled himself. Did he believe he had locked the past in that chest?

Geraint broke his fast in the great hall. It was no formal assemblage. The king and queen were not there. Men and women came and went as they would, filling the chamber with voices, laughter and even snatches of song. The air smelled wonderfully of warm food. The servants handed around bowls of porridge and trenchers of beef, fresh bread and, because it was high summer, fresh fruits: cherries, pears, gooseberries and slices of delicate melons. Geraint surprised himself by eating heartily. His reputation for silence stood him in good stead, and those around him, who had surely by now heard of his early-morning conference with the king, did not bother asking him more than once what had happened. Agravain sat across the hall, stiff as a poker, putting off his neighbours with a quick snap from the look of things.

If he doesn't resign himself, this will be a long journey. Geraint shook his head. Resignation was not a quality Agravain was noted for.

It did not matter. This was his journey. Agravain could make of it what he would, but Geraint would see it through, wherever it led.

Which left only one thing to do. Geraint stood up from the table, nodded his farewell to his fellows, and took himself out from the hall.

As at Camelot, Merlin lived apart from the great hall in a humble dwelling, a cottage with a thatched roof and wattle and daub walls. He could have had a whole stone fortress to himself had he asked the king for it, but this was where he chose to stay. It was an ordinary enough looking place in the day, but Geraint knew that it was no more an ordinary house than Merlin himself was an ordinary man.

The door, which was normally shut fast, stood ajar. Geraint smiled a little at his own trepidation as he pushed it back.

The shutters were all thrown open to catch the daylight, but Merlin's work chamber was still a place of shadows. Bundles of herbs hung from the roof beams, perfuming the air and causing Geraint to duck his head to avoid them. In the centre of the room there was a low, stone well, tightly covered. It was a favourite pastime among the squires to tell tales about what waited at the bottom of the well, here and at Camelot, and to dare each other to venture inside for a look at it. As far as Geraint knew, only Gawain and Gareth had ever done so.

Merlin himself sat in a carved and cushioned chair. A great book, bigger even than the bishop's scripture, was spread out before him. He looked up, his face mild and unsurprised as Geraint entered, and he shut the tome before Geraint could make any sense of the runes and pictures written there.

'And what would you with Merlin, Sir Geraint?' inquired the sorcerer.

Geraint stood there for a moment. Until he had walked through the door, he had thought he knew what he was coming here for, but now, faced with Merlin's lined and ancient visage and his deceptively clear eyes, he was suddenly uncertain.

'What has happened to the Lady Elen?' he asked finally.

Merlin ran his hands over the tooled leather binding of his book. 'I do not know for certain. She is held captive. Something prevents her from speaking plainly. If it is Morgaine, it is most certainly a binding or curse that holds her.'

'How may it be broken?'

Merlin stared into space. He grew straighter, his face seemed to become younger and although he did not move, it felt to Geraint as if he became more distant. The air around him grew heavy and thick. Fear, as real and immediate as a child's fear of the dark, rose in Geraint's throat, and to his shame, he felt the prickle of perspiration on his brow and neck.

At last Merlin said, 'By courage. By truth. By a last act, freely undertaken. These will free the woman.'

Geraint blinked, and Merlin was only an old man again and the air was only air, and all of Geraint's fear crumbled into simple frustration. 'You see far more than you say, Merlin. Why do you not speak plainly?'

But Merlin just shook his head. 'You of all of them, Geraint, know the value of silence.'

'I do not keep silent when my words might help.'

Merlin pushed his chair back from the desk. His hand lay in his lap. The fingers were long and brown and knobbly as old twigs, and the blue veins pressed against his skin like roots beneath flagstones. That hand looked like it could not lift a pen, let alone the staff that leaned against his writing table. 'I keep silent, because words have power, Geraint. Because in the act of speaking, I change the balance. What is seen changes because it has been seen, and if I speak of the change, it changes again. I see only what might be, and what might be might also be changed, even by so small a thing as a word.' His smile was small. 'There. Now you know the weakness of Merlin.'

And I do also understand what it is to be unable to speak. Something eased inside Geraint as he thought of that. 'I know no such weakness.'

For a moment, he thought he saw gratitude in the old man's eyes. In the next heartbeat, it was gone and he thought he must have been mistaken.

'Beware pride, Geraint, beware anger. These are the things that will bring the downfall of the most godly man.'

Geraint bowed his head. 'Thank you.'

Merlin said nothing to that, and Geraint knew it was time for him to leave. He turned to go, but Merlin's voice stopped him in his tracks.

'It is not by accident that you are the one who inherited your mother's eyes, Geraint. Do not shrink from that.'

Geraint's shoulders stiffened. Memory flickered across his mind, of a corridor and darkness, of tears and bad dreams. He closed the door behind himself. If Merlin needed it open again, then it would be open. He hurried across the yard, suddenly eager to be gone.

SIX

Elen woke, but she did not move. She was curled on the pallet at the foot of Urien's bed, a prisoner in the hall that had been her home. Urien now slept in the carved bed that had once belonged to her parents. He had ordered her to sleep at his feet. And when he woke he would order her to dress him and serve him his food, and he would stroke the hawk and she would feel his touch soothing her skin.

She wanted to be sick. She wanted to die. For four days she had been bound to this existence, and it felt a lifetime. *You have been heard*, Merlin swore, but as the nightmare days stretched on, that promise was harder and harder to hold on to.

She risked opening her eyes, and, as had become her custom, she looked to the hawk. She was restless on her perch. The leather chafed her leg and she scratched herself. She flapped her wings hard and Elen felt the rush of the wind on her skin. She wanted to fly. She wanted to kill. The raw meat Urien fed her satisfied her hunger, but not her longing for the hunt. Elen felt all this in the hollow centre of her, and she welcomed it, because it was better than despair.

Urien snorted and shifted on his fur-heaped bed. He yawned loud and long and Elen heard the shift and rustle of his bedding as he sat up.

'Awake, Elen,' he said. 'Dress yourself. Poke up the fire, bring me water and tell Wyx and his woman that I am ready to break my fast.'

So began her morning, as it had for each of the days she had been Urien's prisoner. She rose, amid the other groggy men and women waking on their pallets, blankets and beds. Her only desire in body and soul was to pull on the clean overdress that had been reluctantly allotted her from the looting of her home, and to kneel before the fire pit and uncover the glowing coals. They were the most beautiful things in the world and her hands all but shook with her desire to coax them into flame as she laid on the tinder and the kindling. The fresh smoke and heat were a delight. Then she must catch up the bucket by the wall and hurry through the back of the hall, empty now of its hangings, its shields and its captured weapons, out into the harsh light of morning.

Wyx was the liar who had spoken up at the welcoming banquet. It was no surprise to find he was also Urien's most trusted servant. He now slept beside Urien, and shared out the booty as his chief directed. Wyx's woman, Elen knew no other name for her, supervised those tending the ovens and great kettles in the outdoor kitchen yard. She was brown from harsh weather, her clothing rough, and her chestnut hair hung in one gnarled braid down her back.

'He is ready for his meal,' Elen said as she passed, her feet hurrying her onward. The water must be brought at once.

Away from the house, the nightmare only deepened. She had to pass through the burned and broken village and watch the brigands and bandits. They had been coming in for days.

They wandered through the homes of her people, squabbling over who got a roof and who got this bit of refuse as booty or that stick of furniture to burn. What livestock remained was shared out among Urien's men for their food, except for a few of the cows and pigs that were kept under guard for Urien's own use. Those with neither house nor cow made their camps on the hillside. An army's worth of men, they squatted by their fires. They drank from leather skins. They combed their horses, mended boots and sandals, cleaned and sharpened their weapons. Not a few had brought their women with them. Some of these were wives or slaves, but others also dressed for battle after the old ways. The air was as thick with their voices and their smell as the hillside was thick with their bodies.

But even that was not the worst of it. The worst was that the urgency her curse brought upon her muted the horror brought by every sight, every smell and sound, and she was grateful for it.

She reached the well and shouldered her way through the men and women who waited there, lounging and gossiping and drawing their own water. Some reached out to pinch or pat her, although Urien had let it be known she was not to be touched. She did not pause to rebuke any of them. She did not have the time. She hung her bucket on the hook and lowered it down. She could have spoken as she worked, but she held her silence. She would do nothing more than she was told, but she hoarded these moments inside her. Here, she could have spoken. There, she could have moved. She could feel her boundaries, and they were broader than Urien knew. One day, soon, he would learn that, and he would find it a bitter lesson.

'See how well she serves her master,' remarked one of the women as Elen drew up the dripping bucket.

'Oh, I'm sure her own well is deep and fresh for him!'

screeched another and laughter erupted from the whole gathering. 'Come, sweeting, how does he plunge his dipper in your water? Tell us all!'

Elen fled, the hard laughter following close behind as her feet carried her to the only place she could go.

Back in the house, the beds had been cleared away and long tables set up in their place. Urien was sitting at one of the trestle tables with a crowd of his men, finishing a bowl of pottage. He wore his blue breeches and green tunic. Elen placed the bucket beside his bench and stepped back. A second bowl waited on the table beside him, and the smell of oats and lentils set Elen's stomach rumbling, but she did not move towards it.

Urien turned so that he straddled the bench, scooped the water up with his hands and gave face and feet a rough washing. Around him, his men kept talking, jeering, eating and watching her. Always, they watched her.

Urien lifted his head, shaking off the water droplets like a dog. 'Bring my towel, and next my cloak.'

Elen did as she was bid, fetching the things from the chests along the wall. Urien dried himself as roughly as he washed himself, smoothing hair and beard down with his hands before he reached for his blue cloak pinned with the brooch Morgaine had given him. Elen's skin crawled each time she saw the thing. She could have moved, stepped back, even sat down, but she did not. She stood still before him and watched as he fastened Morgaine's gift at his throat.

She too will fall. I will find a way.

The hawk on her perch preened her feathers. She creeled and stretched her neck, begging Urien for her food. She was glad to see him, and her gladness seeped into Elen who saw for a moment that Urien was swift in answering her need. He took her gently onto his gauntleted wrist, dipping his hand into the bucket of scraps he kept just for her, feeding her the dainties tenderly. He loved her, he saw her beauty, her strength. He would set her free to fly soon. He would see she must fly.

The fetter. Elen closed her eyes. *You do not love a thing you keep fettered. Remember that. Oh, mother, help me remember.*

She made herself open her eyes again, and she saw Urien watching her, the only still figure in this crowd of rough men and women going about their mornings.

'Follow me.'

Obedience fell on her, and she followed him, out into the sunlight of the yard. The world milled around them, all the strangers laying claim to their small scraps of her home.

'It is not me you should hate, Elen,' said Urien. 'I wish you would understand that.'

He stroked the hawk's back and to Elen it was as if his touch glided over her flesh, warm and gentle despite the rough fingers. The hawk creeled softly. A whimper filled Elen's throat. She wanted to hate, she tried and tried, but the hawk did not hate. The hawk only longed.

Remember the blood. Remember your mother. Remember Yestin. Remember these four days.

It came: hatred. Slow and thick, but it was there, and it brought warmth in place of the blood that flowed in her no more.

'You could order me to hate whomever you would,' she said, her voice harsh from disuse.

Urien ruffled the hawk's feathers ever so gently. 'I could, but I do not wish to. It pains me to have to chain you even thus.'

Although the pit of her cried against it, Elen felt the kindness he used on the hawk and could not hold her tongue. 'Then do not do this. Keep me with you if you must, but set me free of this spell.'

Urien sighed sadly. 'And if I do that, will you give up your vengeance of me? Speak the truth.'

Because it was an order, the words tumbled out of her and she felt only the rightness of speaking them. 'I will not give up my vengeance until I stand over your bleeding corpse and know its life has fled.'

'So you see.' Urien shrugged. 'I cannot free you.'

'Kill me then.'

'Nor can I waste you. You will not ask that of me again.'

The new fetter settled over her mind and tongue. Elen turned her face away.

'Master Urien!'

Urien lifted his head at the sound of his name. Wyx was stumping across the busy yard. Three men, two with black hair and one with the colouring of a fox, followed close behind him. 'Here's some outlanders would join the throng.'

Urien smiled as he always did when newcomers arrived for his army. He was counting warriors in his head, matching them against his foes. It was a dream he enjoyed. 'Let's see them, then.'

Wyx stood back and the three men strode up to stand before Urien. All were dirty and unkempt from days of travel, with unshaved chins. The shortest of them, the fox-haired one, had a tangled beard and hair that would have fallen into his eyes were it not bound with a leather thong. The second was taller by at least a head, a lean man with amber eyes and a disapproving glower. Something in his face was familiar, but Elen could not say what it was. The third . . . Elen bit down hard on her tongue to keep from gasping out. The third was Sir Geraint, Arthur's silent messenger, with his deep blue eyes. A black beard of several days growth obscured the strong lines of his face, but it was him. As his blue eyes looked at her face, she saw at once that he knew her as well.

How could he come here? Urien would know him in an instant. He'd be killed and she would be able to do nothing but watch.

But Urien was clapping the fox-haired man on the shoulder. 'Ifor! It's good to see your ugly face! Who've you brought me?' He beamed at the other two.

'Men of Gododdin. Found 'em on the road, looking for work. This clerkish one's Ahern.' Ifor jerked a thumb at the lean man with amber eyes. 'And his dumb brother there's called Gavan. I wouldn't give you much for either of them, but they both bring their own arms and say they know how to use them. Or rather, Ahern says his brother says. I've not been able to get three words out of the man in three days!'

'I'll wager I can get three words out of him!' Wyx bellowed merrily, and he swung his fist out, straight for Geraint's stomach. But Geraint stepped neatly aside, kicking at Wyx's ankle while grabbing his arm and pulling him forward so he slammed into the ground. In the next heartbeat, Geraint was kneeling on the squat man's chest and his knife was in his hand.

'You lose,' he said quietly.

The whole yard erupted in laughter, for many had stopped in their tracks as soon as Wyx swung his fist. Urien slapped his leathery hand against his belly in approval. The hawk shrieked at the noise, and Elen winced.

'Let him up, Gavan. He's a fool, but he's useful to me.'

Geraint stood back and Wyx rose, the hard look in his eyes promising there'd be payment. Geraint did not even appear to notice.

'If you're as fast as your brother there, Ahern, I'll be glad to have you both with me.'

'My brother,' said Ahern dryly, 'shows off more than's good for him. He's as known for that as for his prattling tongue.'

Urien laughed again. 'A wit too! This will liven things up here. Go on and find yourselves a place. I'll soon follow and then you'll hear of some good sport that will test your mettle.'

Elen felt herself go suddenly cold. It had come then. It was today.

She had been listening to Urien and Wyx make their plans since he brought her back to Pont Cymryd. It seemed they had been thinking of this before they even came with spears and clubs to take the hall. There was to be a tourney, here, below the ruined village, where the wild men would fight for the loot and slaves that Urien promised. Thus would Urien see the strength of those who came to him, and they would know his generosity as lord and leader.

Of course, such a great tourney would have a great prize.

Sir Geraint and the other man – was this Ahern really his brother? Yes, he might be, there was something about their faces, their eyes – bowed to Urien. Geraint caught her gaze with his again for one swift instant before he straightened and followed Ahern and Ifor from the yard.

Urien laughed happily, delighted with himself and the glorious day that shone out over his plans. The hawk flapped her wings and Elen shivered. She tried to rouse hope in herself. She had been heard in truth. She had been heard, and help had come. But so too had Urien's great day, and the fear of that laid itself over the hope that was struggling to grow.

Urien turned to her, surveying her with a critical eye, as if doubting her presentability. 'You will come with me,' he said. 'You will stay beside me, and you will keep your silence until I bid you otherwise.'

The fascination fell over her again and she followed, docile as any lamb, as he left the yard and made his way through the earthworks. He climbed to the top of one of the dykes, standing tall and proud on the little hill that had been made to keep the high house safe.

Urien nodded to Wyx, who had been ready for this. He raised the horn that hung from his side and blew it long and loud. The gabble and riot that stretched down the hillside stilled for a moment, and then resumed as the men surged forward, crowding together to hear what their master had to say.

Our master. Sorrow and fear filled Elen. The hawk on Urien's wrist flapped her wings and cried out, and Elen felt the desperate urge for freedom knife through her. But the geas was stronger and she could only stand and suffer with the captive bird.

Urien himself was smiling, showing all his sharp, dirty teeth.

'Behold!' he cried, sweeping out his arm to encompass the mob. 'Urien's round table!'

Shouts of laughter and raucous jeers battered against Elen. She looked for Sir Geraint, but could not see him in the sea of bellowing strangers.

Sir Geraint is there. I am not alone. I was heard.

'Arthur the Bastard thinks he will rule this land. He thinks he and his outlanders can ride into our mountains and sweep all before them. These mountains have seen outland kings come in other days, and they have seen the men of the west drive them back.' Cheers and oaths split the air. Elen felt her heart beating very fast and its fear filled her. She wanted to run, she wanted to fly. Tears threatened because she could do nothing but stand.

'So it shall be with the Bastard!' More cheers and the wild yips and screams of men longing for battle. Urien grinned broadly. The sound swelled him to greatness. 'But more than that! Once we have driven him from our hills, we will pursue him to his own hole! The Bastard will see his fortress looted, his lands burned, and our men getting sons of his women! Nor will we stop until the whole of this land is wiped clean of his works!'

The cheers doubled at that, and doubled again. The whole world was filled up with the roaring voices. The hawk screamed over it. Elen's fear was overwhelming. It was only the strength of Urien's order that kept her upright.

'But Urien shall have none at his table who is not a true man! Each of you shall have a chance to prove his might against his fellows, and the prize for he whose striving proves him best will be threefold. First, he will have my favour in all things! Second, he will have this fine hawk!' He raised the bird high for all to see. Not that any man there was likely to know how to hunt or keep such a bird. It was a gift fit for a prince. That was all they knew. 'Third, he will have this maiden who stands beside me for his own, and with her he shall have her dowry, which is all the land he sees here about him!'

The cheers rocked Elen back on her feet. She felt a thousand greedy eyes drink her in. The air seethed with their thoughts of what they would do once they had won her.

No. She closed her eyes. *No. Mother, help me. None of them will have me. None. I will find a way.*

'Go to your camps. My men will come and count you off in groups of fifty and you'll be told what turn you take on the field. The hundred men who show their best will fight again tomorrow, and of those the best twenty will fight the third day for the great prize!'

The cheer that went up was deafening. The mob boiled, churned and scattered, men streaming down the hill. There was one only who held his place. Sir Geraint. He looked steadily at her, making certain she saw him. His mouth moved, silently shaping a single word three times before he swiftly turned and followed the rest of them, vanishing into the roiling crowd.

'There's one who'll fight hard for you, Elen,' laughed Urien. 'You should be flattered.'

But he did not see what Elen saw. He did not see that Geraint had given her a message.

Well, he had said. *Well.*

He would meet her by the well, and she would find a way to get there. Tonight, she would start down the path to Urien's downfall.

In her mind, Elen smiled, and beside her the hawk let out a loud hunting cry.

Yes. Tonight, finally, we begin the hunt.

It did not take Geraint long to catch up with his brother. Together, they made their way down the hill amid the crowd of gleeful men heading for their own piles of gear and weapons. Agravain did not seem inclined to talk yet, and Geraint was glad. Rage at the sight of proud, beautiful Elen standing so meekly beside Urien the Bull closed his throat, and he did not believe he could have said a word had he wished to.

Their partly completed camp was on the edge of the woods. It was a bad spot for midges, but at least there was some shade and a bit of untrampled grass for the shaggy, unruly horses they'd traded their finer mounts for once they were well on their way from Caerleon.

Once they stood among the neat piles of their own gear – there was no need for subterfuge so great that it could make Agravain sloppy – Agravain turned and surveyed their fellow warriors and the ground they occupied. His head was already full of calculations, Geraint could tell. He was memorizing the lay of the land, the defences of the high house and what weapons and horses could be seen.

'This is good.' He nodded. He spoke the old, mellifluous language they had grown up with, and that they had none of them spoken since they left home. It was frightening how fast it had come back to his tongue. 'We will make a count of the men here, lose our mêlée and be on our way tonight.'

'No,' said Geraint.

'What?'

Geraint nodded up the hill to where Urien stood with Elen at his side. The swift and light maiden he had seen so recently was gone. Elen was drawn with pain and sorrow. Whatever had been done to her, it was almost more than she could bear. That was terribly plain.

Predictably, Agravain groaned. 'Don't tell me you're going to start taking after our brother in matters of women too?'

He meant Gawain. It was as a friend and champion of women that Gawain had made his fame, even before the story of how he won his bride from a foreign sorcerer became known. Geraint just looked at his brother. Then he sat down and rummaged in his saddlebag until he found his whetstone. He soaked it in the bucket that they'd left for the horses to drink from, and then pulled his sword from its sheath. He set the edge against the stone, and began to draw the stone down its length.

'That's both ludicrous and dangerous,' said Agravain flatly. 'Come back with an army behind you. That is how you will save the girl, and if that is not enough for you, we have a duty to the king to warn him of this.' He studied the mass of men heading towards the plain. 'This is no small thing.'

'You will lose in the contest today and leave,' said Geraint simply, not looking up from his work. Slowly, carefully, with attention to each stroke against the grey stone. That was the way to gain a keen edge. 'I will leave tonight, with Elen.'

Agravain made a strangled noise, half anger and half shock. 'You're going to steal her out of Urien's arms with a thousand armed men all around you, who have all been promised she's *their* prize?'

Slow, careful, methodical strokes. The familiar whisper of metal against stone. Yes, Donal had done this before he'd left Caerleon, but it was something that needed doing again. He must have the sharpest edge on this deceptively clumsy looking blade. 'I will meet her tonight.'

'You're mad,' said Agravain flatly.

You're right, brother. It was like a madness, the outrage that burst inside him when he looked on Elen's helpless state. Was this what Gawain had felt when he'd championed some lost damsel? He'd never asked. 'Nonetheless. You will go tell our uncle what he must know. I will follow as quickly as I can.'

Agravain squatted down and seized Geraint's wrist so that he must still his hand. 'Geraint, it is foolish,' he whispered urgently. 'You will only get yourself killed, and probably her with you.'

Geraint at last looked up at his brother. Agravain was furious, and uncomprehending of heart's feeling as ever, but he was also truly afraid. Inwardly, Geraint smiled at his brother. There was more heart in Agravain than he permitted any to guess. Outwardly, he kept his face still and open. *See me clearly, Agravain. Understand me.* 'I will not leave her here.'

Agravain stood, throwing up his hands to Heaven in exasperation. 'Geraint, you will do nothing at all for her if you die!'

'I will have tried,' he said simply. 'I will have given her hope to sustain her until you can return with our king's men.'

Agravain shut his mouth like a box and then turned away. 'Lord God, why have you given me three idiot brothers?' he muttered. Geraint grinned. Agravain would let himself be beaten today, and be on his way under cover of false shame, with a count of the men and beasts safe inside his bosom. Geraint himself would count the men with his sword this day, and tonight . . . tonight, he would steal the meaning of their false tourney out from under their master.

Geraint returned to his work, drawing the stone along the blade. *Be strong, Elen. Tonight you are free.*

SEVEN

Elen lay awake on her pallet. Above her, Urien snorted and turned over. Around them, men and women snored and muttered and shuffled in their sleep to find more comfortable positions on the dirt floor or thin straw mattresses. The hawk sat on her perch, her head tucked beneath her wing. Her sound sleep dragged at Elen, but she forced her eyes to stay open. A puddle of silver moonlight filled the distant doorway. It was a clear night, bright enough for what she needed to do.

It was dangerous. If Urien woke while she was gone, he would ask where she had been, and she would have to tell him, and Geraint would die. But she must take the chance. She must take action, or she would run mad. Worse, she would fail under the weight of all the burdens her spirit now carried.

The day had been endless. Urien had made her sit beside him while he watched his 'tourney' on the river plain. The noise had been worse than a hundred thunderstorms while men shouted and swords and clubs clashed again and again. There had been no sense or order to the fight. The men just attacked each other with a merry viciousness, leaping over their fellows when they fell, or kicking them aside to reach their next foe.

And Sir Geraint, her hope made flesh, was in the middle of it. Sometimes she caught glimpses of him in the crush, but never for long, not until the end. When Wyx had chosen the day's winners – sometimes with no more than a 'And you there, with the crooked nose!' – Sir Geraint had stood with those hundred, although his brother did not.

Then came the feast. Urien had ordered one of the remaining cows slaughtered the day before, and it was roasted and shared out for his new 'champions', along with great draughts of strong ale. She'd had to serve Urien during the whole of the raucous feasting, and could not do more than glance towards Geraint. She did not once see him look in her direction.

It did not matter. He waited out there now. Urien had staggered to his bed once it had finally been set up in the hall, and she had divested him of his clothes, and laid down on her own pallet without being ordered. Bemused by the ale, he did not order her to sleep. So she was awake, and in the smallest of ways, she was free.

Slowly, Elen rolled from her blanket. She crouched on the ground, trying to be nothing more than a shadow. The compulsion on her mind stirred, but Urien did not. Days of holding herself still made her legs tremble at the thought of moving, but move she did. She flitted between the sleeping bodies to the doorway. The hawk's sleep made her feel light and unsteady, but she saw the moon above, and she felt the wind on her face. She moved of her own will, and it was a victory. That victory gave her strength. Elen snatched her cloak from the chest beside the door and ducked into the night. In the hall's shadow, she squatted down and left her water behind. Then, she stood, and she ran.

I want to wash myself, she said in the silence of her mind, over and over again. *I want to wash.*

Her bare feet drummed against the rough earth. Stones stubbed her toes and cut the soles of her feet, but she did not slow down, even as she wrapped her cloak like a shawl around her head. Anyone who saw her would think she was a slave on some errand, and they would be right. But this errand was not her captor's.

I want to wash, that's all. I want to wash.

The fires burned low before doors and tents, glowing coals adding their orange light to the moon and the stars in the sky. Here and there, the dark shapes of men and women sat hunched beside them, talking the night away, passing skins of drink back and forth. In the distance someone raised their voice in drunken song. If any kept a true watch, Elen did not see them. The night was cold and her bare feet were soon numb, but she didn't care. All that mattered was that she was not stopped.

At last, she made out the low, curving wall of the well. She reached its side, panting, clutching at the ends of her cloak and shivering with the cold from which her sluggish blood could not relieve her.

There was no one there.

Could she have been wrong? Elen turned in a circle, trying to see through the darkness, but there was no movement, and the only human sounds were from the distant and fading celebration. Could she have mistaken the word or its meaning? She did not dare search the camps for him.

Despair washed through her, but then the bracken rustled with more than the night's wind. A figure slipped out of the darkness. 'Lady?' he murmured, and it was Sir Geraint's voice.

Elen nodded, weak with relief.

Sir Geraint looked sharply left and right. She thought he

would lead them into the forest so they would not be seen, but he instead came up to the well. A moment later she realized this was the better course. Even at this hour, it was a plausible thing for two people to come separately to the well, and if anyone approached, they would see them long before they were overheard.

Sir Geraint planted both hands on the side of the well. He gazed out across the night, looking up at the fires and the ruins of her home that stood stark in the moonlight. 'What has been done to you?' he murmured.

For a moment, the words stuck in Elen's throat. Would he believe what she must tell him? He was a city man, and surely a Christian one, like the priest who had doubted the bridge on Midsummer's eve.

No. She must trust him. She had no choice. 'I am cursed. Morgan the Fae placed my heart in the hawk that Urien offers as prize with my body. I must obey whoever is the hawk's master.'

Geraint nodded. His jaw worked itself back and forth for a time and his eyes continued to watch the hill, but the quality of his silence did not change, nor did the determination in his face and the set of his shoulders. He believed. She could read it in the very carriage of his person. Relief came again, and a little wonder that she could be so sure of what went on in the mind of this man when he had said so little.

'Can you come with me now?' he asked the moon where it hung at the pinnacle of the sky. 'We could be well away from here before sunrise.'

Yearning overtook her, but at once Elen felt herself rooted to the spot. The vileness of the notion was as filth in her mind, burying all other feeling. She must leave here, now, at once. She must return to her house, her bed, her master, her heart. She should not be here. She could not be here.

I am only at the well. I may go to the well! Elen shuddered, but steadied and was able to speak again. 'No. He has ordered me not to try to escape him.'

'Then how is it you could come here?'

She swallowed. *Go back, go back, go back.* The words rumbled in her. 'It is hard. I . . . there are small ways to fight this curse. I tell myself I am only at the well, only speaking with you. Nothing more.'

Sir Geraint's jaw shifted again. 'Can you part from the bird?'

Elen shook her head. 'If I did, he could call me back to him at any time.'

The knight's gaze searched the hillside. Someone shouted. Someone laughed. A light flickered up, and died quickly away. A wisp of cloud scuttled across the moon. Elen watched the man beside her as he watched the darkened world. She saw the line of his jaw beneath the black stubble of his beard, the curve of his neck, the slope of his shoulder and the line of his strong arm beneath the rough tunic. She felt the intensity of his concentration as he turned the problem over in his mind and willed the answer to come.

When Geraint spoke again, it was clear he chose his words with care.

'Could you bring the hawk here?' he asked at last.

Light dawned within Elen, and at the same time the revulsion, the fear, the rigidity redoubled. She closed her eyes, mustering all her strength. Bring the hawk, nothing more. To this place, no further. No further than the well. She was allowed to come to the well. He had said nothing about the hawk. He had not ordered her away from the hawk.

Perspiration rolled down her brow. Ashamed, she wiped at her face, and opened her eyes. 'I will try.'

For the first time, Sir Geraint turned towards her. His face was little more than silver and shadow. It was in his voice that the gentleness, the concern waited. 'Tomorrow night then. I do not relish the idea of being hacked or bludgeoned to death for Urien's amusement.' She heard rather than saw the small smile that came with those words.

But Elen felt no answering smile in her. She was too cold, and too afraid. She felt his strength, and she knew her own, but would it be enough? Still, they would try, and she was not alone any more. That was what she must cling to now. 'Thank you, Sir Geraint,' she said, and she could only hope he knew how much she meant by those words.

He looked at her for a long moment, and she wished she could clearly see his eyes, his face. He reached out and brushed the back of her hand with his fingertips. Then, without another glance, he slipped away into the darkness.

Elen stayed where she was, feeling the line of heat on her skin where he had touched her. For a moment, she could imagine she felt her heart beating inside her, stirring her blood and restoring the warmth of her body. For the briefest moment, she felt free.

Reluctantly, she shook herself, wrapped her makeshift shawl more tightly around her and started up the hill. The celebrations were fading like the coals from the many fires. The lucky few who had tents had mostly gone to them. The rest hunched by the remains of their fires, or slept stretched out on the hard ground. Elen tried to prod her reluctant feet to move more quickly. The danger of the night would not be over until she was lying back where Urien expected her. But she moved slowly – cautiously, she told herself – breathing the cold night air, for this one blessed moment under no compulsion but her own.

'Land, he promises. It'd be a fine thing . . . Set up in the high house. That bridge must bring in good coin.'

Elen froze for an instant, startled. The voice came out of the dark, from nearby, but she was passing between two tents, and ahead and behind were more little sites with their bundles of gear piled up so high they were hard to tell from the silhouettes of the humans hunched near the fires for warmth.

'Coin and kine. Aye. Think on it, my man.'

Outrage swelled in Elen. *These are my lands. They belong to my people. How dare you count their profits for yourself?*

'You'd not mind the woman, my wife?'

'Pah. That scrap? Sell her off to the highest bidder once he's given you her lands.'

Rage burned, filling her with its intensity. She suddenly wanted to find the speakers and tear them apart with her bare hands, to work on them all the violence she could not bring to Urien.

'Well, I tell you and none other, I don't know. There are some mighty men here.'

'Don't you think I'm watching? You'll do well on the morrow. You're better than most still standing. After that, well, my man, there are ways.'

Elen struggled to master her fury. *Move on, move on. What good does standing here do? You'll only be seen. Get back to Urien. You cannot give him cause to question you.*

Elen forced herself to move, but the soft voice followed her.

'I thought there might be. A man is blessed to have such a woman beside him.'

The woman laughed, a high, harsh sound. 'Win this contest of Urien's, and you'll have no cause to say otherwise.'

Even as she tried to close her ears to the night's greedy musings, Elen's feet began to run. She had to get back to the house. She had to. She could not even think of stealth or delay. She ran, her lungs gasping for air as she tore up the slope. She knew what had happened, and fear all but blinded her.

Urien stood in the doorway of the high house, his shoulders hunched around his ears and his hand leaning against the lintel for support. He watched her running to him and frowned deeply as she stood before him panting, a guilty, straying slave.

'Where did you go?' he demanded.

The need to speak made Elen shudder, she gulped air, but she also gathered her will. *Where did I go? That's all he asked. That's all I must answer. That's* all. 'To the well.'

Urien's frown deepened. 'Why?'

Mother, help me. 'I had a call of nature and wanted to wash myself afterwards.' The compulsion grumbled and it growled, prowling her mind, but the force, the fascination of it did not come.

Urien grunted, rubbing his head, which was surely still muddled with all the drink he had poured down his gullet. 'You use the water in the bucket next time. I can't have you wandering among these ruffians. They may spoil you before the games are over.'

Elen bowed her head.

'Come back in. Lay down, go to sleep.'

Elen did, and as she lay herself on the blankets, she savoured her triumph. This much was done. This first step had been taken, small though it might be. She would find a way to take the next.

Blackness took her, but for the first time in so many days, her last conscious feeling was that of hope.

Elen dreamed.

It was the dream she'd had before, the dream of the hawk in the sky, of her body being torn open and her heart lifted free by the magnificent bird, of the blue-eyed horseman and the great spear in his hand, of how he killed the bird, and how Elen felt her heart split open.

She woke in the morning with tears on her cheeks and pain in her belly, and there was nothing she could do.

The shackles of her slavery settled over her again. She had thought she could bear their weight more easily now that there was a plan of action, but she found she only strained against her captivity all the harder.

She ran to the well and she toted the water back. She fetched and carried for Urien, who was red-eyed and tender-headed, and she ate when she was permitted. All the time she was in the hall, she found herself stealing glances at the hawk. Inside, the bird was not hooded, and it preened itself and fluffed its feathers, flapped its wings and longed for its freedom, as she longed for hers. Did it feel her? Did its yearning for the sky and the hunt reflect the yearning she felt to run, to fight, to drive Urien and his men before her and see them flee like frightened rabbits? Did it know who owned the borrowed heart that beat within it?

Then Urien hooded the hawk with careful hand, and she felt its impatience with the sudden darkness and its acceptance of it.

It is only for now. Just for now. It will end. As these thoughts passed through her, Elen found she was not sure whether they were for herself or for the hawk.

Fortunately, Urien was engaged in transferring the hawk from her perch to his gauntleted hand and did not notice her staring. He wrapped the jesses around his wrist and grunted, 'Follow me,' to Elen, and Elen did.

The morning was chill and grey with a heavy lid of clouds overhead. The wind brought the smell of rain. Elen shivered beneath her cloak as she followed Urien down through the encampment. Men cheered as he passed and he raised his free hand, playing the gracious leader. Elen's stomach curdled, and she tried to see nothing more than the ground in front of her, but she could not shut out the sound of the cheering men, nor the way they called his name. 'Urien! Urien the Red Bull!'

The makeshift field for Urien's tourney lay by the river. It was a great stretch of mud cornered off by four stones set in the middle of the trampled grass and meadow flowers. It was a busy place already, ringed by a great crowd, talking, laughing, exchanging wagers.

She shivered again and wrapped her arms around herself. This was her home they were gaming for. It was so wrong it made her gorge rise. She saw memories like ghosts before her inner eye. There should have been flocks of sheep grazing here, and herds of kine being led down to drink at the river. There should have been carts and travellers passing over the bridge. She saw Carys beside her, carrying the basket of offerings. This was a place of peaceful passage. This was her home and it was for the life and support of her people. It was not this trampling and yelling and casual blood. It was as if they defiled something holy.

The bridge waited silently nearby, grim and grey beneath the unwelcoming sky. For a fleeting moment, Elen dreamed of snatching the hawk off Urien's wrist and fleeing across it calling for the fae to open their gates and take her in. Let Urien chase her down the twilight road if he dared.

The men who meant to try themselves this day ranged across the field. Most of them were half-naked, clad only in kilts or breeches, leather belts wrapped around their waists to hold their knives or swords, if they were lucky enough to have them. A few carried spears almost as tall as they were. Fewer yet had bucklers in their hands, or guards for their arms or shins. This battle was in earnest. A tiny war to see who was worthy to stand beside Urien and claim what he swore he had to give. Men had died yesterday in this contest. More would die today, and those around would cheer and curse and exchange their bets, and Urien would think on how he would throw the survivors against Arthur's legions, and he'd smile.

As a final insult, Urien had father's chair brought down from the hall and placed on the slope just above his field. Wyx, ever faithful, had even rigged up a perch for the hawk and Urien set her on it with great show of care. Elen was given a small plain stool beside him.

You'd think he'd want a better setting for his jewel, she thought with a kind of resigned bitterness as she sat where she was bidden. She clasped her cold hands together and peered between the trunks of milling bodies, trying to see Sir Geraint.

It did not take long to spot him. His raven-black hair stood out in the sea of red and brown thatch. The others swarmed about, greeting friends, jeering at enemies, brandishing their blades, strutting for their watching women. Sir Geraint did none of these things. He stood at the corner of the field, one sandalled foot planted on the marking stone, and he watched them all, his face set and still.

She remembered the night of the feast, when Urien had leapt to his feet. The others had risen to answer him, but Geraint had held still, watching then as now, watching Urien's hands, the way he held his body, measuring and judging the man who might become his attacker but wasting no motion himself and giving nothing away.

They'll know, she thought, her hands gripping each other so hard she thought she might bruise her own flesh. *They'll know he isn't one of them. How could any not see it?*

But it seemed that none did. Urien nodded to Wyx who blew a hard, harsh blast on his horn. A cheer went up, and the onlookers on the field pulled back, leaving just the combatants in a ragged cluster in the middle of the mud.

The horn sounded again, and the men scattered, taking up positions at the edges of the field, each making sure he had his back to the crowd, not to the other combatants. Cheers, whistles and catcalls rose from the spectators.

'Twenty on the Dunwalt!'

'Go on, Tag!'

'You can take 'em, Deny!'

Elen found herself suddenly thinking of the two voices she had overheard last night. She wondered which of these half-naked, fierce warriors with their blue tattoos was that man, and which of the cheering, wild-eyed women was his. What was that woman watching for today, and what would she do when she saw it? Elen felt a stab of envy for that unknown female who sought to claim her home. She could act when and where she would.

Sir Geraint had claimed the field's northeast corner and stood with his back to the stone. Elen could not see his face, but she saw the way he held his arms loose at his sides. He had drawn neither sword nor knife yet. He was still waiting.

Urien nodded once more, and once more Wyx blew his horn. Now the cheers rose from every throat, and the men on the field began to move.

Some of them charged roaring at their neighbours, weapons held high, falling on their targets and flailing at them, trying to take them down by sudden brute force, or run them off the field while they were still close to the edge. The clash of metal and the sound of flesh and bone slamming together sounded over the cacophony of the witnesses. Others walked warily into the fray, choosing their victims with care, stepping in, circling their man, judging him before making the first slash or stab, or raising the first parry.

And still, Sir Geraint had not moved.

'Yah! Gododdin!' bellowed Wyx. 'Get your coward's ass in there!'

Geraint looked over his shoulder, right at Wyx, marking him. Then, slowly, almost casually, he drew his knife. For a moment, Elen thought he was going to barge up the hill. But he faced the field again, crouched low, and charged.

He fell on two men locked in their own fight, slashing his

knife deep in the nearest man's arm, making him scream even as he shoved him to the ground. His opponent, who gripped a spear in both hands, stared, stunned for a moment, and that moment was all Geraint needed. He kicked the man's leg, and caught the spear as its owner fell, stabbing down swiftly. Elen could not see where the blow fell, but it raised an enormous cheer from the crowd.

Sir Geraint was better armed now than he had been, but had also made the others take notice. They came to him now, and he fell back, retreating to the stone, where none could circle him without leaving the field. They came in twos and threes, those who dared. They came with knife and sword, and Sir Geraint knocked their weapons from their hands. He stabbed at arms and legs, ruining their balance, their grip, their chance. None could get inside his guard to close with him. The cheers grew louder, and the attacks grew fiercer, and Geraint held his place and let them come.

The fight wore on. The wind whipped up and the first rain began to spatter down. Urien showed no sign of calling a halt to his contest, and the crowd's frenzy did not abate. Elen bit her lip to keep herself silent. She wanted to be on her feet. She wanted to shout out Geraint's name and urge him on. He must tire soon. Someone would stab him – belly, heart, hand – it didn't matter. Wounded, he might not be able to ride, they would be trapped here another day, and another.

He might die. For her and her need, he might be killed by one of Urien's brutes. The thought cut through her, and tears of anger and helplessness pricked at her eyes.

You do not have to win. You have done enough to show you are no coward, she thought desperately. Someone would make him stumble. Someone would strike him a blow that would send him reeling out of bounds. Then he would be safe, and they could make their escape tonight. They could ride to Caerleon and return with Arthur's army at their backs.

But none did make him falter. Most of them turned their attention to easier targets on other parts of the field where they had room to dance their vicious dance, where they could close and grapple and throw their enemies down into the deepening mud. Rain dripped down Elen's face and the ends of her hair. It began to soak through her cloak and her sleeves. The cold raised goose pimples on her skin, but she did not look away. She could scarce remember to blink. All of her attention was riveted on Sir Geraint and his struggle. Time stretched out into an eternity, and still the fight went on.

At last, at long last, Urien raised his hand and Wyx sounded his horn. The men on the field fell back from each other, panting and wiping sweat and rain from their faces. Geraint staggered, falling back against the stone, doubling over, dropping his spear and putting his hands on his knees. It was all Elen could do to keep her seat. She imagined his breathing, harsh and ragged. She imagined his muscles shaking and twitching beneath his skin, and how his own heat burned him, despite the cold and the rain.

Urien got to his feet. 'Hail Urien's champions!' He lifted his arms as if to welcome to his embrace all the men standing up to their ankles in the field of mud.

The crowd cheered them yet again. Urien waited for the sound to die.

'Tomorrow, only one of you will be left standing here! Tomorrow we will know who wins himself this hawk and this bride!' His hand fell onto Elen's head, and she bowed under the weight of it. The cheer from the crowd rolled over her like thunder.

'But tonight, we celebrate your courage and strength. Tonight, you men come to the house of Urien and learn what a feast should truly be!'

There were more cheers and more noise, and the crowd began to part, slowly at first and then more quickly, as if they only noticed now that it was raining. The men on the field fought through the muck to reach the waiting arms of friends and family, but not Geraint. He remained alone, straightening himself slowly, painfully, fighting to pull his feet from the mud as hard as he had fought any other foe that day.

Help him! cried Elen in her mind *Will no one help him?*

But no one did, and alone, leaning on his captured spear like a an old man's staff, Geraint limped from the field.

'Well now.' Urien chuckled in her ear. Startled Elen looked up to see him smiling broadly down on her. He had the hawk in his hand, and the waterlogged bird hunched there miserably.

'I see you watching my men.' Urien winked and jerked his head towards the emptying field. 'Which of them do you hope for, eh? Which do you want for your new master?'

Just in time, Elen caught her tongue. Obedience was becoming a habit, and she cursed herself for it. 'I want no one for my master,' she said. 'I hope as many of them die as can, so you will have that many fewer men to take to your wars.'

Anger clouded Urien's face. 'You'd better hope my humour towards you improves, girl, or I will tell your husband you said that when I give you to him. We will see what he thinks of it. Come with me.'

Elen followed as she must, but she risked a backward glance, hoping to see Geraint one last time, hoping to see that he had found his strength and stride.

But Sir Geraint was already gone.

The feast that night was much as the previous one had been. Two slaughtered pigs had been roasted, and their flesh was hacked off and shared out with strong beer. Elen found herself grudgingly impressed. Someone had kept fires going in the rain long enough to get the beasts cooked. She tried hard not to think that all the ale going down those greedy throats was from her house. Urien's men must have emptied the cellars.

Urien's champions crammed themselves at his trestle table and the loyal followers who'd come with him to take Pont Cymryd filled the benches on either side of the hall. They ate and they drank and they sang. The hall stank with unwashed men, seared pork and ale fumes until Elen thought she would choke. Her only consolation was that Sir Geraint was there as well. He sat at the high table straight and calm, eating and drinking his portion. A purple bruise spread out across the back of one hand, and he held one shoulder a little higher than the other, but otherwise he seemed whole, at least as far as she could see from the little glances she could steal when Urien wasn't making her run back and forth, and when the others weren't crowding her so close.

They were bolder tonight, these men. They patted her and poked at her as she passed between them. Several times Urien growled at them, and they fell back laughing.

'Patience!' he bellowed. 'You want her, you wait until tomorrow!'

'If you're still upright, Tag!' shouted one of the others.

'He's upright now, that's for sure!' sneered another, and the laughter was deafening.

Elen clenched her teeth and kept silent. She'd be gone tonight. Tonight, she'd fly.

'And what of you, Gododdin?' A burly ox of a man elbowed Geraint in the ribs, sloshing the beer in his noggin. 'You going to be upright tomorrow?'

In answer, Geraint smiled a smile Elen would not have guessed could be his. It was slow and it was cold and sharp as a sword's edge against naked skin. It was a promise, that smile, of regret, of violence and revenge, and it silenced the room until the ox dropped his gaze and drank deep from his cup.

At last, their day's work and the heavy drink overcame them, and Urien's champions began to stumble from the house to seek their own beds. Some men just slid unconscious to the floor and were left where they fell, or were dragged out by bleary-eyed companions.

Geraint walked out on his own two feet. Elen watched him leave with a combination of fear and anticipation. It was her turn now. The hawk sat on her perch, restless and discontent. She had snapped viciously at Urien's offerings of food and refused to be soothed by his touch, something Elen felt grateful for. She did not want that insidious calm distracting her from her purpose now.

The last of the champions stumbled towards the door. All around, the occupants of the hall prepared for sleep, rolling themselves in their blankets, shoving aside benches and tables to make more room rather than taking them down. Urien's stolen bed, of course, was set in its place. Wyx, drunk as he was, would not permit his master to be neglected, but it seemed he could do no more than that. He sat stupidly on the floor and slowly, comically tilted to one side until he was sprawled like a dog at his master's feet.

Urien sat on the bench beside the table, nodding and chuckling at some joke that had probably been told a full hour before. Elen stood beside him with the pitcher in her hand. She had been ordered to serve, but had no new order. It was dark. The fires were almost dead. The rush lights and torches had been allowed to burn to nothing. She stood in the shadows, afraid to move, uncertain of what to do. She could see Urien needed to get to bed. The compulsion needled and it nagged, but it stayed in the lower reaches of her mind, and she did not want to show initiative, even now when he was surely all but blind.

Urien's head nodded lower, and lower, until his cheek pressed against the tabletop amid the bones, greasy scraps and spilled beer. His mouth fell open, and he began to snore.

As gently as she could, Elen set the pitcher down on the table. Her hands felt like lumps of clay, her body cold and inflexible. Slowly, she inched her way around the bench, and then through the narrow space between the bench and the bed to the perch, and the hawk.

She could barely see the bird, but she could feel her, sitting there sullen in the darkness. She burrowed her head under her wing, angry at the noise and riot that kept her from sleep. She did not want to be disturbed again. She wanted only to sleep.

I'm sorry, but we must leave together, you and I.

She wrapped her hand in the sleeve of her dress, and put it up to ease the hawk from her perch.

'Come with me,' she whispered. 'Come bring my heart.'

The bird lifted its wing and glowered at her. Elen put her hand near the hawk's talons as she had seen Urien do. 'Come, step up,' she whispered.

The hawk croaked, and snapped, and didn't move.

'Step up,' she murmured, urgency swelling, and mixing with the hawk's anger. 'Step up.'

But the hawk didn't move. Elen's heart beat inside it, fast and indignant. It wanted to sleep. It wanted her gone. Elen tried to think. She backed away to the table and her fingers scrabbled on the splintery wood until she found one of the scraps from Urien's feast.

'Come, girl,' she whispered, holding up the titbit just out of the hawk's reach. 'Come, step up.'

The hawk lunged, flapping her wings. Her beak snapped at the meat, and Elen's fingers. Elen snatched her hand back without thought, and the leashes, which she had forgotten in her hurry, jerked the hawk back. The bird screamed in pain, impatience and indignity as she struggled to regain her perch.

Urien snorted hard and jolted his head up. Drunk as he was, he saw her at once.

'What are you doing?' he roared, lurching to his feet.

'I . . . I . . .' Elen backed away, her wits deserting her. The hawk had righted herself, but flapped her wings, scolding and cursing Elen with her cries. *We could have been free!* she seemed to say.

Urien reeled towards Elen. 'You will not touch the bird. It is not yours, nor is what it holds.' He grabbed her shoulder. She could have dodged him, but she didn't dare. 'You understand me? Speak!'

Around them, bleary heads lifted uneasily to see what the new fuss was.

'Yes. I understand,' she answered. He held her hard, his fingers digging deep into her flesh.

He leaned close. His breath was hot against her skin and heavy with the fumes of his drinking. 'You are a lovely thing, Elen,' he whispered, his voice full of desire and menace. 'Do not make me mark you.'

'No,' whispered Elen.

He smiled, his gaze raking her from head to foot. 'I could order you to lay down for me, you know. I could order you to like what I would do to you then. I could make you scream your delight so everyone would hear.' He leered at her, shaking her shoulder. 'I could do that right now.'

Elen swallowed, trying to get her reeling wits under control. 'But then all would know I was spoiled goods,' she said, forcing her voice to be steady. 'What of my value as your prize then?' She forced her gaze to drift to the drunken witnesses, who grinned and leered, enjoying the show.

'Ah, yes.' He stroked her hair with one rough finger. 'You begin to understand. You begin to accept what you truly are.'

'Yes,' she said, although the word was foul in her mouth. 'Yes, I do.'

'Huh. Had your mother been so wise . . .' he shook his head and lurched back to his bed. 'Help me.'

So, Elen did what she must, and she blessed the darkness so that he could not see the tears that ran down her face as she pulled off his sandals and tunic and brought him water and yet more ale as he wallowed on the featherbed. She could barely even force herself to look at the hawk without revulsion now. She could remember the plan to take it to Geraint, but it was like remembering a nightmare. Each time her thoughts veered that way, her hands shook and weakness took her.

Maybe all was not yet lost. Perhaps she could lead Geraint back here. He could . . . he could . . .

But Urien was not finished with her yet. As she reached to take his cup away, he dropped it, and grabbed her instead. His hard arms wrapped around her and he pulled her down beside him. 'You stay here tonight,' he whispered in her ear. 'For tonight, you're mine. *She* said I could take you if I wanted. Maybe I'll do just that.'

The paralysis took her and Elen closed her eyes. She could do nothing now. She was too numb even to despair. She could only lie there and feel his crushing embrace, the smell and rush of his ale-soaked breath. Fortunately, the drink was stronger than Urien's lust, and he fell into a stupor. But still she could not move.

I'm sorry, she thought towards Geraint. *I'm so sorry.*

The night settled over her, and Elen could do nothing but wait for the morning and try to remember there was such a thing in the world as hope.

EIGHT

Geraint waited in the darkness of the thicket at the wood's edge. He watched the moonlit hillside and listened to the sounds of the drunken revelry that came from all directions.

Would that we could fly with the speed of wishes, he thought, looking up at the waxing moon. *If Agravain and whoever he brings with him could be here now, this would be over in a moment. There is not one sober man in this whole cantrev.*

He pictured his brother, sour and silent, pushing his mount for all it was worth down the old Roman road to Caerleon. He wondered what Gawain would think when he heard Geraint had stayed behind. And what would Agravain say of his reasons? Would he say it was all because of Elen?

And how wrong would he be if he did? Geraint shifted his weight silently. Elen's face haunted him. But there was more than just the blow of true beauty there. He'd known beauties before, although he was not the most glorious of knights. If the truth were told, he had few deeds of his own to boast of, and he was certainly not Gawain for charm or Gareth for looks. He was of the Round Table, though, and nephew to the king, and that was enough to ensure that he had no lack of ladies willing to flatter him and offer up their modesty. But in Elen he saw a dignity and a fierceness that reached into his soul and touched its very centre. To see her so foully bound to Urien . . . it was as if someone had put a chain around a lioness.

His mind shied away from thoughts of Morgaine, who had made that chain. The name alone could chill his blood.

Am I such a coward in my heart? His jaw clenched. *I should be swearing vengeance. I should be vowing to track her to the hills of Hell itself.*

It was what Gawain would do, and Gareth, though he was only a squire. Agravain would stand back, fold his arms and watch them go.

And Geraint? He looked up to the moon with her tattered skirt of clouds again. *What would Geraint do?*

The moon had no answers, and Elen still did not come. Geraint shifted himself carefully again. He ached in every muscle. Some of the bruises were bad, but thankfully none of the cuts were. It had been a long time since he'd been in such a brawl without any sort of armour. It was no help that this was his second night without much sleep. His mind was beginning to feel heavy and slow, and his patience was ebbing.

Where is she? The moon was inching past the sky's pinnacle, heading down towards the horizon. By this time last night she had been and gone already. Had Urien grown suspicious and stopped her? Had he questioned her? Surely not. They'd be searching the camp for him even now. *So where is she?*

Geraint bit his lip. Unwelcome thoughts flashed through his head. Urien was very, very drunk. Elen said her geas permitted her to refuse no order . . .

Suddenly, Geraint could no longer stand still. No one would think it odd for him to be wandering the camp. A number of men were still up and about, looking for willing women, more drink, or just the place where they'd left their own gear.

Geraint strode up the hillside towards the ruined hall, taking care to walk a wandering path, angling only gradually upward so that he might not appear too deliberate or hasty in his actions. He did not want to draw any attention to himself. The noises were winding down now as the fires were dying. One voice raised itself in loud and off-key song.

'. . . *And merrily she asked of him,*
"Wherever are you bound?"
"I'm out to hunt the bonny black hare,
Where e'er it's to be found!"'

The singer's companions sniggered and shouted and raised their skins and horns for more drink. Geraint passed them by and not one noted him. He left the tents and camps and came to the houses. He wondered what had happened to the folk that had dwelled here. Had Urien slaughtered them all? His throat and hands tightened at the thought. He'd seen no sign of hostages save Elen. Was she all of her folk that remained?

The earthworks were completely unguarded. Geraint threaded his way between the dykes. Fires blossomed here and there across the yard, surrounded by shadows that barked out unsteady laughter and slurred voices. But for all that, the yard was not crowded, and as Geraint made his way forward, none turned to hail him, bound up as they were with their own drunken company.

Ahead, the high house rose black against the night sky. The open doorway looked like an open mouth to Geraint. He shook his head.

No fancies, you fool. Now is the time to see what's in the mortal world.

Fresh voices and laughter erupted from across the yard. Someone had heaved himself to his feet and begun a staggering dance, much to the loud amusement of his fellows. Geraint stole swiftly through the doorway, pressing himself into the shadows, listening hard. He heard no break in their laughter or change in their talk around the yard.

Geraint held himself still, letting his eyes fully adjust to the surrounding dark. The hall was a wreck, with tables and benches pushed every which way, men sleeping where they fell, most without even a blanket over them. Geraint threaded through this unsavoury maze, until he was close enough to make out the one bed that had been set in place in the whole hall.

In that bed lay Urien, and with him, Elen. He clasped her tightly in his arms. She looked up at Geraint, and he saw tears glitter in her eyes. He reached out, his hand trembling, but she made no move, not even to shake her head. Urien snored so that his whole body shuddered, his breath making such a stink Geraint could smell it even where he stood.

Geraint looked to the hawk. It slept on its perch, head under its wing. This was the lock for Elen's chain. If he could take it now . . . but his was a strange hand. He'd never untie its jesses and lift it without waking it. The startled animal would raise a cry, and try to attack, and even if he held onto it, even if that made him the bird's master, what then? In the hall, someone coughed, nearly retching with the force of it. Someone else cursed in their sleep and rolled over again. Could they actually leave this place without rousing the hall? Drunk they might be, but, none of these men were the sort to stand by while Geraint made off with the prize dangled by their new master.

Geraint looked to Elen again, and saw the shame and rage in her tear-filled eyes.

He swallowed. Slowly, he approached the bed, planting each step carefully. Urien snorted and grunted. Geraint froze. Urien shifted, rolling onto his back. Now only one burly arm draped across Elen, and still she lay there, limp as a doll, only her eyes moving, watching Geraint as he approached, the tears flowing freely now.

Geraint bent as close as he dared. 'Lady, can you rise?' he asked in his lightest whisper.

The mute and helpless look she gave him was answer enough. He nodded to show his understanding.

'Has he hurt you?' He hated himself for asking that question, but he could not help it. If Urien had ravaged her, Geraint knew he would kill the man, here and now, no matter what the consequences.

But she did not look away, and Geraint felt a knot in his heart loosen.

Why not kill him now? I have the knife. I could slit his barbarous throat, and we could be gone.

Gone into a camp of armed men. They were sleeping all around him, and more singing was drifting in from the outside. Could he be sure to do it silently? Could they leave this place without being seen? The singing was getting closer.

'Hey, Hewe! Hey! Is that a keg there?'

Geraint froze again. Panic filled Elen's eyes. Urien's steady snores faltered and he grunted again.

'Away, ye slugs. You've had your fill tonight.'

'Awww . . . .come on, man. It's bad manners to keep it all for yourself!'

There was a slap, and a crack of wood, and a shout. Urien snorted and jerked, and his arm tightened around Elen.

Go, her eyes said to him, fear overtaking all other emotion there. *Go!*

But first, he knelt before her. 'Endure,' he whispered, wiping away the tears that trickled down her cheeks with as gentle a touch as he could manage with his calloused and trembling hand. 'Know I will not fail you.'

Then, he did the hardest thing he had ever done in his life. He turned away and left her there. Once outside the cursed hall, he strode across the yard and down the hill in a straight line and did not care who saw. He knotted his hands at his side to keep them from his knife.

His rage blinded him. He did not pay attention to where he was going, and it was not until he stumbled over a stone that he was able to make himself stop and look about. The moon would not be up much longer. He needed to get back to his place or he would be wandering among the encampments all night, and then what use would he be to Elen on the morrow?

Geraint took his bearings. He was close to the well and the wood beyond it. He could hear the river. He had drifted too far to the east. If he turned his path . . .

'It's the Gododdin. He's the danger.'

Geraint started like a rabbit, and then crouched down, trying to be no more than a stone or a stump in the darkness.

'Here, let me see that . . . ah, you've taken worse in play. Too much drink's blurred your eyes. And don't worry any more about the Gododdin.'

He saw the small camp where the voices came from. There was a canvas shelter, and a low fire, and two figures moving back and forth, a man and a woman, but he could not see them clearly. The man was burly and bearded and he stretched out his leg to the woman who crouched beside him. She was slender, and her hands moved cleverly, binding a cloth around his shin.

'What have you done, woman?' asked the man so softly Geraint had to strain to hear.

The woman tied a final knot in the bandage. 'You should know better than to ask that, husband,' she said archly as she sat back on her heels. 'But there are things that may be found out by those with eyes to see and ears to hear.'

The man withdrew his leg. Geraint saw glimpses of pale cloth, brown hair, hard hands resting on naked thighs. 'And what do you know now that you did not before?'

'That which our would-be lord Urien will be glad to know.'
Geraint thought he heard a smile in the woman's voice. 'Now
be quiet and let me see how this other is doing . . .'

The man stretched out his other leg, and the woman bent
over it, tending to his hurts in silence.

Softly, slowly, Geraint stole away. He felt as though cold
water had been poured over him, turning the heat of his
rage to ashes.

What did the woman know? Who was she? Did she know
his true name and office?

Has she told Urien? No, she couldn't have. Not yet.

Geraint came to his own camp. His fire was stone dead.
He had not banked it carefully enough. His tent was little
more than a canvas awning to keep off the dew. His horse
stood nearby, asleep in its hobbles. Nothing here to offer
comfort, no one to offer wisdom.

Geraint wrapped himself in his rough cloak and sat beside
his dead fire. He should retreat. He would do no good to
Elen if his name and errand were exposed. At best, he would
be taken hostage with her. At worst, he would be killed by
Wyx or Urien himself. He should not have attempted this
foolishness. He should have gone with Agravain and come
back at the head of an army.

*I should have never come. They were right. This is not work for
me. She needs a champion. Gawain, or Bedivere, or even Lancelot.*

But none of them were here. There was only Geraint,
who, if he had any sense in him, would flee like a thief in
the night.

Geraint looked up to the sky. The moon had almost set.
The stars shone overhead in their millions: silver, blue red
and gold.

Help me, he prayed. *Lord, who knows when even the sparrow
falls, help me. I cannot leave her to him. Not even for my life, I cannot.*

No answer came, nor any sign, but a kind of peace stole

over Geraint, and he was able to stretch himself out on his
blanket underneath his awning, and sleep.

Urien commanded Elen to dress as a bride.

Since they had looted the treasury, it now pleased Urien
to adorn her with what he had stolen. Mother's green gown
of fine wool, trimmed with ribbons woven with apple blossoms, was taken from Wyx's grumbling woman. It was belted
with Elen's own girdle of bronze and enamel, each link in
the shape of a small bird with peridots for eyes. The necklace made in the shape of a flowering vine that had been
Arthur's gift to honour their family was hung about her neck,
while rings of gold and silver were placed on her fingers,
with no care as to which was hers, or her mother's, or even
Carys's. Her hair was brushed loose to hang past her shoulders and crowned with a wreath of hawthorn and green
ribbons. Once this was done, she was set on a stout, brown
horse, which was then led by Wyx down to the field.

Through it all, she waited still and silent, because she was
ordered to. But even in the midst of the fascination, and the
dread, she felt hope, for she remembered how Geraint had
come last night. He had seen her shame, her helplessness,
but he had not flinched. He had knelt before her instead. He
had sworn he would help her.

Today was the day. Today, Urien would lose the first of
his prizes, and soon he would lose his life. It would happen.
She would make it happen, and much more. Wyx too would
join his master in death, and there were others . . . the gory
tally rolled through her mind. Then, at last, when her lands
were hers again, and her people safe in their homes, she
would find a way to repay Geraint's steadfastness.

The morning had dawned bright and clear. The wind blew
gently as she followed Urien down the hill. The summer air
would have been fresh and glorious, if not for the reek of

the encampment with its smoking fires and unwashed bodies. The crowd cheered mightily as they passed, parting for them as they made their way down to the churned and rutted field. The festival mood was palpable and Urien himself expansive. He paused often, greeting men by name, laughing and slapping them on their backs, or striking hands with them, every inch the great leader of men. The hawk on his gauntleted hand flapped and shrieked, and thrust its neck forward when any came too close, snapping at over-eager fingers. Elen suppressed a grim smile.

Yes. Do what I cannot.

Someone had brought out mother's great chair. Bride that she was, she could not huddle on a stool today. The horse was loosely tethered beside Urien's chair and immediately began nosing at the grass.

Elen sat in the chair and her hands gripped the carved arms. She must not move, she must *not* move. She must not speak, lest she give something away. Urien must not see what she held close inside her. He must be given no reason to suspect her. This escape would happen only if he was taken unawares.

Urien's champions stood waiting on their trampled field while the crowd ringed its edges. The spectators whistled and called out bribes and threats. The champions waved and winked, and shouted back. One man grabbed a woman from the crowd, planting a heavy kiss on her mouth.

Urien laughed out loud at this display, and raised an answering chorus from the crowd. Elen felt herself flinch, and looked to Sir Geraint instead. He stood with the others, one of them and yet still seeming a little apart, as before. Today, though, his stillness was gone. His gaze roamed the crowd, looking for some person or thing. He shifted his weight from foot to foot, and his hands tightened and loosened at his sides. Elen's throat knotted. What had taken his composure? Was it what he had seen last night? Had he come to decide she had sought Urien's embrace?

No. Do not even begin that thought.

Urien set the hawk on her perch beside his chair. The bird ruffled her feathers and drew in her neck, glowering at the unruly crowd. The horse whickered in annoyance at the bird, and the bird looked disappointed that here was something too big to eat. She wanted so much to be free, to fly far away, to hunt and to feast. Her hunger gnawed at her constantly. The heart beating within her was like a distant drum, faint, but insistent.

Wyx sounded his horn. The crowd quieted, but the hawk shrieked. Elen bit down on her tongue to keep the answering shout inside her.

Urien stood, fists planted on his hips, surveying the gathered mob and the assembled champions, a lord well pleased with what he saw.

'Now has come the day!' he cried out, and the cheers that answered him were deafening. 'On this field we will find which among you is the best of men!'

More cheers. Names bellowed out to the heavens.

'Madog! Madog!'

'Eynon!'

'Gododdin!'

'Today, you shall each fight in single combat,' Urien went on. 'The winner of each fight will be the man standing, or the one who makes his enemy yield. The winners will be matched against each other until there remain only two. The one who wins this last fight wins all!' He grasped Elen's hand and held it up high. The crowd cheered. Elen tried to still the fear that prowled within her. Sir Geraint was too nervous. Urien's smile was too broad, the day too bright. There should be a sign of his doom. There should be a carrion crow, an owl abroad in daylight, or some other ill omen. There was nothing but the brightness of summer and the sweet wind from the river.

On the field, each man paired off with his neighbour, and took his stand. Sir Geraint faced a bullish man in a leather vest who seemed to have no neck to keep his head on his shoulders.

'Lay on!' cried Urien and Wyx let loose a blast on his horn.

The fight began with the shouts and clashes of metal and cheers from the mob as it had on the previous days. But today held a great difference. Today, Geraint did not wait and watch as he had done before. Today he attacked with a speed and ferocity that shocked his opponents, catching them completely off guard. The first fight was over in moments, and judging from the cat-calls and hisses under the cheers, there were heavy bets lost.

The second fight went the same way. Geraint's opponent was a great, shaggy bear of a man who planted himself squarely before Geraint and looked as though he would not shift for even a flood or a god. Geraint, though, dodged under sword and shield and drove his blade into the other man's side. As the bear reeled back, Geraint tripped him up so that he crashed flat on his back. The move elicited jeers with the cheers, even as Geraint planted his knee on the other man's chest, and the bear held up his hands to signal that he yielded.

Geraint stood back and let his defeated opponent limp off the field, clutching his wounded side. Elen saw how Geraint watched the field as well as the defeated man, whose face was dark with anger and shame. He ignored those who shouted and reached out to him, calling the name he had given out, seeking to share his triumph and prove themselves his friend.

There was only one other combat happening now. The men circled each other warily. Both were naked to the waist, their skins slick with sweat and scored red with blood from the cuts they had taken. One was a wiry man armed with a short, fat sword such as the Romans used a generation ago, the other a squat badger holding a knife in either hand. They feinted and dodged, rushed together and fell back again. Urien leaned forward, his face fierce as he watched each new attack. Elen could not tell which of them was gaining the advantage. She wondered desperately what Geraint saw.

'Lord Urien! Lord Urien!'

A stick-thin woman elbowed her way sharply through the crowd. One of the guards dropped his spear to bar her way, and she struck it back with one raw-boned hand before she dropped to her knees before Urien. 'Lord Urien! Stop this contest!'

Elen's mouth went dry. Who was this? What did this woman want?

Wyx stepped in front of his master, blocking her way. 'Who are you? Why should Urien the Bull do anything at your word?'

'I am Gwin, the wife of Eynon.' The wind whipped her dark hair across her weathered face and she pushed it back. 'And you should stop this because there is a traitor on your field. A traitor, my lord!' she cried.

Elen all but choked on her breath. The hawk creeled once from her perch. Urien did not hesitate. He threw up his hand. 'Hold!' he shouted. Wyx sounded the horn. On the field, the men parted, startled, and turned to stare at Urien. The crowd fell silent. The hawk settled sullenly onto her perch, watching all.

'What is this?' Urien demanded of Gwin. 'Who do you accuse?'

'Arthur's man, my lord. Here, seeking your favour so he can spy on your plans and report them back to the Bastard.' Was she looking at Urien or at Elen? Elen's mind reeled. What could she do? She could not even move. The hawk screamed again and her fear was Elen's fear and the two redoubled inside her.

'Who, then?' thundered Urien. 'Give me a name, woman, or by the heavens I'll . . .'

The woman's eyes sparkled beneath her wide, brown brow. 'The man of Gododdin, Lord Urien,' she said, loud enough that all the hushed crowd could hear. 'The one who calls himself Gavan.'

Hope fell away from Elen so fast and so hard that the world seemed to spin before her eyes. Geraint, though, pushed his way through the crowd, coming to stand straight before Urien, his naked sword still in his hand.

No. Run, thought Elen desperately, trying to catch his eye with hers. *Run away.*

But he was looking at Urien, and at the kneeling woman. 'Who speaks my name?' he asked, his voice low and dangerous. The mob, all of them Urien's men, closed in behind him, making a unbreachable wall of bodies, crowding close to hear what came next.

Gwin got to her feet. She was tall as well as lean, and she drew herself up to her full height now. 'I do,' she said, triumph colouring her harsh voice. 'I say you are Arthur's man, and that you are a liar and a coward, and will be off to tell the world what our lord does here as soon as you may.'

Geraint's stillness finally returned to him. He might have been an altar statue for all he moved. Urien's men were not so still. Behind Geraint, they reached for knives and swords, muttering and hissing. They crowded closer. Urien himself stood, his bulk looming over the woman, his burning gaze all on Geraint.

A man stepped up behind the woman. One of the three remaining champions, he was at least as lean as the woman, with drooping red-brown moustaches and a beard that spread across his glistening chest. His arms were ropy with muscles and almost as hairy as his face.

'She speaks the truth, Lord,' he said.

Urien looked as if he had swallowed poison. Elen tensed herself. Geraint watched his hands.

'What proof bring you?' Urien whispered. A lord of men did not rear up and strike off a man's head without pause. But his hand was moving towards his sword, Yestin's sword. Geraint saw that, and so did Gwin and her man.

Gwin smiled. She raised one bony finger, and pointed it at Elen. 'Ask her, my lord. She met with him by the well, and last night he came in secret to your door.'

Urien rounded on Elen. The fury on his face turned her blood to water. It was over, it was done, and she could not even reach his knife to strike any sort of blow. Behind him, Geraint's eyes were sharp and calculating. He meant to strike, but he'd die as soon as he did.

'What is this?' roared Urien. 'Speak!'

And speak she must. But she had not been told what to say. Desperation lent speed to thought. 'This woman seeks to save her man who, might otherwise be unable to stand against Gavan of Gododdin and win the prize you offer.'

'Do you say my wife lies!' bellowed the lean man, Eynon, the veins on his neck bulging with his fury. Or was it fear?

Elen bowed her head. She could not look at them and gain control over the trembling that filled her throat.

'Speak!' ordered Urien.

In his anger, Urien had forgotten to order her to speak the truth, but Elen still chose her words with care. She lifted her head, keeping her gaze on Urien, but seeing Geraint, watching and ready behind him. 'Those who cannot be victorious by honest struggle resort to art and subterfuge.' Her heart should have been pounding, perspiration should have prickled her skin, but Elen felt only cold. Around them, voices swelled and the noise of the crowd turned to ugly mutters. Wyx's hand was on his knife now, and the others around

Urien clutched sword hilts and raised spears. They watched the lean man and his wife.

'She lies!' cried Gwin, outraged. 'She . . .

Elen did not give her the chance to level any other charge. 'I cannot lie to my Lord Urien. I can speak only as I am commanded.'

Geraint saw his chance then, and took it. 'These two use my name. Give the man to me.'

The crowd drew in yet closer. The whipcord man and the suddenly pale woman looked to each other. Behind them, the other champion, the one Eynon had been fighting when the uproar began, still stood on the field, digging the heel of his hand into his side.

Urien nodded. 'It will be Gavan of Gododdin against Eynon Gwachul, and the winner shall show the truth and earn the prize.'

The roar that broke over them was loud with approval, but grim. Gwin touched Eynon's arm, her lean face hard. The crowd parted. Geraint stepped back to let Eynon precede him down the slope.

Elen shivered with the cold that filled her. She wanted to feel her heart hammer, to hear her blood sing in her veins as she watched Geraint step onto the rutted field, but there was only the cold.

He had no shield, no buckler, no armour, not even of leather. He was bruised and a cut on his neck made a red thread against his throat. His weapons, the scarred sword held easily in one hand and the keen knife in the other, seemed frail at this distance. Eynon was lean and alert as a hunting hound. His sword flashed more brightly than Geraint's as he raised it. Leather protected his wrists and shins. Gwin stood beside Elen's chair, so tense her hands quivered. Elen feared her there, feared the bared teeth and the face tight with concentration.

There was no signal to start. Eynon charged suddenly, swinging his blade down. Geraint countered the blow easily, but Eynon stepped back so neatly, Elen saw it must have been a feint, a test to see if Geraint had speed and wit about him. Now the men circled each other, their swords up, watching, waiting.

Eynon attacked again. The crowd cheered. He was a blur of speed, keeping Geraint, who was the bigger man, constantly on the move. He danced an elaborate dance across the field, forcing Geraint back and around, stabbing and striking at arms, at legs and head, whatever target was open to his flashing blade. Geraint beat the attacks off, but only just. Even Elen could see that. Eynon's fat blade worked itself ever closer, until with one hard stroke it slashed across Geraint's knife arm. Geraint shouted, blood poured down from his arm and the knife dropped to the ground. Gwin cried out, raising her fists high. The hawk screamed, 'Ki! Ki! Ki!'

Eynon dived into the opening, his blade stabbing up, seeking to drive itself between Geraint's exposed ribs. But at the last possible moment, Geraint turned, and as Eynon fell past him, Geraint brought his pommel down hard against his enemy's skull. Eynon toppled face down in the mud. The crowd roared, and Geraint pressed the point of his sword hard against the fallen man's neck.

Beside her, Gwin's mouth drew back into a scowl. Her eyes flicked towards Elen and Elen saw the pure hatred burning there, and the naked promise.

She is not done. She has not shot her last bolt yet.

But Geraint only held his place, sword ready to drive into Eynon. 'What say you now?' he asked through gritted teeth.

Eynon raised his head. The tip of the sword must have dug hard into his flesh at that gesture. 'I yield me,' he gasped. 'You are the true man.'

Gwin spat at the ground. *You'd rather your man died*, Elen

realized and her fear deepened, even though now around her the air split with cries of 'Gododdin! Gododdin!' as on the field Geraint stepped back, sheathing his sword. Eynon pushed himself up into a sitting position, but could not seem to get further. Gwin shot Elen one last poisonous look and waded through the crowd to get to her stunned man.

All attention was now on Geraint. The crowd made a lane for him and cheered mightily. Even Urien's men shook their spears over their heads. Urien stood, holding his hands out. Blood, blazing scarlet in the summer sun, still ran down Geraint's arm. It was all Elen could do to hold her place.

Fortunately, Urien felt this was a detail that should be attended and signalled Wyx's hard-eyed woman, who came forward with cloths to bind up the wound. When she was done, Urien embraced Geraint roughly, and held his hand up high for the crowd to cheer.

'My champion!' he bellowed. 'Let the Bastard's men tremble at the name of Gavan!'

The mob shouted their approval until the sky shook with the noise and the ground trembled with the stomping of feet. All were caught up in the festival atmosphere, ready for further displays of Urien's generosity and boldness. They grinned and leered and eyed Elen in her riches and her bridal crown. And although this was the moment that would free her from Urien, Elen could only feel sick.

'Now.' Urien turned to face her, his smile so broad it showed all his teeth. 'Stand before your master, Elen.'

Elen stood, her body cold as winter although the summer sun shone clear overhead. Urien took Elen's hands and placed them into Geraint's. Desperate for some reminder that this was what should be happening, she looked into his eyes. Geraint's eyes were so very deep blue, the colour of the sky in the last light of day. His hands were calloused, but they were warm, and that warmth seeped into her skin, easing the cold within her. He did not shy away from her cursed hands. He did not look sorry for what now happened, or as if he would speak word of apology. He only looked steadily into her eyes as he folded his hands around hers, enclosing them with an easy touch. For the space of a single breath, Elen forgot it was Urien who had laid her hands in this gentle resting place.

'As lord I am of this cantrev of Pont Cymryd, I give this woman Elen, daughter of Adara to you, by the oldest laws. *Kynnywedi ar liw ac ar oleu.* She is yours, with all her goods, price and fee. In token whereof I give you this hawk.' Wyx held out the gauntlet for Geraint's hand and Urien unwrapped the hawk's jesses from the perch. The hawk eyed him sullenly and creeled in annoyance as Geraint held out his wrist to receive the bird and take hold of the jesses.

She thought she would feel something with the transfer, but there was no change in the cold, no lessening of the weight. The distant beat of her imprisoned heart remained as before. It did not matter then who the bird's master was, her condition was the same.

Geraint held the hawk high so all could see the bird and cheer at the gracious act of giving. She saw in Geraint's eyes what he meant to do next, even before his hand began to pull her to him. She trembled and the cold threatened to overwhelm her, but it was the expected thing, and she lifted her face. They were cheering and hooting all around, and Geraint dipped his mouth to hers and kissed her. She did not want it. Not like this, not with Urien and his men grinning and filling the air with their japes, and yet, and yet, his kiss was gentle, unhesitating and honest. It was like the touch of his hand against her face when he had wiped her tears because she could not move.

They parted and the world returned with a rush. Geraint was regarding her with a gaze so full she could not fathom all that lay within it. Urien slapped him on the shoulder and opened his mouth to say something sly.

Then, a voice called, 'How is she, Sir Geraint?'

Geraint turned, naturally and easily, to see Gwin, who'd been forgotten on the field. Now she stood behind them, supporting her stupefied man on her arm and grinning her sharp and triumphant grin.

Silence fell like a stone.

'Geraint,' she said again, releasing Eynon, who swayed but managed to keep standing. Gwin walked slowly forward. No hand moved to stop her as she waded through the crowd. 'What man of Gododdin would come from Arthur's court? Which would he trust? Why those who are kin to him. But which of the four sons of Lot could it be? Not Gawain. Gareth would be too young and Agravain gone back already to warn Arthur while you stayed to claim the prize.'

'Woman, your man lost,' began Urien. 'The matter is proven . . .'

Which was too much for Gwin. 'Look at him!' she shouted, all pretence at humility gone. 'You great fools! Look hard! He was here before. You dined with him! See what's before you!'

To Elen's horror, they did look, but Geraint did not wait for them to see. He opened his hand, tossing the hawk up into the air. The bird screamed sharp and high and flapped her great wings to catch the wind. Those closest ducked down. Geraint grabbed Elen's hand and broke into a run, dragging her behind him. Hands snatched at her, ripping her from him and she kicked out, sending her captor reeling. Urien grabbed her from behind, whirling her around, his knife out.

The hawk screamed again, and dived, talons out. Urien roared, and threw up his hands, dropping the knife and knocking the bird sideways. Blood poured from his scalp into his eyes, blinding him. The hawk caught the air again and climbed high once more. Elen snatched up the knife. The hawk dived, sending men scattering on all sides. Geraint vaulted onto the back of the horse that had borne Elen to the field and drew his battered sword, swinging it wide, keeping clear the path the hawk had opened.

'The bridge!' Elen cried. 'We must get to the bridge!'

Geraint dug his heels hard into the horse's sides, hauling on the reins to wheel the beast around. Blood flowed freely out from under his bandage. Elen ran, pelting down the hill, the knife before her, swinging wildly, blindly, her breath coming in gasps, her vision blurring as she saw herself from above, saw the ground swoop closer and then further away, felt the raw hatred of the men who ran behind, and attacked again with talons out. Geraint, on the stolen horse, passed her, barrelling into the mob that tried to gather, breaking them apart, sending them tumbling and lunging to both sides.

The bridge was close but the horse balked at its steps, rearing and dancing. The hawk circled overhead, crying, uncertain. Elen charged past Geraint.

'Hold them off,' she called as she passed him. 'When I call you, come fast, no matter what you see!'

'I will!'

It was insane what she meant to do. It was dangerous beyond words. It was their only hope for escape. She heard the shouted orders, heard Geraint's name called and cursed, heard the horse's hooves on stone.

And she could think of none of it now. She must concentrate on the way ahead, the way she had travelled once before. She must gather the magic her mother had willed to her. She must find the words to bring it forth.

She raised her hands. 'By the blood of the queen, I call the western gate to open!'

Nothing happened. Steel clashed behind her. Voices roared.

Steel. Iron. She still held the knife.

'Elen!' called Geraint. The hawk screamed and Elen felt her plunge.

Elen cast the knife away and raised both her hands again. 'By the life of the babe delivered into my arms, I call the twilight road! By red cow, white pig and the white mare, I call to the other side of the world! Open to my word and show me the true way!'

The wind whipped around her head. The air was hot, then cold, and then absolutely still, and in that stillness, curls of mists formed on the river. They rose up, white and cold as corpses' fingers, wrapping her in their embrace, blotting out the sight of the world. She heard men shout to their gods. Fear sent her mind reeling, but she held her ground. The mists twisted and thickened. Hooves clattered against stone. She felt the panic of the hawk before she heard her screech.

The change of masters had broken all the old bonds. *Come to me!* she willed desperately, holding up her wrist, and to her surprise, the bird did, but the pain of its talons digging hard into her wrist was a new shock and almost shattered her concentration. She must not lose the bridge. It was all they had. 'Geraint! Throw away your sword! You cannot make the passage with the sword!'

Geraint was behind her, pulling his horse up short to keep from trampling her. She heard something splash into the river, and gave thanks that he had listened. The horse was one of Urien's mountain beasts and was therefore unshod. They did not need to abandon it. She grabbed the horse's bridle with her free hand, and as she did, she saw Wyx kicking his own horse up the bridge's steps. Elen hardened her will and began walking into the whiteness. Wyx was on the bridge. he kicked his horse again. The animal reared. Wyx kept his seat, but barely, and still he urged the horse forward.

A wall of whiteness rose up between them, and he was gone.

NINE

Elen and Geraint stood alone on the narrow strip of stone in a world of writhing whiteness. The horse neighed, balked and swung its head, trying to break Elen's hold on its bridle, but Geraint kept his seat. He patted the creature's neck and murmured to it until it calmed. Elen swallowed, grateful for his expertise. She did not want to think what would happen were he thrown into the mists.

On her arm, the hawk creeled softly, shifting her weight back and forth, her talons digging into Elen's unprotected flesh. Now that she held the bird, she could feel her heart pounding hard and strong, and the sensation was dizzying. She gritted her teeth and held tight to the jesses. She could not falter now. She would lose them all.

When the horse was calm enough to follow her lead, Elen began walking forward. The world around them had fallen silent. There was only the noise of hooves on stone and the sound of their own breathing. Even the rush of the water beneath the bridge had faded away.

Geraint's breathing was harsh. The horse whickered constantly. Elen could not find the words to explain where they went. They just had to keep moving. It was so cold. If they slowed the mists would have them. There was no way back, no way out . . .

No. Just keep moving. Keep moving.

So slowly that she thought it was her eyes playing tricks, the way ahead began to lighten. Shadows appeared in the white mists, then shapes, then colours. Finally, she saw a grassy bank, bright with morning dew, and the stone steps leading down.

Elen's fear loosened, although perhaps it should not have. The place had changed utterly since she last saw it. Daylight had come and the sky was a brilliant blue, but there was no sun, and there was no shadow under the straight, white-trunked trees. Only the road was the same, spreading out before them, white and unflawed. The perfume of the blossoms and the green scents of the trees and loamy earth were intoxicating. Flowers in all the colours of the rainbow winked from clusters of emerald grass and dusky fern. The sparkle of dew was on each blade and leaf. The colours and the flora said that it was high summer, and yet it was cold enough that Elen shivered.

'Where is this place?' whispered Geraint.

Elen licked her lips and chose her words carefully. 'If I say it is the home of our good neighbours, will you know what I mean?'

Geraint's face went white and absolutely still. It was only a moment later that he was able to nod.

'Be alert,' she said to Geraint. 'Do not question anything you are shown. Accept neither food nor drink. Be as courteous as you would to a king to whomever we meet. Tell no lies, and do not under any circumstances say your name.'

Geraint nodded again. He dismounted the horse. The animal was twitching and trembling and the whites of its eyes showed. With much patting and gentle coaxing, Geraint led the animal down the steps to stand on the grassy bank.

The hawk, now that the fuss of their pursuit was over, clung contentedly to Elen's wrist, her heartbeat calm and serene. She was hungry. Soon she would be ravenous but Elen did not dare let her fly in this country.

We cannot stay here. But neither could they cross the bridge to home again without help. Few truths were known of the land where they now stood, but this much her mother had told her: human power meant little or nothing here.

Of one other thing she was sure. Those who did wield the power in this place knew they were here.

Geraint stripped the gauntlet from his hand, offering it to her.

'The hawk is yours now,' he said quietly. 'You will be carrying her.'

Elen accepted it, her voice gone mute with the strength of her gratitude, and was able to ease it on, garnering protection from the hawk's talons.

'How is your arm?' she asked.

He squinted down at the streaks of blood staining his tunic. 'Bad enough,' he said. 'But it can wait until we are on more familiar ground.'

Elen nodded. For all the beauty of the woods around them, she felt no urge to linger in this place. She was cold within and without, her hands and mind growing sluggish. 'Come,' she said, grateful her voice held steady. 'We take the road.'

Their feet made no sound as they stepped onto the white road. Not even the horse's hooves thudded against its surface. The trees grew close together, but the wood remained as bright as the grassy bank had been. Despite that, when she looked down the road, she could see nothing clearly. It was as if a shimmering curtain had been drawn across the horizon. The profound wrongness of the place tightened Elen's throat and hands. The hawk watched all suspiciously, and Elen could not rid herself of the sensation that they were watched in return. It was as if unseen eyes peered at them from all directions. From the corner of her own eye, she thought she saw motion – in the trees overhead, beneath the leaves of the ferns and the cups of the flowers, but if she glanced directly at any one thing, the movement stilled, leaving only the faint rustling of leaves and a faint stirring of the fragrant air. What made everything worse, was that she knew this was not mere fancy. In this place, these things were as real as the hawk on her wrist and the road beneath her feet.

The effect of the place on Geraint was marked. He led the horse by the halter, not the reins, keeping close to its side, ready to swing himself onto its back in an instant. His free hand kept straying to his empty sheath, and he kept forcing it back down. All the while, his eyes darted left and right. His urgent need to see what surrounded them was palpable. Elen wanted to say something to calm him, but she had no reassurance to offer, and she knew in the pit of her stomach that any word, however mild, would be overheard.

A distant thunder shivered the air. Geraint jerked his head up at once, grabbing at the air where his sword's hilt should have been. Elen jumped. The hawk screeched its indignation and flapped its wings.

'Hoofbeats,' she whispered, but there was no relief in the realization. All it meant was that the masters of this place were coming for them.

They came in pomp and glamour. They appeared on the road as if they stepped from a fog. There were six of them, all riding tall white horses whose flowing manes were braided with gold. Gold trimmed their harnesses and their saddles. Gold banded the spears they carried and sparkled on the wicked black tips. Gold rings glittered on their leather corslets and gold etchings of fabulous beasts and birds adorned their silvery helms. They were all tall and fair and delicate beyond even the reach of dreams, their skin and hair so pale that they shimmered in the sunless light. They were each alike, and yet different, as the blossoms on a single rose tree might be, and if they were not those who had first brought Elen to this place, they were their close kindred. All around them the world filled with a whispering and a rustling, though no breeze blew to break the still air.

The horse shied at their approach, dancing back and trying to buck, whinnying loudly in its fright, forcing Geraint to grapple with it. The hawk cried in protest, and launched herself to the limit of her jesses, then fell, dangling ludicrously, beating her wings and screaming at the indignity.

The elven knights drew their beauteous horses up before the mortals and their terrified animals and watched with cold, pale eyes as they falteringly brought the creatures under control. Anger filled Elen, and the desperate urge for flight, but she swallowed it down, and pulled the hawk back onto the unsteady perch of her wrist. Geraint laid his hands over the horse's eyes, whispering to the trembling beast. Its nostrils twitched and flared, but it at least was still now.

'Our Lady and Our Lord would speak with you,' said the leader of the knights, his voice as hard as his eyes. 'You will come with us.'

Elen bowed her head. 'We will follow you to your Lady and Lord.'

The six elven soldiers wheeled and backed their mounts with impossible precision, creating a lane in their midst. It was quite clear what Elen and Geraint were to do. Geraint coaxed the horse forward, and Elen kept her grip tight on the hawk's jesses. Awkward and encumbered they walked into the middle of the formation of knights, who closed in around them – two in front, two behind and one on either side.

When they had their charges safely surrounded, the elvish knights touched up their mounts and walked forward. Elen and Geraint had no choice but to do the same. The bright, perfumed woods passed slowly by them. The hawk beat her wings again and again trying to gain the air. The horse moved only due to Geraint's constant coaxing and the blinkers of his hands. Elen felt her heart drumming insistently inside the hawk, and the urge to fly became increasingly unbearable.

At last, the knights led them from the road. The trees still seemed as close together as the wildest woods on the hills of home, and yet they all passed beneath them as easily as if they were still on the open road. The grass was soft as down under Elen's feet. The canopy of green leaves overhead was filled with the rustling of unseen motion. A high piping that might have been birds, or might have been laughter, drifted down.

Ahead, a broad green meadow opened up. Elen had thought they would be taken to the hall where she had been before, but she was mistaken. The Lady and the Lord, clad in white and gold, sat on thrones of white wood beneath two towering thorn trees in full bloom. The scent of the flowers went straight to Elen's blood, stirring and troubling it even more than the dislocated beating of her heart.

More of the cold and pale knights flanked the Lord. Ladies clad in magnificent gowns in every shade of green surrounded the Lady. They were as fair and delicate as their men, all but one. Her flesh was pink and her hair was brown, and she was short, and stolid and earthy amid the airy beauty that surrounded her. Her eyes were wide with wonder, but somehow insensible. In her arms she held a blanket-wrapped bundle that could only be a swaddled infant. She dipped her head and smiled, crooning sweetly to the baby, but when she looked up again, her eyes were still vacant.

Elen swallowed. They had found another to nurse the child she had birthed. Where did that earthly woman think she was?

Elen's knees shook as she knelt to show her respect, grateful that the hawk had stilled itself at least for the moment. Geraint did the same, more smoothly, remembering to bow his dark head.

'You return to us, Adara's daughter,' said the Lady. Her voice was strong and heady, like the scent of the flowers. It was almost impossible to hear it and think at the same time. 'You were not called.'

'No, Lady.' Elen's throat was dry. Words came with difficulty. 'I fled the man who slaughtered my family, stole my lands and drove off my people. The bridge was my only hope of escape.'

'Our lands are not a highway for your folk,' said the Lady sternly. Elen's whole frame shuddered. 'You should know that.'

'I do, Lady. I fled for life and soul. I ask your indulgence of this trespass, remembering the peace and aid that has long passed between your folk and my family.'

Silence descended. Elen tried to gain control over the tremors that shook her. At least the Lady spoke no more words of condemnation. But did they understand at all? Did they care?

'Who is this stranger?' asked the Lord abruptly.

'A knight only,' answered Geraint. 'I am the younger brother, the quiet one.'

'Are you?' Amusement touched the Lady's voice. 'Well, you are a pretty thing, Sir Quiet. Will you stand?'

Geraint did. Elen stayed as she was, for the invitation did not include her. She bit her lip hard to keep her silence as the Lady rose and glided forward. She was so impossibly beautiful, it was as if a star had come to earth to stand before them. 'What brings you here?'

Geraint kept his gaze firmly pointed towards the meadow grass. 'The word of my lady.'

'And who is your lady?' inquired the Lady archly.

'She to whom I am pledged and given,' he replied. 'And who was so given to me.'

The Lord laughed, a sound as beautiful and awful as the tolling of bells. 'Worthy answers, Sir Quiet.'

'Worthy indeed.' Elen thought she would melt at the warmth of the smile in the Lady's voice. 'You choose your companions well, Adara's daughter. Now do you stand also.'

Elen got to her feet. To her shame, her knees were still shaking, but she stilled them. They had passed the first trial. If they were not welcome, they were at least not now unwelcome, and that was no small thing.

The Lady returned to her seat, settling there with the grace of a swan. 'You say your lands are taken. Who has done this thing?'

Elen hardened herself, and answered. 'I believe you know, Lady, Lord. It was your doing that kept me safe from them.'

'Do you fault the fulfilment of our promise?' An edge crept into the Lady's speech. Each word seemed to draw itself across Elen's skin.

Mother dead on the floor, lying in her own blood, the scent of smoke all around. . . but Elen only said, 'No. You did as you promised and I must render you thanks for that.'

Silence again while those words were closely considered. *Careful, careful,* Elen reminded herself. *Feel what you must, but do not let it show. You know not even a tenth of what they could do to you for giving offence.*

'We have watched this one who rode across your land,' said the Lord. 'He has a powerful protector.'

Greatly daring, Elen said, 'One who is known to you.'

'Yes.' The word was plain, showing neither regret nor enthusiasm.

'Do you hold him right to do what he has done?' Geraint's voice rang harshly in Elen's ears, and she winced, at the sound and the question.

It was the Lady who answered, her voice like ice. 'What you do in your lands is of no concern to us in ours.'

'But he is protected by one who has your strength, and under that protection he does great wrong.'

The Lord rose to his feet. Elen saw the golden sheath that hung from his robe's jewelled belt, and the hilt of the golden sword within. Had that been there before, or had he summoned it to him now? The tips of the black and gold spears of the knights glittered in the light.

'Take great care, Man. You know nothing of what you speak.'

Kneel, Geraint, Elen urged silently. *Make your apology.*

But Geraint held his ground. 'I speak only of what I have seen.'

The Lord stepped forward, face to face with Geraint, his pale eyes looking into Geraint's blue ones. *No. Do not look.* But Geraint did look, and he stood still and solid.

'Of what you have seen,' said the Lord. 'But not of all that you have seen with those eyes.'

Geraint made no answer, but neither did his aspect change. The Lord had put no working on him, then. Probably. Was there any way to know?

'You speak as if you would have us right these wrongs, Sir Quiet,' said the Lady, mildly. 'Is that so?'

Now Geraint bowed his head. Elen saw his hand tremble with the effort of his words. 'That is not for me to say.'

'Then who can say? Adara's daughter?' Elen felt the silken touch of the Lady's gaze upon her.

She swallowed. Her head was too full of what she had seen and heard, too dizzied by this place and these beings. Only slowly did the proper words assemble themselves. 'If I were to speak of this, I would ask how these wrongs may be righted.'

The Lord turned to his Lady. The silence between them was deep and heavy as winter's snow, and yet Elen felt some chord of communication singing between them.

At last, the Lady nodded once. 'It would be a worthy question, if asked. What would you give for its answer?'

'What price would be required?' countered Elen.

The Lady gave a show of considering, but the feeling grew in Elen that the decision was already made. Perhaps it had been made before they even set foot on the white road. 'There is beyond the borders of our dominion a thing that was taken from our hands. We would have it returned.'

Elen's mind raced, trying to remember the whole contents of the treasury. What could they have taken from the fae? Neither of her parents were foolhardy enough to knowingly keep anything that belonged to such as these. The story of Maius the Smith and his fate was too well known.

'Why do you not take it yourselves?' asked Geraint.

The Lord's face soured. 'It was freely given. It can only be freely returned. This is the law.'

That word here meant much more than the word of men written in a book or remembered by the elders. Rather, to those who stood before them, law was a thing like the rising and setting of the sun. It must be because the world itself was so ordered.

Elen wondered how this thing they sought had come to be given away, but she knew far better than to ask so much.

Geraint was looking to her. The Lord and the Lady also watched, waiting for her to speak. She must be careful. What she said now would be irrevocable. It would be as set as the stars and the sun in their courses. She must not be mistaken in this.

She licked her lips again. She was so thirsty. She was so

tired. She wanted to make any promise, just to leave this bright, cold, beautiful place. She looked again at the mortal nurse and her vacant eyes and a shiver of fear ran through her.

'Should I find this thing,' she said, 'and should it not defile the honour, name or life of me or mine to return it to its proper place, I swear before all the gods that I will do so.'

The Lady and her Lord were still as death, and yet waves of anger rolled from them, crashing against Elen's mind and soul. Geraint touched her arm, but she could not tell whether it was to give or to receive reassurance. Yet, she stood, and as her breaths came and went, the fear ebbed. Had she not been within her right to make such a qualified promise, she would have fallen before the strength of that anger, but despite her tremors, she stood.

At last, the Lord said, 'Very well. The thing you seek is in the hands of Gwiffert pen Lleied, called by men the Little King. He carries with him a certain spear, sometimes named the spear of Manawyddan. One virtue of that spear is that it will strike whatever it is aimed at, and return at once to the hand of he who wields it. When it does strike, it will kill even the deathless. This is the weapon that will defeat Urien and his works in your land, and do you swear to give it to our hands afterwards, you may use it against him.'

Manawyddan? Elen was startled to hear the name. It came from legend. Manawyddan was husband to Rhiannon and had suffered with her many strange adventures when they were taken into slavery by an evil power. She could even now hear poor Beven's voice as he sang the lay, speaking of how Manawyddan's cleverness saved wife and friends.

Elen set that aside and bowed deeply. 'Then I do so swear. Thank you, Lady, Lord,' she said. To other mortals she might have added assurances that she would keep her promise, but with these two there was no need. A promise to them would be kept, one way or another.

'My thanks as well,' said Geraint, bowing from the waist in a dignified fashion that he surely learned in Arthur's court. 'I add my word to this lady's, and her promise is mine.'

Gratitude and fear warred with each other inside Elen. Could he possibly truly understand what his words bound him to? But it was too late. He had spoken, and it was done.

The Lady smiled at his words, and the smile was both languid and contemplative. 'So very brave, Sir Quiet. It is a shame you and I did not meet before you became so much promised.'

Elen swallowed. *What answer can he make?* But Geraint made no answer at all, he only bowed, his face grave and his eyes downcast. But surely he felt it, the heat of thinly veiled promise in those words. The Lord certainly did, for shadow seemed to gather about him as he frowned.

'You will have to look sharp to find what you seek,' he said shrewdly to Geraint. 'But I think you see more than most. From whence came your eyes that see so much?'

Geraint's jaw tightened and for a moment, Elen thought she saw fear in him, but before she even had time to wonder about it, it was gone. Those words were for the Lady as well, and whatever they conveyed, turned her languid smile into a frown.

We must leave. Now. Before the anger had a chance to grow, before they became more deeply tangled in these threads.

Thankfully, the Lady seemed to think the same. 'Our knights will set you on your road,' she said, before Geraint could make any reply to the Lord's cryptic words. 'Fare you well, Adara's daughter, Sir Quiet.'

There was nothing then to do but kneel again in respect, and wait while the knights on their white horses came forward again to surround them. It was only with considerable coaxing from Geraint that their poor, over-frightened horse was able to move again. It plodded forward, sweating and trembling from the strain of being in this place. Elen knew exactly how the poor beast felt. It was as well the hawk was only hungry.

They had not gone many yards before Elen glanced back and saw that the Lady and Lord and all their retinue had vanished behind the shimmering haze. Another few yards, and she looked back again, and the knights behind them were also gone. Then, between one eyeblink and another, the knights to left and right disappeared, and there were only the two ahead. And she saw that the white road beneath their feet had turned to rutted dirt and old stone, and she saw that the tree trunks were black and brown and speckled with moss. There were once more shadows beneath their branches, and the air was warm, and the breeze blew in her hair.

And at some time while she saw all these things, the last two of their escort vanished, and she and Geraint were alone in the world.

TEN

Elen looked about her, dazed. They stood in a sloping wood. The air around them was full of the warm scents of summer and growing things. The sounds were all the everyday sounds of singing birds and small animals. Oak, beech, chestnut and hazel grew close around them. Wherever the sunlight fell through their branches, ferns and bracken spread their leaves to drink it deeply. While relief flooded her, Elen was still dizzy. The transition from the land of the fae to the mortal world was abrupt and her mind reeled at it.

Beside her, Geraint was breathing heavily as if he had just run a great distance. His face hardened, and slowly, determinedly, he began to master himself, quieting his breathing, stilling his shaking hands.

When he could speak again, he said, 'We should seek the high ground. We should view the country over and see where . . . they have brought us.'

Tired as she was, Elen could not fault this, so she nodded her agreement. They climbed slowly up the steepening slope, leading the fractious, balky horse. The forest around them was old enough that there was very little undergrowth – only drifts of brown leaves and the rustling of branches and the sudden motions of the startled animals. They found a stream running down a culvert and they stopped to drink deeply. The horse also had its fill, and afterwards was more ready to co-operate. The hawk flapped in agitation, her hunger sharpening at the sight and sounds of the forest's animals. She would grow frantic with that hunger soon. So would Elen. She was uncertain what to do. They had nothing but the clothing on their backs. Geraint's arm had begun bleeding again, and her wrist throbbed where the hawk's talons had cut it. Climbing one handed was awkward, and the hawk's irritation pressing on her mind was becoming harder and harder to ignore.

At last, the gloomy woods gave way to open hillside, a sea of grass and a riot of wildflowers. Mountains stood out smoky blue against the horizon in every direction and the air was fresh. The smell of the wind told of a dry night to come.

In the middle of all of this empty beauty, there stood a horse.

It was a tall, dapple-grey gelding, fully harnessed and saddled. It must have been there for some time, because it had worked its wooden bit loose and was chomping steadily at the meadow grass. It looked up when it saw them, and then, unperturbed by their abrupt arrival, returned to its meal.

Geraint and Elen stared at each other for a moment. Then, Geraint handed Elen the reins for their horse and walked over to the grey. He caught the beast easily by the bridle. It made no move to flee him, only snorted in annoyance because his handling interfered with its grazing. He patted its neck, and in return it nuzzled his shoulder. Finding nothing of interest there, it returned to grazing.

Geraint cast about the meadow, but like Elen, he saw no sign of another human, nor any sign that anyone had recently passed this way. Elen approached with the other beasts. The horse was too busy with its meal to take any notice of them. A grey blanket roll behind its saddle looked thick and clean. Its plain leather saddlebags were bulging from their contents. The saddle itself was also plain, except for a small design of knots and birds around its edges. Elen bent closer.

'There is something written here.'

Geraint came beside her. '*Liber Donatus Sum*,' he read. 'I am freely given.'

Elen stared at the beast, understanding coming to her. 'It is from the Lady.'

Geraint looked at her, and looked again at the horse. 'Why?'

Elen's mouth bent into a wry smile. 'She likes you.'

That thought did more than make the knight uncomfortable. A vague trace of fear flitted across his face.

Proving yet again you are no fool, Sir Geraint.

'Is there harm in it?' was all he asked aloud.

'More harm if you reject her gift. That,' Elen ran her fingertip over the inscription, 'says there is no obligation with this.' *Gods all, let me be right.*

Geraint nodded, but he also patted and stroked the horse again, as if to satisfy himself by touch that it was a real creature.

The hawk cried piteously, stretching her neck towards the sky and beating the air so strongly with her wings she almost broke Elen's grip on her leashes.

'She must hunt,' Geraint said.

'Yes.' The hunger was constant now, and the growing frustration. She wanted to fly this moment, to fill her hunger and ease the constant ache of her wings. But there was also the beating in the hawk's chest that resounded in the empty place within Elen. 'I'm afraid what will happen if she does not come back,' she admitted.

Geraint nodded, his face serious and gentle. 'I think she must come back.'

He was right. The bird too was a prisoner of this curse. Despite that, Elen's hand shook a little as she unwrapped the jesses from her gloved wrist. As soon as the slender tethers loosened, the hawk flapped her wings and rose high into the darkening sky, calling out her freedom once before wheeling around to catch the wind and vanishing over the trees.

Elen shivered. She felt herself straining, but towards what she could not say.

'Are you . . . well?' asked Geraint.

Elen shook herself. She was cold, but she was used to that now. Her heartbeat was gone, and there was not enough sound or motion in the world to make up for that lack. 'I don't know,' she admitted. 'But I don't think I am any worse.' *Move*, she ordered herself. *Do something. Do not stand here looking at the sky.*

'A pity she's not trained. She could bring us dinner.'

Elen was a little surprised that she hadn't thought of that. The hunger in her belly was now fully her own, and it was no less sharp than the hawk's had been.

'Perhaps she might yet.' Elen turned to the horizon. She reached with her mind, seeking the beating of her heart that was now so far away. For a moment, the world blurred, and over the sight of trees and the stream nearby she saw brown and green sweeping past beneath her, and then all slowed and dipped and stilled. In a meadow of sunburnt grass and drowsing wildflowers she saw a brace of brown rabbits, loping slowly, nibbling at the grass. The rabbits saw nothing, smelled nothing. She was still, she was still, and she folded her wings, and she plummeted for the ground, talons outstretched.

Elen felt the animal's back snap in two in her hands and

that sensation brought a rush of triumph so great it was almost unbearable.

Elen pulled herself away. She was shaking again, she realized, but this time from the intensity and delight of the successful hunt.

Geraint watched her and his silence was almost more than she could stand.

'I can reach her,' she said, fighting to keep her voice under control. 'I think I can . . . suggest that she bring us a meal.'

'Has she a name?' Geraint asked abruptly.

'None that I know.'

Geraint squinted up at the sky. 'She should have a name.' He turned away then, and began an inspection of the grey's saddlebags. There were flints for striking a fire, clean white cloths for bandaging, good white bread, wooden spoons and bowls, a clay cooking pot and a skin of beer. There was also a stone-bladed hatchet and a matching knife.

'No metals,' remarked Geraint, testing the edge of the hatchet blade with his thumb. 'Is the food safe for us?'

The bread was fresh, and the smell of it set Elen's mouth to watering. 'I think so. I think in this she means us . . . you . . . well.'

'In this,' repeated Geraint.

Elen turned her mind again to the hawk. Instantly, she felt the warmth of rich, raw meat in her mouth and felt muscle tear and bone break under her fingers. It should have been appalling, but instead it redoubled her own hunger until her stomach cramped up within her.

Then it was done, and the hawk lifted her head. Elen collected herself and composed her thoughts. She imagined the ecstasy of hunting, of the kill, and she thought of the comfort of the hawk returning, and of the thump of prey landing at her own feet.

The hawk cried once and launched herself into the air with a dizzying rush. She would do her bidding, Elen was sure, and there was a kind of freedom in that certainty. In her mind's eye, she watched the trees beneath her, amazed at how distinct each leaf appeared even as they rushed past beneath. She watched the deer and badgers, the squirrels and the ground birds that scurried into the trees as her shadow passed over them. The part of her self that was still in her body realized she wanted to feel again the joy that came with the kill, and the shock of that understanding brought her abruptly back.

Geraint was watching her again, a clean strip of cloth held loose and forgotten in his hands.

Elen wanted to speak, but she had no words. Instead, she walked to him and took the cloth. He held out his arm for her attentions. His blood stained his tunic sleeve, which she rolled back. The arm beneath was caked with gore, but the wound under that was fairly clean. There was no sign of pus or angry flesh, and no smell to it. Elen bound it with the clean cloth and noted his skin was warm under her ungloved hand, and that his arm was smooth and well-shaped. She thought of his kiss, and how his embrace had been strong, yet gentle. At another time, her cheeks would have heated up, but such blushes seemed beyond her abilities now.

She began to turn away, but Geraint caught her wrist. She stared, uncertain of what he meant to do, her own unbidden thoughts of their kiss still swirling in her mind. He took her gauntleted hand, and carefully, he began to remove the glove. She thought she did not want him to see the wounds on her wrist, but she made no move to stop him as he pulled the glove off. There was no blood. The flesh was torn badly in several places and it was red and pink, but it did not bleed as it should have. The gaps were obscene somehow in their nakedness. Geraint did not flinch at the sight. He turned her hand in his, examining the wounds, which in all other ways were clean.

'I think if this had bled you would not be standing now.' His voice was thick. He swiftly brought out another bandage and bound her wrist quickly and competently.

But then, he would be used to such work. She watched his bent head and shoulders. He smelled of horse and warmth and salt sweat. She wanted to touch him again, wanted to press against him and feel his heart beating against her.

'Thank you,' she murmured.

Geraint bowed over her hand and she felt the warmth of his fingertips where he touched her. Again, a memory of their kiss shivered through her body. Elen caught his glance and in the depths of his blue eyes, she saw that he was remembering too.

Neither of them spoke. What could be said at that moment that would not be either perilous or absurd? Instead, in unspoken accord, they set about the tasks of making a camp. There was no going further today. Too much had happened. They needed rest and food. They needed calm for a space, and Elen, if she was honest with herself, needed time to remember that shared peril and the need that survival brought could mimic the passions of love. She had heard of this in tales her mother told, but she had not before understood how strong the feeling could be.

Geraint began seeing to the horses at once – removing their harness, rubbing them down with twists of meadow grass, checking their hooves for stones and their legs for any hurt they might have taken. Elen ventured into the woods with the hatchet and gathered up armfuls of deadwood. She cleared grass and litter away to make a place for a fire.

She was striking together the flints over a small heap of dead grass when the hawk made her second kill.

Triumph, joy, breaking bones and red, red blood. Elen

wanted that blood. She needed it, for her own ran no more in her veins and its absence was like the absence of light. She felt that, she understood it with the whole of her being as the hawk rose again with her prey tight in her talons. If she ate now, Elen would know her satisfaction. Her heart would beat hard with exertion and delight. She would be replete with the blood and the kill.

Her hands shook so hard, the flints slipped from her fingers. Geraint looked up questioningly. She only shook her head, and picked up the flints again.

I will master this, she thought as she struck the stones together again and again. *I will become used to it and the strength of it will fade. It will.*

It must.

The fire caught at last, and Elen laid on the tinder and then kindling. Even as she fed the flames, she felt the hawk returning. She stood, staring up at the sky, until she saw the bird. Her heartbeat was strong, steady and compelling. She was full with her feasting and her flight. It was only a mild annoyance to have to let go of the pheasant she carried so it fell with a thump at Elen's feet. The hawk skimmed past, heading straight for the trees, easily finding a branch, and lighting down. She looked down at Elen, seeing her clearly. They stared at one another. Elen knew precisely where the hawk was although her eyes could not pick out the bird's form from the mottled tree bark at this distance. Elen was breathing hard, as if she had herself been flying. Now that the bird was close and she could sense her own heart easily again, some measure of calm slowly returned.

It was then she realized that Geraint had come to her side, and that she had not felt him near her. He looked at her now, his face filled with concern.

'It will pass,' she told him. 'It is already fading.'

It will come again. You should tell him that too.

But she did not. She picked up the pheasant. 'May I have the knife? Our meal will take some work yet.'

She saw clearly that he was disappointed with this trivial statement, but he gave her the knife and kept his silence. Elen cleaned the bird and spitted it on green sticks to roast in the fire that had burned down to its coals. The scent of the cooking fowl was so delicious as to be maddening, but not as maddening as the sight of the offal had been, or the feel of the bones under her fingers. She hunched by the fire tending their meal while Geraint cut branches to make a shelter from the leather awning he'd found in the blanket roll. He laid the blankets down, making a pallet for each of them, and, she noticed, leaving as great a distance between them as the tiny shelter would allow.

When the bird was cooked, they ate it gingerly with their fingers, sopping its juices with the good bread and sharing the beer skin between them.

Through the whole meal, Geraint did not speak. At first, Elen did not mind, but gradually the silence began to weary her. She wanted, no, she needed, human contact, to wash away the memory of the hawk's hunt and the elation it had brought her.

She looked towards the bird. The sun was sinking towards the horizon now, and she was sinking towards sleep; secure, well-fed, content. Her heartbeat grew slower and heavier.

'Calonnau,' said Elen, almost to herself.

Geraint looked up.

'Her name.' Elen nodded in the direction of the tree where the hawk waited. 'Calonnau.'

Geraint appeared to consider this. 'Heart?'

Elen nodded. 'You speak our tongue well.'

He set his bowl of bones aside. Elen looked away from them, concentrating on Geraint's face. 'My Uncle Arthur insisted we learn as many tongues of the land as the monks could stuff into our heads. I'm not as fluent as Agravain, or Gawain.' He paused, watching the shifting colours of the coals for a moment. 'There was something Urien said, when he held us together, that I did not understand.'

Elen knew exactly the words he meant. They were old, and not commonly spoken. She pulled her knees up to her chest, wrapping her arms around them. The cold deepened within her. *'Kynnywedi ar liw ac ar oleu.'*

Geraint nodded, and waited.

She could lie. He did not know, and he did not have to know. His ignorance could keep her free of this much at least. But no lie would come to her, and Geraint was still waiting. 'It means . . . many things. It means given without consent, or abducted . . .' She bit her lip, and then she said, 'It means because he is lord of the land, I may be given to whomever he dictates without my consent or that of my kin.'

Geraint's face was stony. 'That is not law.'

'It is.' Tears stung her eyes. *I will not cry.* 'He is . . .' Mother, dead on the floor. Yestin's sword in Urien's fist. 'He is made chief of Pont Cymryd by conquest. By the law of our people, for seven years I am your wife.' Given before witnesses, hooting and jeering at her, with her people killed, captured and scattered, her mother dragged away and buried she knew not where, if she had been buried at all. But still, there was not a judge or chief in the West Lands who would say that Urien had not conquered and held what he had taken.

'For seven years?'

She nodded. 'At the end of that time, I may leave you if I wish it.' She looked at the stained and battered skirt covering her knees as she said this. Somehow she could not look at his face and speak of leaving him.

After a long moment, Geraint said, 'I think the bishop at Camelot would not approve of these laws.'

'Then tell him to argue with Urien,' snapped Elen. 'Arthur does not rule here yet and your white Christ did nothing to stop the slaughter of my family. For seven years no man of my people will see me as other than your woman.' The tears came now, for anger and for loss, that Urien had stolen even this from her, and for the part of her that rendered her unable to lie to this man.

But Geraint just accepted her anger. It neither startled nor shocked him. 'Lady,' he said softly. 'What would you of me?'

'Nothing.' She wiped the tears away for shame. He had seen too many of her tears. She looked at the twilight sky instead, and listened to the sounds of the nightjar rising from the meadow. Soon the evening star would shine and the moon would rise. It was getting colder. 'There is nothing to be done but what we do now.'

Geraint laid another stick on their fire. He watched the flames cradling the fresh wood. Her gaze traced the line of his jaw beneath its black beard. She saw the way the fire-light reflected in his eyes, the broad slope of his shoulders and the way his arm rested on his thigh. She told herself to look away again, but she could not make her gaze leave him, and so she was still watching him when Geraint turned, and met her eyes.

'I stood beside my brother Gawain when he was married,' said Geraint. His voice was hoarse and Elen felt her lungs, throat and hands all tightening at his slow, careful words. 'He wore green silk and a gold belt about his waist and a gold chain over his shoulders, and his bride Rhian was all in red and gold. Queen Guinevere walked with her. The court ladies sang in chorus to accompany Rhian to my brother and even . . . even Agravain looked content as the High King put their hands together and took their pledge one to the other. She was so brave, so proud, so beautiful, and smiling as if she looked on Heaven itself, and my brother's face shone with the pride and wonder of it all.' He paused. 'When I stood with you, that is what I wanted for you. That was what was in my heart, and I promised . . .' He dropped his gaze, looking down to his calloused, sun-browned hands. 'I promised God that was what you would have one day. That when the work we had was done, I would . . .' He faltered. 'I did not know what he had done then. I did not know . . .' Abruptly, Geraint got to his feet and walked away.

Elen stared after him. He waded out into the meadow grass, and stood there, his back to her, facing the southern mountains. At his sides, his hands opened and closed, knotting themselves over and over again into fists. His shoulders heaved and shuddered with the strength of his breathing.

Leave him be. You have no place or right to do otherwise. You will only make things more difficult.

Despite this counsel, she got to her feet, and she crossed the distance between them. She stood beside him, looking over the retreating foothills, feeling the cooling air and the evening breeze, hearing the noises of night growing louder as the light grew dimmer.

'I told myself I would not speak of this.' Geraint hung his head. 'I have never before had trouble guarding my own tongue.'

'How could we not speak of it?' She tried to say the words lightly, and failed. 'We are here, together. What happened . . . happened.'

'Yes. What happened.' He whispered those words to the evening, and then he turned to face her. 'Elen . . . Lady . . . I must know. Do you see yourself as wife to me, here, now, as we are?'

Her tongue cleaved to the roof of her mouth. *No,* she meant to say. *No, of course not. What happened was forced and false.*

Yet, she knew the law. She had watched her father, and

her mother uphold those laws. She had always known one day she would sit in judgement herself and she had striven to learn how to judge well. She had never thought to live outside her people and her lands, or to be governed other than by the old ways.

But she was not the Fae Lady. Law was not blood and bone to her. It could be broken. She could deny it. People did. Judges and chiefs denied it and bent it as they chose. She was trying to deny it even now. She was a human being and free to make that choice. What had happened was not right. It was one more wrong worked on her by her enemy.

But it was real, and she had not lied. It was she who had told Geraint that what had happened had its foundation in law. If she held that law in such light esteem, why had she done that?

'Yes,' she whispered. 'I do.' *Because I am daughter of my people and cannot be otherwise. Even to try would be the ultimate falsehood. I will not give Urien that. Never that.*

Geraint let out a long shuddering breath. He still did not look at her.

She tried to guess at what he must be feeling. His sense of duty was strong, she knew that much, but they had not been married according to his customs, or the dictates of his god. He could not feel as she did. But surely, he would at least look at her as he told her that. If he did not acknowledge the marriage, that would give her freedom. He could cut this cord. He did not have to wait the seven years. That would be best. Surely that would be best.

Surely. She could tell him that. Her tongue did not move.

'I thought I knew hatred before,' whispered Geraint. 'I thought I knew it when I saw you in his arms. But that was just the shadow. This is hatred. This is the wish to see another soul in Hell. That he should force you . . .' Words choked him. His face was livid. 'That he should force what would have been the sweetest of all gifts, what I would have striven for with all my might.'

The fervour in him rocked Elen back. She wanted at once to comfort him. He did not deserve this pain. But what comfort could she offer? *Tell him. Tell him there is a way out for him.* 'You will not feel so for long,' she tried. 'You do not . . .'

'No.' He cut her off, shaking his head. He looked to the woods, he looked to the heavens, and in the end, his gaze came back to her. 'Elen, I love you.' His voice cracked. He was close to tears. He stood before her and he trembled. But slowly, slowly, that trembling eased, and he was master of himself again, and yet the strength of his words did not diminish. 'I loved you when I first saw you at your mother's side. I loved your grace, and your strength and the light in your eyes when you looked towards me. It was because of my love I begged the High King to let me return to Pont Cymryd and because of my love that I did not leave with my brother. All I have seen of you has only deepened that love. If it is a fool's love, then so be it. I am a fool, and I will live and die one, for I will live and die with my love for you.'

What could she say? She could not turn this away . . . and yet she could not accept it either. To do so would be to accept what Urien had done to her, to them. Worse, it would be to welcome it. No good could come from his evil.

Tears threatened again. She felt split in two, as when Morgaine had plunged the sword into her, but this was worse, because this was as if she'd begged for the blow. Her mind was so full of swirling, raging thoughts, she felt as if it would burst. Her hands had gone cold as ice.

'I don't even know if I can love,' she said bitterly. 'Love is ruled by the heart, and my heart was taken from me.'

'So was mine.'

She did not deserve this pain. Neither did he. He loved, she did not, could not doubt that, but what did he love? She was shattered and bloody. How could she ask him to cleave to her as she was?

'Elen.' Geraint turned to face her. 'What do you want?'

The question startled her. She wrapped her arms around herself. What did she want? She wanted blood. She wanted Urien and Morgaine dead as pheasants at her feet. But he knew that, and she did not think that was what he really meant. And there was more she wanted beneath that base hatred. 'Warmth. Wholeness. Freedom. I want . . . to be free of my hate, and my shame.'

'You have done nothing to be ashamed of.'

'Perhaps not, but it is there all the same.' She looked up into his blue eyes and saw how exactly their colour mirrored the colour of the darkening sky over them. 'I want you never to have seen me helpless or afraid. I want to be rid of this geas and this need for vengeance. I want to be fair and proud and easy in my home with you seeing all that is best of what I have and what I am.' This was not reason. It was beyond reason. Now she was the one who was trembling because the truth was threatening to burst free, and she could not with all her strength hold it back. 'I want to be free to love you, Geraint.'

Whose hand reached out first? Elen didn't know. She just knew Geraint pulled her close and he kissed her, and she returned that kiss. In it was her pain, her desperation and her confusion, but it also held all of her need for him.

Then it was over, and he drew back, but he did not let go.

'I'm sorry,' he breathed, because it was right that he do so. He was giving her the chance to pull away, to stop this thing here. If she did, he would stop too. She saw that in his eyes. 'I had no right. I'm sorry.'

Let him go. Let him be free.

But she did not want him free, and she did not want to stop. She wanted the passion she saw in those blue eyes. She wanted the love that lay beneath it. She wanted to give him the love and the need that ran through her veins. She wanted so much she could scarcely breathe for the strength of her wanting.

'Be you my husband, Geraint,' she whispered. 'I will be your wife.'

He smiled. She realized she had never really seen him smile before, and his smile was full and warm and it lit his face even in the darkness. 'Be you my wife, Elen,' he answered. 'I will be your husband.'

They kissed again, and it was joyful. Life itself was in that kiss and the sweetness wrapped around her with his embrace. Elen pressed against him and his heart beat against her breast. She took that heartbeat into herself and returned it over and again as the night covered them in its darkness and the stars came out to stand guard over the marriage bed they had made for themselves.

ELEVEN

Customarily, when Morgaine, called the Goddess, the Sleepless and the Fae, rode out from her home, she went in stealth and disguise. This time, she chose to ride in state. Two score men marched in procession with her, wearing bright blue cloaks trimmed with beaver fur. Her tall, black horse had a blue blanket beneath its saddle and blue ribbons hung from its gleaming harness. Blue ribbons also adorned the spears her men carried, showing them to be ceremonial, for all their tips were sharp and keen. The four women who rode behind her on grey palfreys also wore blue, with more blue ribbons plaited in their dark hair and woven into crowns.

Morgaine herself wore a gown of rich black. The sleeves fell to her fingertips and the hems trailed nearly to the ground. Silver girdled her waist and wrists and banded her brow. Straight and proud, she rode through the open gates into Gwiffert's stronghold.

For all he was called the Little King, Gwiffert pen Lleied was a man of stature, golden-haired and blue-eyed. Frequent and warlike exercise had made him strong and broad in the shoulders and trim in the waist. The clothing he wore was of deep, blood red, well-fitted. A golden chain hung from his shoulders, the links made in the shapes of hunting hounds. A golden torque circled his throat, made to look like a tusked boar, chased with silver and with garnets for eyes. In his right hand, he held a spear as another man would have held a staff. Its tip glittered black and keen in the summer sun. Its butt rested on the toe of his boot. Its shaft was banded with silver and carved with runes that Morgaine itched to read and understand.

With Gwiffert stood an impressive host of disciplined men, all in leather corslets and armed with sword and spear. Closest to him, however, were eleven men in mail coats with silvered grieves on their shins and silver cuffs on their wrists. Each of them wore a helmet that concealed his face down to his jaw. Each was made differently, and gave the wearer the appearance of a horned demon. Their swords were naked in their hands, held in salute for her procession as it came to a halt before the master of the stronghold.

A servant hurried forward and placed a stool for her feet. Morgaine dismounted and approached, making her curtsey before Gwiffert, who bowed in return.

'Morgaine,' he said. 'You are, of course, most welcome here.'

Morgaine arched her brows. 'Of course?'

At that, Gwiffert only smiled. He beckoned to another servant who came forward with a silver tray holding gilded cups of red wine. Morgaine took the one offered her and she and Gwiffert saluted each other and drank. The wine was warm and richly spiced, but all the tastes were familiar ones. Morgaine smiled now. She had not in truth thought Gwiffert would offer poison, but he was not one to be trusted, or underestimated.

'Come,' he said, holding out his free hand. 'A feast has been prepared for us. My people will see to the comfort of your men and the beasts.'

Impatient, but understanding well that courtesy must be
followed, Morgaine allowed her host to take her arm and
lead her into his hall, her women trailing two paces behind.

Gwiffert's fortress was a strange and labyrinthine place of
branching corridors and many walled courts. It was rumoured
to have been built or stolen for him by the various demons
under his command. The great hall to which he led her now
was painted with fantastic designs. Great hearths blazed in
each of the long walls, filling the hall with the smells of
smoke and applewood. A table had been set on the dais and
laid with brilliant white cloths. It held a variety of fragrant
meats – salmon in butter, wild boar and parsley, and roasted
goose. These they ate with breads of flour, oats and herbs
spread with new butter and honey. To accompany these
homey dishes were delicacies made of truffles, and softly
boiled eggs and pine kernels. For drink there was small beer
and bright white wine. The food was all excellent, and
Morgaine did not stint in her enjoyment of it. There was no
reason not to find pleasure in the moment, even when there
might be discord in the future.

Gwiffert did not once set down his spear. As he ate, he
laid it across his lap. When he finished, he took hold of it
again, nestling it easily in the crook of his arm as the servants
cleared away the dishes and departed. Morgaine nodded to
her women, and they withdrew from the dais to sit on the
benches before the nearest hearth, alert for their mistress's
signal, but out of hearing of her words.

'Now then, Morgaine,' Gwiffert said pleasantly. 'What
great business brings you to my home?'

'I have come to deliver a warning, Your Majesty.' If
Gwiffert wanted to style himself a king, it did no harm to
give him the use of the name. 'There are thieves approaching
your door.'

'Thieves?' His surprise was false. Morgaine did not know

if this was because he already knew who was coming to his lands, or because he suspected her of hidden motives. Still, it was best to play this game as it had begun.

'Two are coming from the lowlands who seek to achieve your spear.'

Gwiffert's hand strayed to the spear's shaft, touching it gently, as a man might touch his new bride's hand, just to make sure she was still with him.

'I see.' He laced his fingers together, and contemplated her for a long moment. 'Tell me, Morgaine, why do you come so far to deliver me this warning?'

Morgaine pulled back. Now it was her turn to show surprise. 'Surely, Majesty, it is to our mutual benefit that we aid one another. We who live on the borders between day and night have common cause.'

'On the borders, we do.' His mouth stretched into a sly smile. 'But you do not intend to remain in the borderlands.'

Morgaine shrugged slightly and Gwiffert sighed. He was ready, then, to cease his pretence. Good.

'You are playing a dangerous game, Morgaine. You need Arthur strong when your son is grown. It is so much easier to lop off one head than deal with a hydra of squabbling kinglets. But he is growing stronger than you anticipated, and rather than lopping off heads himself, he's leaving them in place to pay him tribute. This is his genius, and it is serving him well.' Gwiffert lifted one finger to make his point. 'If, for a small price, kings such as Mark and Lot can keep and hold their thrones, and have aid against their enemies, why should they rebel?' He levelled that finger at her, sharp as a law man in high court. 'You cannot risk Arthur's lordship spreading further north and west than it has already gone. You will be found out if it does.'

Morgaine was expecting all of this, and said nothing, but could not hide her eyes quickly enough. Gwiffert of course saw the flicker in her glance and leaned forward. 'Unless you have already been found out?'

'Arthur has seen a shadow, and is starting at it. Neither he nor his know anything in truth.'

'Your shadow?' Gwiffert cocked his head. 'Or only your lover's?'

You are as insolent as you are clever. Be careful, Gwiffert. My patience with your play will last only so long. 'They are one and the same.'

'So you would have Urien believe, I am sure.'

Morgaine felt her blood warm. *Softly, softly,* she counselled herself. *Let him believe he knows what brings you here.* 'You are very blithe, Majesty, in your mists and glamours,' she answered sharply. 'But it is Arthur who sends these thieves. One is his own nephew. It is only the first attack. When Arthur himself comes marching in the full blaze of sunlight with Merlin and his knights and his laws, then what of you? I know well his willingness to do whatever he must to hold and keep his lands, whether it violates the laws of man or his own god. Can you be certain Arthur will recognize these borders where you live? Or will you pay him the small price that he asks?' Her face went hard as stone. 'Remember well, the price he asked of me was the life of my son.'

Gwiffert's mouth twisted into a smile of wry humour. 'Why should I allow them into my lands at all? The last enemy you sent me has been a sore trial to me.'

'Do not fault me for your weaknesses, Majesty.' Morgaine added the title slowly. 'It was you who let him live long enough to have a son who could become your rival here. If you are going to play the fool, a fool's reward is what you deserve.'

Gwiffert sat back. Morgaine nodded. He was angry at her slight, she could see as much in the set of his jaw.

Nonetheless, she had reached him. His next question confirmed this.

'What are their names, these thieves?'

'The man is Geraint. The woman is Elen. It is she of whom you must take the most care. There is magic within her, and for all she bears my curse, she still walks free.'

Gwiffert got to his feet, planting the butt of his spear on the floor. 'Let us see what comes, then. You will excuse me for a moment, my lady.' He bowed, not without a trace of mockery. Morgaine tipped her head towards him and waited just long enough to see the anger and concern rising in his eyes. Then, she nodded her assent at being left. Gwiffert was uneasy at her calm acceptance of his command. He left the hall, marching with stiff shoulders and a tight grip on his treasured spear.

She smiled as he disappeared through the archway and composed herself to patience. She would not delve into the secrets of her host, at least, not while she was his guest. But let him fear she would. Those who feared what would not come grew careless with what might.

Gwiffert's home held many secrets, even more than Morgaine's own. The place was a marvellous warren of doors locked with keys and enchantment. As to what waited within, she had only yet been able to uncover a few secrets.

Do you venture into one of those sanctums? she wondered idly as she took a sip of the white wine remaining in her goblet. *Or is it to one of your towers you go? Perhaps to that empty mews you keep? What flies from there, Little King? What returns?*

You have worked so very hard to make this place. She drank again, smiling at the place where her host had been. *You hold it so tight and fast. Surely you are secure from all enemies and prying eyes.*

It was no hardship for Morgaine to wait. She had learned patience long ago, and under circumstances that made this a heaven of comfort by comparison. Her ladies sewed their fine work. Folk came and went from the hall, never looking up at her, their shoulders hunched, their backs ready for a blow. They always hurried, even the children, as if they feared they might be noticed if they stayed in one place too long.

She shook her head slightly at this. *Those who do not follow willingly will betray when they can, Gwiffert. This is the open door to your hall, but you don't see that, do you?*

Eventually, Gwiffert returned. His eyes were glassy, and his steps faltered a little. Perspiration shone on his brow. Wherever he had ventured, it had been far away. She signalled one of the waiting women, who scurried forward with a jar of wine to fill her king's cup as he sat down.

The wine revived Gwiffert quickly, bringing him wholly back into the room.

'So, Majesty.' Morgaine smiled. 'What do you see?'

Irritation crossed his face, but was smoothed quickly away. Of course she knew, she could all but hear him thinking. 'I saw a man and a woman. He carries the burden of blood. She carries a hawk and the burden of hate. I saw strength and weakness. I saw honour that may yet crack in the firing. I saw hope and fear and blood and love. I saw the balance, and the balance may tip.'

Do you seek to riddle me? 'What would tip that balance?'

Gwiffert smiled, sly and tired all at once. 'What will tip the balance for most men? Gaining what they believe is their greatest desire.'

Morgaine nodded. *It does not take an oracle to see so much. You could have spared yourself your efforts.* 'Can you make use of this knowledge?'

'Oh yes, with a little extra that can easily be found.' He wiped his brow, and looked shrewdly at her. 'Tell me of the hawk.'

Ah. You've seen that too have you? So gifted. Morgaine hesitated for a few heartbeats, as if choosing her words. 'The hawk holds Elen's heart. Whoever is master of the hawk is her master.'

'But she carries the hawk. She herself has mastery of it.'

'Clever girl that she is, yes,' admitted Morgaine, not without grudging admiration. 'But what she does not know is that should she lose the hawk, or should it stray too far from her, her sensibility will leave her, her caution and her righteousness. She will become a wild thing of unmoderated feeling, and that feeling will overwhelm her. She will die eventually, but she will run mad first.'

Gwiffert returned her a look of wonder, and, Morgaine thought, a little fear. 'All this to one girl who crossed you.'

Do not let his fear grow. 'Urien's life was not hers to take,' she said bitterly.

Fear turned quickly to cleverness. 'Is it yours?'

Morgaine was silent at that.

'Is it?' asked Gwiffert again. 'You know there will be a price for these deaths you ask me to bring about.'

She turned her head. 'If there is a price, I will pay.'

Gwiffert considered her carefully for a moment, and then nodded. 'Yes, I expect you will.'

It is you who should beware the unpaid debt, Gwiffert, not I. She kept this thought silent, and Gwiffert, confident in his power and prowess, asked a question that must have seemed good to him. 'Tell me, how might this fearsome spell of yours be broken?'

'Oh, no, Gwiffert,' she answered flatly. 'That you shall not know.'

'So be it.' Gwiffert got to his feet, cradling his spear. 'I know what must be done here. What of you?'

Morgaine unfolded herself smoothly and stood without aid. *See, I am strong even here.* 'Urien readies his army. I will help as I may. We will stop Arthur's men at the river and

drive them back into their own lands.' She smiled. 'You were
right. He overreaches, and too soon. My son is not yet ready
for the throne, although it will not be much longer.'

'And what then?'

'That will depend on how well you play your part.'

He did not like being called an actor in her mummery,
she saw that plain enough, and it sharpened his mind against
her. 'You are a bold woman, Morgaine.'

'I am as I must be.' That much at least was unvarnished
truth.

'As are we all,' answered Gwiffert, and for the barest
instant, Morgaine heard genuine sympathy in him.

She looked him full in the face. *Heed me, Gwiffert. Hear all
I say.* 'You would do well to kill them, and quickly, Little
King. There are four lives here that they may change, and
do they change them and do they save them, all that you
have woven will unravel.'

He heard, and he thought, and while he kept his face
careful and closed, he had already dismissed her words.
'Leave this matter to me. They may reach this place, but they
will go no further.'

*Ah, well. None can say I did not behave as I ought towards my
host.* Morgaine curtsied. 'Thank you, Your Majesty. I knew I
would find faith with you.'

Gwiffert bowed, and Morgaine saw the gleam in his eye
as he did so. Why not? He believed he had her gratitude
now, and in his heart he was surely already dreaming of how
he would spend that coin. So, she only smiled, and let the
Little King dream.

TWELVE

Geraint woke with the sunrise, dishevelled and content. The air against his skin was cold with morning, and heavy with dew and the promise of rain. Their rude awning had begun to sag above them and it brushed Geraint's head as he sat up. Beside him, Elen slept, curled in on herself, her arms crossed protectively over her breasts. She was scarred there. He had kissed that scar afterwards, and she had told him how it had come to be, and he had held her while she cried.

In sleep, her face regained its nobility and was without the air of a hunted she-wolf that overcame her in waking hours. In sleep, at least, she was as she should be.

God be my witness. She will be free and we will stand before my uncle and all the world as man and wife.

Man and wife. Geraint drew up his knees and rested his forearms on them, looking out at the brightening world. Dew-drenched cobwebs covered the hill like a blanket of mist. Flowers lifted their heads here and there, opening themselves cautiously to the leaden sky.

What was this thing he had done? This vow he had sworn? His love was true, he had no doubt, and he would stand by her. But what would they face when he returned to court?

What of my uncle, Arthur? What of Agravain and, Heaven help us, Uncle Kai? Will even Gawain understand? Will she be able to stand firm when they counsel me to set her aside? He smiled. *Yes. That much I think will happen.*

What of the rest? What of all I have not said?

He imagined the look he would see in her eyes when he told her he was kin to the one who had bound her so foully. He thought of her turning away from him, breaking the so-fragile vows that held them together. He thought of her coming to fear him. He shook his head. *When she is free of this curse, I will tell her. When she can once more breathe and think freely, without the threat of the geas haunting every moment. Until then, she knows full well that her enemies are my enemies. It will be enough.*

Will it? Be sure of that, Geraint.

Elen stirred and stretched. She opened her forest-brown eyes, looking up to him. For a moment, Geraint's heart beat hard. What would she see? Did she regret the choice she had made? Did her dreams speak to her of evil done?

But no, she smiled at him, and her smile lit the world.

'Good morning, my husband.'

Husband. The word swelled Geraint's heart with pride. 'Good morning, my wife.' He brushed his fingertips down the length of her arm where it lay atop the blankets, taking delight in the smoothness of her skin. 'You are well?' *Do you regret what you have done?*

Her smile did not falter. 'I am well.' She sat up, brushed her dark hair back from her face and made as if to pull the blanket aside, but she paused. 'Husband?'

Worry touched Geraint. 'Yes?'

Elen was looking warily at the edge of the blanket he'd spread beneath them. 'There is . . . another thing you should know.'

He quirked his eyebrows up. There was a hint in her voice that seemed to say she was teasing, but he could not be sure.

Elen gathered the upper blanket closer, sheltering her scar, or hiding it. 'It is the custom among my people that the wife is permitted to ask for a gift from her husband before she leaves their bed on the first morning. If she does so, whatever it is, he must grant it.'

'Very well,' Geraint said solemnly, but he suddenly felt keenly aware of his own nakedness. Not just in the matter of clothing, but of possession, of friend, of sign of rank and title and property. He had only himself now. He waited. Elen licked her lips, looking at the edge of the blanket, listening to some argument within herself. This was real then, not just some tease on the part of a new wife.

The whole of her body had tensed. 'If anyone steals Calonnau from me . . . you will kill her.'

Geraint froze, stunned. A dozen possibilities had flitted through his imagination, but this . . . 'Will that kill you?' he asked.

'I believe it will, yes,' Elen replied softly.

'You ask this of me?'

She did. She faced him squarely and spoke without flinching. 'I cannot again be under the command of an enemy. I cannot again be made to work against my home . . . or you. This is what I ask, husband.'

No! With an effort, Geraint quieted the refusal that threatened to burst from him. *I do understand. It is only selfish desire that makes me wish to refuse. But oh, Elen, it is a cold and bitter thing you ask.*

These thoughts too, Geraint shut away. He looked into Elen's eyes. 'I promise before God and Jesus Christ and Mary who is his mother, that if I must, I will do as you ask.'

'I would that I never had to speak so to you, husband.'

'I know,' he answered simply. What more was there to be said?

She scrambled out from under the blanket and reclaimed her battered and rumpled dress. Clothed once more, she went out to the fire, poking about in the ashes with a gnarled stick to see if any coals remained. Geraint let her go.

It will not come to it, he tried to assure himself. *God is kind. It will not be so.*

God was kind, but Morgaine was cruel, and the wrongs done blood to blood were very strong.

Repenting quickly the sin of doubt, Geraint pulled his tunic and breeches on and then he too left their shabby wedding bed.

There was little enough with which to break their fast. They ate bread and drank some more of the small beer. Gooseberries grew at the edge of the woods. Elen had gathered some to help eke out the meagre meal while Geraint led the horses to the stream for a drink. The mundane task of caring for the beasts helped settle his spirits. The invisible world was always near. He and his brothers had more cause to know that than most. There was nothing to be done but face it. Gawain had done so, and his bride was safe at Camelot, waiting to be delivered of their first child. And Gawain had seen at least as much as Geraint.

Hadn't he?

It is no accident that you are the one who inherited your mother's eyes, Merlin had said. *From whence came the eyes that see what you see?* the elven lord had asked.

The past closed over him so suddenly, Geraint felt as if he would drown. He was standing again in the wide stone hall, in the dark, his bare feet twitching against the frigid stones. He saw his father reeling from his chamber.

He saw his mother follow, his mother who was years dead,

and saw how she laughed soundlessly at his father, who fell onto his knees, grovelling before her.

And now that vision turned to look at him, and he saw that his mother's eyes had turned black.

Geraint shook himself hard. Now was not the time for such memories. Now he must focus on the way before him. There would be a lifetime and more for the dark past.

Elen insisted on checking Geraint's wounds. The cut on his arm seemed to be healing cleanly and the bruises had already begun to fade. The same could not be said of her own wounds. Beneath the binding, the tears on her wrist remained fresh and open, just as they had been the day before.

'Does it hurt?'

'Yes,' she admitted. 'But it is nothing I cannot bear.'

Neither of them spoke the worry that as she was, she might be unable to heal.

Merlin will solve this riddle. I will see her safe to Camelot and all will be set to right.

But the road was long between here and there, and where it ran . . . Geraint frowned at the distant hills.

'Even Gareth would have something to say to me about my choice of priorities,' he sighed. 'Elen, do you know where we are?'

Elen smoothed her sleeve over her re-bandaged wrist and looked north. The mountains that had been misty blue yesterday were today grey with low clouds and the threat of rain. She looked south, where the land was more gentle and green.

'I think Pont Cymryd is far on the other side of those.' She pointed towards a trio of green mountains that clustered together as if gossiping. 'You can see them in the distance when you stand on the bridge. They are the highest of the Black Mountains. More than that, I cannot say.'

Geraint puffed out his cheeks, considering their options. There were, in truth not many.

'North and west then,' he said.

She cocked her head. 'To seek a thing neither of us knows anything about, we should go to a place neither of us knows?'

He nodded. 'If we follow the stream down the valley . . .' he pointed to the silver thread meandering through the valley's dark green fabric, 'we may come to folk who have heard of this Little King.'

Elen folded her arms, her lips pursing in approval. 'It is as sound a plan as any.'

Geraint felt his mouth twist into a wry smile. 'Faint praise from my wife.' Elen bowed her head in such a show of humble apology, he could not help but laugh.

While Geraint saddled and harnessed their horses, Elen packed up their meagre camp. Her hands seemed clumsy this morning, and she dropped the bowls and spoons more than once. When she saw Geraint's questioning glance, she turned away, her unbound hair falling across her face, hiding her from him.

'It is Calonnau,' she said. 'She knows we are leaving. She does not want to be out in the gloom when hunting will be poor.'

For a moment, Geraint had allowed himself to forget the hawk. She had sat still and invisible in her tree since he had woken. Elen, however, could not forget her for even a moment.

'She will obey,' said Geraint. 'She will accustom herself to these things. You are her mistress.'

'No, I'm not,' answered Elen, and her voice was very small. 'Her keeper, perhaps, or her fellow prisoner, but I do not master her. If anything . . .' she would not finish the thought. She only bowed her head again so he could not see her face and continued to pack the saddlebags.

But Geraint found he could not let it go at that. 'Does this . . . way of being pain you?'

'No. It frightens me.' Elen looked over her shoulder towards the wood. What did she see there? 'We talk of noble beasts. What I feel in the heart she carries for me . . . there is no nobility. There is no thought. There is hunger and fear and anger. She is content when fed, and when she kills . . . it is all mindless. Being close to this . . . I fear that I will never lose the taint of it, even if there is a way to break this curse.' She rubbed her arms and hands, trying to wring warmth from them. Her flesh had been cool beneath his hands the night before, growing warm only slowly. He had not thought before how very cold she must be.

'There will be a way. Merlin will know it if no other man does.'

'I pray you may be right.' There was no faith in her voice. She pulled the laces on the saddlebag tight and knotted them, and would say nothing more.

She insisted he take the grey horse they had dubbed 'Donatus', although he offered it to her. She was no horse-woman, she said, and the Lady had given the beast to him. She let him tie the reins of the small brown to his saddle and was content to be led as they made their way down the sharp slope towards the northern valley. He could not help but eye her seat, and agree, she was clearly unused to horses. The people of her country kept few ponies, using the rivers or their own feet to make their way through the mountains. Perhaps, when they returned to Camelot, the queen would agree to a tutor for her. The thought of riding with her to hounds and on May Day made him smile.

The weather did not threaten for long, but fulfilled its promise. By the time they reached the valley floor, a cold, misting rain began, the sort that seemed to rise up from the ground as much as it fell from the sky. The grassy hillside quickly turned slick, requiring Geraint to get off his horse and lead both animals to help them keep their feet. The broad valley held no trace of human habitation and the rain had silenced even the birds. To keep their northward course, they had to climb the next hill, and descend again. No cloak was thick enough to keep the rain out and soon they and the horses were all soaked and shivering. Calonnau could not fly in these conditions, so Elen carried the hawk on her gauntlet. The bird hunched miserably in on itself. Elen was beginning to pale with the cold and she bit her lips constantly. They would have to find shelter and fire soon.

This new valley was sharp and narrow. The hills rose like earthworks on either side. The horses would not be able to manage them. So, Geraint set them to following the chill, pebbly stream that snaked through the grass and reeds. The brown fish that swam beneath its waters had pressed themselves against the bottom, trying to escape the falling rain. The ground was level, so Elen and Geraint could ride again, but the horses plodded so listlessly, walking might have been faster.

Geraint began to eye the stones scattered here and there, wondering if any were large enough to put their backs against for some slight shelter. Then, he caught a faint scent on the wind. Elen caught it too. She lifted her head, equal measures of fear and hope kindling in her.

Smoke. There were hearth fires burning nearby.

'I'll ride ahead,' Geraint told her. She slipped the knot that tied her horse to his. He urged Donatus into a canter, kicking up clods of mud with every step.

At last the rain began to slacken. The wind picked up, sending the grey clouds rolling across the sky. It also blew straight through their sodden clothes. Hills and stream bent, forcing the valley around a corner, but then the way broadened. The stream spread out to become a small, reed-choked lake. Through the sullen mists, Geraint saw the shape of a small hamlet – half a dozen houses crowded between forest's edge and new cleared field. No more than half the acres were green with grain. The others still sprouted stones and burnt stumps.

In the middle of this detritus, an old dame and her man struggled with a large stone. They had tied it with ropes, and while the old man pulled, the dame tried to slip a sapling pole underneath it to lever it out of its bed. They were alone in their labours, and Geraint guessed that whatever fellows they had in this place had sensibly taken shelter. He found himself shaking his head at the fact that these two oldsters were left to this heavy work on their own.

Elen caught up with him, reining in her horse to stand beside his. She saw the aged pair and the distant houses. There was hunger in her face for that shelter, but she nodded her answer to his unspoken question.

Geraint dismounted and walked forward. Such was their attention to their labour, he was almost beside them before the old man noticed he was there. The man straightened up quickly, and the woman, gasping as she took in the new arrivals, did the same. They both bowed their heads humbly for a bare instant, then the old man examined him with narrowed eyes.

'What do you want here, Sir?' There was suspicion under the acknowledgement of rank.

'Shelter for myself and my wife,' Geraint answered. It felt odd to say those words aloud, and yet fresh pride stirred as he did. 'For which we would be most grateful.'

'You shall have it and welcome, Sir,' said the old man smartly. 'That's our house, the closest you see there.' He pointed back towards the cluster of cottages still blurred by the mists. 'Shout at the door and they'll let you in.' He moved to pick up his ropes again.

'Come, let us get out of this,' said Geraint, sweeping out his hand to indicate the way to the cottage. 'I will lend my strength to yours as soon as it is fair again.'

The old man held his ground. 'Nay, Sir, and thank you. This has been left too late as is, and it must be done.'

What is this? 'Surely . . .'

'No, Sir,' said the old man, who seemed all at once as stubborn as the stone. 'I've said this will be shifted today, and it will.'

It was clearly no good to argue, and it was more than discourteous to leave their hosts out here to do the work. In this rain and cold it was dangerous. The damp could take either or both of them. Elen dismounted from her horse. She came forward to take Donatus's reins while Geraint rolled up his sleeves and inspected the old man's lashing with hand and eye. It was skilfully done, and there was little he could add to it.

'No, Sir, truly,' began the old man, flapping his hands, as if trying to shoo Geraint off like a straying hen. 'Get you into the warmth. This is no work for such as you and your lady. Get you in by the fire. We will . . .'

Geraint ignored him. He picked up the ropes and Elen led the brown over to him so he could tie them to the horse's harness. He joined the oldsters behind the stone, firmly taking the sapling pole from the old woman's loose grasp and digging it into the mud between the stone to be moved and the stone placed as the fulcrum for the lever.

'Sir, please . . .' began the old man, now wringing his hands together. 'Your . . .'

'Walk on!' Geraint called. Elen clucked her tongue and urged the horse forward, a little awkwardly for she only had the use of one hand. Calonnau complained constantly at this disturbance from her gauntleted wrist. The horse protested, balked, and then walked. The ropes creaked. The stone tipped. Geraint dug the pole further underneath it and heaved. The oldsters, apparently resigned to being helped, put their shoulders to the rock's sides and added their strength. The horse pulled and whickered. The mud squelched and shifted beneath Geraint's sandals as he leaned hard on the pole.

The stone came free with a huge popping sound and rolled perilously close to the horse's hooves. In the hole left behind, something shone gold in the watery light.

The two old ones stood back, their heads bowed, looking for all the world like guilty children. Slowly, Geraint reached down into the cold mud, and his fingers closed around a sword hilt. It came easily into his hand and he held it up. He could not see much of it between the terrible weather and the filth that covered its blade, but it felt well balanced in his grip and there was gold on its hilt and pommel. There was no scabbard.

Elen stared. Calonnau screeched a complaint and shook her whole body hard.

Geraint lowered the blade. The old couple had edged closer to each other, their fingertips just brushing. He watched them carefully for a moment, standing there under the brightening sky, but they did not look up at him. There was mystery here, and it was only growing deeper. Warning rang slow and solemn through his mind.

'It's yours now, of course, my lord,' muttered the old man, turning his face away. 'Thank you for your help.'

Geraint opened his mouth to deny this, but Elen was quicker.

'Come, now.' She held out her free hand, sounding for all the world like she was warm and dry in her own home rather than shivering in a half-cleared field in the foul rain. 'We have all been long enough in this weather. Let us take shelter and you can tell us the tale of this thing you've found and how it came to be here.'

'It is no good for such a fine weapon to be in the damp,' said Geraint in swift agreement. 'Will you take it in with you, my wife, while I see to our horses?'

Elen received the sword, giving him a glance that said, 'Well thought of'. At the very least, this should reassure the old folk that they did not mean simply to ride off with this treasure. There was more than one riddle here. Given the nature of the quest he had sworn himself to, Geraint knew it was not wise to leave such a mystery gaping open behind him. Mysteries were dangerous. They could turn friend to enemy, and drive families to madness.

'If you will please show me the way?' said Elen to them, smiling and patient for all she was also shivering with cold.

It was clear neither of them wanted to, for all their previous offers, but also clear they felt they had no choice.

'You go with the lady,' said the old man to his dame. 'I'll help Sir with his horses.'

The woman made her obedience to Elen. Together they tramped across the muddy field. Geraint tried not to see how Elen slipped and struggled with her flimsy slippers and trailing hems. *She has eyes of her own, and more power than you. She will be all right.* He turned his attention to the horses, untying the ropes from the brown while the old man undid the other ends from the stone. *She will see better than you. She will not be caught unawares.*

'How may I call you?' he asked the old man as he passed him the rope to coil up.

'Cob,' he answered tersely. 'How is my lord known?'

'I am Geraint of Gododdin, Lot's son.'

The man grunted and slung the rope over his shoulder. Geraint's name clearly meant nothing to him. Geraint turned back to his work, but did not miss the way Cob glanced towards the horizon. The clouds were thinning and some late-afternoon sky was beginning to show through their curtain. For a moment, Geraint thought Cob was noting the improvement in the weather.

It was then he heard the hoofbeats.

They rode out of the gorge, two of them. They had helmets on their heads, leather corslets covered with scales of steel, and thick grey cloaks clasped with silver. One carried a spear. Both wore swords on their hips. Their horses were tall, but poorly fleshed. Geraint could all but count the creatures' ribs.

They reined their skinny horses to a halt before Geraint and the old man. The left-hand one, who had the spear, wore a helm of leather banded with steel that had been chased with oak leaves. Along with the short sword on his belt, he wore a black-handled dagger.

What sends you out so heavily armed, my lord?

The right-hand one had horses for his decoration, and two gnarled scars on his wiry arm. That old wound must have affected his grip, because he held the reins tightly in his left hand and wore his sword on the right, where his left hand could reach it most easily. Beside the sword, a knobbly club of blackthorn had been thrust through his belt.

'Well now, Cob,' drawled the oak-crowned one. His gaze swept from Geraint to the stone and the muddy hole. 'What's this?'

Cob blanched, and bowed his head humbly. From the corner of his eye, Geraint saw, Elen had paused, her hand on the old woman's arm.

''Tis nothing, my lords, nothing,' Cob was saying. 'Only the field must be cleared while there's still some hope of planting this season, mustn't it? And this stone . . .'

'You knew you were not to move this stone, Cob.' Oak Helm rested his spear on his boot and leaned over his saddlebow. His voice was deceptively smooth. Horse Helm had his hand on his club. The old woman was tugging at

Elen's sleeve, saying something urgently. 'Our lord charged you and yours most particularly.'

Cob looked blank, taking refuge in the appearance of stupidity. 'Was this the stone, lord? I never knew. In the bad weather and all . . . I'm most sorry, lord.'

There were so many things wrong here, Geraint could not begin to count them. There was no recourse but to be bold.

'What cares your lord for a stone, Sirs?'

Oak Helm turned towards him, as if seeing him for the first time. 'Who are you to be asking?'

'Geraint of Gododdin,' he said patiently. Oak Helm had dark eyes. He shifted his grip on the spear, but not on the reins, yet. 'Son of King Lot of Gododdin and nephew to Arthur, the High King,' he went on. If these were to be his enemies, they might hesitate more at killing Arthur's nephew than they would at killing one unnamed and unknown. 'And I am the one who moved the stone.'

'Are you?' Oak Helm sat back, but his grip on his spear did not change nor did it loosen. The old woman was still tugging on Elen's sleeve, obviously urging her to come away. Elen was not moving. The hawk shrilled and shook itself, preening frantically. Horse Helm looked over at them, frowning. His hand stayed on his club. No danger there yet, though. It was Oak Helm's attention he had to keep. He was the leader of the pair.

'Cob,' said Oak Helm harshly. 'Did you explain to this lord that this stone was not to be moved?'

Cob hung his head further down, and drew his shoulders in, trying to make himself as small as possible.

It was absurd that they should be standing here discussing the moving of a stone. Rather, it would have been absurd, were it not for the spear and the club, and the fear in Cob and the old woman, and the gold-hilted sword that Elen now carried.

'He had no chance to explain,' answered Geraint, which was true enough. 'I ask again, Sir, what cares your lord for the moving of stones?'

Now Oak Helm changed his grip on the reins. His horse felt them tighten and lifted its head and stamped. Horse Helm was trying to divide his attention between Cob, Elen and Geraint.

'That is my lord's business, Son of Lot, and none of yours.'

Geraint had no weapon. He had no armour. He was as good as naked before these two. Even if Elen ran forward with that sword now, he could very well be dead before she reached him.

'Is it the stone he cares for, or the sword?' Geraint asked mildly.

Oak Helm's frown grew thunderous. Incongruously, the first of the birds began to sing, alerting their fellows that the rain was over. 'Where is the sword?'

'It waits here,' answered Geraint, keeping his gaze fixed on Oak Helm's face. They knew where it was. They did not need to give more attention to Elen, who still had not moved. The old woman plucked constantly at her. 'Cob was most insistent that it not be removed from its bed, but I did not know what such as he would have to do with such a fine weapon.'

Oak Helm raised the spear and tucked it under his arm so the point was levelled at Geraint's heart. Horse Helm moved his mount closer so Geraint faced a wall of man and beast. 'You will give it me,' said Oak Helm.

Geraint did not permit himself to flinch. 'Assuredly, if it be yours. Wife!'

Cob's woman moaned and clapped her hands over her eyes. Elen came forward calmly, the sword in her right hand, the hawk on her left wrist. 'Husband?' she inquired coolly, as if there were nothing wrong at all.

So brave. 'These two claim the sword you carry belongs to their lord.'

Elen blinked. 'An' that be so, we must give it them.' She held the weapon out to Oak Helm, hilt first.

Now it was Cob who moaned. Geraint looked again from Cob to the riders. The day was brightening all around them. The horses, the riders, even the stone threw their faint shadows across the grass. There were too many things wrong. Far too many. He should step away. His concern should be Elen's safety and his own. Oak Helm most likely had the right here.

But he does not do right. And Geraint made his decision.

Oak Helm took the sword. With the blade in one hand and the spear in the other, he had no hand left for his reins. Horse Helm smiled, although Oak Helm did not. Horse Helm also loosened his club from his belt.

Oak Helm laid the contested sword across his thighs and said grimly to Horse Helm, 'Teach Cob and all his kin what it means when they fail to defend what is our lord's.'

Horse Helm swung his club for Cob's head. Elen saw the blow coming and shoved the old man aside, knocking them both to the ground. Calonnau screamed and flapped free, landing on top of the stone.

Geraint grabbed Oak Helm's sleeve, and kneed the horse in the side. The horse reared and Geraint yanked Oak Helm towards him. The rider's foot caught in the stirrup and he dangled ridiculously over the horse's side. Geraint caught the spear as it fell from Oak Helm's grip and let the sword thud to the ground. Oak Helm's horse whinnied high and frightened and danced in a tight circle, trying to throw off the struggling weight. Geraint and Elen's horses answered with snorts and whickers and both danced back. Oak Helm hollered and cursed, and Horse Helm shouted his own curses, trying to manoeuvre his beast past Oak Helm's to get a clear swing at Geraint.

Geraint leapt backward. Elen scrambled to her knees. She snatched up the sword in one hand and her skirts in the other and ducked quickly behind him, heading for Donatus before he bolted. Cob was on his feet, hobbling to his wife as fast as his legs could carry him.

Geraint thrust the spear at Horse Helm's mount. The beast had no taste for a fight and shied, coming down within an inch of Oak Helm's head. He hollered, and it shied again. Elen hauled Donatus up to Geraint, and Geraint swung himself into the saddle.

Oak Helm at last kicked himself free of his stirrup and landed on the ground with a thud. Horse Helm had mastered his beast, and urged him around his fallen captain. But it was not Geraint he headed for. It was to Elen, standing on the grass, the sword held awkwardly in her hands.

Geraint put Donatus between Horse Helm and Elen and thrust again with the spear. Horse Helm knocked his blow aside with the club and turned his horse in time, passing by Elen, and wheeling about to try his charge again. Oak Helm found his feet and limped towards her, fighting to draw his own sword. Geraint made his choice and swung at Horse Helm. Elen saw the opening he gave her and ran past. Horse Helm dodged Geraint's spear again and drew up short, landing a blow above Geraint's knee. The pain shot stars across Geraint's sight. The next blow caught his arm, and he dropped the spear.

Oak Helm howled and caught the spear up, swinging it around. Hoofbeats beat the ground. Elen had run only far enough to mount her little brown, and now she charged at Oak Helm, who levelled his spear. Geraint cried out, and only barely managed to duck the fresh blow from Horse Helm.

Elen veered off her course, swung the sword, and threw it at Oak Helm.

The blade spun end over end. Oak Helm ducked. Horse Helm stared. Geraint kicked his horse hard, sending it plunging forward. Holding tight with his knees, Geraint swung out his good fist to catch Horse Helm hard on the temple, just below his cap. The man reeled. Geraint grabbed his club from his hand and slammed it down against Horse Helm's weak right arm, which was all the man had to guide the horse. He felt bone give and heard the crunch, and Horse Helm screamed as his horse reared and lurched and he fell from the saddle.

Oak Helm had grabbed the sword and abandoned the spear. He thrust the weapon into his belt, the naked blade dangerously close to his leg and his horse's side as he swung himself back into the saddle. But the fight seemed to have gone out of him and Oak Helm turned his horse about, sending it galloping up the narrow valley way.

Geraint, arm and leg weak and burning with pain, urged Donatus to follow as best he could. Oak Helm shouted something Geraint did not understand. Thunder roared and the ground shook. Donatus screamed and stumbled. Geraint barely kept his seat. When his mount recovered, Geraint saw that one of the green hills now gaped open wide. Through the gap waited another valley where the sun shone bright and the air was clear. But he saw these things only for an instant, because Oak Helm charged through that ragged, earthen gate.

It shut behind him, and he was gone.

THIRTEEN

As soon as Geraint rode past her, Elen grabbed up the spear. The fallen man had his knees bent and was struggling to rise. She shoved the spear at him until the point rested over his heart. Corslet or no, he had reason to fear the weapon held this close. For a wild moment, she had an urge to stab his chest, just to reach the heart that he did not deserve. She uttered no threat for she did not trust her voice. Calonnau flapped her wings atop the stone, and continued her frantic shaking and preening. The hawk's distress mixed with Elen's fear for Geraint and the near-panic the battle raised. For all that, her hands and gaze held steady, and the man with the horse helm and the broken arm held still.

Calonnau shrieked. Elen heard the approach of a single horse. She did not let herself look up. Despite his injury, Horse Helm was watching her closely from where he sat, looking for his chance.

The horse halted, and someone dismounted. She knew it was Geraint before he came into her field of view. He circled the captive until he stood opposite her.

'Who is your lord, villain?' he asked quietly.

Horse Helm turned his face away. Geraint knelt. He

removed the captive's helmet and tossed it aside. Underneath, their man had a thatch of brown hair and one eyebrow was made ragged by an old scar. But that was not all. Someone had burned the man's forehead with a brand, leaving behind a livid white scar shaped like a sealed knot.

Elen's stomach turned at the thought of the pain such branding must have caused.

Geraint did not pause for such matters. He drew his knife and held it to the man's cheek, right below his ear. 'I have no time for quizzing. I know not whether you are a mortal man, but I know you can be hurt. Tell me whom you serve, or you will have much more to regret than the pain in your arm.'

There was no menace in Geraint as he spoke these words, only cold promise. Elen swallowed, but held the spear still. She thought she could feel the man's heartbeat making the shaft quiver like a harp string. She gripped it tight and gritted her teeth.

The captive ran his tongue over his lips. 'My king is the lord of the hidden country and the narrow way. If you know him not, you will soon. You should fear the Great King.'

'Names and riddles again,' muttered Geraint. He looked to Elen. 'Whoever he is, their lord will soon know what has happened here. I lost this one's captain.'

Elen could only shake her head. 'He knew we were coming, Geraint. This was all a ruse.' She risked a glance away from their captive. The last of the fog had lifted, and now she could see the empty meadow. The cottages and burnt fields had vanished with the mists, leaving behind only the tall grass, the silent lake, and a fringe of young forest. Elen was not surprised. 'The old ones were here to make sure we stopped. These two were sent to make sure we went no further.'

'I know,' said Geraint ruefully.

'You saw?' Elen had seen what was amiss as she was walking with the old woman. The illusion had been complete, except that the brightening day showed no shadow under the woman's feet.

'Not soon enough,' muttered Geraint. He pressed the edge of his knife more closely to the flesh of their captive. 'You spoke of the Great King, villain. Do you know the one called the Little King?'

This man was more than mist and expectation. Perspiration sprang out on his face. Yes, he feared both spear and knife.

The captive made to shake his head, but stopped as he felt the movement brush skin against blade. Then he smiled, a death's-head grin.

'Kill me, then,' he said. 'My king will raise me up whole and perfect again.'

Geraint pulled his head back, for the first time showing surprise. 'You are a Christian knight?'

Horse Helm laughed, and there was a high edge to the sound. 'I spit on your weak Christ. He swears some strange future day of fantastical beasts shall come and then you shall rise from ashes. My king will raise me up before I am even laid in the grave.'

The sealed knot on his brow seemed to glow whitely in Elen's sight as he spoke these words, and cold worry settled over her mind. Geraint's brows knitted tightly together, but rather than try to answer this boast, he looked up at Elen.

'Elen,' said Geraint without letting his knife stir from its place. 'Can your gifts make him speak?'

Elen considered. There were rumours, things her mother had spoken of late at night, of magics that were grey and black and had more than a little poison in their purposes. There were too the three gifts she was allowed to bestow. 'It can be done.' *If it must.*

This declaration took all the boast from their captive and the blood drained from his face, leaving him pale. 'No,' he whispered. 'You cannot make me.' But the words were spoken in hope, not in belief, and his dark eyes were filling fast with fear.

Of his lord, or of my husband? She felt her eyes narrow. *Both, and the Little King is a third. What warrior finds himself with so much to fear?*

Geraint shrugged. 'You will speak, villain, now or later, by pain or by enchantment.'

The captive's eyes flickered from Geraint to Elen and back again. His jaw moved back and forth and in the silence of the day, Elen could hear his teeth grind together. 'You would truly go to the country where the Little King dwells?'

'Yes.'

He clutched his arm more closely to his torso. Elen's hands tightened their grip on the spear. 'More fool you. I will show you the way.'

While Elen held the spear ready, Geraint relieved the captive of his arms and made him strip off his corslet. This Geraint claimed, along with the helmet and the grieves on his legs and guards on his arms. He dressed himself in the armour. The fit was tight for their captive was a slender man. For all that, Geraint seemed to relax a little more with each piece of armour he put on.

As if he's found his own skin again.

Geraint belted on the captive's sword. The grey cloak he offered to Elen, who accepted it gratefully and clasped it about her shoulders, sinking into the warmth of the dry wool.

Geraint trussed the man's good arm behind him with rope from the saddlebag while Elen rigged a sling with one of their precious bandages for the broken one. Geraint mounted Donatus and took up the spear as Elen passed it to him, and Elen knew that for the first time since the welcoming banquet she saw Geraint whole and complete. He was a knight, a warrior on horseback. She had not thought what it was to be deprived of the tools to which he was so much trained.

All the while Horse Helm watched them with his dark eyes and said not a word.

Elen sheathed Horse Helm's knife at her waist and reclaimed Calonnau to her wrist, despite the bird's shrill protests. She mounted the captive man's dapple-grey horse, which was of better blood than her little brown, and moreover had a real saddle. With Geraint levelling the spear at his back, Horse Helm trudged up the valley way. Elen rode behind, leading the spare horse and carrying Calonnau on her gauntleted wrist.

They came to the place where the hills bent and bulged, making a corner as neat as any on a highway built by men. The captive stopped there. He seemed to hesitate, but then he looked back at Geraint. To Elen's surprise, a smile twisted on his lips. The captive leaned forward until his mouth was almost kissing the slope before him. He whispered a single word three times, and straightened.

With a sound like thunder, the hillside shuddered. The ground trembled. The horses screamed and danced. Calonnau screeched and tried to fly. Elen fought to keep her seat and some control over bird and horse.

The hill split open, a gaping black hole tearing through the wholesome green. A moment later, sunlight and warmth poured through the cleft, as through an open door.

Geraint looked back to Elen, silently asking if she was ready to do this, and Elen, who had crossed knowingly into the fae's lands, found herself afraid. Premonition surged through her. There was danger beyond this doorway, danger of loss beyond death. She knew it and she could not keep that knowledge from her eyes as she looked back at her husband.

*There must be another way. The Lord and Lady did not tell us
this was the only way.*

But there is no time to find another way.

So Elen nodded to show her readiness, and Geraint
prodded their captive with the point of his spear. The man
walked forward into the cleft, and Geraint followed him, and
Elen followed her husband.

It was like walking through a ragged archway. It was dark
and smelled of earth. The floor beneath them sloped down
sharply, causing the horses to balk, and then step cautiously.
Roots as thick as Elen's thumb dangled overhead. Then, they
stepped out into the fresh sunshine of a summer afternoon
with a broad green meadow sloping down before them.

Behind them, without a sound, the passage slipped shut,
leaving only the wild hillside.

Whatever this place was, there was no returning by that
route.

The captive giggled. Elen's head whipped around and she
stared at him. He threw back his head and laughed to the
sky, shaking in his mirth.

'You think you have come with open eyes,' he gasped.
'You think yourselves wise and clever. You know nothing of
my lord. You are his already and you know it not.' The man
laughed even louder, and his laughter echoed off the hills.

Then, he was gone, melted away like ice, and the ropes
they had used to bind him fell on the ground in a useless
heap.

Elen stared. Geraint made a gesture she had seen only
rarely. He crossed himself.

'Are we in the place of the good neighbours?' he asked.

Elen shook her head. 'The sun is in the sky, and there are
shadows around us.'

'Aye,' muttered Geraint. 'There are shadows around us.
That is the very truth.'

Elen smiled with dark amusement. 'What should we do?'

Geraint sighed and scanned the way westward. 'Will you send up Calonnau?' he asked. 'Let us see what she sees.'

Elen nodded. Calonnau was itching to fly anyway, urged on by the sight of the clear sky after so long in the rain, and she was more than ready to spy out a wayward rabbit or pigeon. Elen wondered if she were moved by her hunger, or Elen's own. It seemed it had been a hundred years since Elen had eaten a decent meal.

Whatever the reason, the hawk took gladly to the sky. Trees and meadows passed under her. She saw narrow valleys and ragged, stony hills. She saw red deer, and foxes, bears lumbering through glens, wolves sleeping the day away in their packs. She saw a stream of brown trout, and she saw a huddle of huts in the middle of cleared fields, but there was nothing in those fields better than mice.

With some difficulty, Elen pulled herself back from the hawk's eyes.

'There's a village,' said Elen. 'Due west of here. A few hours' ride, perhaps.'

Geraint glanced up at the sun. It stood a bare finger's width above the horizon and their shadows stretched long behind them. Elen was weary and she was hungry. They'd had only bread since the morning and the beer was not going to last much longer, and these might be the least of their worries.

'And between there and here?' Geraint asked.

'Wilderness only.'

Geraint lapsed back into silence. Elen did not blame him. She did not like this place where a man of flesh and bone could vanish in front of their eyes. She did not like ignoring the premonitions she felt so strongly.

Nervous, Elen tried to call Calonnau back to her, but the hawk had decided that if mice were what was nearest, mice would be enough. She dived and she struck, and the sickening

delight coursed through Elen. As she tasted blood, she realized what else she had seen and horror rocked her backward.

The mouse, the creature Calonnau was even now tearing
to bits, had no front paws. Rather, it had human hands.

'Elen!' Geraint caught her, steadying her. 'What is it?'

But Elen could not answer him. She pushed away, stumbling past the horses and was abruptly, violently sick. While
she retched, Calonnau finished her meal and launched herself
again to look for fresh game.

Geraint knelt beside Elen, waiting for her fit to pass. He
handed her a twist of grass to wipe her face. His eyes begged
her to tell him what she had seen, and she did. Without a
word, he folded her in his embrace.

'It is your heart within her, Elen.' He held her close. 'Your
heart.'

My heart but her desire. Elen swallowed. *It does no good.*
Helplessness pooled inside her, but anger poured in behind it.

*Call her back. Call her down. It is your heart. Whatever has been
done to you, you remain yourself. You are Adara's daughter and
you will not let your heart run wild.*

She squeezed Geraint's hands and stood. She raised her
gauntleted wrist and stretched out her will. *You will return.
You will return now.*

Anger surged through Calonnau. She fought, as she fought
the jesses, but she wheeled on her wingtip, and soon Elen
saw the hawk's shape approaching from the bright blue sky.
She landed heavily on the gauntlet and scolded as Elen caught
up the jesses again.

Endure, she said silently to the hawk, using the word
Geraint had used for her. *I will find a way to free us both as
soon as I can.*

But such promises meant nothing to the wild creature
before her, and Elen felt only Calonnau's anger in return.

The light was dimming quickly. There was no going further this day. They set their camp beside a broad stream. Geraint saw to the horses, removed most of his armour and took a thong, a crust of bread and a loop of fine wire worried out of Elen's belt to try to catch them some fish. Elen could not bring herself to use Calonnau for hunting again. She made a makeshift perch of Donatus's high-sided saddle and lashed the jesses down. Calonnau grumbled, snapped and complained. Elen ignored her as best she could and went to kindle a fire.

Geraint was successful in his efforts and brought back three silver trout. One they gave to Calonnau who tore into it greedily. The remainder they cleaned and gutted and roasted on a flat stone. They were dull without salt, but they were filling and made a decent meal rounded out with the last of the bread and beer, and such fruits as Elen had been able to find on the bushes growing nearby on the hillside.

But even as she sat beside the fire, and picked at the last of her own meal, Elen felt Calonnau swallow the raw fish guts and her satisfaction of them was greater than even her own pleasure at the cooked food before her. Elen shuddered again. She turned away when she saw Geraint watching her. She did not want to see the growing distaste in him for the feelings she could not govern.

I should never have told him how it was. I should never have tried him so far so soon.

It seemed, however, she had misjudged the thoughts in his mind. Instead of pulling away, he reached out and touched her hand. 'It is not easy, to have no control over a part of yourself,' he said carefully. 'My father was a good man, but he could be brutal in war. Cold mad, some said. When mother . . . left us, he was driven more and more into that part of himself, until it was not just in battle that he was so mad.' His gaze drifted towards the sky. Gauging the weather, or simply not wanting to look at her? 'When I held my knife to that man, I felt my father's madness in myself. No matter whether he spoke or not, I wanted to cut him, I wanted him punished for my pain, and even more for yours.

'I do not take what you are lightly, Elen,' he said. 'But nor am I ignorant of the power within to turn it aside.'

'You have none to blame for who you are,' she muttered. She was being churlish and she knew it. She did not wish to be so, but she was exhausted and frightened and she did not want to be either of those things either.

'Do I not?' murmured Geraint. 'Had I neither father nor mother, nor brothers, nor aunt, nor uncle, what you say might be true. But I have all these things and more besides.'

'There is no one without blood or past, but I am under geas, and I know not what compulsion may be laid on me next.' This was the root of her fear. This was what drove her to ask such a boon of him as she had that morning.

'And yet even so, you freed yourself,' Geraint said gently. 'Your heart that was taken from you is yours again. Your enemies are for the time confounded. No.' He stared straight ahead of him, remembering something long past. 'I have heard the priests say otherwise, but I believe God always leaves a choice.' Then, very softly, so that she barely heard him, he murmured, 'I must believe.'

What does that mean, Geraint? she wondered, but she let him lapse into his silence. This was hard for him. It was a hard way to give comfort, to show weakness and worry. It went against pride. Yet he did this for her, to show how he understood.

'It is the fear that is worst,' she whispered. Honesty for honesty. It was the only way to repay him for what he now offered her. 'I fear for myself, but also for you. What will I do to you, or cause you to have to do? You have already faced death to save me.'

Now he smiled, and it was his true, quiet smile that was so new and so familiar at the same time. 'All I have done, I have chosen to do, and I chose gladly.' His expression turned to mocking pride. 'If nothing else, the story I will have to tell when next I sit at the Round Table will earn me a verse from the poets, and such a one as not even Gawain's name has been put to.' He put on a face of such stern and noble vanity that Elen laughed loud and long.

Elen watched him as he settled back into his attitude of calm and serious study. She tried to imagine life with this man. She tried to imagine the years stretching ahead: the work, the sharing, children . . . but it was beyond her power. She could not even imagine the shape tomorrow would take. That pained her. She wanted to see that future, to have that premonition singing in her stilled blood, but it would not come.

'I wish you could have known my mother, Geraint,' she said suddenly. 'I believe she would have liked you.'

'From what I saw that night, I know I would have liked her.'

'Your mother is gone?' she asked curiously.

Pain flickered across his face. 'Yes.'

'I am sorry for it.'

'So am I.'

'And your father?'

'He lives,' Geraint sighed. 'Though perhaps he should not.'

I should not press. It may be too much. There are years ahead for us to know one another. And yet . . . 'What is his madness that you spoke of?'

'Many things, but the worst of it is murder.'

Elen's tongue froze.

He watched the way straight ahead of him, seeing past the dark meadow and the grasses waving in the night breeze, the approaching edge of the wood, and the steeply rising land. What his eyes looked on was black and bitter, and he spoke haltingly. 'I had a sister once. She . . . there was a man, and then there was to be a babe. When she would not name the father, our father threw her from the ramparts of Din Eityn.'

'I am sorry, Geraint.' The words felt feather light. They would blow away without touching him at all.

'This is the blood that runs in me and my brothers,' he went on grimly. 'We each one of us fight it as we can. Gawain, he became so noble, so proud, that the blood rage could never touch him. Gareth . . . he's done it by denying our father, I think. He's seized on another to show him how to be a man. I hope he's been wise in his choice.' He shook his head. 'And then, Agravain . . . he became cold and hard. I doubt not he'd take out his own heart if he could. But then, he's the one of us who must go back there. When father dies, he's the heir of Gododdin.'

Oh, husband. 'And what of Geraint? How do you fight it?'

'With silence,' he said.

The stars were coming out overhead. Elen watched them for a long moment. She saw the familiar patterns, and took heart. They could not be too far gone from the world if the stars above held their familiar courses.

'I hope you will not ask me to fight such a battle with such a weapon,' she said lightly, hoping to turn his thoughts. *We have heaviness enough between us.* 'I'd lose in an instant.'

Geraint chuckled. 'You are a woman. You have your own weapons.'

'Tch,' she clicked her tongue. 'You'll call me shrew next.'

Now there was mischief in his eyes, for all his voice was solemn. 'Of all the names I'd call you, that is not one.'

Elen cocked her head, one hand on her hip in an imitation of impatience. 'What are these names then?'

But Geraint fell silent, with only the smallest of smiles

playing around his mouth, and Elen found she could laugh at that and be glad for a precious moment.

For a while they sat with arms around each other, watching the stars and breathing in peace. When the time came for sleep, Geraint took first watch. They slept in shifts that night. It was cold and dark but the moon was nearly full. Owls hooted in the forest and wolves gave tongue to their fellows, but nothing untoward came about and the stars wheeled overhead in good order.

Elen found breathing easier. Above her she saw the mother's white face, not yet turned away. *We are not alone,* she told herself. *Not even here.*

In that thought Elen found strength enough to watch the night and wait for the morning.

When the morning came, they fished again to break their fast, then rode together down the rolling slopes towards the valley Calonnau had seen. Had it not been for their means of arrival, Elen would not have known it from any other part of the West Lands. The tall mountains brooded blue and purple behind them, and if the land before them was rough, it was green. Thick, dim forests of oak and alder alternated with meadows bright with summer flowers. The birds sang, calling and warning. A fox yipped. In the distance, a stag crashed through the underbrush, startled, and launched on some adventure of its own. Calonnau, her hunger sated by the fish, followed them, flying from tree to tree, circling occasionally overhead, untroubled by this new place. She saw prey for coming meals. She saw a fox that had blue eyes, and a quail that had golden feathers in its crest. That these things looked strange troubled her no more than the mice with their delicate hands did. They were food and the hunting of them was as it should be.

The day wore on, and they passed through meadow and

wood, up gentle stony hills and down them again. The bread and beer were gone and they had only water and tiny wild apples and a few currants the birds had missed to sustain them through the afternoon.

They came to a strip of thick wood and had to dismount and pick their way through the gloom and the rattling bracken. The light slanted sharply through the trees. Evening was coming fast. They needed to find shelter or make camp soon.

Elen opened her mouth to say so, but Geraint held up his hand, stopping her. She listened, and she heard it, the thick, heavy sound of hoes striking earth. A faint shout rose over them, and another answered it.

Together, they waded into the underbrush, moving towards the welcome human sounds as quickly as the horses could be coaxed between the trees.

They emerged from the forest and found themselves in fields bright green with grain that rose as high as the horse's bellies. People, sun-browned and sturdy in loose, rough clothes, worked here and there among the wheat, chopping weeds with wooden hoes, or carrying out buckets of water to the workers. An old man herded geese into the rows to eat the insects and weeds. The scene was as familiar to Elen as her name and her throat ached to see such a homely place.

For all the fields appeared prosperous and long-established, the settlement beyond had a rough and wild look. Elen could not see one proper cottage, let alone a hall or great house. There was at least one long, windowless building with proper walls washed well in lime, but Elen could not imagine that such a strange place could be the high house.

A rutted lane ran from the woods to the village and they set themselves and their horses on it. Elen held Calonnau close, swallowing the hawk's anger. The bird's hunger was growing again. She'd find it a meal soon. Calonnau was not going to hunt in these fields.

A man straightened his back from his labour. He saw them coming and stopped to stare. Geraint raised his spear in salute. The man shouted something to his fellows. All halted their busy labours then, and all gaped as if stunned. Elen fought the urge to shrink near Geraint in the face of all these strangers watching her. It reminded her too much of her time at Urien's side, with the hungry-eyed men measuring her worth.

While she pushed this thought aside, the fields burst into commotion. A gaggle of children raced to the village, calling out in shrill voices. Their elders all hurried to line the road.

'What do we do?' she asked, discomfited.

'We greet our hosts,' replied Geraint.

They rode at a gentle pace through the fields. As Geraint and Elen passed, every one of the serfs knelt and bowed their heads. Those who wore hoods or headcloths doffed them at once.

What is this? Elen wondered. Outwardly, Geraint seemed to take it in his stride, bowing his head this way and that whenever someone risked a glance upward. It was only the small furrowing of his brow that told Elen he too was surprised.

When they reached the village, they found it was indeed a poor and dishevelled place. Hovels of mud and bark hunched beside an open-walled pavilion of thatch and poles with the bark still on. Some dwellings were no more than tents of hide on frames of willow wands. The only buildings that looked dry and sound were the four long, windowless houses with their bright, white walls.

There were many pens full of fat animals – sheep and goats, a fine herd of shaggy cows, pigs, with even a white piglet wallowing among the others in the mud as their fat sow watched benevolently. But while kettles hung on chains over open fires, and a few clay ovens smoked, Elen smelled only boiling pottage and vegetables. No scent of meat leavened these other fragrances.

A small cadre of old men waited nervously for them in the shade of the enormous chestnut tree that grew beside the broad well. Like the workers in the fields, they knelt as Geraint and Elen approached, their hoods in their hands. Those hands were black with ancient dirt. Their tunics were rough and undyed. They were shod in bark-soled sandals. Their beards were untrimmed and uncombed. Elen stared from the fat, well-tended animals to their lean and filthy keepers and had to work to keep her jaw from falling open.

A boy wearing nothing but a loose and much-mended tunic ran forward to hold Geraint's horse while he dismounted. Elen watched Geraint's eyes and knew he saw all she did, but he held his face absolutely calm. He walked up to the man who seemed the oldest among those who knelt in their ragged line. His bald pate was bronzed, mottled and shining from all its time in the sun. His ragged-nailed hands shook as Geraint approached.

Geraint said something in a tongue Elen recognized as Latin, though she understood none of what he said. The head man just shook and made no reply. Geraint tried again, this time in a guttural and less measured tongue. Still the man said nothing.

Geraint tried a third time, speaking in the tongue of the West Lands that Elen knew.

'I thank you for this good welcome,' said Geraint gently. 'My wife and I are in need of food and shelter for the night.'

'Wife?' exclaimed the man, his head jerking up. He stared for a breath at Elen sitting on her grey horse and wearing her grey cloak, and he dropped his gaze instantly. 'I'm sorry, my lord. Of course, my lord,' he stammered. 'It is no more than our duty.'

Elen frowned. Who were these people who went poor in

the midst of plenty? The accent was familiar to her. His tongue
had learned to speak not far from Pont Cymryd. She thought
of the man who had worn Geraint's armour. Was it the one
they feared so much? Or were there others?

And why the surprise that such a one should have a wife?

But Geraint was holding his peace, and so Elen decided
to hold hers. They were now the centre of a flurry of activity.
More boys came for the horses. Elen let Geraint help her
dismount. The children led the animals to a trough where a
stooped and wiry man stood ready to see to their care. A
few old women scuttled into houses coming back with chairs
that were set in the shade. Another man hobbled back
towards the fields, hollering for all to come in and see to the
comfort of my lord and my lady.

All their faces were stark white. All of them trembled
whenever they glanced in Elen's direction. The wrongness
of it all left a sour taste in Elen's mouth.

The old men all got to their feet. Bowing deeply, the bald
one they had singled out gestured to the chairs. 'If you and
your . . . lady would care to take your ease, my lord. You will
see how well we have tended the king's plenty. All is yours.'

'May I know how we may call our host?' Geraint asked.

That startled the man as badly as naming Elen his wife
had. 'A . . . Adev, my lord.'

'Adev. Thank you.' Geraint inclined his head once. He took
Elen's hand with so stately a courtesy it would have been
flattering, had they not been surrounded by people wide-
eyed with fear. He led her to one of the chairs, seeing that
she was seated before he was. She took a minute to lash
Calonnau's jesses to the chair's slats since she had no other
perch for her. She was not letting the hawk away from her
now. She needed the steadiness of her heart beside her, even
with the hawk's anger pressing hard against it.

Women brought pitchers of small beer and wooden

noggins, which they filled, and then they backed away, hastily bowing, trying to get out of sight as quickly as possible.

'What has been done to these people?' murmured Elen to Geraint. 'We do not dare ask.'

Geraint shook his head. 'We watch.'

So, watch they did as the folk came flooding in from the fields. No person stopped to salute, much less speak to them. Mothers and granddames pulled their children into the rude houses. Men brought out trestles and boards for a table which they set in front of Geraint and Elen. Only Adev stayed at their side, and he kept his eyes fixed rigidly ahead. His brow was bright with sweat and his eye bright with fear.

People went into the long white houses and emerged with all manner of foodstuffs. These were clearly the stores, but Elen had never seen anything like this. Stores were for grains and preserves, not for bread, or cheese, or the fresh fruits.

Snatches of furtive conversation reached her.

'. . . the whole thing, here . . .' A father said to a child as that child brought out a round, ripe cheese.

'. . . bring the best . . .' called one woman to another as she hurried forward with an armload of cloths to spread on the table.

'. . . That's all . . .' said a man's quavering voice behind them.

'No matter, bring it,' answered another, deeper voice.

'But . . .'

'Hush! Would you tempt the wrath? They'll know if anything's held back!'

She wished for a way to reassure them, a way to understand what plagued this place where they were so clearly afraid for their lives. They were heaping the table in front of them with food – breads and cheeses and steaming bowls of stew, fresh fruits, and last year's apples. Her stomach churned with its hunger, but all the same she could not believe her eyes. Whole barrels of beer were being rolled out of the strange, white storehouses, and huge piles of nuts were stacked beside them. Two people could not possibly eat so much, yet no chair was set at the board for any other to join them, let alone any long bench. What were they doing? Paying tribute or toll? Some hard tax?

She thought of the old pair by whom they had been distracted on their road. This was what that illusion had been taken from. This was the truth of that shadow play of fear. She thought of the man whose armour they had stolen, and of the twisted brand on his brow.

'Geraint,' she whispered. 'Take off your helm.'

He understood at once. 'It is a risk.'

It was, but it was a way to show who they were to those who would believe no less a sign. 'It is better we should be open about who we are than that we should try to hide and fail.'

Rather than waste words of agreement, Geraint simply undid the strap under his chin and removed the banded helmet, running his hand through his black hair as he did.

Each and every one of the villagers froze in their tracks, and they stared at Geraint's open and unmarred face.

'He's not . . .' began a tangle-headed child. A woman grabbed her from behind and clapped a hard hand over her mouth.

Adev was also staring, his jaw slack, his brown eyes wide. 'But . . . you carry the spear . . .' he stammered. He took one step back. 'She wears the grey . . . how is this . . .'

'I won this armour from one I defeated in battle,' said Geraint evenly. 'So too the cloak and spear.'

'Defeated?' The word choked Adev, and he could say nothing else for a long moment. He swayed on his feet, torn by his different fears. Geraint waited; his patience seemed infinite. All around them the people murmured, their fear taking on a new, sharper pitch. Whatever danger they expected, this was not it. Was this worse? What did it mean?

'Who are you?' whispered Adev.

No names, Elen mouthed to Geraint. There was too much magic in the ground of this place. They must hold off giving their names as long as possible.

Geraint saw her warning and answered Adev. 'We are strangers to these lands.'

For a moment, Elen thought Adev was going to faint. A woman gasped. Had this not been so horrible, it would have been comic.

'A stranger, bearing the grey . . .' Adev wagged his beard back and forth. 'No. No.' He gripped his head in both hands, shaking it hard, as if trying to dislodge some unbearable thought. Behind them, someone had begun to weep, the choking hiccoughs sounding unbearably lonely in the still air.

When Adev could look up again he croaked, 'My lord, I beg you, leave this place. Leave us in peace. Please. He must not know you have been here.'

Geraint remained seated. 'He? Who?'

'My lord, please!' Adev fell to his knees. 'Leave us! Leave now! We have done nothing to you. Please! He must not know!'

Around them, others were looking to the fields and the track. There was no movement that way but the waving of the green wheat. Some husbands were shooing wives into the houses, but mostly young and old huddled closer together. They were afraid for their lives, afraid and help-less.

Unable to sit still any longer, Elen rose and walked forward. 'It is your king you fear, Adev?' she asked, as mildly as she could.

Adev bowed his head, biting his lip. Elen thought of Urien,

and how he sent fire and slaughter down on Pont Cymryd, all because his will was denied.

She knelt so she could take the man's hands, cursing the coldness in her own. She would share human warmth, that most clear and basic communication, with this man who was almost mad with his terror. 'What will he do when he finds we have been here?'

'He . . . he . . .' Adev licked his lips. 'All is his. That we offered what is his to strangers . . .'

What overlord grudges his people hospitality?

Elen nodded, although she understood nothing of this place. She stood, raising the old man to his feet. 'Then you must not give us what is his. Take away what you have brought. Instead, we will host you.'

Geraint was watching her, wondering what she was doing. The truth was, she was wondering the same. At home, she would not have even contemplated what she was about to do. It was a thing out of legend. But here, in this place, legend surrounded them and such power as should have belonged only to the gods simmered in the air of the fair summer evening. The prophecy her mother's ghost had laid upon her was everywhere written, and it came to Elen that to refuse to do this thing might be more dire than to attempt it.

Slowly, haltingly, Adev managed to look up. Weak hope sparked in his eyes. He looked to the crowd, the husbands and wives in their homespun tunics and dresses. They all had a worn and hollow-eyed look that made them appear so alike as to be of a single family. Not one was fat. Not even the babe bundled at his mother's hip. Not even Adev the headman. 'Take this away,' she said again, gesturing to the food on and around the cloth-covered table. 'We would not bring trouble on you.'

They did not need more urging. As swift as the food had

been laid out, it was now snatched away, hurried into the stores and some little into houses, to be hidden perhaps, or to be eaten so it could not be taken away again. This was madness. This was a nightmare worse than any vision Elen had ever seen. What had done this? These were people of the soil. They should have been as tough as tree roots, and as hard to pull from their place. The right of blood flowed both ways, and a chief who was too hard . . . there were torches in the night and a high house burned as well as any other. Elen had heard stories at the summer fair in Abergavenny of such revolts. Those who laboured for their lords would stand only so much. Even if revolt did not happen, it was not unknown for entire villages to simply . . . disappear. Whole families, or indeed whole clans, might take to the hills looking for a new life, and a new chieftain. Strong backs and skilled hands could find homes more often than not.

What, then, had driven these people mad with fear, but not driven them to rebellion?

When the board was empty, Elen said, 'I saw a white piglet in the pen. Bring it to me. I swear it will not be harmed nor taken from you.'

Habits of obedience, it seemed, ran deep here, even over such a strange request. Or maybe it was that hope had not been completely driven from them. She had promised to feed them, and they wanted to believe. A square, mud-stained man with gnarled hands stumped to the pen. He reached unafraid among the noisy swine and with an expert twitch grabbed the tail of the white piglet as it nosed his hands to see if he'd brought food. The animal squealed and kicked comically in mid-air, but no one laughed. They only drew back as the man came hesitantly forward.

All this time, Geraint kept his seat, and his false calm. She could feel the tension pouring from him. He did not know what she planned and he did not like this place. His keen eyes watched the road, looking for danger from that way even as the folk around them watched it, leaving her free to work.

Elen took the squirming, kicking, piglet, holding it tight in her arms as she had so many others in spring. It was not pure white, having faint brown dapples on its skin, but it was near enough.

She knelt, gathering her concentration, reaching back to that place where her mother's gifts lay. Her heart beat strong in Calonnau. Around her the air was heavy with portent and premonition. It reached into her blood and it made her strong. Weary in her fear and her loss, she accepted that strength and drew it into herself.

You shall be allowed to bestow three gifts, her mother's ghost had told her. *Well, this shall be the first.*

'Mother Don, Mother Rhiannon, look with favour on this.' The prayer steadied her, and she felt the touch of the other world on her shoulder. Certain now that she would be heard, she whispered into the swine's ear in the oldest tongue she knew. 'Cousin mine, go you and tell your grand-mother that Adara's brood is taken hard by hunger in the far country.'

The little pig was still in her arms for a moment. Then, it wriggled free, and she let it go. But it did not run back to its pen. Instead, it trotted up to the table, calm as a dog in his master's hall. It circled the table, once, twice, and once more, and touched its snout to the cloth.

What happened then happened between one eyeblink and the next. Where there had been a bare board, there was a bounty of food. Baskets of berries and apples. Rounds of nutty breads, fresh and hot. Roasted quails and grouse steaming in their juices on wooden platters. Clay tureens full of stews of fish and vegetables. Pottages of pease and wheat, crocks of butter, honey and cream, pitchers of foaming beer. All the wealth of the land was spread on that board.

The piglet squealed high and sharp and bolted back to its sow. The strength left Elen's knees at the same moment and she collapsed. Geraint caught her before she hit the ground.

'Stand me up,' she whispered. 'Make no sign.'

He did not like this, but he did as she asked, lifting her and steadying her on her feet.

One, said a woman's voice in Elen's mind.

Elen swallowed. *So be it*, she said in silent answer.

'Please,' she said, spreading cold hands to encompass the whole village. 'Accept this gift.'

She found she could stand again. She squeezed Geraint's hands as she took them from around her waist. She said nothing. She did not want any of those who crowded around to see that aught was wrong.

They did stare, in wonder and in trepidation. They looked to each other. They looked to Adev. Their chests heaved at the sight of the bounty loaded upon their spare board, and at the warm, heady scents that rose into the evening air. Mothers clamped their hands on children's shoulders to keep them from scrambling forward.

'It is none of your lord's,' said Geraint. 'It is freely given to you.'

A spasm very like pain crossed Adev's face, but gradually, his resistance melted away.

'Yes,' he whispered. 'Yes, we do accept this gift.' He turned to his folk gathered there, reluctant to believe, fear delaying understanding. 'We do accept this gift.'

One by one, parents holding back their children stepped forward. Older children edged ahead of younger ones. They came to the food with hesitant hands, plucking apart bread to dip into gravies or scoop into butter, picking up the fresh gooseberries one at a time to pop into mouths. But as the taste of the food, its scent, the reality of it spread, the fear ebbed, and they crowded round the table. Chairs, tables, benches and knives were fetched. Children sat under trees with split loaves heavy with butter and cream between them, their mouths now full, sticky and laughing. They all ate as if they were starved, and not just for the food, but for the fellowship the feast provided. They smiled as if for the first time in years. They came to laughter as they had come to the food, hesitant and fearful, but gradually accepting and grateful.

The day dimmed around them. Geraint and Elen sat in the chairs they were given and ate their fill with the rest, setting by worry and questions both to satisfy the basic needs of self and soul. Elen fed Calonnau meats from the tip of her knife. The hawk snapped and tore at them, eating without relish.

Slowly, the feast was worn down to crumbs and bones. The pitchers were drained, and the folk around were eased with the repleteness that came with satisfying hunger nursed too long. They lolled on their benches in the dim light, holding each other, coming and going from houses slowly, happily.

Hopefully.

Adev drained his noggin of beer a final time and wiped the foam from his tangled beard. Geraint, sensing opportunity, leaned forward. 'Father Adev, I ask you as one who means only friendship to you and yours – what is it you fear in this place?'

Adev started, and the wariness leapt back to its place in his eyes. 'You must know. You met . . . you fought one of them.'

'Even so,' agreed Geraint. 'But all I know is that we met a man in a grey cloak with a brand on his forehead.'

Adev's eyes shifted left, then right. '*Gwerin Llwyd*,' he whispered. Grey Men.

'What are they?' asked Geraint, but Adev turned his face and would not say.

Elen tried another route. She spread more butter on a last slice of bread, tore it in two and laid one half before her host. 'Adev, you speak the tongue of the West Lands as we use it in Pont Cymryd.'

Adev's mouth moved, repeating the cantrev name sound-lessly, savouring it. 'We belonged once to Llanthony, in the Black Mountains.'

Llanthony? Now it was Elen's turn to stare. She'd heard . . . it was years ago. Her father had still been alive, and she'd been shooed out of the hall before she could hear the whole of the story from the solemn messenger, but she'd eavesdropped on plenty of gossip in the following days. Llanthony had vanished. There'd been a battle. They must have been burned out by the men of Honddu, folk said, but there was no ash, no sign of fire . . . and no one had ever heard more tidings of them. The good neighbours were blamed, but mother did not believe this. It remained a mystery, and became a ghost story for a time, and then faded away altogether.

Elen said none of this. 'How came you to be here?' she asked instead, trying to keep her voice as mild as if she were asking about the conditions of the road ahead.

Adev shook his head. 'I may not say. It will . . . some things are heard farther away than others, Lady.'

Elen nodded. She did not press, but her anger deepened. These were her cousins chained and cowed here. Geraint's face had gone hard. He felt it too. He was a king's son and a king's nephew. He knew the responsibilities of blood and birth at least as well as she did.

Adev looked from one of them to the other. He looked to his empty cup and the bread that lay before him untouched. Elen could not read all the emotions that flickered across his face, but she felt he reached deep within himself, past even the place that remembered courtesy. Trying, perhaps to remember friendship, or loyalty.

Or courage.

'We were at war with our neighbours,' he said. 'They had killed Cadugan. He was the son of our chief, Cadog. Blood demanded we fight, but we were too few. We were going to be overrun. We were set to flee our homes.

'Then a stranger came. He told us he could save us all, if we would but swear our fealty to him. Our chief was dead. We feared not death,' he said quickly, firmly and Geraint nodded his agreement and understanding. 'Never clean death, but to be taken in slavery. . . the shame . . . we took counsel and we agreed we would swear fealty to the stranger, if he would save us.'

Elen shivered at this. She too could understand what had driven these people to make such a choice. Oh, yes, she could understand it well.

'We thought he would lead us in war,' Adev went on, his voice growing heavy with memory and regret. 'But he did not. Instead, he rode seven times around our homes, crying out in some tongue none of us could understand. We all fell into a deep sleep. When we woke . . . we were here, and safe we were, from all things save our new king.' These last words were spoken with a bitterness that ran bone deep.

Geraint said nothing. Elen said nothing. Adev pushed the bread away from him. 'He keeps . . .'

Before Adev could say more, a shout rang out from the fields.

'They're coming! They're coming!'

FOURTEEN

Adev shot to his feet, his face suddenly deathly grey. A man was running in from the fields. In the distance behind him, Elen could make out a group of riders on horseback. She counted five, but at this distance could make out few details beyond shining armour, grey cloaks, and one black horse leading four greys.

The indolence and contentment of a moment before were gone. Everyone was on their feet now. Parents snatched up children and ran into their rude houses. Husbands and wives clutched each other. An old woman began to weep, an oddly birdlike noise. All stared at the board and the remains of the feast in horror, wondering what they had done.

Adev gripped the table edge as if hoping to draw strength from it. 'Get you gone,' he whispered to Elen and Geraint. 'I will meet them.'

Geraint did not waste his breath on refusals. He put the helmet back on his head and picked up his captured spear. Elen reclaimed her gauntlet, loosened Calonnau's jesses and set the complaining hawk on her wrist. She also took the knife from where it lay on the table and returned it to the sheath at her side.

Adev saw all this and it seemed to move him beyond words. He swallowed hard and turned his face towards the riders, but even as he did, Elen thought she saw shame in his eyes

For something you have done, or something you will do? I wish I could ask, for it might mean our lives. She found a moment to wonder at her own calm as she thought this.

The riders came closer. Four of them were large and bullish men, dressed and armed in the same style as the others Elen and Geraint had met. Two of them wore the sort of half-helms they had seen before and the other two wore full-helms that covered their faces and were decorated with horns and lines that gave the wearers the appearance of demons approaching in the light of day. The steel was chased with silver which formed the shapes of runes on the masks like tattoos on skin, but Elen could read none of them. Cold and fearsome, they came on steadily.

At their head rode a dwarf. This was not a little man, like Tor who lived at the edge of the village and worked as hard as any man twice his height, nor yet was he like the fools who sometimes came with the minstrels to play at the summer's fair and were astounding in their mastery of music and juggling. This was a mean and apeish creature. His head was topped with tangled black hair and a black beard covered his jutting jaw. He held a black whip in his hairy hand. His clothes too were black, except for the cap on his head which was a dull, rusty red.

At the sight of the dwarf, Adev's nerve failed him. He fell to his knees as if he'd been struck. Geraint planted his feet firmly, at the width of his shoulders. His hand shifted on the shaft of his spear, readying for what might come, but making no openly threatening move.

The dwarf reined up his black horse. The soldiers, clearly the Grey Men Adev had spoken of, halted behind him. They and their horses stood absolutely still. The faces of the two wearing half-helms were set in hard and contemptuous lines. Of the others, she could make out nothing at all. They might have been twins for all the difference between them she could see. The dwarf's gaze swept from Adev to the villagers huddled like sheep behind him and came to rest on her and Geraint. His glittering black eyes looked more like those of a bird than of a man. Calonnau screamed, high and sudden, and launched herself from Elen's wrist. Elen lost control of the jesses, and the bird soared into the sky, coming to land in the branches of the chestnut tree, shrieking with anger, but even more with fear.

The dwarf chuckled.

'Welcome!' he said, leaning on the edge of his saddle. His voice boomed strangely loud and deep for so small a creature. Elen could not name him a man. She almost expected to see he cast no shadow on the ground. His shadow was there, however, black and solid in the waning evening sun, no different from hers. He was flesh, whatever else he might be. 'Welcome my Lord Geraint! Welcome my Lady Elen!'

So much for hiding our names.

'My lord king has been waiting for you,' the dwarf went on. 'Right glad he was to hear you had come safe to his lands and found hospitality already among his people!' He grinned at Adev and his fellows. The old man's shoulders slumped in defeat.

It was Geraint who replied. 'Adev thought us sent from his lord king. He treated us only as he should. When he learned we were strangers, he refused to give us what was his lord's. All you see here,' he gestured at the board, 'is the working and gift of my lady and none of theirs.'

'But of course, my lord!' said the dwarf expansively. 'Adev and all here,' he beamed with a sharp-edged benevolence

on all assembled, 'know their place well. They would have
done nothing else.'

'Please . . .' Adev blurted out the word.

'Adev,' said the dwarf quietly. 'It is not your time to
speak.'

Adev fell silent at once, and bowed his head, but Elen saw
something in his old eyes that had not been there before.
Anger.

The dwarf tapped his whip restlessly against his thigh.
'Now, Sir Geraint, Lady Elen. My king bids you come to his
hall, where there is room and cheer fitting for guests of your
rank.'

'We are anxious to accept that hospitality which is freely
given.' Geraint's voice was mild, but he watched that whip,
and watched it carefully. 'But I fear that darkness is coming
on and we may not reach your king before nightfall.'

The dwarf grinned at them. 'You may well fear, Sir Geraint,
but our king does not. It pleases him for you to ride with
us, and to know that you and your good lady will reach him
before the night does.'

The sun was just at the horizon. In moments, it would
begin its final descent. There was no hall on any hill that
they could see.

'Who is your king?' asked Elen bluntly. This false courtesy wore on her. It reminded her too much of Urien standing
before her mother, and of Morgaine in the goatherd's
cottage. It was another illusion and she'd had a bellyful of
all such.

But the dwarf only grinned at her. 'He is himself, as you
will see.'

'Why will you not name him?'

'Because I do not choose to, my lady. You will come with
us now.' This last was spoken sternly. It seemed this creature too had had enough. He made a small gesture with one

finger. One of the Grey Men, the one to the dwarf's left, nudged his horse so it walked forward, just a few steps, so its shadow fell across the way before Elen.

Geraint also stepped forward, so he stood just in front of her. No challenge entered his manner or voice, there was just that small change of place. 'Perhaps it would be best if you rode ahead to announce our coming. My lady is mightily fatigued from the day's travel and needs rest.'

The dwarf's hand curled more tightly around his whip. The tapping was loud, like an angry heartbeat, and as insistent. 'She shall have rest when she reaches the hall of my king.'

Geraint held his place, and his courtesy. 'We will follow in due course, you may be sure.'

'But I may not be.' The tapping whip stilled, and the dwarf leaned forward, his bird's eyes narrowed to slits. 'You will come with us, Sir Geraint. We will accept no other answer or action.'

Before Geraint could reply, Adev spoke. 'Please, lord,' he said. The words were nothing more than a throaty whisper at first, but they gained in strength as he went on. 'Please, lord, we have made them guests here. We have shared bread and board. Let us keep them this night. You know we will not fail the king . . .'

'Do I know that?' smiled the dwarf. He folded his arms on his knee. His oddly delicate fingers rolled the little whip back and forth. 'So anxious are you for guests, Adev. So ready to feed the hungry . . .' He paused, and cocked his head, considering. 'My horse is hungry.' The dwarf jumped down from his saddle, landing neat and square on both feet. The point of his red hood barely came up to Geraint's shoulder. 'Indeed, I believe all of us here are hungry. Will you feed us?' A mocking querulousness overcame his voice, and behind him, two of the riders smiled.

Adev swayed on his knees, and Elen thought for a moment he would fall. 'Lord, please!' He stretched out his work-worn hands. 'It is only . . .'

'You knew we were coming,' interrupted Geraint. 'Why did you not meet us on the road?'

'Because it was our master's wish to know how Adev and these others would comport themselves when you came. He is not at all pleased that he would have fed you when his majesty's true servants were going hungry. Very hungry, Adev.' The dwarf pursed his lips and shook his head. 'I believe I cannot restrain him in his hunger.' The dwarf touched the black horse's side, and it whisked around, more kitten than horse, and trotted to the edge of the field of grain, the grain that would surely pay the tributes this king demanded, that would feed the village in the winter. Someone screamed, a sound quickly muffled by hands. A child wailed, high-pitched and fearful. Adev closed his eyes.

The black horse began to eat. It moved like thought, like a dream. Where it had been, the grain was gone, leaving only stubble behind.

The villagers watched, open-mouthed in horror. Two of the Grey Men, the ones horned like demons, dismounted from their horses.

'So very hungry,' said the dwarf again.

The grey horses joined the black, tearing up great chunks of grain, swallowing them down, each move clear, and yet devouring all with a speed that no mortal steed could have matched.

Nor was that the end. The two Grey Men in full helmets marched swiftly, smoothly into the village, to the sacks and barrels and piles of food that Geraint and Elen had refused. They leaned their spears against the chestnut tree, and they too began to eat. They ate like famine made flesh. They ate like the dreams of gluttony. They swallowed apples, cheeses, loaves of bread whole, they lifted barrels of beer as if they were wooden cups and drank them down.

'No,' whispered Adev. 'No. The king . . . we cannot pay . . .'

Their fellows in the half-helms stood beside their master, their arms folded across their chests, and they laughed.

Calonnau screamed from her place at the top of the tree, and below her Elen cried out. 'Stop this! They did nothing! They gave us nothing!'

'But they would have,' said the dwarf quietly, folding his own arms in satisfaction. 'Oh yes, my lord is most displeased.'

Geraint looked from the dwarf and his mirthful guard, to the villagers in their huddle, to Elen. She thought she understood the calculations passing swiftly through his mind. He saw the spears on the ground and the swords in their sheaths. He saw those used to torturing the cowed and broken, who did not know what man stood beside them now.

'Stop this,' he said. 'Or I will stop it.'

The dwarf turned to him with raised black brows and a mocking smile on his lips. Geraint gave him no warning. In a single deadly move, he whipped the shaft of his spear around and brought it crashing down on the dwarf's whip hand. Elen ducked in and caught up the whip as it fell. The people cried out and scattered. The dwarf screamed as Geraint locked an arm around his thick neck, dragging him backward off his feet.

'Stop!' Geraint roared. 'Or your captain dies!'

The two half-helmed men jumped back, hands reaching for swords. Around them men and women fled their homes, crying, screaming, weeping to the gods to save them, save them, save them!

'One more move and he dies,' said Geraint in his certain, steady voice, jabbing his spear towards the dwarf's throat. 'One more.'

The demons froze in place, bent over their thieving feast,

watching him with their hidden eyes. Elen would not have believed living men could stand so still. In Geraint's arms the dwarf hung with his feet dangling, his menace gone, for a moment looking nothing but small and ridiculous.

'You think we are an enemy to fight like any other?' His voice was merry, almost gleeful. 'Show him!'

Elen went cold. Slowly, making certain Geraint saw every move, the first of the demon-helmed men reached up. He plucked off his helmet, and he cast it aside. For a moment, Elen's bewildered eyes thought his head was bald, or grey haired. Then she saw it was the bare and mottled bone of his skull. The only flesh left was withered and wrinkled around his jaw, and the teeth bared by his withered lips were ragged and yellow. His eyes were rheumy and clouded with the death that should have laid him down long ago. Yet he stood. He too was marked as his living counterpart had been. The brand had burned into the bone.

Terror sent Elen reeling backward. The dwarf laughed, shaking hard in Geraint's embrace. 'Do you think any of us care for your spear? Take him!'

The nearest man clapped hand to sword, and Geraint threw his spear, but the man dodged, and the weapon struck the earth harmlessly. The other raised his sword, but Geraint had twisted and drawn his own with the same motion that threw the spear, and now held his blade to the dwarf's throat. The touch of the steel seemed to make the creature go limp as a babe and no more orders came from him.

Perhaps you should fear us after all, thought Elen wildly.

Half-helm was frozen where he was, but behind him, the one still in his demon helmet lifted his head and gave a shrill whistle. Hoofbeats sounded from behind. The horses were coming in from the ravaged fields.

Elen recovered herself and reached out with her will.

Calonnau screamed and she fought, and she hungered, and she dived.

The creatures were enchanted but they were horse enough to fear for their eyes. Calonnau swooped again and again, devilling them, making them rear and strike out uselessly with their hooves and fall back as she wheeled overhead. Elen felt the wild beauty of the dive, of the strike, and her soul sang with the power of it. She took her knife into her curled hand and stood ready, ready for blood, ready for the strike and the feasting . . .

Half-helm dragged the spear from the ground. More hooves sounded, this time from their right, and Elen jerked her head around in time to see two horses, one brown and one grey, run from around the white storehouse, where Adev peered from the corner.

Adev had freed Donatus.

Geraint slammed the dwarf down to the ground where the creature lay stunned and broken, and he mounted the tall grey. He rode at once into the demons, bowling them both down, swinging his sword. It caught one of the half-helms, spinning him around, sending him toppling to the ground. But he picked himself up at once, as Geraint wheeled around and froze at the sight. Such a blow should have broken him, if not killed him.

Beside Geraint, the second half-helmed demon grabbed hold of his spear, and the stillness was over. Geraint swung Donatus around to dodge the coming blow. The first demon now had his sword out, and he lunged for Elen. She swung the dwarf's whip, but it glanced off the helm and he sliced down at her side. The blow caught only her cloak and she pulled herself away, stabbing up with her knife into his sword arm. She caught the space between corslet and guard, and living or dead, he had blood enough.

A blow fell hard from behind and Elen crashed to the

ground, the world suddenly blackness and sparks of bright light. Her knife skittered from her hand. Geraint screamed, Calonnau screamed. Awash with pain, Elen could not move. Thunder roared in her ears. It seemed the ground shook. There were voices, the grinding of steel and wood.

Before she could move again, the red-capped creature was beside her, a knife at her throat.

'She dies!' he thundered. 'You like this game of hostages now, mighty lord? You strike one blow more and it is she who dies!'

Geraint wheeled the horse around, and froze. Elen cast out all her strength of will, and called Calonnau. The hawk screamed and dived down, talons extended, but the dwarf ducked sideways, and the hawk missed him narrowly, swooping up just before reaching the ground and fighting to climb again. Geraint tried to charge forward in that moment, but one of the Grey Men blocked him with his spear. The dwarf bared his teeth, and drove the knife into her.

Pain tore through her. Geraint cried out to shake the heavens. Calonnau's scream mixed with his. Elen heard the sounds of battle, heard shouts, too many and not Geraint's voice. Dead? No. There . . . She could not see properly . . . she reached up with one hand, and pulled the knife from the dwarf's hand, and sat up.

There was no blood. Pain, but no weakness, and she held the knife.

'Do you think any of us care for your knife?' she croaked.

The dwarf bared his teeth at her and scrambled backward. Elen stood slowly, the knife in her hand. Its blade was clean, she noted. Of course. There was no blood to flow. She stalked forward. He had tried to kill her, he had tried to cause Geraint's death. Pain sang through her and drove her on. 'Help me,' wheezed the dwarf. 'Help me, lord king!'

A stranger. A stranger on horseback, a spear in his hand

and a black cloak billowing from his shoulders. The dwarf
looked at him in terror. The stranger cast his spear, and the
dwarf fell, impaled on the weapon for an instant. Then the
spear was gone and there was only the body at Elen's feet.

'Elen!' Geraint threw himself from his horse to run forward
and grasp her shoulders. 'How . . .'

With a shaking hand, she touched the clean edge of her
bloodless wound. Revulsion gathered in the pit of her stomach.
*What am I become? Am I a corpse? Like the Grey Men? I cannot
die because I am already dead?*

But Geraint only drew her to him. She closed her eyes.
She could not look at him. She could not return his warm,
living embrace.

What am I?

'We must go!' shouted the stranger. 'Now!'

Geraint released her, and pulled her towards her horse.
He boosted her into the saddle. She should have been dead,
at least unconscious from the blow, but she was only cold.
Deathly cold. Corpse cold. Elen recovered enough of herself
to call down Calonnau, but her hands were shaking too badly
to hold the reins. Geraint saw this at once and snatched them
up. The stranger, his spear once again in his hand, turned
his horse's head due west and urged the animal into a full
gallop. Geraint dug his heels into Donatus's sides, and Elen
kicked at her reluctant brown, feeling the daze wearing off
her.

The horses ran into the deepening night. Elen hung on
grimly to the saddlebow and the hawk's jesses. It was all she
could do. Her breath was harsh and ragged. Her throat burned
and her wrist throbbed beneath the bandage. Every jolt of
the horse's hooves sent fire through her. The countryside
passed in a blur of shadows. Geraint did not even look back
at her. All his concentration was on keeping up with their
rescuer.

At last, the stranger slowed his pace for a moment. He raised his spear and shook it, calling out something Elen could not understand. Ahead of them, the world seemed to twist, blur and change as in a dream, and time grew long and then short, and then she could see that on the hill rising from the darkening night there was a fortress wall.

She could not even find it in her to be surprised. Of course they rode forward, threading through the earthworks, their rescuer hollering up at the gates. Of course the gates opened to reveal a dusty yard. A sprawling house of stone stood against the night sky. Calonnau cried out in fear and beat her wings. Elen's vision wavered. She saw shadows, she saw bones where there should have been timbers.

Where's the knife? she thought stupidly. *Where am I?*

Then, she felt herself falling, and she could do nothing about it.

FIFTEEN

When Elen woke, she found herself lying on a narrow bed in the midst of a forest grove. Calonnau stood on a sturdy perch beside the bed, flapping and crying in frustration. Geraint was just rising from a plain stool to cross to her. The ground beneath him was flagstone and rushes. She blinked hard, then she saw the trees were only painted on the high walls around her.

She stared at all these things, trying to reconcile them with where she had been a brief moment before.

'Elen?' Geraint took her hand and sank onto the bed beside her. 'Are you well?'

She was, she realized, for all that pain lingered in her throat. She felt the clean touch of cloth that told her someone had wrapped a bandage about her neck to match the one binding her arm. She did not touch it.

'How long have I slept?' Her voice was harsher than it should have been. She did not want to think about the cause of that.

Geraint laid a hand on her cheek, checking for fever, or perhaps just reassuring himself she was still flesh. 'Not long, and much of the time you were in a natural sleep. It is the morning of the day after we were brought here.'

Her wits had cleared enough that she could look past Geraint to see something of this place now. The trees were masterfully drawn on lime-whitened walls. A little watery sunlight and a breath of air trickled in from a narrow slit up by the ceiling. A brass brazier gave off some warmth as well as charcoal smoke. A table waited beside the stool Geraint had abandoned, and a plain wooden chest stood beside that with some clothes neatly folded on its lid.

But it was the trees that drew her eye. She had never seen such decoration in any place. They were more marvellous to her than any tapestry would have been.

Geraint followed her gaze. 'Beautiful, is it not? Wait until you see the corridors outside. I have only heard stories of such places. Uncle Kai spoke of paintings like these when he told us tales of Rome, but he said that much of their art had been lost.'

'Where are we?' she asked, marvelling still. The trees were caught at the height of spring. They seemed to grow out of rich and mossy ground. She could even see a bird's nest in one, and a fox's face peeping out from behind another.

'We are in the home of Gwiffert pen Lleied, also called the Little King.' Elen stiffened immediately, and Geraint laid a hand on her shoulder, pressing her back against the featherbed. 'It was he who rescued us, Elen.'

Without thinking, she looked to Calonnau on her perch. The bird was, as always, frustrated at being leashed and confined but her heart beat steady and strong. If there was immediate danger, neither the hawk nor the knight felt it. The fears brought on by waking in so strange a place began to ebb.

'How came the Little King to rescue us?'

'I don't know,' admitted Geraint, leaning his elbows on his thighs. He looked towards the door, which had been painted cunningly to become the trunk of a great oak spreading its branches over the smaller trees. It reminded Elen of the Lady's door with its decoration of apple trees in fruit and flower. 'I have so many questions I cannot number them, but what is plain is that all is very different from what I first thought.' Geraint smiled thinly and she pressed the hand that held hers. 'Are you well enough to stand? The king our host sent word that he would be breaking his fast in his hall at this time, and should you wake, we were to join him there.' More softly he added, 'I would know what you see in him.'

Elen searched her husband's face for a moment. 'What do you suspect?'

Geraint's smile grew tight. 'In a place where men vanish into thin air and die without making a sound, everything.'

Elen could not fault this. Instead of answering, she pushed back the furs that covered her and eased her legs over the side of the bed. She stood, as relieved as Geraint to find her legs steady underneath her.

The clothes that had been laid out for her were simple but well made – a brown dress of wool trimmed with a border of oak leaves, as seemed fitting for the grove she had lain in. There was also a linen under-dress and good shoes to replace the battered slippers that had carried her this far. What there was not was any woman to help her. So Geraint, with many a wry smile, undid her belt and helped divest her of her torn and filthy finery. She laid the old clothes carefully on the chest. Perhaps they could yet be cleaned and mended. She could not bring herself to part easily with anything from her home.

Geraint also had new clothes – a long tunic of rich blue, fine grey trousers and cross-laced sandals. He had washed his face, hands and hair, but he had not been shaved, and his beard was rapidly becoming full and black to match his waving hair.

The clean clothes felt wonderful. A wooden comb allowed her to work the worst of the tangles from her hair and re-braid the plaits that hung on either side of her head. With her belt, necklace and rings all in their proper places, she felt ready to be seen. She did not come as a supplicant, but as a daughter of chiefs, worthy of respect and hearing, even in this magnificent place.

Geraint nodded his approval and reassurance, and held out his hand for hers. At that moment, Calonnau shifted restlessly, and cried once. Elen suddenly did not want to leave the hawk behind. She put the gauntlet on her hand, and lifted the bird from her perch. Geraint made no remark at this. Elen was glad. She was not certain she could have explained.

Gwiffert's fortress was a far different place from the high house in which Elen had been raised. Rather than one great hall, it held a warren of narrow corridors lined with more doors than Elen had ever seen, all of them closed. As Geraint had said, the walls here were painted with decorations far more fabulous than her little grove. Whole orchards of trees grew floor to ceiling, followed by fields of ripe grain. Herds of cattle grazed in green meadows. Ancient kings rode in chariots of bronze pulled by white horses.

Geraint seemed to navigate the place easily enough, and she was glad of his touch against her arm. The stone seemed to lean against Elen, and the still eyes of the paintings watched her far too closely. The pain in her wrist and throat throbbed in time to her heart's insistent beat, as far away as that was in Calonnau's breast, and she found herself near desperate for a glimpse of true sky or a breath of wind.

Where are the people? Someone must live in this warren. Where are they?

At last, they rounded a corner and walked under a soaring

archway that opened onto a great hall. The hall looked as if
it could have held her house and had room for a dozen
cottages. Fires roared in four man-high hearths, filling the
chill stone room with a warmth even Elen could feel. Spitted
meats roasted over the flames, and the sizzle was as appe-
tizing as the scent.

Here were the people Elen had missed. Men in leather
jerkins sat at long tables with dogs lolling about their feet.
A cluster of women sat in a corner, distaffs and carding combs
busy. Children turned the spits and stirred the pots under
the eye of a stout and stern woman with her grey hair plaited
and bundled tightly behind her ears. Still more people flitted
back and forth on their own errands. The hall was as full of
their voices as it was of the scents of cooking food. They
were better dressed than the folk of Adev's village, and better
fed. They worked or ate briskly, busily, as people will when
they have steady, true purpose.

All around the walls where Elen would have expected
tapestries, or war trophies, were more of the paintings. These
looked newer to her awe-struck eyes, more clean. They
imitated the ribbonwork she had grown up knowing, and
they showed such symbols as were part of her daily speech.
She saw the white mare there, here a white sow and a black
boar, there men in bronze helmets and spears of familiar
work, and there, a man beneath a black owl, its wings spread
wide. Apple branches made a border for the space nearest
the floor

Geraint touched her arm, and Elen realized she was gaping.
She drew her eyes back down to the hall. At the far end
waited a dais where a single, long table had been set. Only
one person sat there – a lean man who held a spear in the
crook of his right arm. This, then, was their host, the Little
King. He stood as they entered, bowing deeply, and waving
them forward.

As she walked beside Geraint, Elen took in more of this remarkable hall. The roof was sloped and buttressed with mighty beams that were black with age. The floor was made of many-coloured tiles laid out to depict scenes of battle as well as great feasts and hunts and animals sporting in the forests.

King Gwiffert came around his table, but did not put down his spear. Geraint brought them to a halt before the dais and bowed as Elen curtseyed. Her first impression of Gwiffert was of a sharp man – pointed chin, long, dextrous hands, lean but wiry limbs. His hair was bright gold and his blue eyes slanted above his sharp cheekbones. There was beauty in that face, but it was of a dangerous kind. It reminded her of something she could not quite remember. His skin was brown, but it was the rough brown that comes after fair skin has been long exposed to sun and harsh weather. His under-tunic and close-fitting trousers were pure white. The over-tunic of rich, forest green was so long it brushed the tops of his sandalled feet. It had been embroidered on hem and cuff with the faces of the moon in white and silver threads. A golden torque in the semblance of a scythe-tusked boar encir-cled his throat.

'Be welcome, Sir Geraint. Be welcome *Chwaer* Elen.'

Elen straightened, surprised by this term of honour that had so recently belonged to her mother, and the elusive memory came to her. Beneath his golden hair and wide brow, Gwiffert had blue eyes like the rider in her dream of death.

'We owe you more than we can say, Majesty,' said Geraint smoothly. Elen's own mouth was dry and her manners confused as she struggled to rise above her dream mem-ories. It was good fortune that Geraint was used to such scenes from Arthur's court, and could speak where she could not.

'I am only glad I could reach you in time. Please, sit with me.' King Gwiffert stepped back gesturing towards the table. 'Food is being brought.'

Geraint led Elen to sit at the king's left hand. He took the place on the right. Elen tried to school her features into polite lines. She tried to concentrate on setting the annoyed and impatient Calonnau on the back of an unoccupied chair and tying her jesses down tightly. Whatever her dreams, she and Geraint were here now and they were dependent on this man's good will.

'I am sorry I sent no woman to wait on you, sister. Despite what you see,' King Gwiffert nodded towards the busy hall, 'we are few in number here, and our women are even fewer.' He shook his head sadly.

'How did this come to be, sir?' asked Geraint. 'This seems a great hall.'

'Seems,' said the king bitterly. 'And should be. Its master was a Roman and brought great builders from the ancient city of Athens, which mothered Daedalus, the greatest of all artisans. He meant to make a great house like no other on the isle of the Britons. It was to stand on the river Severn, a symbol of his lordship over those he called barbarians.' He smiled. 'But he fell in love with one who should have been his slave and made her his wife. She raised them up a son and she made sure he learned the best of both halves of his blood so that he might rule righteously over his lands.'

As the king spoke, Geraint's careful eyes drank in the man in front of him in a way that might have been thought of as too bold, but the Little King did not seem to notice.

What does he see?

'Your father?' asked Geraint quietly.

Gwiffert turned his face away and gazed about the hall with its ribbonwork and bestiary so familiar, but their way of making so strange. 'Such grand plans, but they were not to be,' he said softly.

'We are a long way from the Severn,' said Elen. The spear

in Gwiffert's hand was carved with ancient runes she did not believe she could read, even if she were closer to them. What she could see was that the windings that held the head to the shaft were silver rather than copper or hide. The tip itself was some black stone that glittered where the firelight touched it.

No iron in its making, then, nor could there be for a thing so enchanted it could be cast out and return at once to its master's hand. This, surely, was the spear they sought. The death of Urien was held in that long hand, and the prize of the fae.

If he saw how hungrily she eyed his weapon, he gave no sign. He only sighed. 'Aye, we are a long way from the river, sister, and have been these many years.'

Two old women and a trio of girls in plain linen brought the food then. All was simple, but filling – stewed mush-rooms, apples, stout loaves of bread and slices of cold venison and pork in jellied gravies. There was beer and cider to drink from bronze cups. Elen ate, and tried not to think too much on Adev's people. What had happened to them? Were the Grey Men gone? Was the wrath of their king averted? Elen fed Calonnau titbits with the tip of her knife, enduring the hawk's impatience. She wanted to fly. She wanted to be out of this stone cavern.

And so do I, but we have work here.

Once they had finished and praised all there was, Elen was able to ask the next question.

'Majesty, how is it your house came to be in so strange a place?'

King Gwiffert hung his head. When he looked up again, it was not at her or Geraint, but down the length of his hall towards the men and women who moved about within it.

If not true shame, a good semblance. The thought brought Elen up sharply. *Why should it be false?*

'It was war,' said King Gwiffert. It was a recitation he

began, a story told so many times the teller knew it by heart. 'A man called Jago sought to become High King over all the land he called Gwynedd. The men of Rhyd Sarn would acknowledge no overlord, and so the fight was joined. But his numbers were greater and his warriors more fierce. There were *scoti* with them even, brought down from the north and over from the west with promises of land and prizes.' A muscle twitched in Geraint's cheek, but he remained silent.

'My father died, hurled from his horse into their mob. I was little more than a boy, and I knew not which way to turn. I did not want to die myself.'

I'm not going to let you die too! Elen dropped her gaze, reliving that last quarrel with Yestin. What the king told was her own story come again – the need to live in freedom, the blood lost for the sake of blood. She bit her lip, and looked at the painted walls, working to keep her face in a plain and polite expression. She felt Geraint's questioning gaze on her, but she did not return it.

The king made no pause for Elen's distraction. Probably he was too lost in his own story. 'Then, one night there came to the earthworks a single man. He rode in a marvellously painted chariot led by a team of white horses. He was no mortal man, but a giant. I had never seen one who stood so like a mountain.'

There was a white horse on the tapestry over his shoulder, a white mare galloping along the twisting road of ribbon. Elen frowned. There was something wrong, something the artisan had done that was out of tune with how it should have been, but she could not quite understand what it was.

'He called my name,' King Gwiffert was saying. His face was hard, his eyes were distant. Behind him, the white mare ran on the bright road. 'He asked to enter. I let him into the hall, and he said to me that he could save us from Jago, me and all that were mine. He said if I swore loyalty to him, Jago would fall before the sun set the next day.'

To choose between one service and another, between Urien and Arthur for her, between Jago and a giant for Gwiffert. Was this the fate of all the people of the West Lands?

'I almost said yes. Perhaps it would have been better if I had. Perhaps then . . .' he stopped those words with a wave. 'But I deliberated that whole night, and I said no. What good was one overlord or another? I still carried the spear of my fathers and all its power. I thought we could yet win through.'

The spear of my fathers? But the Lady and Lord had said that spear was theirs. Did the king lie now? Or was he claiming descent from Manawyddan?

Or was it just that the Lady and Lord neglected to say how that spear came to be in their hands? Such as they did not lie, no, but neither did they easily tell the whole truth.

'I refused him as courteously as I could, and he flew into a rage. He said he would have me for all my pride. I should have stopped him then, but I let him leave my hall. He returned to his chariot, and although the horses had not been harnessed between its shafts, still he rode that chariot seven times around our walls, swinging the great club he carried, calling out in a harsh tongue that no man knew.'

So it was with the story Adev had told. Elen could not help but wonder what the extent of this land was, and if there was in it a place for Pont Cymryd. Would this giant have come to her if she had not run to the fae?

'I ran to the walls to see his working. I meant to cast down the spear, to stop him, but I was too late. Too late,' he repeated, anger filling his voice and face. 'As I watched, the world around us melted away like butter in the sun.'

Elen remembered the winding mists on the bridge. She remembered the fear and the sense of utter loss as the mortal world fell behind.

'Then, I and all those who were within the walls of my house . . . we were here, in these hills, in this country that has no name.'

'What then?' asked Geraint quietly. He leaned forward, hands on the table, all his attention on the Little King's words.

Gwiffert shook his head. 'Then, the giant came again. He shouted up at me that I was his now, and he would come for me when he was ready, and he rode away.'

You are his, but you do not know it.

'What then?' Geraint asked again.

The king laid a hand over his spear, as if he feared it might be wrenched from him. *Perhaps he sees our need after all.* 'Since then, he has taken us by ones and twos. No matter how strong our earthworks, or how many armed men ride out with our people to find food or fuel, the Grey Men come. Women, old men, children, they take. Fighting men, they kill or steal to swell their ranks, and I can do nothing, nothing at all.'

Geraint continued to watch the Little King closely. What he saw though, seemed to trouble him. His question showed Elen why. 'Why does he not take this hall, if he is so powerful?'

King Gwiffert's smile was rueful. 'I think he means to wait until I am alone. Then he will come for me at last.'

'You will wait for this?' Geraint was clearly surprised, and appalled.

'I have no choice. I cannot find him.' The king spoke now from wounded pride. The hand that gripped the spear had whitened around its knuckles. *This is true*, she thought to herself. *This much is wholly true.* But again she could not understand why part of her might think her host a liar. 'We have searched the countryside as far as we dare for his fortress.' He sighed, the hand relaxed, and the eyes cleared. Did Geraint see all this? Surely. 'But there is nothing, save the other people he has claimed for his own.' Gwiffert struggled with some thought for a moment and went on. 'Always the story is the same. There is war, and there is the promise of safety in return for loyalty. Whether it is accepted, or it is refused, all are brought here. Only the nature of the slavery is different.' Whatever thoughts crossed his mind behind those few words, his face tightened in the attempt to contain them.

'We heard much the same tale from Adev and his people.' Elen paused. 'Has he a name, this giant?'

Gwiffert shook his head. 'If he does, I have never heard it. I wish before all the gods I had. Had I his name, there are arts I could employ to find him.' Again came that rueful smile. 'Any who speak of him call him the Great King, as I am become the Little King.'

The Great King. The one the Grey Men spoke of. *You should fear the Great King.*

'You have no help?' asked Geraint.

A spasm that might have been pain, but might also have been laughter, crossed King Gwiffert's sharp face. 'No true help. All those you see about me are here because the walls are strong, and I carry the one weapon that has held off the Grey Men and the Great King. I am told my name has reached the mortal world, but save for yourselves, none has come from there.' His eyes glinted, and Elen saw suspicion there. Was that new, a thought come to him on speaking these words, or was it something he had been able to hide until now?

Geraint did not miss the sharpening of King Gwiffert's demeanour. 'You must wonder about us, sir.'

'Yet you seem to speak freely,' put in Elen. Calonnau flapped her wings once beside her. 'Sir,' she added.

This met with a long silence. Between them, the bones and crumbs of their meal waited untouched. The women stood in their places, twisting their hands. 'I had a dream,' said

Gwiffert at last. 'I had a dream of a hawk that accompanied a man on horseback. Where they rode, the world split open, and through the cracks, I saw the land of my fathers shining through. I resolved to ride out and look for this hawk and this man, and it was thus I found you so beset.'

A dream. Do your dreams also hold blood and terror? Mine do. Blood and blue eyes. 'Can you tell us what the Grey Men are?'

Gwiffert's face twisted into a mask of disgust. His hand curled more tightly around his spear. 'Only in part. Some say they are the dead, but I don't believe so, at least, not entirely. I think they are soldiers bound to their lord, and that while he lives, they must walk in this world and follow his will, whether their bodies truly live or not.'

The pain in Elen's throat sharpened as he spoke, and her right hand twitched.

'If he could be found,' said Geraint. 'What would you do?'

'Do?' Gwiffert's gaze focused on Geraint again, and the anger in him rose. 'What would any man do? I would fight with all I had. I only wait for my enemy because I have no choice.'

No choice but to wait. Elen remembered how she had waited at Morgaine's word, without choice, without question, how she had waited again at Urien's side, and in his arms, and how that curse waited on her even now. Now there must be more waiting yet, waiting until they could speak plain to Gwiffert, waiting until they could find a way back to their proper home. Waiting, always waiting . . . the anger of it filled her belly as surely as the good food did, and turned all to bile.

'Sister?' said Gwiffert. 'What is it?'

Elen realized she had clenched her hand into a fist, knotting up a great bunch of the table cloth. She did not remember making the gesture and she stared at her cold hand as if it belonged to a stranger.

Geraint answered for her. 'Our road here has been hard and strange beyond the telling. My lady is overwhelmed.'

'Of course,' said King Gwiffert at once. 'I am discourteous to keep you here talking when you both must still be worn from your trials. You should take some rest.'

Although she had slept a full night, weariness still dragged heavily at Elen's body and mind. The idea of sinking again onto that bed was as beguiling as the thought of a waiting lover.

Gwiffert got to his feet. Elen and Geraint also rose, and the Little King took Elen's hand. 'We will talk later, Sir Geraint, sister,' he said seriously, looking deep into her eyes. 'I confess it is my hope you will be able to aid us here.'

She wanted to help him, and the strength of that desire stunned her. She wanted all he said to be true, and all she felt of lies and suspicion to be the dream. *Why?* she swallowed and her throat stung as she turned and fumbled with the knots on Calonnau's leash. *What is this man?*

Gwiffert gestured over their heads and an ancient retainer came scurrying up to the foot of the dais and knelt there. 'My man will take you and your lord to your chamber. I will find a woman who can wait on you, Lady Elen. If there is anything needed for your health or comfort, order it at once.'

Geraint bowed in thanks. 'We had not thought to find so much welcome here, Majesty.'

'Well do I know it,' replied the Little King.

With that as their farewell, Elen and Geraint were taken from the great hall down to the room she had been given, to rest and to try to understand all that had passed.

Gwiffert watched the pair depart the hall, Elen clutching the hawk's jesses and her man's hand as if for dear life. He smiled as they turned the corner and disappeared to be kept safe and close within the heart of his home.

The slaves passed to and fro, intent on their own work, all of them having been well taught to take no notice of their master unless he had a use for them. Gwiffert sat, gesturing for one of the women to come fill his cup. It was done instantly. He sipped the small beer, watching his doorway, and considered what had passed at his table.

The woman was strong. He doubted that she herself knew how strong. Despite that, she was plain and open. She wanted her revenge, her home, her heart. All these were simple enough to bestow. She would be his without much struggle.

The man with her . . . he carried a secret in him, down under the depths of his long silences, and this was something Gwiffert had not expected. It could be nothing. It could be everything. It was most certainly more than Morgaine had told him, and that alone made it worthy of discovery.

Gwiffert left his hall. He walked his corridors, turning left, then right, then right again, until he came to a broad, dim stairway winding up into one of the three squat towers that decorated his home. At the top waited a single door of ashwood banded with bronze. Gwiffert drew a ring holding two keys out from under his shirt. One was silver, the other was gold. Gwiffert took the golden key and unlocked the door.

On the other side waited a single, round room filled with the scents of straw, old droppings and dust. Sunlight streamed in from three arched windows, each so large two men could have stood abreast on their stone sills. It was a mews. There were perches and nesting boxes enough for a dozen birds here. Jesses, hoods, lures, and all the tools of the falconer's trade lay untouched on a table that had been made to fit against the curving wall. Only one bird was kept here now, and it opened its round, yellow eyes at once as he entered.

It was a great owl, black as night. Its hooked beak was as sharp and wicked as the talons that clung to its perch. It gazed at him imploringly and hooted urgently.

'Hello, Blodwen.' Gwiffert drew on a pair of gauntlets, and with a deft motion lifted the bird from its perch, settling it onto his wrist. He ruffled its feathers and it shifted testily for a moment, but then calmed as he carried it to the window. 'I have a task for you, my lady.' Daylight blazed outside, but that made no difference to this bird. 'You must hunt me out the truth of Geraint the son of Lot Luwddoc.'

He loosed the jesses and held the bird up to one of the windows. She hooted twice more and spread her great, black wings. She plunged from the window ledge until the wind caught her and bore her up on its back.

Resting the spear in the crook of his arm, Gwiffert sat on the windowsill, as any man might who wished to rest for a time, enjoying the view of his country and the warmth of the sun on his skin. A moment's pause in all his busy doing, a moment's contentment with all that had been done. His house was secure and all he owned was sound. Before him lay that which was new and waiting only to be properly dealt with. What better cause for contentment was there than this?

After a while a shadow emerged from the top of the distant forest and became Blodwen. As she soared near, he saw her talons were extended, the long jesses trailing behind them.

So you have brought me more than a dream this time.

He stood back from the window and Blodwen swept through, dropping her prey with a small thump onto the rushes at his feet as she swooped down to her perch. First, Gwiffert made sure her jesses were secured, that he had praised and fed her from the bucket of scraps that he himself renewed daily. Only then did he turn to what the black owl had brought him.

It was a mouse, a small brown field mouse, its fur and

whiskers sleek from its foraging in the fields. It lay on the floor, stunned by the flight, the fall, and by finding itself still alive when it could have expected nothing but death. It was only by looking closely that one could discern that its tiny white forepaws were not the claws of a mouse, but the hands of a human made in perfect miniature.

So. Gwiffert pulled up a stool and sat, planting his spear on the floor. 'Rouse yourself, Llygoden. You gain nothing by testing my patience.'

As he spoke, the mouse changed. It shifted and it stretched. Fur became skin and the hands became those of a man, their backs sprinkled with fine brown hairs to match those on his head and chin.

The man lifted his head. His bones were small and his features delicate. Had it not been for the beard on his chin, one might have taken him for a woman, and the long, belted tunic of rich brown wool he wore for a dress.

The man spoke no word, his jaw set tight in anger, but he did pull his knees underneath him and climb slowly to his feet, leaning heavily on the low windowsill.

Gwiffert nodded his approval and folded his hands over his spear. 'Llygoden, you saw much of the world before you came to my service . . .'

'Slavery,' said the shape-shifter.

Gwiffert allowed this rebellion, for there were no other witnesses. 'As you will. What can you tell me of the son of Lot Luwddoc?'

Llygoden spread his hands, a smile of grim merriment on his face. 'Whatever you will, my king. I am entirely yours.'

'Ever the trickster, you.' Gwiffert made sure his disapproval was plain in his voice. 'So much the mouse even in the form of a man. Speak clearly, I have other business and will not waste my time here.'

But the smile did not fade. 'I could sit here for days and

augur on many matters of that family. Ask a better question, my king.' Llygoden bowed his head down in mockery.

Which was too much. Even Blodwen did not get so long a lead from him. 'Be wary of your tongue, Llygoden.' He planted the spear. *Take a look at your doom, mouse. You can bring it down whenever you choose.* 'Do not think because I permit you to keep your little games with jars that are forever full of their milk, that I cannot take what remains of your art as easily as stretching out my hand. And do not think I will spare that wife of yours no matter how great with child she has grown.' He grinned. 'Would you like her to be mouse forever, that pretty pot-keeper wife of yours? Would you like my Blodwen to know her name?'

That made the mouse-man go pale with rage and, more importantly, with fear. Gwiffert nodded. 'Yes, Llygoden. Remember yourself. Now. A better question. Fair enough.' He considered. 'What is the secret that Geraint, son of Lot Luwddoc, carries in his blood?'

Llygoden frowned, his eyes narrowing as they looked into the distance, seeing back through the long years, back before he had made a gamble that now displeased him so.

'Two girls,' he said in a soft voice. His gaze did not move. Augury, then, or just the long sight of one who might see what all his own people saw. 'They run on a hillside, holding hands and laughing. They are alike in face and form, so that no man could tell them apart, save that one has blue eyes and one black. The blue-eyed sister will have four sons blessed in birth by a man who will love her, and then hate her. The black-eyed sister will have one son whose father will not know him until it is too late.'

Black-eyed, a single son . . . Is that Morgaine herself? Morgaine has a sister? A twin?

He thought. Lot's queen had been . . . Morgause, he remembered now. Morgause, the daughter of Uther and

Igraine, the half-sister of . . . and Gwiffert laughed out loud.

Morgause was half-sister to High King Arthur. Arthur had married her to Lot Luwddoc to bring about an alliance with Gododdin against the Picts as well as the Saxons. She had mothered his heir, Gawain, and Gawain's three brothers: Agravain, Gareth, and Geraint.

Gwiffert shook his head, his jaw loose with the force of his wonder. Morgaine, Morgan the Fae, was sister to Arthur the High King. And Geraint, this man she had coaxed him into agreeing to destroy, was her blood kin, her sister's own son. No wonder he looked at the world so closely. He carried the blood of the Sleepless One and all its power in him.

Small wonder she wanted him dead.

Oh, little Elen, do you know what you have fastened onto? He smiled. *I think not. You would not ally so readily with the kin of your enemy.*

Gwiffert laughed again.

'I trust, my king, I have served you well?' said Llygoden, all sincere solicitation.

'Better than you may know, my mouse.' Gwiffert stood, holding the spear easily in his hand. 'As was ever your way. You may go now, but be ready. I will be sending you someone soon. I expect you to serve her even better than you once served Rhiannon.'

Llygoden's jaw worked itself back and forth, but he bowed his head, because he had no choice.

'Be of good cheer,' said Gwiffert consolingly. 'This is no friend I send you. She permitted her hawk to hunt among your people. You may take her life as your due.'

Llygoden lifted his head, and there was a gleam in his dark eye. 'Then at least we may strike at one enemy.'

Gwiffert shifted his grip on the spear, slightly, but deliberately, making sure Llygoden saw. 'Go, little slave.'

In return, Llygoden smiled, and his white teeth were very sharp. 'Slavery within slavery, worlds within worlds. Beware, Gwiffert, lest you find yourself locked in here with the rest of us.'

Gwiffert let it go. Words from a mouse were nothing to him. Llygoden shrank and plumped, brown wool and brown hair becoming fur and whiskers again. Blodwen watched, hooting in her annoyance as the tiny creature scampered along the floor and disappeared into a tiny chink in the wall.

Smiling Gwiffert left the mews, closing and locking the door behind him. Smiling he walked down the stairs. Let Llygoden rail. He had what he needed. The way was now clear. He would have Elen, and he would have Geraint, and in time, they would ensure that he had Morgaine herself.

SIXTEEN

Once Elen sank into sleep on the narrow bed she had been given, Geraint found himself pacing the tiny room. Calonnau watched him suspiciously from her perch. He thought of what Elen had said about the hawk having only anger and corporeal need in her. He thought he understood that now. His vaunted patience was failing him in this place, and for all he was concerned for Elen's health, all he wanted to do was get out of it. He needed to be doing, not wondering, not fearing.

A tentative knock sounded on the door. Geraint stilled himself before his tongue could form a sharp rebuke. The door opened, and a woman, well into her middle years stepped in. She dropped a nervous curtsey to him.

'His majesty would walk with you,' she whispered as if afraid of being overheard. 'I'm to sit with the lady to attend her when she wakes.'

Elen lay still, curled in on herself as she did when she slept beside him. Calonnau preened on the perch. He did not like the idea of leaving Elen alone, but he had no good excuse to offer should he refuse this request from his host. The woman clutched her skirt in both hands, worrying the cloth with her gnarled fingers. She was afraid, but she met his eyes nonetheless. So, not afraid of him.

'Where shall I attend His Majesty?' he asked.

'At the walls by the main gate.' She curtsied, her relief obvious in the stillness of her hands as well as her voice.

Praying this was not the wrong choice, Geraint took up his cloak and strode out to meet once more with the king of this strange hall. After a few false starts in the labyrinthine corridors, he found his way to the yard. The day had grown close and grey. The wind tugged impatiently at the edges of his cloak. The yard had been covered in straw, in an attempt to hold back the mud the rain must bring. The smells of the place were all as familiar to Geraint as his own name – horses, hearth smoke, the acrid stink of a tannery and the metallic tang of a forge. Men, women and children hurried about their tasks. They seemed content enough, but underneath their everyday appearance he thought he saw something furtive, an unspoken fear in how the women hunched their shoulders, and how the men scolded the children ferociously and clouted them hard for doing nothing more than play a little too long. No, all was not right in this oh-so-homelike yard.

Gwiffert pen Lleied waited by the gate, a massive affair built of timbers that were as broad as a man's two hands. Not even Camelot had such a portal. The walls that held the gate were stout stone with stairs leading up to the ledge where the sentries might survey the land all around.

This place has been built to do much more than hold in secrets.

'Ah, Sir Geraint, thank you.' King Gwiffert stopped Geraint with a gesture before he could kneel. He still held Manawyddan's spear, cradling it in the crook of his arm. 'How does your lady?'

'She sleeps, Sir,' Geraint replied. The king carried his spear comfortably, almost tenderly, as if it were no more than a treasured ornament. As one became used to its presence, one might almost forget it was a weapon of war.

Geraint found himself wondering if that were not part of the reason Gwiffert did not put it down.

'Sleep is the best thing for her now,' said Gwiffert. It was a polite murmur, nothing more. The way he watched his tightly closed gate and the men standing sentry above it said he had other matters on his mind. 'Forgive me for taking you from her, Sir Geraint, but I am in need of your help in more ways than one.' His eyes shifted sideways, as if this were an admission that cost him pride to make, and well it might be.

Geraint bowed in his best courtly manner. 'Your request honours me.'

The king nodded absently. His attention was still on his walls, as if he could see through them to the country beyond. 'As I told you, I was . . . brought here while a young man. My schooling in the arts of war was never completed, but even I had heard of the prowess of the Round Table.' He rested the butt of the spear on the toe of his boot. He twisted the weapon in both hands for a moment. 'I would ask you to view our defences with me, tell me where we may strengthen what we have, and what new tactics we might employ. Every detail helps us. The Great King will attack again before winter.' Whatever Gwiffert had been when he came to this place, he was not young now. There was no grey in his golden hair yet, but his hands were hardened and browned from the work of war, and the veins stood out on their backs. His face was seamed with fine lines that would only deepen with time, especially around his eyes.

Geraint bowed again. 'I will be glad to render what help I can.'

Together, they climbed the stairs to the walkway that

circled the walls. The sentries, with their spears in their hands
and their horns at their sides, knelt for their king and then
went rigidly about their watch, without any of the gossip
and joking Geraint would have expected. He and the king
followed the narrow way with careful steps, for it was a long
fall to the yard below. Beyond the hall, they overlooked the
rugged country of steep valleys and dark, crabbed mountains. They paused often to contemplate the earthworks,
discussing the use of ditches and terracing in readying a hall
for siege. The king spoke with great feeling of the attacks he
had so far endured and Geraint watched him closely as he
spoke. He talked of the loss of this man and that, of women
carried off as they foraged in the woods, of villages frightened into helping the Great King in his betrayals, of the
constant threats and fear that his dwindling folk must live
under.

He spoke emotionally, with the detail of a man who had
seen the tale he tells. He talked angrily of his attempts to
find the other king, and his repeated failures. As he spoke
of these things his hand tightened on the shaft of his spear,
the knuckles turning white with the strength of his grip.

They stood at the northwest corner of the walls. The wind
whipped around their ears, bringing the smell of more rain.
Below, the country sank into a crooked valley, only to rise
again into stony peaks covered in red earth and dark trees.
It was very different from the green and gentle scenery
Geraint was used to, or even the hard and rocky hills around
his childhood home at Din Eityn. It was as if the land itself
spoke of the blood and secrets spilled there and crowded
close to keep both for itself.

Geraint shook off that thought, and searched for a way to
compose the questions stirring inside him. 'I confess I am
surprised that you have not been able to do more against
your enemy, Sir. With the weapon you carry . . .'

At the mention of it, the king curled his arm more tightly around the spear, drawing it close. Geraint was not even certain King Gwiffert was aware he did so. 'It is all that has kept us safe thus far. I am still but one man against his hundreds. My enemy can fetch more to replace what he loses. I have only those around me.'

To be without allies, to be a ruler and yet a stranger in this land of blood and magic. . . there was reason enough for his fear, and his anger. 'None other will rise up with you?'

King Gwiffert shook his head. 'I have no claim of fealty here. Even if I did, they are afraid, and rightly so. They have seen the Grey Men too.' Slowly he turned his gaze from the lands beyond, as if he feared to turn his back on them. He took a deep breath, planting his spear against the ledge. 'Sir Geraint, if this war were yours, what would you do?'

Geraint considered, staring off across the cramped and crooked countryside. There was so little open ground, so many steep hills. 'If I had but a few men, I would not hurl them at a fortress. I would seek to draw out the enemy and spring what trap I could on him.'

The Little King's eyes narrowed. 'Yes. That would be the way. But what trap? And how to bring him out? It is in this that I have failed for so long. He comes and goes as he will, whatever of my urging or insult.'

There was a way. Geraint saw it as clearly as a candle flame in a darkened room. 'What if he believed you would soon have help?'

King Gwiffert started. 'What help?'

'Arthur, and the Round Table.'

Gwiffert stared at him for a long moment. 'Tell me.'

It was a shaky thought, and Geraint knew it, and yet it could be made to work. It would play on the one thing this Great King must count on, that Gwiffert had no ally. 'If the

Great King could be made to believe that Arthur had found the way to breach the borders of this land, that he was coming with all his might at your urging . . . would he not attack before they could come here, while you still seemed weak?'

The king licked his lips. Geraint watched the hand that held the spear. His fingers drummed restlessly, uncertainly against the shaft. 'It would be a terrible chance to take. If he came with all his power . . . it could drown us.'

'I wonder, Sir.'

The fingers stilled. The runes were shallower beneath them, worn away by his grip. How many years had it been since he had set the spear down?

'How is that?'

'No one lets an enemy sit on his doorstep merely to toy with him.' As Geraint spoke, the thought gained strength, becoming sure and solid within him. 'The only reason not to defeat an enemy is that you cannot.'

'You do not know the one I fight,' King Gwiffert murmured.

'No, Majesty, I do not,' Geraint admitted. 'I know only war and the ways of war.'

Grim and silent, the Little King stared out over the mountains that hemmed in his hall. His fingers clenched tightly around the spear, releasing, drumming uneasily, clenching again, the visible sign of the disorder of his thoughts. 'Can it be?' he whispered. 'Can it be this whole long time I have been deceived in this too?'

Geraint held his peace. He felt agreement growing in the other man, felt it shift and settle into place. He saw it in the way his shoulders relaxed, in the way he held his spear away from his body, as if he no longer needed it quite so close to protect him.

When he turned to Geraint again, his eyes were bright

and keen, very like the tip of his spear. 'Sir Geraint, will you take charge of my men? Will you lead us against the Great King? I have done all I can, and I would not wait like a teth-ered bull for my doom when there might be a way to defeat it.'

Despite all the caution in him, Geraint's heart swelled at these words. That he should lead, that his skills should bring such a victory as this must be . . . to take this back to Camelot and stand when the Round Table gathered and speak of his own deeds for once rather than his brother's. As much as anything, that was what had taken him back to Pont Cymryd. He had said as much to Gawain, and now his chance had come.

Be careful, Geraint. Be very careful. This was a great request to make of a stranger, desperation or no. Yet it had been made, and the words rang very true.

'You yourself told me I do not know your enemy, Sir,' said Geraint, tempering his own desire with a vital truth before he himself forgot it. 'I do not know if I could lead your men well.'

The king bit something back. A hint of impatience smoul-dered in his eyes. 'Sir Geraint, I ask you this as a man who has nowhere else to turn. I cannot see beyond the maze that has trapped me for so long.' The king reached out with his free hand and gripped Geraint's wrist. 'You yet have clear eyes. You can find the way.'

Geraint froze in place, unsure of how to answer. Arthur had never touched him so, nor for such a reason. But Arthur was king in his own court and his own lands. He had not known such fear as the Little King knew in many years.

A feeling of pettiness came over Geraint as he realized what he must next ask. He could not forget the other quest and the promises gone before, and yet, it felt as if he were haggling over the price of market goods. Still, Geraint rallied himself. 'If I do your bidding, Majesty, I would ask a boon of you.'

'Anything within my power.'

How to ask for the only true protection this place had? Reluctance stirred in him, but he was too far gone now to turn back. 'I am pledged to defeat the ones who stole my lady's lands from her. The only weapon that will bring them down is the spear of Manawyddan.'

The Little King swallowed. His free hand flew to the spear's shaft, covering it as if he thought to hide it from sight. *It was too much. A misstep, but I had to try.*

But the Little King bowed his head to Geraint. 'Very well,' he said, and for all he hung his head, his voice was more resolute than Geraint had heard it yet. 'If you will free me from my enemy, the spear of Manawyddan will free you from yours.'

Geraint drew himself to attention and laid his fist over his heart in the old Roman salute. 'Then let me see your men, Majesty. Let me speak with your captains, and we will begin.'

A smile, broad and confident, spread across the Little King's lined face and unhesitating, Geraint followed him down.

Elen dreamed.

She dreamed the dream of the hawk in the sky, of the blue-eyed knight, and her blood flowing free, but instead of waking as she fell, she fell into a new dream. In the dream she saw Geraint. He ran through the woods of Pont Cymryd. Behind him ran a herd of red swine, their teeth and tusks shining yellow in the darkness. Geraint ran until his breath came in gasps and his eyes were wide with terror, and still the swine ran hard behind him. He tripped and fell, and the great red boar that led the herd reached him with its tusks sharp as swords and Geraint screamed . . .

Elen woke to darkness. The room was utterly black around

her. She heard Calonnau scolding on her perch to the right and felt the agitated pulse of her heart, but she could see nothing. The scent of brazier smoke was faint. Only one star shone silver-bright through the window slit. Elen curled up against the darkness. Her lungs felt tight, her mind constricted.

Geraint. She must find Geraint. She threw the covers off and planted her feet on the stone floor. Calonnau scolded once more, angry about being woken, but already she was calming, getting ready to sink back into her own dreams of open skies and clean wind.

Elen was used to navigating dark rooms and shuffled to the brazier. She prodded at the ashes with a stick and found one coal with enough life in it to be coaxed into flame. From this tiny fire she kindled a rush light plucked from the basket nearby.

In her memory, Geraint screamed, and screamed again.

She hurried into the corridor. It was cold. Elen almost felt she should have been able to see her own breath. The walls were so close she couldn't even straighten both arms out across the breadth of the corridor. The painted images crowded her, squeezing her mind and gripping her wounded throat and wrist. Yet it was those images she followed out to the great hall.

Despite the holding's many rooms, the king had found it was necessary to lodge Geraint in the hall with the servants and the men of war, so Geraint had told her, with many apologies. Their host seemed to think complete quiet was necessary for her healing and it would be discourteous to contradict him. Elen bridled at that, but she knew he was right. So, she remained in her grove and he went to the great hall, and now she hurried after him, biting her lip, trying not to see the boar's tusks flashing before her mind's eye.

At last, she came to the great open archway, and she saw

a pile of men's bodies. She froze, then looked again, and saw
they were only sleeping, crowded together on pallets, sharing
blankets, lying this way and that. A few women lay bundled
with their husbands. If they followed the same custom as
back home, the unmarried women would sleep elsewhere.
There were only a few beds, plain things with thick mattresses
that might well be straw rather than feathers. What she did
not see was a bed for the king. However, the plain pallet by
the nearest hearth held Geraint. He lay on his side, his arm
pillowing his head. His face relaxed in sleep, his strong arms
bare to the faint glow of the banked coals.

Looking at him, so soundly asleep there, the urgency of
her nightmare bled from Elen. He was only as tired, as worn
as she was. He had sworn himself to hard labour, she knew.
When he had come to her chamber during her brief waking
that evening, he had told her what he had promised the
Little King, and for what price.

'Mother Don protect . . .' she had gripped his hands hard.
'Geraint, what have you done?'

'I've bought us an honest chance, Elen,' he answered,
wondering at her anxious exclamation, as, in truth, she did
herself. 'Now we may get what we need, and what your
people need, without deception, or betrayal of our host.'

'But we also swore we would give the spear back to the
Lady and the Lord,' she breathed. 'How may that now be
done?'

'You swore if it did no dishonour it would be done,' Geraint
reminded her. 'If it is the spear of his fathers, we surely
cannot give it to their hands without dishonour.'

She bit her lips. Her throat hurt too much for more speech.
Her weakness shamed her. She was afraid, but she could not
tell why.

'Deception fails before truth, Elen,' said Geraint firmly. 'If
we act honestly, honour will shield us.'

In other circumstances these might have been the words of a naive boy, but there was so much magic here . . . Before the gods and the fair folk, what he said was true.

She drew back, moving out of the doorway, leaving the people in the great hall to their own dreams. She would tell him her nightmare in the morning when they could think on its meaning together. He was safe. Surely tonight they were both safe. What could touch them this deep in the heart of so much stone?

Elen rubbed her eyes and took herself back down the corridors the way she had come. When she at last reached her own door, she paused. The thought of returning to that room was suddenly smothering, like the thought of climbing into an open grave. But neither could she stay here. So much stone kept her safe, sure, like a cage kept one safe, like a cell. The painted world around her brought no relief. She needed to see the moon and the stars, to know if it rained or was fair. Even a single breath of free air would be some relief.

Gradually, Elen became aware of a noise. It was soft, but insistent. A double beat, very like her heart in Calonnau, but sharper. Metallic.

A forge? It sounded like a hammer on metal. But within the walls? How could that be? She held herself still, straining to listen.

Ching-ching. Ching-ching.

Yes, it was a smith's hammer, but not a hammer for iron. Something lighter, more delicate. What was being worked so late at night?

The noise nagged at her, making her uneasy, like an itch just beneath the skin.

Ching-ching. Ching-ching.

Part of her said that she was being foolish, that she should go back to her bed and let the night spin itself out as it would.

But part of her felt she had been too long abed already. The stone walls oppressed her. She could not go back tamely to her false grove. She needed to know she could still move.

The strange sound continued, never speeding up, never slowing. It was as if it had always been there. It was only now, when the busy sounds of day were silent that she could hear it.

Ching-ching. Ching-ching.

She glanced back down the hall. To the right, the wall was painted with a field of grain and trees heavy with fruit. To the left was a pasture of cows and bulls, their heads held up to the sun. She drifted down the right-hand way, only to hear the noise grow fainter. She turned around, and followed the other way.

The walls flickered in the rush light, so that their painted images moved in an eerie parody of life. Trees shifted in the light as their natural counterparts would in the wind. The hides of the cattle and horses rippled. Men's eyes blinked. The hammer's ring led her around a left-hand turning and then a right. Doors passed her shoulders on both sides. How could one place have so many doors? So many tiny rooms holding . . . what? Were the people of this place behind those doors? Or was there treasure? What could anyone want to keep so hidden?

Although the floor beneath her feet stayed level, she had the sensation of sinking more deeply into the earth. The stone around her became darker, the air more still and damp. The paintings became steadily stranger. The scenes of prosperity and abundance now held fantastic monsters – a horse with a man's torso carrying a screaming woman in its arms, a snake with a dozen heads, a woman in a chariot pulled by great dragons.

Her lungs laboured to breathe. She could not feel her heart. She should not have left Calonnau behind her. The absence distracted her mind, worrying at her, even more than the sound she followed.

Then, beyond another left-hand turning, Elen saw light. She rounded the corner. Ahead, one of the doors was open, just enough to let the red glow of a fire spill out across the stones.

Ching-ching. Ching-ching.

Cold with fear, Elen hesitated. She had come so far, and she knew so little. There was some secret here, and it was unwise to spy on such things without protection. But perhaps this secret could help her and Geraint understand both this place and their host, who spoke so freely, but kept so much shuttered behind his eyes. She gathered her courage and stepped into the wedge of light that spilled into the corridor.

A wave of heat rolled over her. Beyond the door was a forge. It was a wide, open crucible larger than any she had ever seen. Flames leapt up here and there, greedy and pale over the bed of livid, orange coals. Beside them, a huge, brown man, wearing nothing but a leather apron, stood behind an anvil that shone like silver in the powerful light. His head was bald and mottled red and black, with only a few tufts of brown hair sticking out. His hammer was a light and slender thing that looked like a toy in his great fist. He brought it down on a gold chain that draped across the silver anvil in a swift double beat.

Ching-ching.

It was wrong that this was here. This space, these stones, were not meant for a forge and its fire. She knew that, instinctively and certainly. The chain shone brassy, almost bloody, in the firelight, each link barely the size of her little fingernail. It was long, impossibly long. It lay in heaps and coils on the floor, in places as high as the smith's ankles. Her gaze travelled its tangled length, searching for the end, or the beginning, and finding neither. It came to her that it was endless, and yet the mountainous man stood wielding his small hammer, and making it longer yet.

As if he heard her thoughts, the smith lifted his head. He turned directly to her, and Elen bit her tongue to keep from screaming. His face was a single massive scar, twisted and lumpish, the skin peeling off from the raw flesh beneath, all slick with sweat. He had no eyes. Blind, he worked on the delicate, endless chain. Blind, he knew she was there, and he grinned, a gaping grin that showed all his yellow, ragged teeth.

'You too?' he said. 'He's got you too, sister?'

Elen's tongue cleaved to the roof of her mouth. The smith's hammer came down again and again, never faltering, his burnt fingers seeing the way where his eyes could not.

'Who are you?' Elen croaked.

He drew in a hissing breath. 'I'm the first one. I'm responsible for all the others. All of them are my working.'

She watched in a kind of horrified fascination as he reached for his tongs. He pulled a fine wire from the forge and laid it against the chain. He pressed the hot metal into place, twisting it with his tongs and his scarred and scabbed fingers. She smelled burnt flesh, but the smith did not flinch. His movements were deft and quick, his touch unerring. He could not be a living man. He could not be real. 'Why?'

'For pride, for greed,' he said, lifting the delicate hammer again. 'For the son who does not understand the gift his father gave.' He lifted the hammer again, beating the new link into place. Yet, he did not work on the end of the chain, for it had no end . . . she shook her head. She had seen what he had done, and yet she had not seen it. Vision. This was vision, and prophecy. She must hold fast. She must not become bemused or she would lose herself. 'Why labour for such things?'

'Because while the fire burns, I labour. So do you, little sister. So do you!' He laughed then, a high-pitched childish giggle that pierced skin down to bone and left pain behind.

Elen's courage shattered. She backed away from the door, turning to flee into the darkness. She shook with the cold of her fear, and behind her she heard laughter over the endless sound of the hammer forging the endless chain. She barely found her first turning. She dodged around the corner, and made herself stop. She pressed her back against the wall so that her trembling knees would not drop her to the floor and tried to regain her wits.

It is a nightmare. A bad dream only. A vision. I have seen worse. It cannot hurt me. It was not a true thing.

Wasn't it? whispered a tiny voice inside her empty breast. *Was it not?*

The tremors increased. *Get outside,* she thought wildly. *Get outside. I need the air and the sky over me. I need to see the moon. I'll know where I am then.*

But which way was the moon? Right then left then right again, and she'd be back in her own cell . . . her room. Where was Geraint? She was alone in this stone maze.

No. Think. You felt you were descending coming to this place. There must be a way to ascend again.

She gritted her teeth and began to walk. There was a way. There was a way. The moon and the sky were there. She would find them. Left and right. She walked. The air grew lighter. The sound of the hammer grew softer. The feel of her heart came to her, strong and sure. The monsters were replaced by cattle, grain and orchards. Not so far from her room then. Right again.

A breeze touched her cheek. Elen froze. Yes. The scent of summer greenery wafted by her. She turned her head. A little past her right shoulder was a narrow archway, so dark that in the failing rush light she had mistaken it for another closed door. But it was another corridor, and a draught of fresh air wafted out of its darkness.

Hope rising in her, Elen hurried down the tiny passage. The image of a lake set deep in black and brooding mountains surrounded her. Ahead, she saw another door, banded with metal that gleamed whitely in the failing rush light. It stood slightly open, as the last one had been, and through this there came the unmistakable feel of the open air.

She did not pause for caution. She flung the door wide open and stepped out into the cool summer's night. The moonlight poured down from the clear sky accompanied by the glimmer of a million, million stars. Elen lifted her face to that light. She inhaled great lungfuls of the night air. The weight of the stones slid from her spirit and the trembling eased from her limbs. She could think clearly again. She could find the calm in herself. She could breathe – Oh, thank the gods! – She could breathe.

'*Chwaer?*'

The sound of Gwiffert's voice startled Elen. Now she saw the Little King standing beneath a grove of trees that rustled in the cold and gentle breeze. She was in a garden, she realized. The lawn beneath her feet was short and soft as wild grass could never be. The trees were perfectly straight. They must have been pruned and tended over decades. Gwiffert stood at the edge of a pond as round as the full moon overhead. It reflected that lady's face perfectly in its still, dark mirror.

'Sir.' She should kneel, she realized. She bent her knee, but the king stopped her.

'None of that, Elen. There is no need.'

So, she stood before the king, head unbowed as he walked around the pond that held the moon and stood beside her. Even here he carried the spear with him. He rested it on his shoulder, easily, like a labourer might carry his hoe. In the moonlight, he was very pale and his hair was more silver than gold. Only his blue eyes remained strong and bright.

'So, I am not the only one who chases sleep this night.' He smiled wanly at her.

Elen licked her lips, truly disconcerted at finding another living person here. It seemed she had forgotten she was not the sole inhabitant of this place. 'I am sorry,' she said, rallying manners and wits together. 'I did not mean to disturb you . . .'

He shook his head. 'I think I wanted to be disturbed. I usually lock the door behind me.' An owl hooted in one of the perfectly tended trees. Elen shivered. Owls were omens of death, and murder.

Gwiffert glanced up. 'Yes. It's a hard night, for all its beauty.'

'What keeps you from your bed?' Elen asked before she could remember again that this man ranked above her, and it was not customary to ask such questions of kings.

But Gwiffert did not seem to mind. 'The future keeps me awake,' he said heavily. 'It has come at last, as I begged it to so many times, but now that I see it, I am not sure I want it.' He looked down into the pool, watching the moon's reflection.

Watching him watch the moon, Elen realized what this place reminded her of. It reminded her of Olwen's well at midwinter, the time of sacrifice and sacred fire, when the gods might be called down for blessing or prophecy.

'You saw . . .' she began tentatively. 'Your Majesty is a seer?'

He frowned at the word. 'I have some skills that let me see further than most men, and I thank the gods for that,' he said. 'Without them, we would have been dead long since, even with the spear.' He turned the shaft against his shoulder.

'And yet you cannot find the Great King's fortress?' Elen's brow furrowed.

Gwiffert shook his head. 'He blinds my sight. Perhaps it is part of the geas that keeps us here . . . I do not know.' He swung the spear down, cradling it into the crook of his arm again. 'But it may be we will find a way even in our darkness. He gives me great hope, your husband.'

Elen felt herself smile softly. 'Yes. He's skilled at that.'

The king regarded her searchingly for a moment, but what he was looking for, she could not tell. Whatever it was, it had taken the little smile from his face. 'He asks a mighty thing of me.' He spoke the words so softly, they were almost lost on the night's wind. 'To defeat my own enemy, only to part with that which has defended my place and people for so long . . . I can scarcely even think that far, and when I try, I feel only a shameful fear.'

Guilt touched Elen, and the memory of the Grey Men surrounding Geraint, the way they rode their silent horses towards her, remorseless death in the guise of life. 'I am sorry,' she said, and she meant it. 'But I too have an enemy that must be defeated. He has slain my family and conquered my lands.' Mother. Yestin. Dead and perhaps defiled. The rest . . . *Oh, Mother Rhiannon, where are the rest?* 'I have been told that only the spear will defeat him.'

'I should have known such a thing would be the price of our final delivery.' The king spoke to the moon's reflection. A breeze answered him, rippling across the water and distorting the shining sphere. 'We make bargains with the invisible and the fantastic, and sooner or later, the price comes due.'

A question nagged at Elen, and as the king seemed well inclined to talk, she decided to ask. 'How came you to hold the spear, Sir?'

'Ah.' He sighed and straightened slowly, as if lifting a great weight. 'That is a long tale. Longer than yours, I think.' He looked down at the spear, fondly, as a man might look at a pet dog, or a child. A spark of mischief blossomed over him and the sideways glance he gave her was sly. 'Longer than the tale of how you came to be in my private garden.'

Had she heart in her, Elen would have blushed at that. 'I heard a sound, it woke me. I saw . . .' she stopped. How to explain the portentous thing she had seen?

But the king was not content with silence. 'What did you see?' he pressed her.

She told him of the goldsmith at his forge, his ravaged face, the endless chain he worked.

All mischief bled away from Gwiffert. 'You saw the smith?'

She nodded. 'What is he?'

King Gwiffert was silent for a long moment, resting his hand protectively against the spear. 'He haunts this place,' he said at last. 'No, haunts is the wrong word . . .' but the right word did not seem to come. 'I see him some nights when I walk the halls,' he said instead. 'I think . . . I think that chain is the fetter. I think it may be what keeps all things bound to this place by his master's command.'

Elen thought again of the blind, ravaged face that somehow saw so clearly. *I'm the first one. I'm responsible for all the others. All of them are my working.* 'I have never heard of such a thing.'

'No,' said Gwiffert flatly. 'I doubt very much that anyone has.'

For a moment, Elen felt lost. She wanted to be of use, but she was alone here, and all that was hers was so far away. She was not sure she even had life to call her own. 'If any can help you against your enemy, it will be Geraint, Sir.' Though she knew these words to be true, they sounded weak in her own ears. 'This much I can promise you.'

'Can you?' His eyes were mournful. 'I pray to all the gods you may be right, sister. It is . . .' He shook his head and tried to laugh a little, but failed. 'It is a hard thing to trust strangers

who come to bear away what I have depended on for so
many years.'

He looked small then, and young, as if he were not much
older than she was. Elen wanted to say they could wait until
all was right here, that then he could ride out at the head
of his own army to Pont Cymryd, but she knew there was
no time. The gods alone knew what Urien had done to her
home and her people. It was too much to hope that Arthur's
men had arrived already, no matter how swiftly Geraint's
brother had travelled. She hated her need suddenly, she hated
all that had driven her to this place, but it was real, and here
she must stand.

'Together we will defeat our enemies,' she said and she
tried hard to believe it.

'Perhaps,' the Little King answered softly. Then he settled
the butt of the spear on the toe of his boot. He seemed to
draw assurance from that gesture. He straightened his shoulders and his smile returned. 'But come, you need your rest
yet. You have been through a great deal.' He held out his
hand to her.

'As have you.' She looked at his hand. It was a city courtesy she knew, but her house had never adopted it. No one
took her hand who was not a member of her family . . . or
Geraint.

'Yes, but I have had many a long night to grow used to
my sleeplessness. Come, lady.' His hand stayed where it was.
It would be brown in daylight, and it was much calloused.
She reached out and took it and found it was warm with
remembered sunlight and the heat that life brought. He held
her cold hand gently and escorted her through the silver-
banded door. Once inside, he let her go to carefully lock that
door with a key he brought out from under his shirt. Then,
taking her hand again, he walked her back down the narrow
corridors to her room. He bowed to her and she thought she

saw something soft shining in his eyes as he did. Then, he left her there.

It was not until she lay down again, and Calonnau was settling back to sleep, that Elen realized Gwiffert had not told her how he came to possess Manawyddan's spear.

When she woke to the dawn, she would not remember that at all.

SEVENTEEN

From around the corner, Gwiffert watched Elen's door until he was certain she would not emerge from it again.

She is safe and quiet. The night is dealt with. It is the morrow you must see to now.

Gwiffert turned on his heel and strode swiftly down the narrow corridor. For him, the way was straight and clear, and he followed it with an unerring instinct, as a bird follows the way to its own nest.

He emerged into the yard. The night was black. Torches flared about the courtyard, giving light in the darkness. There were boys here whose job it was to walk the walls all night and make sure the lights did not go out. There should always be light about Gwiffert's hall. He was most clear on this command. Too many things were made bold by darkness, even if he had them conquered by daylight. It was not his wish to have to fight old battles over again.

Two of those boys hurried by now, heads down, feet flying, clutching their lanterns as close as they could to their bodies without burning themselves, clearly hoping to pass unnoticed. Gwiffert stopped them with a word and their faces went pale as they approached and knelt.

He pointed to the first of the boys, whose red brows and freckles stood out sharply against his snow-white skin. 'You will find me Taggart and Rhys and tell them I await them at the barrows.'

The boy was on his feet in an instant and running as fast as he could for the hall. Gwiffert spared him neither glance nor thought. He turned to the other boy. 'You will bring that lantern and come with me.'

The boy gulped and stood, shaking. But his fear of his king was worse than his fear of what waited outside the gates. Gwiffert had seen to that as well, and the boy made no sound as he walked beside him to the gate, carrying the bright spark of man-made fire.

Other halls had small openings in their walls so that men and horses might pass easily one at a time when the gate itself was sealed against the night or coming war. This hall had none such. No one came or went save by the gate, and none without the master's knowledge or permission. He stood before the heavy portal and knocked on it three times with the butt of his spear. The great gate flew open and outwards, the gust of wind buffeting Gwiffert where he stood. He walked into the dark night, his spear resting on his shoulder, with the little lantern-bearer beside him, his bare feet making no noise on the cold ground.

To the north of the hall grew a dense wood of thorn and rowan trees, so thickly overgrown with brambles and nettles that passage through it would look impossible to any passerby.

But that same tangle opened before Gwiffert as easily as the gates had opened, and he walked without hindrance. So too did the trembling boy. The woods were still and stuffy as a closed hall, even when they emerged into the clearing of the barrows.

There were twelve mounds, rising in a ring. Each hillock

was of a size and shape that it might hold a single man as he lay in repose. One of them was open, exposing a hollow bed of naked black dirt. One of them was always open.

The boy crouched on the ground, trying to be small enough to hide behind the fire he carried. Gwiffert stood in the circle of that light and raised the spear, holding it like a bar in both hands over his head.

'Come!' called Gwiffert to the night. 'Caddrig, Caddugo, and Celanedd! Your master calls!'

Before him, three of the mounds shuddered and shifted. Then the ground parted sweetly. Out they came, three Grey Men, mounted on their lean steeds, their horned helms on their heads, their silver swords naked in their fists. They rode towards him, swift and silent as ghosts, bringing with them a tang of metal, blood and earth. They reined their horses to a halt before him and raised their blades in salute. They held that pose, waiting, ready to serve their lord and master in all things.

The boy bowed his head and shut his eyes tight. Gwiffert turned his back on the motionless riders without fear, and waited. Then, a new spark appeared on the track his passage had opened. Taggart and Rhys, the two seasoned fighting men he'd styled his captains, approached. Taggart was the taller and the older of the two. Both his long hair and beard had gone stone grey. He held a torch high to light the way. Rhys was still brown-haired. His rough hands were tattooed with sacred signs that had never once saved him. Both men saw the three riders arrayed behind their king, and they froze in their tracks, their living bodies balking at the nearness of the dead. Gwiffert smiled and lifted his free hand, beckoning them forward. Rhys closed his eyes, his mouth moving. Did the man still pray after all this time? He should know full well that Gwiffert would not permit any god to hear such a prayer.

Taggart, wiser, or perhaps more resigned to his fate, knelt and bowed his greying head. Rhys, holding the torch before him, as if it were a shield, also knelt.

'You summoned us, Majesty?' asked Taggart. His voice was hoarse, betraying the fear he had kept from his demeanour.

'I did.' Gwiffert smiled benignly over the men. 'I wished to commend you for your conduct with our outlandish knight, Sir Geraint, this day.'

Taggart licked his cracked lips. 'Thank you, Majesty.' He did not lift his gaze from the ground. The torchlight flickered and shivered as Rhys's marked hands shook.

'Tomorrow you ride out with him, in search of an enemy, do you not?' The inquiry was casual, the answer known to all. It was not knowledge Gwiffert sought to gain in this audience.

'Yes, Majesty,' said Taggart, his voice fainter now.

Gwiffert spoke slowly, giving the men time to fully understand his words. It would not do to have them forgetting a single one. 'It is vital that he believes the Grey Men to be the Great King's followers, do you understand? There must be no hint in word or deed that it is otherwise. It is the Great King that they follow and whom you fear.'

'Yes, Majesty,' breathed Taggart.

'And you, Rhys, do you understand?'

Rhys bowed his head, but that was not enough.

'Rhys. Look at me.'

For a moment, Rhys could not bring himself to obey, and Gwiffert wondered, amused, if he would have to lay his hand on the man. But then, the head jerked up and the brown eyes opened. They were bright with tears, as if the mind behind them were still a child's. Gwiffert's smile broadened, knowing his captain saw so clearly the three riders behind him, and how still they stood, how well they waited.

'Do you understand your charge, Rhys?' he asked again, softly as the night's own whisper.

'Yes, Majesty,' he rasped.

'Good.' Gwiffert nodded. 'Because Rhys, it is you I will hold responsible if Sir Geraint wavers in his understanding.' A single tear slid down the man's sallow cheek. 'Yes, Majesty,' he said again.

'Good,' said Gwiffert, fully satisfied. 'Now, walk with me,' he gestured towards the path with his free hand. 'It is past time we all sought our beds, is it not?'

The men before him bowed their heads as he passed them by. The boy rose carefully to his feet, turning as fast as he dared so as not to see the men, the living and the dead, who followed behind. All together, they walked to the edge of the tangled wood, the king and the boy leading the way, the riders guarding the rear with their silent presence and their scent of the grave.

At the edge of the wood, Gwiffert paused briefly and turned to his riders. They raised their swords and sheathed them, knowing all their commands without need of clumsy words. They touched up their silent horses and rode away from the light until the darkness swallowed them up.

'Come now,' he said, turning his attention back to his men waiting silently with him in the circle of golden light. 'Let us all go home.'

The moon was well past its zenith by the time Adev, headman of Llanthony, son of Hova the Black Hova who had once wrestled a breeding wolf to the ground, reached the edge of the wood. Above him, the wind blew across the bare crest of the mountain, bending the grass so that it rippled silver and black in the moonlight. A single standing stone pointed itself at the stars, its moonshadow stretching long and grey beneath it.

This was said to be the exact centre of the Little Country.
This was the place, they said, where the Little King stood
and worked his fearful enchantment, raising up the mountains and bringing down the sky to fence in his captives and
fence out the gods.

Adev didn't believe it. One like the Little King – Adev
didn't even like to think his name – would not leave the
heart of his working so exposed. If there was a centre to this
place, it was inside the king's hall, buried deep under its
stones and its spells. It was not out here where any fool,
even Adev the Fool, could reach it.

Adev's feet ached. His body stooped in its weariness, for
he had taken no rest since he set out, nor had he brought
more than a crust of bread for his journey. His wife had wept
to see him go, for they both knew he did not expect to return.

At least, not as he was

He tried to tell himself it did not matter. All that mattered
was that he, Adev, even in the winter of his years, had come
here.

He knew to come here on the night of the full moon the
way one knows a story told in childhood. Even in the land of
the Little King, there was gossip. Whispers were passed
around the hearth with the beer jug. Wives talked to each
other over the loom or the birthing bed, and some of them
whispered in their husbands' ears in the time just before dawn.
They spoke of the king's enemy, and how he rode out on such
nights, looking for those in thrall to Gwiffert, to kill them, or,
if the lightest whispers were to be believed, to free them.

His hall was full of the living, they said. His enchanted
wall was the one thing that could blind the Little King, and
he could have stayed safe behind it, but he rode out still, as
his father had. So they said.

Adev would have dismissed this, if he had not seen it.
Once, when he was a boy, he had run from the village. He

had seen his father, whom wolves could not kill, ridden down by the Grey Men. Fear and fury had driven him out to find the borders of the land, to find a breach, a tunnel, a secret road that would take them all home. Instead, he had found the black owl and the Grey Men. He would have died had not the Great King in his chariot come, swinging his war club, scattering the Grey Men like dolls, while Adev cowered on his knees. When he could stand, did he follow the Great King to take up arms with the one who saved his life? No. He ran back to the village to live a slave, because he'd seen the grinning faces beneath the helmets and the naked skulls with their sealed brands, because he saw how Gwiffert stole even honest death from those who displeased him.

Now, here he was again, looking out on that high, bare hill, exposed to the moon and stars, and whatever eyes King Gwiffert had sent out into the night. He panted, his lungs wheezing and stinging from the effort of his climb. His belly, used to hunger though it was, added to his pains.

Old man, old man, his trembling heartbeat said. *Too late, old man.*

Not yet, he told himself in angry answer. *Not yet.*

He heard the sound of hoofbeats over the other side of the hill, and his heart froze. But with it came the rattle and clatter of chariot wheels, and before he could move or remember to breathe again, two great horses appeared over the rise, followed hard by the Great King and the slim boy who was his charioteer.

He was tall and broad, towering over even the standing stone beside him, just as Adev remembered. He could not tell whether the boy before him was the one whom he had seen all those years ago. He might have been. Time was a strange and shifting thing in the Little Country. There was no road to bring them here. All roads belonged to Gwiffert, and they came and went as he ordered them and would not hold still even for the chariot's iron wheels. Only the wild ways remained, and yet the chariot, its bent-wood frame painted with triskelions and other signs of the gods and goddesses, seemed to have found no obstacle climbing to this high place. The charioteer reined in his dark horses, and they obeyed, stomping and snorting to show that like their master, they still had spirit.

The Great King carried his war club easily in his huge hand. He looked down on Adev, his bearded face dark and grim.

'I remember you, Adev.' The giant's voice rumbled far deeper than that of a man of natural stature, and yet there was a gentle note to it, and something sorrowful. 'Why are you here?'

'Great King.' Adev knelt. 'I came . . . I would . . .' Long years and the hard climb brought his breath out in gasps, but his hesitation was more than that. Habit and fear even now shackled his tongue. He had thought the journey would loosen such chains, but still he stumbled. 'I came to tell you that the wall is breached. Strangers, a lady and her knight, have come from the larger world.'

'I know,' replied the king, as Adev had suspected he would. He too had his spies. Everyone who wearied at last of Gwiffert's rule had two roads to take. One led to the Great King, and the other led to a hidden grave where it could be hoped they would not be troubled. 'And Gwiffert has rounded them up already.'

Now came the treason. Now came the last bit of good he could do his own. 'Sir . . . the knight will be let loose against you. Sir . . . I am asking you not to kill him.'

The Great King paused a long time before he asked, 'Why should I not?'

Yes, why? Come, Adev. You rehearsed your pretty speech all the way here. 'Because he may yet do us all good. They . . . when they came to us, they sought to save us trouble. They fed us, Sir, from food that was none of the Little King's. They fought the Grey Men for us. The king does not yet own them. He fears them, I swear it, and he is lying to keep them tame.'

But the king only sighed. Adev could see nothing of his face in the night's shadows. 'What lie does he tell?'

'He claims all your deeds as his own, and lays his deeds at your feet.' *My cousin Rhys risked his life when he told me this, when I crept up to the king's walls to try . . . to try to help those who helped us. Please, do not waste this.* 'It is only these lies that make the lady and her knight hate you.'

'What of it, Adev? This is Gwiffert's way.'

Here it was. Here was the hope he had never thought to find in his lifetime. 'If they could be shown the lie, they would turn against him. They have power. The lady is gifted. The knight is strong. They came in from the outside of their own will. They might be able to show us the way out from this place.'

But the Great King only shook his head slowly. 'They have been taken into the hall. You know as well as I do they are his now, Adev. Whatever they were before they entered those gates is turned now to his purposes.'

'But not yet . . .'

The Great King did not let him finish. 'I'm sorry, Adev, but you have lived under his rule, and you know how swiftly he works.'

Anger, heady and unfamiliar, surged through Adev, quickening his old blood. 'You are like us. You have come to believe he is a god. You are as afraid as we are, who crouch in the mud unable to raise a hand against him.'

The Great King turned his face away from the accusation and said only, 'You should have come before, Adev. I looked for you, all those years ago, after I saved you from the Grey Men. I would have done my best to protect you and yours if you had come to me.'

Shame for shame. I should have expected no less. 'Before I thought we could live as we were, but now . . . now we will starve with the winter, and there is nothing left to lose.'

'He may come for you before then. The owl searches for you even now.'

'I know,' said Adev simply. 'So at this last, I have remembered I am a man.' He stood, bones and joints creaking from cold and long travel. 'I am going now, and I will do no more in life. What will you do, Great King?'

He did not wait for an answer, but turned stiffly on his old feet and stumped down the hillside, coming again to the darkness beneath the trees. He knew if he looked back, he would see the giant no more, so he did not bother. Instead, he turned his path down the north-facing slope, his face set in determination, his eyes ahead, as a man will who knows his road by heart.

Presently, he heard an owl hoot, and he nodded. He lifted his chin and spoke to the trees. 'You may tell him you were in time. I have spoken to no one.'

Adev sat down on the ground, borne down by the heavy years of his life, and he waited patiently for the sound of hoofbeats.

EIGHTEEN

Geraint awoke knowing it was dawn. He felt it in his bones, even though the broad hall with its painted walls offered no view of the sky. The coals burned redly beneath their blankets of ash. In their dim light, he saw the men around him begin to stir, rolling over, grumbling, scratching, trying to decide if they could burrow under the blankets for just a little more sleep. Despite its size, the hall smelled strongly of human warmth and unwashed bodies.

Some of these men would soon march to war with him if all went well, and he knew none of them. The thought troubled Geraint as he eased himself out of the bed and reached beneath it for his tunic and sandals. Before he attended to that disquiet, though, he needed to see Elen. He badly wished they had not been separated, but he had been mindful of the need to avoid offence to their host.

Her door was slightly ajar when he reached it. From the other side, he could hear cloth rustling, and Calonnau's complaints. He knocked softly.

'My wife?'

There was a pause. 'Come in, please, my husband.'

Inside the room, Elen stood between the bed and the

serving woman Gwiffert had given her, smoothing down her
unbound hair. She wore a borrowed dress of fawn-coloured
wool that had been twisted with darker threads to make
black flecks amid the brown. Its colours startlingly matched
Calonnau's feathers, and Geraint wondered if it had been
chosen by their host on purpose.

'Good morning,' she said, but her smile was tired. 'Meg,
you may go break your fast.'

The woman bridled, but in the end, turned and left the
room. Elen sighed as she did, but her stance relaxed as the
door closed.

'How was the night?' he asked.

Elen shook her head and sat down on the bed. Concerned,
Geraint sat beside her, but it was a long time before she spoke
to him. She stared at Calonnau preening on her perch and
stretching out her talons.

'I could not sleep, and, I . . . walked the halls a little. And
I saw . . .' She pressed her lips together, cutting off the words
that wanted to emerge. 'I found the king in his courtyard,'
she said instead. He listened carefully while she described
her conversation with him, and how he had returned her to
her room through the twisting corridors.

When she fell silent, he asked, 'What else did you see?'

Elen frowned. 'I tell you true, husband, I am not sure. It
was a nightmare, but I'm not sure it was a dream.' She stared
at the painted trees that surrounded them. 'I don't like these
walls. They prey on my mind. The king, he does his best, but
this hall of his . . . I don't know what it was made to hold.'

'What do you suspect?'

But Elen only shook her head once. Wisps of hair drifted
in front of her cheeks and she brushed them back impatiently. 'I don't even know that much.'

Geraint took her hand. There was no other comfort he
could give her. 'I wish I did not have to leave you here.'

That drew a smile from her and she was able to look at him. 'So do I.' She covered his hand with her cool palm. 'Do you know where you're going?'

'King Gwiffert's captain, Rhys is his name, has some thoughts, but the man is badly afraid. I don't believe they've ever hunted the Grey Men or their cohort before. I cannot get much out of him. I wish . . .' It was his turn to shake his head. He remembered standing on the walls with Rhys and Taggart the day before, and the short answers the men had given to his questions, and how little they could say about anything that lay beyond the terraced hillside. It was as if their idea of the land ended at the last ditch. That, more than anything else, worried him. What sort of warrior did not know the land around his home like he knew his own name? The first and simplest explanation was that neither captain wished to speak with this stranger who had been set over them. That boded only ill for their riding into battle together.

'What do you wish?' Elen asked.

'I wish Gawain were here,' Geraint said with bitter honesty. 'He's a born leader, my brother. I've seen him rally a troop that the day before didn't know him from Adam, but once the battle began they'd follow him to the gates of Hell. Such gifts are not mine.'

'You will do what you must, Geraint. That is your gift.'

I wish I could believe as you do. 'It is hard, Elen,' was all he said aloud.

'I know.'

They stayed like that for a little while, holding each other's hands, surrounded by a stranger's stone walls, bound by promises made perhaps in foolish haste. He could not have said why so many doubts plagued him this morning. Yesterday, he had been certain of what needed to be done, and he still could see no other way, and yet . . .

In his brooding silence, Elen spoke. 'Let me send out Calonnau to view the country. She is anxious to hunt, and she may show you where your quarry can be found.'

'A good thought.' It was. Geraint berated himself for not having had it himself, although he was reluctant to ask her to do such a thing, knowing how the hawk's flight, and more, its hunting, affected her. Another thought now came to him. 'Although, I do not like the danger. They have spears, these Grey Men. They may have arrows.'

'And why will they waste them on a hunting bird? Come, Geraint.' She shook his shoulder gently. 'This place does not know all our secrets.'

'Yet.'

They looked at each other for a long moment before Elen got to her feet and went to the perch. 'So we should make use of them while they are still ours.'

They stood there together, the grimly determined woman and the sullen bird, with their brown robes and their dangerous eyes.

'I cannot argue with this.' *Would there was an argument to make.* 'Let her fly then, and let us see.'

Outside, the morning was damp and grey with mist. Despite this, Geraint felt better in the fresh air. The doubt and brooding that had taken him since waking were easier to shake off. He was still himself, after all, and he knew wars and he knew the men who fought them. Elen stood beside him. He would do as he promised. A way would be found.

Despite the early hour, the yard was busy with animals and their folk, and all the noisy chaos of an overfull house. The great gate stood open. The walls were thick with men on watch. Four stood on guard at the gate. As Geraint and Elen approached, they raised their spears in sharp salute.

'I must ask where you are bound, my lord,' said the tallest of them. His cloak was clasped with silver rather than the bronze the others wore. 'It is not safe past the gate.'

'My lady's hawk must hunt or it will pine away. We will not go beyond the shadow of the walls.'

The man's face twitched nervously as he struggled with himself. Some order had been left with him, and he was unsure how closely to apply it to these guests.

'Let them pass,' said one of the bronze-clasped guards roughly. 'For Heaven's sake, Ren, let them go.'

Ren looked sharp at his fellow, but his pained face stilled and he nodded. Geraint and Elen passed between them. The pressure of her fingers against his said she also noted this strangeness and wondered about it. They both held their silence as they walked through the archway.

Once they were outside the walls, Calonnau stretched her neck towards the sky and gave her sharp, pleading cry. Elen loosened the jesses. The hawk beat her wings hard, taking to the air at once. The heaviness of the mist and clouds made no difference to her. She soared high, wheeling around, and, making her course over the fortress, she swiftly disappeared into the gloom.

Elen stared up at the sky for a long time after the bird was lost to sight. The wind rose, sliding between her and Geraint, bringing the mists with it to prickle their skins with cool and insidious damp.

'Will you stand near me?' murmured Elen at last.

Geraint moved closer, putting himself between her and the freshening wind. She was so cold.

'She is going to kill again. I do not want to be alone.'

He wrapped his arms around her, making himself a cloak for her shoulders. He felt her breathing, felt her ease herself closer to him. But there was no heartbeat. Her heart was as far away as her gaze, and that truth brought a deep and increasingly familiar sorrow. The stillness at her centre was an everpresent reminder of the wound he did not know how to heal, and of the things he had not yet said to her.

This place does not know all our secrets . . . Yet . . . So we should make use of them while we keep them . . . Or we should set them free.

She was not aware of him now. She had the wild hunger in her eyes that belonged wholly to the hawk. Her hands crooked and her head strained forward. He tightened his arms around her. Her hands grabbed him suddenly, her fingers digging deep into his flesh until he winced with the pain. Then, it was over, and she was back with him, her face tight with shame.

'It's getting worse, Geraint,' she whispered. 'I thought it would ease, but it's getting stronger.'

He had no answer. He could only stroke her hair and hold her close, and curse his helplessness. He would tear Morgaine apart with his bare hands for what she had done. He would slit Urien gut to gullet. He would do everything, and he could do nothing.

'We will finish this battle quickly. I will take you out of here and we will go to Merlin. There is a way to break this geas. There must be.'

'Yes.' She rested her hands against his chest, struggling to master herself again. 'You are right, of course.'

He waited. Gradually, she was able to lift her head and smile a little, to step away and stand alone. He let his arms fall to his sides. She was gazing into the distance again, seeing whatever it was Calonnau saw. Although he could have reached out and touched her easily, he felt as if she were a thousand miles away.

But she did return, her eyes focused on what was before them both, the slackness in her features replaced with her own vitality. 'I . . . she saw them. To the north.' She pointed to one of the ragged hills, black and white in the morning's mist. Geraint took note of its shape and where it stood among its fellows. 'They are moving towards that hill, coming in our direction. She just saw the valley beyond it. There were a dozen of the Grey Men, half those in the full-helms, half of the other kind.'

Half still living, half already dead. 'Thank you,' breathed Geraint. He did not want to acknowledge what must come next, but as with so much else on this darkening adventure, promises had removed choices. 'We must go at once if we are to have a hope of catching them.'

She nodded, biting her lip. He thought she was going to tell him to take care, to come back to her, but she just pulled him down and kissed him with a fierceness that spoke more clearly than words.

When she let him go, he strode away into the hall, and did not dare look back.

Elen was still standing in the shadow of the fortress walls when Geraint and his men rode out. They were twenty altogether. They looked better armed and more sternly martial to her eye than the men of Pont Cymryd would have, but less so than the ones from Arthur's court. She knew this from the rueful look Geraint gave her as he passed. She waved to him, blowing a kiss in imitation of the great ladies she had heard of in the songs and epics. He bowed gravely to her from the saddle, saluting with the spear he carried. Then, with harness and corslet jingling, he was past her, leading his men down the hill and through the earthworks, to find the enemy and set his plan in motion.

When they reached the level ground, Geraint raised his hand, making a motion as if casting a stone. His horse broke into a canter, and all those following him did the same. The sound of hooves was distant thunder. From her height, Elen could see nothing but the colours of the horses and helms, but she watched them as they flowed away from her, a living river along the valley floor. The hoofbeats had faded to a faint thudding like rain on a high roof by the time they reached the forest. The trees admitted the tiny band to their shelter, and they were gone from sight.

Elen rubbed her arms, but it did no good. She was cold, inside and outside. Still, she did not make any move to return to the yard, much less the hall. She lingered in the damp and mist. She could breathe out here. She could see the sky and the land beneath it. She could not let herself be closed up in stone again. Not yet.

She paced beside the walls, breathing the fresh air deeply. Calonnau was sated now, and settled in some distant tree, viewing the land with her sharp, predatory eyes. She would venture no further in the damp than she must. Elen found herself wishing the hawk would fly, so her mind could go with her. The illusion of freedom would be a fine thing now.

I am becoming used to this, she thought and worry settled heavily on her mind. *How soon before I forget the way I used to be?*

She did not know how long she stood there in the shadows, her mind swinging between that question and her fears for Geraint. She could order Calonnau to follow him, and watch where he went, but she was afraid of that as well. She feared the more she made use of the hawk, the closer they would grow, and the harder it would be to remember that she wanted to be free.

'Lady Elen.'

Elen jumped and turned. King Gwiffert stood beside her, a serving woman in tow. She carried a basket over her arm. The odour of fresh bread wafted from under its covering of rough cloth.

Elen swallowed, suddenly ravenously hungry. The king nodded to the servant. She came forward and held the basket out at arm's length to Elen with a respectful curtsey. Elen took it, and, grateful she did not have to watch Gwiffert watching her, she gave all her attention to investigating its contents. There was fresh, warm bread, broken open and spread thickly with new butter and honey. There were two winter apples, wrinkled and sweet, and a wedge of bright, white cheese.

'I hoped if you would not break bread in my hall, you would consent to eat in its shadow.'

Shame took hold. She could not have spoken disrespect more clearly than to have neglected to come to her host's board.

'I am sorry, Majesty. I was . . . much distracted.'

He nodded, hearing what she had not said. 'It is hard for one born in the open country to be so long in a house of stone.'

She smiled a little to hear her feelings so neatly described. 'Forgive me.'

'There is no need.' The king returned her smile. 'Perhaps you will do me the favour of breaking your fast with me now.'

'Gladly, Majesty.'

Playing the role of hostess, Elen shared out the contents of the basket. If the bread was a little coarse, it was good and filling, and took the edge off Elen's cold. The apples were sweet, the cheese mild and refreshing. When they were finished, she gave the basket back to the serving woman, whom the king dismissed with a glance. When she had scurried off out of earshot, he rested his spear against his shoulder and looked up at the leaden sky.

'Where is your hawk?'

'She goes to hunt, Sir,' Elen said, trying to sound as if this were an everyday matter. 'I cannot keep her sated with butchered meat for long.'

But despite her show of unconcern, Gwiffert's eyes grew sharp and knowing. 'Cannot keep yourself sated is what you mean, my lady,' he said softly.

Elen took an involuntary step backward. 'No.'

But he shook his head, dismissing the word and the obvious lie behind it. 'You are the one who longs for bloody death. And why not?' His words grew mocking now. 'In every pigeon, every rabbit, there is your enemy.'

'Your Majesty judges me unfairly.' But he did not. That was something she had not been able to tell even Geraint. When Calonnau killed, when she felt the delight of the bones and the blood, she also felt her revenge completed, each and every time.

'I too have eyes, sister.' A bright-edged chill filled King Gwiffert's voice. No answer came to her, save the painful tightening of her wounded throat. The wind blew hard, and it was thick with the smell of rain.

'You learn to take refuge in silence, as does your man,' muttered Gwiffert. 'How many sins such silence covers.'

He gripped the spear, his fist growing first red, then white. 'You are bound to that hawk, and yet you will not speak of it to me. You come to my hall and eat my bread and offer deception in return.' This was what lay behind his offer of food. He knew it would shame her all the more to hear this charge so soon after she had broken bread with him. It was a wonder he'd brought no salt.

'No, Majesty, it is not so.' *When did you learn this?* she wondered. *Why did you not speak last night?*

Where did your sight take you after I left you?

There was no way to ask any of these questions.

'Not so?' repeated the king, his voice heavy with sarcasm. 'Then why will you not speak of your nature?' The question was sharp, and the accusation deserved. The fate of King Gwiffert and his folk hung in her hands as well as Geraint's. He knew now that she was no natural thing, and that she had not told him so.

This place does not know all our secrets. Her own words came back to her and her cold deepened. *Was I wrong?* He had gifts of sight, this Little King. How much did he see? How well and how often?

But then, what man harbouring two strangers at such a time and such a place would not look to see what they were?

Around them, the mists were lifting. The sun's warmth penetrated the clouds, burning away the fog. Overhead, the guards called the all clear to each other. The king waited, twisting his spear where it rested on his shoulder, rolling it back and forth. Words came to Elen, slowly, haltingly. 'It is not a thing of which I may speak easily. It was nothing I sought, but was forced on me by my enemies.'

Gwiffert nodded slowly, his face still grim. Elen realized that he already knew this much. He had wanted to see if she would lie. 'And who are these enemies? You do not speak their names.'

'No.' *Why do I not? Why not proclaim them far and wide?* The answer came to her almost at once. *Because I do not want this man to know more of me than he must.*

But why? This time there was no answer. Her wrist hurt. Her throat hurt. Her head was beginning to ache.

She shook herself. The king was waiting. She had been revealed. Honesty was the only defence remaining. 'They are Urien the Bull and Morgaine the Sleepless, she who is also called Morgan the Fae.'

Surprise slackened Gwiffert's face. 'Morgaine? Morgaine did this to you?'

Elen nodded. 'And more. I beg you,' the pleading word

tasted strange on her tongue, but she spoke it regardless, 'do not ask me to tell you of that.'

'No . . . no . . .' he fell silent. 'Morgaine.' He whispered the name now. His hands turned the spear's shaft between them, twisting it tightly.

'What do you know of Morgaine?'

'What does anyone truly know of Morgaine?' he shrugged, straightening and returning the spear to the crook of his arm. 'I have seen her, and I have heard her. It is because I crossed her will that I am trapped here.'

'You crossed Morgaine?'

He laughed grimly. 'Oh yes. The first of my many mistakes.'

She waited, her tongue pressed tightly against her teeth. The noises from the yard seemed suddenly very loud. She wanted to ask, but she could not. She must wait. If he wished to tell her, he would. She could not question her host as to his shame. That bold she could not be.

The Little King kicked at the dirt with his boot heel, looking very young, even as he had standing in the moonlit garden. 'How should I tell this story?' he mused. 'Were I a bard, I would speak the tale of the coming of the king most fair. I would say that Morgaine came the night after he had helped raise his father's cairn and his hands were still raw from that work. A storm was rising, and she came. I would say he thought of ravens when he looked on her with her black cloak and black hair . . . She said to that young boy that his father had made a bargain with her. She said that he had sworn that on the day of his death, she would have a levy of certain treasures that had come from old Rome. For the protection she had given his house, she said, but she would not say what that protection was.' He scowled at the ground, seeing the sorceress as she stood before him then, perhaps; perhaps seeing himself as he stood before her. 'And I would say how that foolish boy denied her.'

Elen said nothing. Neither did Gwiffert for a long time. It occurred to Elen that he was retreating from that youth whom he had seen so clearly in his memory, trying to remember again that he was man and king. 'Oh yes, that new-made king was young and was lost in arrogance. Once he had spoken his folly, Morgaine said, "If you will not give it to me, you and all your house will vanish from the world."'

Vanish from the world. Into this other world with its own hills and valleys and Grey Men. 'This is her curse, then?'

'Her curse that brings the king to the Little Country.' He laughed once. 'Her allies, you see, are not of the mortal world. It was after she said this that Jago began his wars. Perhaps he was hers too.'

'Why so . . .' but the rest of the question died away. She had meant to ask, 'Why so terrible a vengeance for so small a thing? Why no bargain?' The flash of the sword's blade in the moonlight, the fury in Morgaine's eyes as she pronounced her sentence, these things were clear before her mind's eye. Why so terrible a vengeance for so small a thing? Because to Morgaine, no denial of her will would be a small thing.

'Do you fear us?' she asked, wrapping her cloak more closely around her. 'Now that you know we too come from Morgaine?'

'No more than before. If anything, it is good to know we have a common enemy.' He sighed. His fingers drummed the spear's shaft gently. 'And you need not fear me, sister,' he said, his words soft but steady. 'I made my promise to your man and I will keep it.'

The wind blew cool and heavy around them. Overhead, the sentries walked their narrow way. The faint shadow of the wall withdrew before the sun as it rose higher behind the clouds, and Gwiffert gazed down the green slope to the distant trees. Bees buzzed unconcerned among the clover flowers. Guards stood on watch while the men and women worked the terraced fields. All of them waited for the next attack and feared the direction from which it would come, including the king beside her.

'You will keep your promise, but you do not trust the one you gave it to,' said Elen, and she felt that this was the truth.

Gwiffert sighed. 'No,' he admitted. 'However much I want to. There are . . . there is . . .' he frowned. 'How long are you and your man married?' he asked abruptly.

Memory of her double-edged wedding ceremony warred with the sudden sight of green forest. Calonnau's view flashed brightly before her own. The hawk perched in a tree, waiting for the time when prey would be most active, waiting for the swallows and the finches to take to the wing so she could soar and strike. She saw nothing of Geraint from where she was, and did not care, however much Elen might.

'It is but days.' She licked her lips. *No. You don't need to say any more. He does not need to know.* But the king's eyes were narrowing. *Too late, Elen. He already suspects and he trusts little enough as it is.*

She wanted him to trust her. They needed true alliance with him. There were too many ways a war chief might see a man killed in a fight. It was not an honourable thing, but all the world knew it happened. 'It was done by Urien. I was given as an abducted bride, without my consent or my kin's . . . Geraint knew not the law when he took me so.'

'Urien wed you to this man,' said the king slowly, as if he did not fully understand what she had told him.

Elen nodded. 'Geraint was victor in a contest Urien staged, and I, to my shame, was the prize.'

Gwiffert considered this. In the distance, the little birds began to call from tall grass. Was she hearing with her own ears or with Calonnau's?

'Yet you esteem him,' said the king.

'I do, and more.' But the word love would not come to her lips. *What holds me back?*

'But he . . .' began Gwiffert. Whatever his thought might have been, he bit it off hard. His face was pinched, and growing white around the mouth with the effort to hold it back. 'No. Forgive me.'

'For what?' She tried to speak lightly, and in some measure succeeded.

'Doubt. Fear.' He clutched the wooden shaft of his spear, for what cold comfort its runes and its power brought. 'For living too much alone in too much danger.'

'You are surrounded by your people,' Elen reminded him, but the words sounded feather-light and frail.

He smiled sadly at this, and that sadness went straight through her, finding its echo within her. 'Sister, I am alone. There is none of my family here. These folk I shelter are strangers, brought here to serve the pleasure of their captor. I am very much alone.'

Mother, dead on the stones. Yestin, dead the gods only knew where. Madyn, dead in a stable. All the others scattered to the winds and the mercy of neighbours, and she here, trying to find a way to fight a war that might already have been lost. 'I understand.'

'Even though you have your husband?'

She bowed her head. 'Yes. Even so.' She had Geraint, and she had the goddess looking down from her high place, but standing here in the cold wind with the strange hall at her back, she knew it. It could never be the same as having mother and Yestin and the others she had known since birth, whose blood went back with hers to the time of Maius Smith and beyond.

'We are not meant to be alone, our people,' said Gwiffert softly, sadly. 'We are meant to be with our own blood, on our lands. We are weak when we are separated from these things.'

Weak. Truly. She felt that weakness. She had felt it ever since she left her own country. She wrapped her arms around herself, gripping her elbows, for there was no touch but her own she could turn to for comfort.

As she thought this, she also thought she felt a trickle of warmth from Gwiffert, and that thought was followed with the realization that he had a heartbeat about him, a distant pulse, a high, faint drumming. It was beneath his breathing, beneath his skin. Now that she felt it, she wanted to draw nearer to him, to feel that warmth drive away her cold, to rest against that heartbeat and let it echo through her hollow breast.

Elen swung her thoughts hard away, and her eyes suddenly saw the world blur green, black and brown, shadow and light, as Calonnau, disturbed by their mixed hungers, took wing.

'What is it?' asked the Little King.

There is no place for my mind to be, she thought for a wild frightened moment. She did not want it to be with Calonnau as she soared into the bright meadow, so alive with little birds calling to one another, each one prey. But nor did she want it back with this king, who was also a man, and whose heart called out to her emptiness.

But neither could she stand here silent. 'Calonnau is flying,' she said. 'She will hunt. Her hunting . . . it is not a pleasant thing.' *Another lie. It is far too pleasant. It fills all my emptiness, and I want it to do so.*

'Distract her then,' suggested King Gwiffert. 'Send her to look for Sir Geraint.'

There would be anger if she did this, and a clash of wills, and she was tired of it. It would, though, be better than standing next to this man and feeling his warmth and words beguiling her while she also felt that awful delight that came with the kill.

So she stretched out her mind, and Calonnau fought, as Elen had known she would, but the hawk turned from her flight across the meadow. She climbed higher, and higher yet, the wind bearing up her light body and outstretched wings. Was it this that made Elen feel her own hollowness so strongly? How could the hawk be so light while it bore the burden of her heart? Perhaps her heart was gone now, dissolved into the bird's wildness.

A ripple of movement crossed Calonnau's vision to the east. She turned into the wind, flapping her wings for more height, catching the warm currents, flying through the cold stillness. The cold within Elen became edged with pain, as if ice cut against her breast as the hawk flew further, and further yet.

She neared that ripple of movement. It spread out into a moving blot on the sloping meadow. She saw flashes of silver and bronze that became men running, frantic, like rabbits after a missed strike, but these did not scatter, they clustered ever more tightly together. She swooped low, and her ears, which were not so keen as her eyes, caught the shouts of men's hoarse voices and the ring of metal on metal.

Geraint had gone in search of the enemy, and he had found him.

She could make him out easily now, mounted on Donatus, for all the horses and their riders around him made a sea of grey and silver. He had ridden into the thick of battle. His spear was gone and he had his sword out to swing down at the nearest enemy. The other man threw up his shield to meet the blow, but staggered underneath it, and Geraint raised his sword again.

Something flashed across the battle, too fast for even Calonnau to see, and a man just behind Geraint fell, his mouth wide open as he screamed. Elen saw the strange, straight branch that had flown to strike him down, and she screamed.

'What is it?' demanded a man's voice. Gwiffert. The king stood beside her, but she could not see him. Flash! Again, the slender thread of swiftness cut across the battle, this one landing harmless and quivering in the dirt, trampled swiftly underfoot by the surging of men and horses. But the flash came again. Geraint turned suddenly, and it just missed him. She saw where they came from now. Two carts had been turned over to make a wall, and behind them two men in half-helms took aim with their bows. Each had a full quiver. Each could be profligate with his shooting. Neither paused in his work, but each nocked a fresh arrow into his string and loosed it again, and again men screamed.

'What do you see?'

'The battle . . . they have archers . . . They have arrows!' The Grey Men held Geraint's people where they were, they only had to keep them from moving forward, only had to keep the archers safe so they could pick the attackers off. A flash of speed across the boil of brown and white and silver, and a horse went down this time. Another. Calonnau shrieked and wheeled. The ravens were coming to ride the winds with her, and she did not care to meet the huge, black birds. She flapped her wings hard, struggling to leave.

Elen fought to hold the hawk where she was, but this fight she lost as she saw the great beaks and the wings longer than her own. They were birds that could fight if they must, and had no love of her kind, and there were so many of them . . . Elen let the hawk dive for cover in a copse of yew trees. The leaves screened the battle from her. The hawk did not care, but Elen's hands curled into talons in her frustration.

'Listen, listen!' Gwiffert's voice was right in her ear. She felt his breath on her skin, but she could not see him. All her straining was to see Geraint through the leaves and branches that hid Calonnau. She wanted to take to the wing again with all her heart, but the bird clung stubbornly to the limb beneath her. 'Listen, Elen! Would you turn the arrows?'

'Yes!' she shouted the word so loud and so hard, Calonnau cried out.

'Will it so! Call them from the sky! It is your power and your right!'

Elen stretched out her hands, hooked like claws. She saw the battle. She saw the blood running from the fallen men and beasts. She saw the flash of the arrows and she hated them. They should break, they should shatter. They should turn on their masters and bite their hands before they touched the one that was hers.

Even as she shaped the thought, she saw it come to pass. *Two* said the voice in her mind, but she paid it no heed. The arrows splintered in mid-air, the shards falling to earth as harmless as feathers in the wind. The enemy was stunned and in that precious instant, Geraint charged, barrelling Donatus through them to the makeshift wall and swinging his sword down hard. Geraint's men cheered and surged forward. Geraint turned Donatus in a tight circle, aiming for the men in half-helms, aiming for those who yet lived. He struck, and he struck again, and they fell, maimed from his blows.

But then they rose. Broken and bleeding they rose from the ground and she saw why he used his sword and held no spear. The spear was no good. No pierced heart would stop them, sealed to their master as they were with the terrible knot that branded their brows. They could not die. They must rise and fight on with their life's blood pouring down.

But they could not fight with tattered bodies, with useless arms and lolling heads. Men who should have lain down to

die, instead turned and ran. It was hideous. It was a nightmare beyond any she had yet seen. Those longer dead held
as they could, but they too fell before sword and knife.

The attackers were calling her husband's name, 'Geraint!
Geraint! The Round Table!' His grin was fierce as he pressed
forward with all his host behind him. Elen cried out in
triumph, the sight of the blood and the wounds bringing to
her all the warm, rich delight of hunting.

'They're running! He's broken them. They counted on the
arrows . . .'

'Follow them, Elen! Follow them and see where they go!'

Strong in her ecstasy, Elen thrust Calonnau from her
branch. The hawk screamed but could not resist, and she
soared above the trees. Let the ravens take the dead. Here
was living prey, here was warm blood, here was the hunt.
Soar high, see clear, see where the rabbits run, know you
are faster, you are fiercer, get ready, get ready, you will strike
soon . . .

'Speak, Elen! What do you see!'

'They run, they run . . .' She panted. She beat her wings.
She was woman and she was hawk, and Geraint was alive
and she had a hunt before her like no other and she was
filled with the glory of it. 'There's another in front of them
. . . He's in a chariot. He's huge . . . it's the Great King . . . it
must be . . .'

'Yes.' The last sound hissed hot against her ear, Gwiffert
was so close. She did not care. She was hungry. She wanted
to swoop, to strike.

'What now? What now?'

Not yet, they are not ready for taking. Not yet. Soon. 'He's turned,
his man drives the horses . . .' Her hawk's eyes blurred
strangely, and Calonnau hesitated, hovering on the air's
warm currents. There was pain in her breast, and it dulled
her delight, her hunger. 'I cannot see . . . it's too far . . .'

'You must see! You cannot lose him!'

No. Cannot. Geraint was below, his pace was slacking. His confusion she could see, but the giant, the Great King . . .

Calonnau, Elen, Calonnau, cried out in confusion, and soared high, until all the land below was a quilt of brown and green, the red of soil, the liquid silver of rivers and the stillness of stone. And there was only Geraint and his men, alone.

'No, he is gone. Vanished.' Elen sagged. The world was spinning. She hurt. How could she have lost what she hunted? She could not lose it. She must find it! 'There is nothing.'

'Damn you!' shouted Gwiffert to the sky. 'Damn you! Gods!' She was aware he shook his spear uselessly, even as she was aware that Calonnau circled and cried, and below, Geraint looked up to see the hawk. 'Why do you hide his name from me! If I had his name I could break that wall! I could see for myself!'

Name, name, name. Elen was weak and dizzy with her efforts, filled with pain and hate and the wild frustration of prey denied, escaping out of reach. *His name, give me his name. Mother, give me his name!*

And the voice answered, and it said *Rhyddid ap Carchar*. And it said, *three*.

Then it was gone, and Elen did not care. She had her prey. She would strike and she would know the warmth and the ferocious, filling wonder.

'Rhyddid,' she said. 'He is Rhyddid ap Carchar.'

Gwiffert threw back his head and he howled, a high, triumphant sound more wolf than man.

'Rhyddid!' he cried to shake the heavens. 'Rhyddid ap Carchar! Gwiffert pen Lleied calls you! You will reveal yourself to my eyes! Rhyddid, you have no more hiding place. I call you by your name Rhyddid ap Carchar, the Great King, and so you shall be known!' And he cast out his spear into the sky, high and straight, as if he meant to bring down the sun itself.

Elen saw the spear vanish into the grey sky, only to reappear in Gwiffert's hand.

Calonnau saw a hall, a long, low hall with a peaked roof, appear on a hillside, and she saw the ditches and the earthworks rippling on its green slopes. She saw the low, crude stone wall that ringed it.

Beside Elen, Gwiffert laughed, long and hard, full and open.

With the Little King's laughter filling her blood and bone, Elen crumpled to her knees.

NINETEEN

Geraint returned as the sun was setting, marching into the great hall with his helmet under his arm and Gwiffert's two captains behind him. The hall's inhabitants stopped their tasks and their talk and stood to watch them pass by. Elen was able to leave the table where she sat with the Little King and walk down from the dais to greet him with gladness and relief. He was bruised on his arms, and had a long, shallow slice over his right brow that was cleanly scabbed, but was otherwise unmarked. He saw at once, of course, how she tottered as she took the three steps, and how drawn her face was. His eyes filled with questions, and she tried to reassure him with the strong pressure of her hands as he bent to give her the chaste and courtly kiss that was a seemly greeting for a knight to give his lady while a king looked on. Calonnau was perched beside Elen's chair. Elen could feel her heart beat once more, and it dimmed her awareness of the other hearts nearby that had so troubled her before. She could reason again, and see with her own eyes, and she could hold herself more apart from the king.

'What news, Sir Geraint?' asked Gwiffert eagerly as

Geraint released Elen to return to her place at the king's left hand.

Geraint, standing with martial straightness at the foot of the dais, described the battle – how they had come across the enemy suddenly in the field, fresh with spoils from some village or hamlet. Geraint and his men charged in at once, but they were repulsed long enough for the archers to take up their positions. Geraint thought they might have to retreat, for try as they might, they could not surround or circle their enemy to reach the archers that were picking them off so swiftly.

'I heard the hawk above us, and then the arrows began to break. I had made it clear that my name and the Round Table were to be used as the battle cry. The Great King heard it. He knows who stands beside Your Majesty, and I believe it will plant the suspicion we need in him. Your men fought well and bravely, Majesty. They are to be much commended.'

'Be assured I know their worth well from today's work,' said the king warmly, looking to Rhys and Taggart who stayed diffidently behind Geraint. Like him, they were dirty and tired and spattered with blood. Unlike him they stood, solid and silent as stumps, accepting the praise, but taking no joy in it.

If Gwiffert saw this, he did not care. He leaned forward, and asked eagerly, 'And did you see it, Sir Geraint? The hall of the Great King?'.

'From a distance I saw, Majesty. It is hard by the valley where we found the Grey Men. It is no great fortress such as this, but more the home of an outland chief.'

Gwiffert grinned as he nodded his agreement. He stroked the spear lovingly. 'You were right in your counsel. It was the ability to remain unseen that was his defence. He has no other. We will be able to ride out and take him without trouble.'

'So it would seem,' answered Geraint carefully. 'We have not yet had the chance to survey his defences, nor do we know how many good fighters he has.'

King Gwiffert shrugged. 'Does it matter? Your plan succeeded. He knows you are here and he knows himself exposed. He will move fast. We must be faster.' The Little King's eyes gleamed. 'Even I know so much.'

Geraint made no answer to this. King Gwiffert beckoned him up to the dais and sat him at his right hand. The two captains he dismissed, and they went to their places down the hall. They sat there at the prepared tables with friends and fellows, and accepted the food set before them. Their voices joined the murmuring river that filled the hall, but no voice raised in cheer, none gasped in delighted surprise at the telling of brave tales of the battle just won.

What sort of king fails to give honour to his men? Elen's gaze flickered about the painted hall, as she fed Calonnau from her knife. She saw the bright paintings, the white mare, the black owl and the red boar all captured in the knotted ribbons of saffron and sapphire. She saw the living people, well-dressed and well-fed, some serving, some sitting and eating. Victory and freedom were promised – freedom from their long fear and confinement. And yet not one of these people cheered or raised a voice in song of praise.

Victory and freedom. Freedom. The word repeated itself in her mind, and yet she could not follow it up with any thought. It soared away like Calonnau on the wind.

She became aware, all at once, that both Geraint and Gwiffert were watching her. They had been deep in talk, and she had not heard a word, having been so far away in pursuit of her own elusive thoughts.

'I'm sorry, Sirs,' she said, quickly, reaching for her cup as if its touch would help attach her to the present moment. 'I did not hear the question.'

'No matter.' Gwiffert waved his knife, dismissing her words. 'A woman may be much distracted when her man goes to war. Perhaps you too fear what may come on the morrow?'

Elen looked to Geraint, bewildered. 'We ride out again tomorrow,' said Geraint quietly. 'I will ride beside His Majesty and we will together meet the Great King before he can make his preparations.'

'Tomorrow? Surely, it is too soon!' She needed time. Time to speak with Geraint, time to understand why her own thoughts scattered like mice. Wars took weeks to plan and to mount, even between small bands in the mountains.

'I do not think it is,' said Geraint softly. 'His Majesty has the right of it. We do not know how swiftly he can call on his Grey Men, or in what numbers. We must not give him time to make himself stronger, or to work some new enchantment.'

'You are right to be surprised, sister,' added Gwiffert, and the king was wistful as he gazed at his crowded hall. 'As it is, such smiths and armourers as I have will be working all night. In another place, there would be great loads of arms to ready, wagons to load with supplies, plans to lay, allies to court. Men would be called up from all corners of the land. But there is only us here. All the men we can call on are in this hall. All the arms we have are in the stores now.'

'Yes, of course.' Elen rubbed her brow. Geraint did not seem afraid at this prospect. Concerned, perhaps, with his careful mind running through calculations, implications and plans. Wishing for more time, even as she did. But he was not afraid. Why should she be? She was not trained to the sword, but she need not be idle either. It was her work that had turned the arrows from him today. She could do it again. The Great King would not last out the day against them. Then, the spear would be theirs and they would go home together and chase Urien from the West Lands. All was right. There was nothing wrong.

Her temples began to pound, adding another pain to the one in her throat. A stray draught brought the scent of cooked meat to her, and her belly heaved over suddenly. The smell was wrong, dead, rotted . . .

She felt herself begin to sway. Her head was too light and her body too heavy.

'Elen?' Geraint grasped her hand.

'I . . . I'm sorry, Sirs,' she whispered. She tried to stand, but only sat down again. 'I must retire. Sir, Majesty, would you . . .'

'Yes, yes. Let Sir Geraint aid you. I will lead you both.'

'Calonnau.' She stretched her hand out.

'I will bring her,' said the king. 'Let Sir Geraint . . .'

'No!' The words burst out as a shriek from Elen. 'Do not touch me!'

'Forgive her, Majesty,' said Geraint at once. 'It is her illness that makes her speak so.' With expert fingers he undid the jesses and set Calonnau on Elen's bandaged wrist. With Geraint supporting her, his arm strong underneath her elbow, and the king before them, Elen staggered from the hall. She clutched the hawk, setting the bird screeching and battering her wings, but she did not let go. Nor did she look up. She had thought she had seen a knowing smile on the Little King's face as he came behind them and she did not want to see it again

Her knees shook so violently she could barely walk. The paintings on the walls moved and pulsed with each wild beat of Calonnau's heart. The white mare galloped on the ribbon road, whickering urgently. The black owl dipped and wheeled. All the eyes, the living eyes and the painted eyes watched her go.

It seemed an age passed before she was in her little grove

again and Geraint laid her down on the narrow bed. The king leaned over her anxiously, and the pain in her head redoubled.

'Have you a healer, Majesty?' asked Geraint as he secured Calonnau on her perch. 'A physic of any kind?'

Gwiffert shook his head. 'None but an old midwife. I have some skill myself. Perhaps . . .'

The thought of him laying a hand on her turned Elen's stomach again. 'Please,' she whispered. 'Please, Sir, just . . . let me stay here, let Geraint stay with me. I will be well.' But even as the words came out, she found she was panting for breath. 'I will be well,' she insisted.

The king looked from Geraint to Elen and back again. 'Very well,' he said stiffly, and left them.

For a time, all Elen could do was lie on her side, panting. Geraint sat on the bed beside her. Behind him, the painted trees swayed before her eyes, tossed by a breeze she could not feel. She even heard a rustling, as if of leaves or small animals seeking their burrows. Calonnau lifted her head, turning this way and that, looking.

No. No. It is not true. Elen closed her eyes. *I must think of what is true.*

The wind was true. The heat and the hunt . . .

No.

'Geraint,' she whispered. 'Talk to me. Tell me . . . tell me of the battle today.'

'Elen, you are ill. It is not . . .'

'Geraint.' She clutched his hand. 'I need strong food for my mind. Please.'

So Geraint began to speak, slowly and softly. He did not speak of battle like a bard reciting an epic. He said nothing of glory, nor even of pride, although she was sure he felt that. From his words, she understood what it was to be in the thick of battle. She heard the clash of steel. She felt the heat and the confusion, and the struggle to keep wit, heart and soul all sound, while body only wanted to fight and flee if it could. She came to know what it was to wade through the small sea of men and beasts while all turned to mud and blood around you.

These things were grim and they were hard, but they were true, and they had nothing to do with the paintings around her, or the Little King. Gradually, they drew her out of herself, making it safe again to see and to turn her thoughts to other matters. The sickness in her ebbed and drained away, and she was able to sit up on her own, with only a mild thirst to remind her of what had happened.

'Thank you,' she said to Geraint.

'Elen . . .' he had spoken steadily before, but now he hesitated. 'Is it possible you are with child?'

She laid her hand across her belly. 'I fear not,' she said. 'But even if . . . even if I could quicken after what I've become, it would be weeks before the sickness came over me.'

For one of the very few times since she had first seen him, Geraint seemed at a loss. 'What then?'

'I don't know.' She pushed her hair back from her face. 'I wish before all the gods I did.'

Geraint sat in silence for a long moment, studying her, searching for what? She did not know. 'We must get you away from here,' he said at last.

It was true. She knew it was true. She wanted to flee from these walls, to fly over the mountains that stood like enemy guards and find the hills she knew. At the same time, it was impossible. 'How? We cannot leave without the spear, even if we knew the road. The only way out is through the Great King.'

'Then that is the road we will take,' said Geraint grimly.

'You are not sure.'

He shook his head. 'I am not the leader my brother is,
nor the planner Agravain is . . . it is my job to order the men,
not to rally them. I ride beside them, and sometimes behind
them. This has taught me some things.' He paused, considering his next words. 'I know how men are when they have
been pressed into battle. They may understand that the war
is their king's but they do not see it as theirs, for it's not their
borders or cattle that are threatened.'

Elen nodded. The greatest argument she had heard against
Arthur was that he would demand men to fight in distant
wars that had nothing to do with Pont Cymryd or her people.

'Such men generally fight well enough. They want to live
after all, but there's no . . .' he waved his empty hands.
'There's none of the heart in it, the bright bravery of men
fighting for their homes and the lives of their families. I would
rather face the legions of old Rome than a man fighting for
his own wife and children.'

'So will these men fight,' said Elen, but she watched him
while he spoke and saw only doubt. 'These husbands have
their families in these walls.'

He nodded. 'Yes, and they all fought well today, but they
did not fight like men with everything to gain. Rather they
were like men with nothing left to lose.'

She thought about this, trying to understand the difference. Calonnau was hungry. The bird's need pushed at her
mind making it hard to concentrate. 'They have been under
siege a long time.'

Geraint's eyes narrowed, looking to a memory. 'Today, I
saw a man . . . he was an older man, not a raw boy. He had
scars . . . Dai, I think he was called. I swear to you he all but
ran onto a Grey Man's sword.' Geraint was confused and
angry as he spoke of it. 'I have seen such things before. Men
will sometimes seek death in battle when death is better than
facing what lies behind them.'

'What does it mean?'

Geraint scrubbed the back of his neck, trying to rub out his impatience. 'I don't yet know, but I am uneasy with this war.'

'Do you fear the Great King?'

Geraint shook his head, contempt overtaking all other feeling in him. 'He is a king without honour. His men, his people, whatever they may be, fought, and he stood behind all and watched. No king, not the lowest chief with four barbarians in his train, would behave so. Now that we know where he goes to ground, we will take him easily, however many of his dead rise to fight for him.' He paused again, thoughts running ahead to the battle to come. 'The terror of them . . . how great can it be? They are unnatural things, and it would give a sane soul nightmares to see them rise up when a mortal man should lie still and wait for Judgement . . . but they can be made to flee before warriors who hold their ground and they do not become whole again when they are broken, at least, not at once . . . how was this not discovered before? After all these years, how are their weaknesses not known?

'I do not like this place,' he said abruptly before Elen could think of any useful answer. 'I do not like this blanket of magic that smothers us. I do not like that there is so much that I cannot *see*.' His fist pounded angrily against his thigh. 'Magic binds you to a wild beast. Magic freed us, magic brought us here, magic directs how we fight this fight. There is a serpent in the darkness. I know it is there and I cannot *see* it!'

'We are neither one of us seeing clearly,' said Elen softly, and this also was true. Calonnau scolded and muttered, dancing on her perch, stretching out her neck. Elen held out a hand to stroke the bird, and only got her fingers snapped at.

'What is it?' asked Geraint, but Elen was not sure whether he referred to what she had said, or to what so agitated Calonnau.

A mouse in the room, perhaps. She shook her head. *Think. What are you trying to say?* Geraint was waiting for her, waiting for her counsel or at least her tale. So she told him what had happened that day; how the Little King had stood beside her and helped her send out her will to shatter the arrows, and how she had used the last of the gifts her mother had bestowed to give him the name of the Great King.

'The name of his enemy gave him great power,' she said. Calonnau's hunger burned. Something rustled. Calonnau wanted to be free, to strike. There was a mouse and she could not get the presence of it out of her mind. It took all the strength she had to remember what she had done. 'He all but wept before I gave it . . . and it broke the barrier between them. Now we know Rhyddid's weakness. Now we may defeat him, and free those so long imprisoned here, but . . . what is not right?' There was a mouse. The mouse was not right. *No. Stop.* 'It is as if we were in a guessing game and asking all the wrong questions.' She rubbed her forehead. 'I am sorry, Geraint . . . I'm tired . . . what was done today was hard.'

He gathered her to him, and they held each other for a time. She drew in his warmth. The beat of his heart made a deep, strong note beneath the high flutter that was her own locked within the restless Calonnau.

Endure, he told her silently. *Endure. We will find a way.*

Yes, she answered with all the strength she had left. *Yes, we will.*

Much later Gwiffert strolled about his fortress's yard. The torches on the walls and beside the doorways blazed brightly. Boys trotted between them with baskets of freshly pitched

branches and tallow-dipped rush lights to replace those that
had burnt out. The sound of the armourers' hammers rang
through the darkness. Men ran to and fro, readying what
was needed for the battle to come. The air was filled with
the scent of fires. The smoke spiralled up towards the waning
moon like an offering to the night's gods. His men would be
tired in the morning, but they would fight just the same.

Gwiffert sighed with satisfaction. It was almost done. Soon,
the one family who had been able to defy him in his own
lands would be gone. He had the name now. Geraint would
lead the fight, and he would die, and Elen . . . What would
Elen do? That was a question. He pursed his lips thought-
fully. It would be a shame to throw away such power, especially when Morgaine desired so keenly that he do so.

Gwiffert left his men to their work. They knew his eye
was on them, whether he stood beside them or not. He passed
through his doors and his great hall, into the painted corridors that led to his private courtyard. There, beside the round
pool, waited Llygoden, already in the shape of a man. It was
not possible to wear disguises before Gwiffert in this place,
which was one of the reasons he chose it for such meetings.

'So, Llygoden.' Gwiffert rested his spear on his shoulder.
'What did our true lovers have to say tonight?'

The mouse-king spoke, repeating all he had overheard.
Gwiffert smiled, and kept smiling, as a man who is pleased
with his children. 'Well. She is clever, that little girl, and her
clever eyes do not like the glamour about her. I see I will
have to give her something else to think on, and that soon.'

Llygoden drew his lips back, just a little, showing his white,
sharp teeth. 'You harbour a serpent in your hall, King
Gwiffert. You should take care.'

'Ah!' Gwiffert raised one finger as if to emphasize his point.
'But serpents may have their teeth drawn, is that not so, my
mouse?'

'So they may,' said Llygoden slowly, looking him straight in the eye. 'It should be done quickly before they become wise enough to grow afraid.'

Gwiffert suffered this insolence. 'Go speak to your people, Llygoden. Bring them home and tell them to stand ready. I may soon have need of them.'

Llygoden knelt, bowing his head without the least sense of deference in the gesture. Then, he stood and crossed the threshold from the court to the hall. As soon as his foot touched the flagstones, he was mouse again, scampering away into the darkness.

Gwiffert clicked his tongue against his teeth. *I think, Llygoden, I have allowed you too much freedom. I think you need some loss to make you properly humble. Well, it may be the little girl will solve that problem also before she dies. If not, Blodwen can easily make up for the lack.*

Gwiffert rose, and walked down his corridors, readying the path for Elen. She must not, after all, be made late for their tryst.

Ching-ching.

The beating of hammer against metal wormed into Elen's mind, burrowing through the layers of sleep that sheltered her, making them soft and fragile until they came apart around her.

Ching-ching.

Her eyes fluttered open. She was alone in the dark. The air around her was stale and warm. She had woken so gently that Calonnau barely stirred on her perch.

Ching-ching.

It is the armourers, she told herself. *He said they would work the night through. Geraint has gone to make sure of them. That is all.*

But even as she thought this, she knew it was not true.

This was a lighter sound, more delicate. A sound that should not have penetrated the stone walls.

Ching-ching.

She knew what it was. The smith was out there, with his ravaged face and his blind eyes. Elen huddled in on herself and tried to stop her ears. It did no good. The sound was as insistent, as compelling as a heartbeat when Calonnau was away from her. It filled her mind and echoed in her blood. It was meaningless, and yet full of meaning. It passed unheeding over her, and it called directly to her.

Let me be, let me be, she pleaded, squeezing her eyes tightly shut. *It is too much. I do not want any more. I want to sleep. I want to be gone from here.* Her cowardice shamed her, but she could not push it away.

Ching-ching.

'Elen.'

Elen pushed herself upright. She heard it again, a man's voice, too far away to be recognizable, and yet what it said was clear. 'Elen.'

Fear left her, replaced by urgency. She did not stop for questions. Elen threw back the bedcovers. She wasted no time with the rush light. She fed the brazier until its flames leapt up, then wrapped her hand in the sleeve of her under-dress and lifted the brass basin high to light her way. She left her door open wide behind her, so she would know it again when she came to it. Calonnau slept on behind her, distant in her dreaming. These noises were nothing to her.

Out in the hall, she hesitated. Was it the smith himself who called? Should she go towards that sound? What if it was Geraint? She did not see him anywhere. What if it was only nightmare?

Go back, go back, she tried to tell herself. But she was weary of mysteries. Elen gritted her teeth, turned to the left and hurried on.

Her hand grew warm from holding the brazier, but the good cloth kept her skin from burning. The paintings flickered in its orange light, and again she was surrounded by monsters – the half-horse, the many-headed snake, the dragons. Again she had the sensation of moving downward, deeper under the earth, although the floor was flat and level. The air grew heavier, colder. She smelled loam and mould, as if she were in an ancient forest. The hammer's sound still led her onward, down further. The paintings around her became dim from grime and smoke. Where was the owner of the voice? Who called her from such a distance? The paintings were harder to make out behind their curtain of age. All she could see clearly were the eyes – the white men's eyes, the yellow beasts' eyes, the red eyes of monsters. Here and there she saw a horn or a hand, but the further she went, the more obscure all became.

Then she heard a new sound, like flowing water. She paused between one step and the next. Was it a river? Was she so deep down that she could hear the spring that mothered the well in the yard? No . . . no . . . it was not only water . . . it was weeping. Someone lost in this darkness was weeping.

Elen turned towards the sound, down a narrow corridor to her left. The walls were painted with scenes of priests at sacrifice, and the blood shimmered red in the brazier light. The weeping grew louder, as did the sound of the flowing water.

Ahead waited the open door. She had expected that. This place had its patterns. Elen pushed the door back and raised the brazier high.

It was a storeroom, filled with great ewers made of white clay, gaily painted with scenes of feasts and harvests, and every one of them open. In their midst stood a woman with long brown hair hanging over her shoulders. Her dress was loose, but not so loose that Elen could miss the fact that she was great with child.

The woman held a red clay jug in her hand. From it she poured white milk into a ewer that stood as high as her waist. Mice, small, quick and brown, scurried without fear around her feet. One even clung to her skirt. She looked up at Elen, and her face was streaked with tears.

She poured the milk out in an endless stream, and the jug did not empty, but neither did the ewer seem to fill.

'It should have fed my child,' she said to Elen. 'How will I feed my child?'

As if in answer to her distress, the mice swarmed around her. They crawled up her skirts and into her sleeves, over her shoulders and under her hair, dozens upon dozens of them, and every one had white hands.

Elen could not bear it. She backed away, to her shame, and she turned to escape the sight of the woman and the mice, and the wrongness of it all.

I should not have tried . . . Get away, get out. Find the courtyard. Yes. Find the courtyard. See the moon and stars. Feel the air. Yes.

Elen held tight to that thought as she hurried along the corridors. She did not dare run for fear of putting out the brazier. The idea of being trapped here with no light, knowing the painted eyes were all around her but not being able to see that they were only painted . . . no.

She passed doors on the left and the right. Again she wondered what was in them. Did each room hold its own nightmare? Its own strange vision and prisoner?

How can this be? How can any of this be? This place was said to be a haven for those stolen away by their enemy. How can it hold such darkness?

But even as she thought this, the air around her lightened. The paintings became newer and more familiar. The walls seemed to widen, letting in more air, allowing her to breathe more easily. She could pause and take her bearings, and listen.

The smith's hammering was gone. When had it left her? When she turned to follow the weeping? But the man's voice had returned.

'Elen.'

She turned. Down the right-hand way, she saw the silver-banded door, and through it, the garden. She went to it gratefully, stepping out into the open air like a child coming home. There, across the pond, stood King Gwiffert.

'Elen,' he said. His blue eyes glowed in the moonlight. 'You heard me. I hoped you would.'

'Majesty . . .' She shook herself, trying to cast off the new nightmares she had seen. She set the brazier down on the cool grass beside the doorway. Its light was almost gone. In another few moments, there would be nothing left but the moon. 'It was you who called?'

'Yes,' he nodded once. He rested his spear on his shoulder. 'I was afraid when you took so long.' The words made him sound very young. His skin was white and smooth under the light of the moon that was just past full. He was a slight man, in truth. It was only his labours that made him otherwise.

'I was . . .' she wanted to tell him, and yet she did not. In another place, she would have wondered if he would believe her, but not here, and yet, she held her tongue. *Why should he not know of the smith and the woman, and that they drowned out his voice? Why?*

She opened her mouth to speak, but she saw him watching her with such an air of weariness that these other thoughts fled her. 'What is the matter?'

'It . . .' The king sighed, twisting the spear. He swung it down, and lay it in his arm. With this, he seemed to reach some decision. He walked forward until he stood beside her.

She felt his heart, and it beat quickly. He was afraid. 'You know I have some gifts of sight? I told you this.'

'Yes.'

'You know also that such gifts are double-edged. They can show both more and less than what one asked to see.'

'Have you had a portent?' Pain stabbed sharp at the base of her throat. 'Have you seen your death?' *Is that what makes your heart beat so fast?* She wanted to lean closer, to understand its rhythm better.

'I wish it was only that.' The king looked out at his garden for a time. The peaceful, green scents of the summer night were mixed with the distant smell of smoke from the busy forges. 'It might be a relief after all this time, if I knew my enemy would die with me.' This cold hope Elen could well understand. 'But no . . .' Gwiffert's attention shifted outward again, and she felt the weight of his gaze on her. 'It was . . . it concerns you.'

'How?' Elen took a step back. What more could come down upon her?

'I thought long . . .' The king rested the butt of his spear on his boot's toe and turned it in his hands. Even in the moonlight, she could see how the leather was scuffed and worn from the many times he had made the gesture. 'I do not wish to bring you yet more pain.' He looked up, his eyes bright, and he stretched out one long hand towards her. 'But I could not see you so bound to your enemy.'

Elen felt the cold creeping over her, the cold that came with fear and confusion. Her blood settled more heavily in her, making mind and soul slow and chilled. 'What is this?'

He let his hand drop to grip his spear again. 'Geraint.'

It took Elen a long moment to understand whose name he had spoken. When she finally did, she laughed, a harsh, sharp sound. 'You say Geraint is my enemy?' She covered her mouth, and tried to compose herself. Relief made her weak and foolish. 'Sir, you are wrong in this. You have mis-understood what you have seen.'

But the king remained absolutely sober. 'Elen . . .' Gwiffert straightened his shoulders. He spoke slowly, dropping each word like a stone between them. 'Geraint, the son of Lot Luwddoc, is kin to Morgan the Fae. His mother Morgause is Morgaine's sister, her twin.'

Elen stared. Her eyes blinked quickly, as if trying to clear themselves of some mote or splinter. Geraint? Kin to Morgaine? No. It was not possible. It was not. Morgaine was the one who had stood over her with the sword and torn her living heart from her. Morgaine was the one who raised up Urien when he should have lain dead on the stones. Geraint had lent her arm, wit and blood when Elen was in thrall to her enemies. Geraint brought hope and help to her conquered people. Geraint had lain beside her at night and given her the safe haven of his arms.

'It is Morgaine's blood that flows through Geraint,' said the king.

Elen shook her head violently. She wanted to clap her hands over her ears like a child being told unwanted news. 'It cannot be. He is nephew to Arthur, he . . .'

'Yes.' That single word cut off all her protestations. 'It is Morgaine's kindred that sits on the high throne and seeks to rule the land over.'

Elen could not stand still anymore. She turned and ran from the king, even as she had run from the weeping woman. She ran to the doorway, and saw only darkness through it. Nightmares waited in there, but nightmares waited here as well.

She gripped the cold stone of the lintel as if she could break it with her fingers. 'If this is true . . .' she turned her head so she would not have to look into the dark mouth of the doorway. 'If he . . . they . . . are Morgaine's kindred, why would Urien try to rise up against them? He is Morgaine's.'

Gwiffert's laugh was grim. 'What could be better? He keeps the secret of their alliance, and he conquers and holds those lands Arthur cannot. He brings to him those men who will not go to Arthur. Then, once all the island is shared out between these two, she rises up to rule her brother and her lover.'

A deep plan, twisted and dark, just what Morgaine would do. It could be worked with glamour and with secrets. It could all be held behind her black eyes and pressed forward with her disguises. Oh, yes. Elen felt certainty like a knife against her skin, waiting to cut deeper. It was very much something Morgaine the Sleepless would do.

But not Geraint. Never Geraint. 'No.' She struggled to bring order to her thoughts. 'Arthur has honour. It is all that is said of him.' Mother had believed in Arthur's honour. So had Yestin.

'Arthur's bards speak of his honour,' said Gwiffert softly. 'And Arthur's kin.'

Elen looked at her hand where it gripped the edge of the stones. Her fingers were crooked, like Calonnau's talons. She felt weak, as weak and as sick as she had felt in the great hall, but there was no one here to help bear her away, save the king who told her these horrors.

Slowly, as if she had become an old woman, she turned to face him. 'Why tell me this now?'

Gwiffert took one step towards her, then another. He breathed like a man who expects each breath to be his last. His heart drummed hard. She felt it beneath her skin. 'Because I cannot bear to see you with him anymore,' whispered the king. 'Because I cannot watch you love one who is so close to your enemy.'

'He is not.' She spoke the words deliberately, making each

one strong. She must be strong. She must hold fast. This could not be. She would not allow it to be.

Gwiffert moved closer. The moonlight showed her his wide, slanting eyes, and they were sad, but there was anger in them. 'Then why did he not tell you who he is?'

'For shame.' She could barely speak. Her throat was a knot of pain. But if it were true . . . but it could not be true. But then did Gwiffert lie? She looked deep into his eyes, and she could find no lie there.

He touched her, laying his hand lightly on her sleeve. 'You say these things because you are proud. Too proud to admit you have lain down with your enemy.'

Gods. Gods all. Could it be true? Elen shuddered. She had stood before Morgaine and seen the sorceress's true visage. She remembered the face clearly, the black hair, the burning eyes, so sharp and watchful, even when she wore the guise of a crone. Those eyes took in each detail, barely blinking, never straying, knife-bright and knife-keen.

Did Geraint have Morgaine's eyes?

No. Gwiffert was wrong. It could not be as he said. But she could not think why. All she could see were Morgaine's black eyes, and Geraint's blue ones, and all became tangled in dream and nightmare whirling together in her mind until she could see nothing at all.

'Elen.' Gwiffert's hand tightened where he held her. 'I am sorry.'

'It cannot be as you say.' She forced the words out, her voice harsh as any crow's.

'Why not? Why else would she have made you so strong?'

'Strong?' *I am not strong. If I were strong I would move from this spot. I would fly. I would know what the truth is. If I were strong, I would not be so afraid.*

'You are deathless, Elen. I've seen that proved in battle. You can reach your will to wherever the hawk flies.'

Gwiffert laid his hand on her cheek, on her shoulder. 'Why would she make you so strong if she had not meant to use you?'

His touch was warm. It soothed her. She felt his heartbeat through his hand, steadying her, filling her emptiness. She took a step closer to him. She was so cold, so still. She wanted to feel living warmth. She needed it. She was afraid, and fear left her cold as the grave.

'Elen,' breathed the king, and his breath was sweet with life. 'Elen, you deserve so much more than this.'

His heart was very loud now, very near. She could reach out and lay her palm over it. It was almost as if it was within her, as if she were strong and whole. His mouth brushed her brow. Warmth. Life to overwhelm the despair. She wanted . . . she wanted . . .

She moved closer. She tipped her mouth up and looked in his bright blue eyes.

And saw the hawk and the spear and memory of her dreams flooded her, sending her stumbling backward into the darkened threshold. 'No!' she croaked. 'No,' she said. She looked at the Little King, wreathed in moonlight, his expression that of a young man wounded in love.

No. Why? Why? 'I will not betray,' she said, drawing herself up. *Remember who you are. Whose daughter, whose hope.* 'Not even for this.'

'What betrayal?' Gwiffert flung his empty hand out. 'He is blood of your enemy. Do you think Morgaine the all-seeing did not know it was his path she set you in the middle of?' Anger poured from him. 'What will you do with this man of yours?' he demanded. 'Take him back and set him up in your cantrev as lord? Morgaine's nephew as lord of Pont Cymryd and its bridge?' He moved closer to her, coming into the shadows with her. 'She cannot lose. Either her lover or her kin will hold your lands over your mother's body.'

'I am his wife, whether I willed it at first or no. It is law and I will not break it.'

'What do you care?' cried the king. 'You do not need him. I can bring you vengeance.' He was so close now, coming to her like a lover. He feared for her, he was as sorrowful at her obstinacy as he was angry. 'It is I who hold your enemy's death in my hand. I will help you, Elen. I will do it for your own sake, not for land or kin or honour or any of these lesser things. For you alone.' It would be so easy. Her heart and Geraint were so far away, and both had already played her so false.

But an older, deeper need held her firm. 'It is my honour,' she said. 'It is the honour of my family, though they lie dead beneath the ground.' She drew herself up. She was so cold, but at least in this she was sure. 'If I break the law, it is them I shame, and I will not do it.'

Gwiffert's gaze sharpened, love and longing falling away. 'Then what will you do, Elen? In the face of all you know now, what will you do?'

What will I do? What can I? Honour. Honesty. Those are all I have left. 'I will tell him what I know. I will hear what he has to say.'

The king shook his head slowly, without taking his gaze from her. 'He will lie, Elen.'

'Then I will know him for what he is.' She turned, facing the black corridors. 'If he has come to me in deception, I owe him nothing.'

She stood there, trying to root herself in those words, trying not to think how it would be if everything Geraint had said was born from the lie of his blood, and realizing, absurdly, she could go nowhere, because she could not see.

Warmth touched her skin. She turned her head a little. Gwiffert stood behind her, holding out a tin lantern in which a tallow candle burned.

She accepted the light silently, and alone she walked down the corridors, heading for the great hall, taking all she knew and all she felt to Geraint. With each step she heard the same words in her mind.

He will lie. He will lie.

Until at last those words entered her blood, and she no longer remembered they had not come from her.

Behind her, the Little King breathed, 'Go with her my mouse. It is not good that the lady should be alone at such a time.'

The grass rustled in response and grew still, and Gwiffert looked into the shadows, and smiled.

TWENTY

The fires burned high in the great hall, washing out the shadows in a flood of red and gold light, and making all the paintings dance in the flicker of the flames. Women scurried to and fro, carrying crocks and blankets, canvas bundles and leather sacks. No one slept this night. No one would. There was all the work of war to do.

She knew these things only distantly. What was most clear to her was that Geraint was not there.

Nor would he be. He will be where the captains are.

Moving like one half-asleep, Elen drifted to the great doors. She had to find him. She had to hear what lie he would tell her. She had to know what she had truly done when she had told him she would be his wife.

The yard was at least as busy as the hall. Horses and ponies were being led from the stables and examined by soldiers and stable hands alike for soundness. Harnesses were being shaken out and mended where needed. Everywhere were the shouts of voices, the reek of fires, the ringing of hammers.

Hammers within, hammers without. Elen held back a wild giggle. *Only I am silent. Only Geraint and me.*

Even through the crowd and the uncertain light of torches and lanterns, she found him easily. She knew him so well now, how he looked, how he stood, how he spoke. All his disguise to hide the blood within him, she knew it perfectly.

He stood in the middle of a crowd of men in plain tunics and breeches. One of them was holding up a wooden tablet, showing him some tally or the other written on its wax face. He did not look tired. He looked strong and in his place, surrounded by the racket of armourers, horses, men, and weapons. Every inch the knight, the man of war. Every inch the commander, seeing to all the details . . . letting nothing escape his eye.

His eyes, his storm-blue eyes. Was it those eyes she saw in her dreams, those eyes that brought her death? She swayed on her feet. She had to see him now. She had to look into those eyes and see Morgaine there.

But it was Geraint who moved. He looked up from the tally book he was being shown, touched the man on the shoulder and left him, coming swiftly to where she stood before the oak doors.

'Elen, what is it?'

How could she even speak? He was so close. She felt his heart shuddering through her frame, the heart of Morgaine's kindred, the reason she was enslaved and half-mad. He stood before her, the husband made hers by stealth and violence.

'Tell me, Elen.'

He will lie.

Then I will know.

She did not want to know that. She wanted to believe. She did not want to know she had given herself to her enemy.

But she was a chief and the daughter of chiefs and such cowardice was no refuge for her.

'I know who you are,' she whispered. Her throat was too tight, too pained to force out any stronger sound.

He made no answer, only watched her. Slowly, the meaning of her words sank into him. She saw understanding form in his eyes, in the way his face moved and reshaped itself, passing from anxious, to grim, to sorrowful.

She expected him to turn away, to look towards the work of the war he meant to wage – for Gwiffert, for her, he said – but really for his kindred. He did not turn. His gaze barely flickered. 'Who told you this?' he asked.

'It does not matter.' Was that itself a lie? Elen found she was not sure.

'No.' Geraint sighed. 'All that matters is that it was not myself.' Now he did hang his head. Now he rubbed his eyes. 'I'm sorry, Elen. I should have told you before we ever made our vows to each other. It was cowardly and I cannot undo that.'

Elen stared at him. He could not have understood her. She must be mistaken in her understanding of what he was saying now. He was thinking up his lie, delaying her with his apology. He could not be admitting to such a thing. He had lied. He must lie. He would lie. She was sure of it. With the blood that surged within him, there was no other way for him to be.

For a moment, Geraint watched the ebb and flow of work around them. He seemed satisfied with what he saw, or perhaps he was only satisfied that no one was paying the least attention to what he said, save for Elen.

'Growing up, I did not know Morgaine, except by name, and that I only heard of once, from whispers between my mother and father that I was not supposed to hear. Three days later, my mother was gone.'

Elen could not speak. Bewilderment turned cold flesh to stone. She had been ready only for denial and a smooth and earnest lie.

He stood there, his hands dangling loose at his sides as if they were dead and useless. 'If I knew how it could be done, I would kill her.'

'Noble sentiment.' Elen had meant the words to be mocking, but they sounded fearful. Here came the lie. He could not deny the kinship, so he must deny the closeness of their bond.

'It is vengeance.'

Vengeance. The word rang in her. She had wanted so much revenge. She pined for it like she pined for her missing heartbeat. 'What has she done to you?'

It was a long moment before Geraint could speak, and when he did, his voice trembled and cracked, as if he had never spoken such words before, and now they came hard. 'My mother and my sister are dead because of her. And what she has done to my father . . .' He looked to her again and she saw such deep fury and despair in his eyes it seemed to her she must be seeing to the pit of his soul.

It is only show, it must be show, part of her insisted.

'I do not know all the tale,' he said, his words breathy, tremulous. 'I do know that before I was born, Morgaine was imprisoned. My mother, Morgause, saw Morgaine her sister had grown mad with years and grief and rage. Morgause enlisted Merlin's aid to set her sister apart from the world of men, where she might not cause harm. Guinevere too had a hand in it, though this was before she became the High Queen. Together they thought her fast bound, but there came a day when she escaped their snare.

'I was a boy when that happened. I knew nothing then. I only knew my mother was leaving us. She called all five of us to her: my brothers, my sister Tania, and myself. Her eyes were red with weeping. She spoke of duty . . . I . . . I do not remember what she said . . . she hugged us, urging us to take care of each other and our father until she returned.'

He stopped. His eyes shone. The tears threatened to spill, but they did not.

'But she did not return.' His voice went flat and dead, as if the only way he could speak now was to hold himself apart from the words. 'No one spoke of what had happened to her. I don't believe anyone truly knew, not even my father. She had been sun and moon to him. He . . . he grew alone and solitary. Sometimes he roamed our hall at night. Sometimes we heard him talking and waiting for answers.

'I spoke to you of his madness? This is where it began. He imagined slights. He raged for no reason. My sister especially felt the brunt of his meaningless rage. We thought it was because she was a woman, and the woman who meant the most to him was gone. We were wrong. Oh, God on High, we were so wrong.' What did he see now? He did not see her. He did not, in the manner of a liar, look to see how well she was believing. He saw the inside of his own heart, saw the memories and the feelings kept so closely there. 'We all tried to shield her, even little Gareth, but it did no good, for at the same time we could none of us fully believe what our father was becoming.

'Then . . . Tania . . . there was a man . . . as I told you . . . Father threw her down . . .' He stopped and Elen knew this time he would not go on with the thought. He did not need to. He had told her that first night in this cursed land. Tania his sister was long dead at her own father's hand.

'That was when Gawain left. He tried to take us younger ones with him, but Agravain would not permit it. They quarrelled badly, but Gawain still left. Once he was gone, Father only grew worse, and I began to fear sleep for the nightmares it brought. I too began to wander the hall.'

She thought she could see him as he was then, a thin and lonely boy in a hall of stone and dirt, directing his footsteps by the patches of moonlight that shone through the high and narrow windows, ready to brave the dark and all it held, because it could not be worse than what he held inside his soul.

'Then one night, not very long after Gawain had left, I woke, and I heard my father's voice. He was in tears, pleading. I could not understand what he said. I was little more than a boy, and like a boy, I got up from my bed to look.

'In the great hall I saw my father on his knees. He was grasping the hem of a woman's skirt, and that woman was laughing at him, mocking him. At first, I thought she was my mother. She looked like her. But when she turned and she looked at me, her eyes were black. My mother had blue eyes.'

Like mine. But he did not say that. There was no need.

'Since Gawain was gone, I told Agravain what I had seen. That took some doing.' For the first time since he had begun his tale, the ghost of a smile passed across his face. 'Agravain too had grown cold, and I thought he would mock me. But he did not. Instead, he sat up with me the next night, and he saw . . . he saw our father, but he could not see the woman. Despite that, he believed me. That morning, he told me to take Gareth and go to Gawain at Camelot. He said he would find a way to free our father.'

Elen thought of the man she had seen beside him the day he came back to her, the lean and frowning man who spoke with smooth and terse words while Geraint stood silent and watched. This stern and clerkish man had sent his brothers to safety while he faced down a sorcerous shade and a maddened sire?

'Agravain has never said what happened, no matter how we . . . how Gawain, in truth, pressed him. He only said that he failed, and father was still mad and driven by the spirit that came to him, the spirit he was made to believe was our mother.'

Geraint drew in a deep breath and let it out in a single gust that shuddered his whole frame. 'This is what Morgaine is to me and to mine. This is what she means to my family. This is why I will fight her in whatever way I can and why her allies are forever my enemies.'

Elen blinked, and tried to pull herself back from the depths of the tale. No, she told herself. It could not be. It was a lie. There was a lie in those steady, dark-blue eyes. There must be. He must lie.

Why? said a soft voice in her mind. *Why must he? When has he lied?*

He lied. He lied when he took her hand. He lied when he said he loved her. He lied because he was Morgaine's kin and he must lie.

But he looked at her, and he saw the thoughts that tumbled within her, and his gaze did not flinch. His face was calm, as it always was when he spoke from certainty. It was keen, watching close, looking for . . . looking for what?

Why must he lie?

Because the Little King said he must. Memory came back to her with a jolt. It was the Little King who had said so much. Gwiffert saw, even more than she did. Gwiffert knew. She must believe him. She wanted to believe, but still, Geraint did not lie.

Pain took Elen. It rippled out from her throat and her wrist, flooding her stagnant blood and radiating out into her skin like fever. She must believe what she had heard, but she could not believe. Why could she not believe? Geraint was a man. Geraint could lie, but she could not see the lie in him. She could not see anything. She was blind, blind.

An owl hooted somewhere. A winged shadow skimmed across the sky. An omen of death. Whose death? Hers? *You are deathless,* said the king in his garden, but she'd heard the owl there too. And seen it. No. Elen grasped her head. Her thoughts were coming too fast, making no sense. But she had seen the owl, and it was important.

But where have I seen it? Where?

'Elen?'

'I saw it!' she cried to Geraint, demanding an answer to a question he could not possibly understand. 'I *saw* it! Where?'

'What did you see?' he asked softly, swiftly.

'The owl. There was a black owl, there was a man and . . .' *And I remember.*

The paintings. Memory became clear as glass, and the world became steady once more. The black owl was in the paintings in the great hall.

Without a word she turned and ran, as if fleeing from Geraint. If he thought that, it did not matter. All that mattered was the great hall and its paintings, and that she could see.

She ran into the centre of the hall, so bright with the light of its fires. The women hurried around her, not stopping to see her pivoting slowly, searching through the hundred images on the fantastically painted walls, until she found the one she wanted – the loop of blue ribbon where the owl flew. She stared at that false owl, watching its ebon wings flicker in the firelight. Its talons were outstretched, and dark lines trailed away behind it.

Lines? Elen walked forward until her toes stubbed the edge of the dais. *Lines? No.*

Jesses.

Beside her, Geraint stood mute, watching.

The black owl that hovered over the man's head had jesses. It flew against a sky-blue background wrapped in royal-blue ribbons. It flew in daylight, the omen of death and murder, and it did so from a hunter's gloved hand.

She turned, and now each way she turned, she saw what was wrong, what she had failed to understand before. She saw that the white mare, the sign of the goddess Rhiannon, ran on a ribbon of gold, but she was pursued by a host of spearmen, and there was blood on her flanks.

She saw that the white swine, the symbol of wisdom and plenty, was pursued by a black boar, and that in turn was pursued by a red swine, its mouth open, its dagger-sharp teeth exposed. She had seen that swine in her dreams with all its packmates, running Geraint to death like dogs after a deer.

She saw the branches of apples and blossoms that bordered the walls nearest the floor. She saw how the blossoms and the fruit shared the same branches, and how those branches were all of them broken in two.

She saw it all now, and she understood. She knew why Gwiffert had been given the spear, and why the Lord could not take it from him. She knew why the Lady and the Lord sent her and Geraint here so soon after the birth of the child she had helped deliver. She knew why Gwiffert made his kingdom here in this other world and not in the mortal lands, which were the middle lands and had the loosest of boundaries, easily crossed by men or gods, or any other who so chose.

She knew that she must believe Geraint lied, because she had shared the Little King's food and looked into his eyes and known his touch, and he had told her to believe just that.

She should have seen it before, in his gold hair, his pale skin and slanting eyes, in his lean bones and the way he could fascinate with a word or a look. For when they came across the bridge, or by their other ways, they came for more than aid, mischief or barter. They came too for love, and there were children born of such love. Was he the Lord's son, or the Lady's? The Lord's, she thought, for it was he who had spoken of the spear. Gwiffert himself had said it once. *The spear of my fathers,* he had said. It was not Manawyddan he was claiming descent from. It was the one who gave him the spear.

Perhaps it had been meant to make him a great hero. Instead, it had made him a monster.

She should have known all these things, for the signs of them were all around her, but, he did not wish her to, and for one such as he wishes had force, particularly in their own houses. But such deceptions could not stand before naked truth, and truth was what Geraint had given her.

The truth was all that Geraint had ever given her.

But now, here they stood in the hall of their true enemy, with his eyes and ears and power all around them. He had touched her with the force of his will and believed he held her in sway. What would he do if he found the sway was broken? What mark would the spear find if she spoke now of what she saw?

But I must speak somehow. I must warn Geraint. She bit her lip. *Words. It has all been a game of words since Urien first came. Words with power, words with double meanings.* 'Nothing here has been as it seems,' she said slowly. 'Nothing.'

'Elen . . .' began Geraint.

She did not allow him to go any further. 'Since we came, I have been shown one thing when another was true.' She faced him, she looked into his eyes. *See me, Geraint. You see so much, you watch so close. See me now.* 'What did you see in me when you kept your secrets, Geraint? Look hard! Did you see a fool to be swayed by your show?'

'No.' His word was sure, but his face confused. 'Never a fool.'

'Did you think I would not find out the truth? Did you think I remain blind when the truth surrounds me?' She flung out her hands, letting her voice grow loud and warm as if with anger. 'Your words were as thin as these images around us. Oh yes, I see, and all is cruel deception!'

'Then you do not believe . . .?' Was that comprehension she saw dawning in his visage? Did he begin to understand?

'Oh, I believe,' she snapped back bitterly. 'I believe the one who presented himself as my dearest friend is my bitterest enemy. I believe all I have been told is the exact opposite of what is true!' *Listen to me. See me. Understand, Geraint. Oh please, White Christ who watches him, make him understand!* 'Blood will tell in all things. A deceiver's child will be a deceiver, a demon's a demon!'

Geraint turned away, putting his back to her. Elen shook with fear and with hope. 'Do you understand me, Sir Geraint, Lot's son?'

When he faced her again, his jaw was set and grim, but his eyes were keen. 'Oh yes, my wife,' he said slowly, letting each word fall before he took up the next. 'I understand you perfectly.'

'Then take that understanding and go from here,' she said, her voice ice and stone.

But he did not move. 'And if I do go, what then?' He slurred the words into a sneer. 'What will you do without me?'

Oh my husband. I should have known a man who understands silence so well would have to understand words as well. 'I will no more be bound as I have been,' she drew herself up tall. 'I am stronger than even my gaoler knows, and I will be free. It is a crime that any should be so enslaved to one who knows only deceit. No one should remain in such chains, and I will not remain in mine!' Her hand trembled as she raised it, pointing towards the doors. 'You have shown me what you are. Now go!'

Geraint too drew himself up, showing himself for a moment all that he was, a true knight and the son of kings.

Then, he strode away, his hands clenched in fists, his shoulders square and strong. He marched through the soaring archway, and was gone, and Elen was alone in the hall, surrounded by the symbols of death and blasphemy.

Even as she watched her husband leave, she heard the touch of bootsoles against the tiled floor behind her. She knew by the feel of his approaching heart that it was Gwiffert who came to stand there.

'So, Elen,' he breathed. 'What did he say for himself?'

Elen did not have to force her eyes to blink back tears. She wanted to turn, to rake her nails across Gwiffert's cheeks, to grab him by the throat and snap his neck cleanly.

Don't turn. Don't look at his eyes. Don't look. 'I did not truly know him before,' she answered, her voice strained by the strength of her feeling. 'I was wrong in so many things.'

His touch on her shoulder was warm and sweet as honey. His heartbeat strong and beckoning. 'I will not let him hurt you, Elen.'

She had to turn now. It would be strange if she did not. *Don't look up.* She hung her head, letting her hair fall about her face to screen her from the king's blue eyes. 'What will you do?'

'My people will all be in danger if I confront him openly before the battle.' *You know the sense of this,* the words told her. They caressed her cold skin, as warm as his touch, and even now, even when she looked at her own feet, she felt herself longing for his eyes. She wanted to look up and see him clearly, to feel more perfectly the meaning of his words.

Remember. By the Mother Rhiannon, by Mother herself. I will remember what he is.

She pulled his hand from her, clasping it tightly between her own. She looked up into his face, letting all her fear show. *Let him think me broken over Geraint. Let him think me the wounded damsel.* 'Promise me you will act with honour,' she said, her voice strained and harsh with her pain. 'Promise me that.'

It was a gamble. It might not work, for the fae blood was only half his, and men might break such promises with ease, but it would be there. A weak shield, but it was more than nothing, and might just save Geraint from a spear in the back before he had a chance to act for himself.

Gently, he took his hand from between hers and brushed his fingers down her cheek. Her tears had spilled without her knowing it. The touch was fire, but it was also memory. Geraint had once touched her so. *Remember that too. Remember that truth.* 'Elen, he does not deserve honour.'

Steeling herself, Elen reached up and touched his face. His skin was soft, his heartbeat strong. She felt light as feather-down, ready to blow away with whatever wind came next. 'But you must not stoop so low. Please, Gwiffert.' His name was acid on her tongue and she shook again to speak it. 'Promise me you will act with honour.'

'Very well. I promise that I will do what I must with honour towards him.'

'Thank you.' *Thank you, Mothers All.* She dropped her hand and stepped back. It was easier to breathe with more room between them, easier to smile shyly, more natural to turn her head away, the coy and bashful maiden. 'You should go. He may come back, and he will wonder.'

'It does not matter.' She heard the fond smile in those words. 'Go back to your room, Elen. Rest yourself now. When I return, all will be made right.'

Yes. Elen let her faint smile be all her answer to him. *Yes. That much I promise you.*

TWENTY-ONE

Geraint waded back into the mass of toil. The torches flared high, sending their sparks and smoke up to the stars. Men milled like ants underneath their lights, talking of a thousand things that suddenly made no sense. The only thing he understood clearly was that he had left Elen in the hall behind him, and that were he a true man he would turn and take her out of there if he had to break down the stones with his bare hands.

Men were asking him questions. He could not hear them. He could not see them. A haze as thick as any glamour of the fae kept him from them.

'Sir Geraint.'

That much he heard. He turned around to see one face clearly. King Gwiffert, his spear resting on his shoulder, stood behind him.

Geraint was glad he was unarmed. In that moment he would have drawn his sword and cleaved the king's skull in two, or he would have tried, and probably died himself, impaled on that spear for his troubles.

Anger ebbed, allowing room for reason again.

'Sir Geraint, the lady told me . . .' he paused, looking about him as if he just now noticed the yard full of busy men. 'But not here perhaps.'

'Majesty,' Geraint's voice sounded thick in his ears, as if he spoke from exhaustion. 'There is much yet to do.'

'I know.' The king laid his free hand on Geraint's arm. It was a familiar touch. It spoke of trust and friendship. How could a man lie so well with a touch? *The same as with a look. The same as with a word.* 'But we must talk all the same. Come.'

Dutifully, Geraint followed the Little King to a corner of the yard. He set his back to the wall so that they could speak without anyone coming on them unnoticed.

King Gwiffert rested the butt of his spear on the toe of his boot. 'Is it true?'

As a grown man Geraint had never spoken of these things with anyone who did not share his blood. To speak of them to this king of secrets seemed suddenly like heresy.

'Who told her these things?' he asked instead, flexing his hands, looking for something to hold onto.

King Gwiffert sighed. 'Secrets have a way of being found out. It may even be that Morgaine or Urien first showed her the truth.'

So this is how it will be done. You have separated us neatly, and now you will make yourself the friend of both. 'And you? Morgaine is your enemy as well.' He thought he knew the answer, but he wanted to watch how the king said it.

Gwiffert held the spear easily in both hands. He and Geraint were almost of a height, so he looked directly into Geraint's eyes. 'The enemy of my enemy shall be my friend. I need you in this fight.'

The trust in those words touched Geraint's pride. He wanted to hear more. No, he wanted to deserve more. 'You do not fear I will betray you?'

'Will you?'

Geraint shook his head to break the grip of the king's gaze.

It did no good. He still yearned towards this man. This was how men felt about Gawain, how heroes felt about Arthur. They wished to please him, to be better than they were because he needed them to be. 'No.'

Gwiffert watched his busy yard for a long moment, as if thinking hard about what he had to say next. 'Will you swear to that?'

So. You will trap me with my own honour. 'Yes.'

Now the Little King watched him keenly. 'By what, Sir Geraint? By what will you swear?'

At these words, Geraint knelt and laid his hand over his heart. 'I swear before God most high and by Jesus Christ his son. I swear by my own right arm and the love I owe my king that I will betray no trust and do only what is honourable in the battle that is to come.'

The Little King's blue eyes glittered brightly. 'Then I do believe you, Sir Geraint, and I do trust you.' He took his arm. 'It is not only her blood in you.'

Those words warmed him, that trust filled his heart with pride. The men were well ordered, and come morning, he would lead at the side of his king.

No, Geraint ground his teeth hard together. *Arthur is my king. Remember that. Remember the vows you have made. Remember Elen left behind in this one's tender keeping while she tries to break his kingdom open.*

These thoughts steadied him, dimming pride and all its glamour.

God help me, he prayed as he walked with the Little King back into the thick of the labouring men, each one of them a prisoner of this place and this man. *God help us all.*

Thankfully, the work was real and Geraint was able to hide himself behind it. Even for such a swift and tiny war, there were a thousand details to be marshalled and assembled, knowledgeable men to be consulted and given their orders.

Scouts had to be readied and sent on ahead, for by now the false dawn brightened the horizon.

But even while he gave his orders and watched over his men, Geraint's mind was elsewhere. These around him were no danger. In truth, he itched to take Rhys and Taggart aside, to speak to them of what he now knew and tell them he would give them his help against their king. Could he urge them to turn against Gwiffert? Convince them to believe that he would defeat the one who had already conquered them all? No. Had he all the power of Arthur himself, there was no time for such things. It would take weeks of careful persuasion. Those around him were slaves to the Little King. Dupes, prizes taken in war, victims of their chieftain's cowardice. They lived in fear of the Grey Men.

He saw that too, now. The Grey Men were not weapons of war. They existed of terrify the helpless, or to convince the blind of the enemy's evil. They worked by fear, by famine and by the threat that was ever in the grave 'See, you will become like I am. So cower in the dark and pray to God to spare you this!'

Why did I not see before?

Because I was in his house, came the answer. *Because it was his wish I should be blind. But he goes now to war, and war is* my *house.*

And what good does that do? Geraint rubbed his face. Weariness fogged his mind as effectively as any of the Little King's glamours. It was the spear that was the danger, the spear that never missed its mark, that could kill even the deathless. It was the spear he must take from Gwiffert's hand. But if he shattered it, they could not claim it to defeat Urien. He had to steal it whole, somehow. But if Gwiffert did not set it down in his own fortress, he would surely not do so on the field of battle.

Set it down. The thought touched him, a half-memory, something seen but unheeded, like so much in this place. *It is not by accident you have your mother's eyes,* Merlin had said to him before he had set out on this madness.

What have my eyes seen?

Geraint looked across the busy yard. The king stood before the steps of his hall. He rested the butt of his spear against the toe of his boot, watching the work around him. It was a familiar pose. Geraint had seen it many times over the past days. Often the king had stood just so in the yard before him.

He will not set it down.

The king stood just so before him in the yard, but not in the hall. In the hall, he rested the spear against the flagstones or the mosaics.

Geraint searched his memory, his first and last weapon. His life had been saved many times before by his close study of his enemy.

Was it true? Did the king prevent this spear, this thing of enchantment, from touching the living earth?

It made sense after the ways of magic, which were not the ways of reason. All spells had a weakness. All weapons of enchantment had a flaw that could not be countered. All the epics and all the ballads told that this was the way. He had heard similar things from Merlin. Was this the spear's weakness? Did the spear lose its virtues when it came in contact with the earth?

An idea came to Geraint then, fully formed and clear as sunrise. The risk was great, but if the other king, Rhyddid ap Carchar came to the battlefield, there was a way. Gwiffert believed he had blinded Geraint with his own pride. Let him believe that still, and Geraint might be set free to act.

The boards were laid in the great hall and food was served. The men ate well. Geraint and Gwiffert sat on the dais.

Gwiffert was cheerful, free of that heaviness, real or feigned, that had lingered at the edges of his manner since Geraint and Elen had first come to his house.

Elen did not come to the table. Geraint did not expect her, but he missed her. He wondered if sleep had found her in her grove of false trees. He wondered how she meant to achieve the quest she had set herself.

He wondered if he would ever see her again.

No toasts were drunk, save those Gwiffert and he drank to each other. Geraint strove to be cheerful, to be confident. Fortunately, the meal was brief and the Little King much distracted by the thought that his enemy was about to be destroyed.

When the last cup had been drained, Gwiffert led Geraint out into the yard where the horses waited, saddled and ready for their masters. In that yard, Geraint armed himself. He donned a fresh corslet, grieves and wrist guards that fit him, a banded helmet chased with images of hunting cats. He belted on sword and dagger, and he mounted Donatus. One of the waiting boys handed him up a spear and a shield painted with the image of a hawk on the wing. Geraint found himself wondering if Gwiffert had chosen the device for him.

Men crowded the yard. More men waited outside beneath the shadows of the walls. They carried pikes and clubs, swords and daggers. They hoisted four-cornered shields of leather stretched over wood and painted with all manner of fanciful designs – dogs and wolves, triskelions, leaping salmon, running mares and great green eyes. Over them all flew the banner of the Little King. It was a spear, of course, slanted across a white tower, as if to shield it from harm.

Or perhaps just to bar its door.

Beside him, King Gwiffert raised that spear in the air. One of the horsemen sounded a horn, then another. Gwiffert pointed the way forward with his spear, and Geraint touched up Donatus. Side-by-side they walked their horses through the gate to meet the dawn. Behind them, slowly, ponderously, the Little King's army began to move.

Morning's grey filtered through the slit of a window over Elen's bed. Calonnau saw it and creeled indignantly. She was hungry. She wanted to hunt. Her restlessness breathed life into Elen, stiff and cold from her waiting. She had not slept. She had worried the night away, alternating between lying awake on her narrow bed, and pacing the tiny room, her ears straining for the distant sound of the smith's hammer.

But that night it had not come. *So be it.* She twisted her hands together. *What I must do, I must do.*

What she wanted to do was go out into the yard and watch Geraint ride away, to gain what reassurance could be had from a glance, a swift touch. But she could not do that and maintain the appearance of the bride wounded to the soul by her husband's betrayal. She must stay here as if sunken in her grief and watch the sky slowly brightening outside her window.

Eventually, she heard a soft scratching at the door. Calonnau cried out sharply, as if in hope that here at last was someone who would take her outside. Elen herself made no answer. The door opened and Meg, the faded serving woman, peered around it.

'Will you come break your fast, lady?' she asked softly.

Elen rubbed her tired eyes. She was hungry and Calonnau was ravenous. 'Are they gone, Meg?'

'Yes, lady.' A look of pity came across the older woman's face. 'They are.'

What tales are told among the people here? wondered Elen tiredly. *What do they find the courage to whisper to each other? Do you know what passed between Geraint and me, or do you just see a fellow prisoner?*

'Help me dress, Meg. I will go into the yard a little, then I will eat.'

Meg bobbed her curtsey and bustled about the tiny room, helping Elen into her brown dress with its oak-leaf borders, brushing out her hair and replacing her jewels and rings.

Armed and armoured, she thought a little ridiculously. *Let us hope it is enough.*

She took Calonnau from her perch. Meg followed her as she walked out into the yard. The place was silent and empty after the busy labour of the night before. It looked grey under the morning's heavy sky. Only the churned sea of mud and straw showed that the small army had passed this way.

The gate remained open, with a quartet of old men for sentries. They did not challenge Elen as she walked between them to stand in the shadow of Gwiffert's walls. She raised Calonnau up before her and looked long into the bird's wild yellow eyes. *Fly to Geraint,* she said. *Stay near him. Watch and keep safe.*

The hawk was angry and confused. She wanted only to hunt. *Fly to Geraint. Take him my heart and keep it close.*

Elen loosened the jesses. The hawk did not stay, but beat her wings hard to gather the wind under them, to lift her up and soar away. Elen watched her go, and ached to fly with her.

No. I am beyond such wishing. I will leave no one bound to this king for my wishing.

She stripped off her gauntlet and turned away from the path of the hawk's flight. If Meg had questions, she did not ask them. The Little King certainly discouraged such things.

Elen walked back to the great hall where the boards were laid. Only a few people still ate, women mostly, with a few youths and children. Meg went before Elen to the table on the dais and served her bread and beer, boiled eggs and pork, and fresh bright cherries. Elen ate without looking up. She felt the paintings all around her, felt their eyes watching her in speculation and accusation. The white mare was afraid, and where was Elen to defend her? The red swine was running fast, coming up behind Elen because she moved too slowly. The air around her fairly pulsed with the power of her enemy. She could feel it thrumming through the floor and in the soles of her feet.

Stop, she told herself harshly. *If you become so distracted so soon, how will you be when the work begins?*

She forced herself to sit and eat and drink well. She needed strength and solidity, for there was no telling how long she would be gone on her errand.

At last, she rose. She left the remains of her meal for the servants and without any word, she left the hall. Meg trailed along in silence, her hands neatly folded over her apron, waiting to be given her orders.

Or carrying them out already. Elen stopped in front of her door. 'I would be alone for a time, Meg.'

'Please, my lady.' Meg's hands knotted into her apron. 'His Majesty told me I was to stay with you while he was gone. He was most clear. You were not to be left alone. He will be angry . . .' she stopped.

Am I not supposed to know how much the king can see? Elen looked at Meg with sympathy and wondered how long the woman had served in this place.

'Where do you come from, Meg?' she asked.

The question startled the older woman. She bit her lip and twisted her hands in her apron. 'From here, my lady. This is my home.' Despite this, all about her told Elen how much she longed to give some other answer.

'Is it?' *Come, sister. I know your tongue as you know mine. You too played on the banks of the Usk as a child.*

'Please, lady.' There was a tremor in her voice. 'This is my home.'

'I understand.' *Forgive me for frightening you.* 'I ask you to understand. Your king has told me my husband is the kindred of my enemy. I am faint with the news and broken in soul and spirit. I need to be alone for a time.'

Meg's eyes flickered back and forth, making the kind of calculations the fearful make, but she clearly did not want to be with this lady who asked dangerous questions and might walk her into a trap of words for the king to find.

'I do understand,' Meg murmured to the floor, and she made her curtsey. 'I will be in the great hall. I will go no further.' *Was that to me or to him?* Elen wondered.

'That will be good.' Elen nodded solemnly. She went into her room and she waited, listening, until she no longer heard the tread of Meg's sandals on the stone.

Mother Don, she is your daughter too. Watch over her, she prayed. *And if I fail, please, do not let it fall more heavily on her.*

If I fail . . . The thought echoed in Elen's mind. *No. Move. Do not give yourself time to think that again.*

Some servant had been in the room while she was gone. The bed was freshly made, the clothes tidied and the brazier lit to add its little bit of light and warmth to the sunlight that trickled through the high window. Elen fed the flames well, making the fire fat and bright. Then, as she had done the night before, she wrapped her hand in the cloth of her sleeve and lifted the brazier up.

She left the door open behind her. She cast back one regretful glance at the empty perch. She was already cold, and she felt the hollow within her as clearly as she felt the pain in her wrist and her throat. Then, she turned and faced the darkened corridor in front of her. All the torches and rush lights were at her back. No one brought light to this deeper way.

Come then, she thought grimly. *All those who have been set to follow me. Let us see where we may go.*

Elen plunged into the shadows and silently they closed around her. She did not dare move slowly. She did not want to give the half-formed fears inside her time to freeze into proper forms. She kept the brazier and her gaze ahead of her, glancing at the paintings only when she needed to be sure they followed the pattern she knew, the plentiful fields, the monsters, the phantoms hidden behind their shrouds of dirt and age.

And always the doors, the closed doors. What would the deepest parts of this place be without the king above them? What would roam free without his hand to keep all the doors closed? Elen wished she had not sent Calonnau away. She felt light-headed. Her feet sounded loud against the stones, and she stumbled again and again against the edges that time had tipped up or crumbled away. The cloth of her dress itched at her and rested too heavily against her skin. The shadows were thick enough to breathe out fear all around her, and yet the brazier's light hurt her eyes. Her nose and mouth filled with the scents of earth, of mould and loam and less wholesome things. Stones pressed against her on either side and weighed down the world over her head.

It is only fear, she told herself. *I have been through so much before. It is only fear.*

Movement flickered in the corner of her eye. *It is the light.* But she could not stop her eye from glancing in its direction.

The painting moved.

Elen froze in an instant, her throat clamped tight around her breath. At her right hand, the wall was black with grime and spotted with mould. Beneath this curtain of filth, the blurs of colour and strong black lines shifted and rippled as if they were alive. They leeched slowly through the grime, as if pressing through a forest's shadows, and became clear.

They showed her a race of people in a hundred forms. They changed to birds and soared through the sky. They changed to fish to swim in the seas, even to the roses that climbed the walls or the stones atop the hills. They sported and rejoiced in their many shapes, and the sun shone down in blessing. In the middle of them stood a man and a woman. Both had bands of gold on their heads. They clasped their hands and raised them high. In her free hand, the woman held a great, curving ram's horn and from the horn flowed a wealth of food, an ocean of milk and golden honey.

This painting was still and placid. The only sign that it had not always been here was the shining newness of the colours.

Ahead, something else was moving, and something beyond that. More paintings, shifting and changing, becoming a tale for her witness. Shadows and the stones crowded close around her as she moved from one to the other.

Next she saw Gwiffert. He was easy to recognize from the spear, the golden hair and the blue eyes. He stood before the man. He was young in this rendering, his face full of mischief. He pointed the spear at the sky. The man and the woman were grinning in return. A game, a bet was being proposed.

The images grew crowded. The man, the king of these wild, enchanted people, assumed many shapes: a stallion, an ox, a bear, a fish, a butterfly, a golden ram. For each shape, Gwiffert took a different one – a rider with a bridle where the king was a stallion, a raging bull where he was an ox, a bear where he was a fish, a hunter where he was a wolf. But it seemed Gwiffert began to tire and his forms grew smaller – a cow, a dog, a quail, and at last, a sprig of wheat, and so the other man became a mouse to snatch up the wheat.

Then Gwiffert was Gwiffert again, and he stabbed the tip of the spear against the mouse's neck, trapping him against the ground, and all the wild ones cringed back and shielded their faces from this horror. The queen threw herself at Gwiffert's feet, pleading for her husband's life.

Now, where there had been the freedom and wonder of a thousand forms, there were only small brown mice with small white hands, and the Little King standing over them all. Their king knelt at Gwiffert's feet beside his queen, his head bowed, his tears spilling out on the ground.

As Elen watched, the dirt crept over the bright colours, hiding them away, turning the mural again to glimpses of colour overhung by shadows. Elen was breathing hard as if she had just run up a mountainside, but it was taking all her strength just to stand still.

Ahead, a door swung open. Elen made herself turn so that none who watched would see her paralysed by her fear. For she was watched. The door showed the cool room with its great ewers as she had seen it before, but this time no weeping greeted her. Instead, crouched between the white clay vessels were a host of people. Their hair was long and brown, and tousled as if from a harsh wind. Around their feet and between their fingers scampered the mice with their little white hands. Elen's stomach roiled at the sight. Their eyes were round and black, and within them was all the wildness, all the hunger, she had ever seen in the hawk's eyes. She had thought herself ready, but she had not imagined all these black eyes watching her, nor the mixture of animal hunger and human hate that shone from them so brightly.

With them stood the woman, great with child, her red jug clutched against her side. Beside her, a tall, slender man leaned against the wall. He too was black-eyed and long-faced, making him appear kin to all the others crouching around him.

'So,' he said, pushing himself away from the wall. 'Murderess. You are come to us at last.'

TWENTY-TWO

'I have done no murder.'

One corner of the man's mouth turned up in a vicious smile. 'But you have. Your hawk killed one of my people. His name was Kedigan. His widow mourns him even now. His children clamour for their revenge.'

Which are they? Elen's gaze darted around all the crouching people. They looked so much alike in the half-light from her sputtering brazier. She could make out no difference in countenance between them. Even their dress – their long brown tunics belted with twisted grey ropes – conspired to confuse male and female. 'It was done in ignorance. Had I known who you were, I would never have permitted such a hunt.'

'Nonetheless, it was done,' said the king.

Remember who you are. Remember why you came. She should not have sent Calonnau away. She could not find her focus. She could barely hold her thoughts in order. 'I owe you bloodprice for this.'

'You do,' agreed the mouse-king, his round eyes narrowing. 'What price will you pay?'

For a moment the fear rushed through Elen that she would

be overheard. *It is too late. You are already a traitor to the king here. Tell him.* 'The life of your enemy.'

The man sneered. 'You do not have it.'

'But I will.'

He laughed, a sound bitter as poison. Around him, his black-eyed kindred smiled grimly. Elen saw the gleam of white teeth as their lips curled back.

'Why do you come here?' Her questioner flung out his arms. 'This is not the place he made for you. This is our prison.' He touched the woman's hand, and then the shoulder of a man who crouched before him.

Hold yourself straight. Remember who you are. You come as lady, as chief, as ally. 'I came seeking help.'

He shook his head. 'There is no help for any of us here.'

'Then we must help each other.'

A mouse ran across Elen's foot. She felt the tiny claws and fingers scrabbling at her skin and she flinched. The mouse king smiled. 'Must we?'

'If it is the only way to freedom, yes.' *Listen to me.* Elen's fingers curled up at her sides. The mice chittered and scrabbled. *Listen to me! There is a way out for us all.*

'Freedom?' He frowned, rolling his eyes towards the ceiling and tapping his chin. 'What a curious word. I think I heard it once, years ago. What does it mean?'

Carefully, Elen set the brazier down on one of the few lidded ewers. Her hands had begun to perspire, the sweat prickling against her palms. An urgency that she could not fully name was building in the back of her mind. 'I can bring him down.'

'No, you cannot. He is older than your nightmares and stronger than your Mother Don.'

'But he can be fought.' She pressed her hands against her sides. Hands, not claws. The air was harsh against her skin, like rough cloth. Its touch distracted her. 'The Great King would not exist if he could not.'

The mouse-king laughed again, once, hard and sharp as flint. 'You know nothing. You do not know the lives it cost to hide the child after its birth so the Little King would not learn its name. Villages died for it. The mother who bore him could not kill herself fast enough and was kept in her starvation for seven years before she was permitted to enter the grave. Her mouth was stopped with earth because she would not speak. You do not know how many paid to find him the secret that hid his hall from King Gwiffert's eyes. Oh yes, he is a great warrior for all of us who are imprisoned and cowed, and perhaps he would have triumphed, but for you and your man.'

Elen closed her eyes, cut deep by the justice of the words. She wanted to be still for a moment. She needed to be still. She needed not to be seen, to be as insubstantial as a shadow against a cloud. 'Perhaps,' was all she could make herself say.

'Oh? Is there a plan, little one? Come.' She heard movement and her eyes flew open. The mouse-king had crooked his finger and he beckoned to her. 'Whisper your plan to the king of mice, and let me take it to my master. He will be well pleased with us both then, and perhaps your suffering will be shorter for coming to your senses.'

'You're . . . you . . .' A red haze blurred the edge of her vision. *You are the spy. You are the one who told him what we said.*

'What's the matter, little girl?' The mouse-king leaned forward, resting his hands on a ewer's open mouth in mockery of her own stance. 'Is something lost? Something gone from you that you could ill afford to leave behind?' The crouching people laughed. They shifted their weight on their feet. Were they armed? There were so many of them, did they need to be?

The mice scurried everywhere, climbing over their fellows.

She could reach out and pluck up any of them, snatch them up as they ran for shelter. She could do it this instant, break their bones, tear their skin.

To her utter horror, Elen realized what the urgency within her was. It was hunger.

'You do not need to do this.' She felt her tongue pressing against her teeth. She felt the sharp nails at the ends of her fingers.

'Oh, but I do.' He drew the last word out, so that she felt it against her skin, as she felt the Little King when he spoke nearby. 'I have been so ordered by our king.'

She saw the mice, the sneaking, creeping, chittering vermin, all around her. Anger and hunger mixed together in her, pressing the breath from her body and the reason from her mind.

'He is not my king,' said Elen through her clenched teeth. *Hold fast. I must hold fast.*

'He is king of us all.' Elen started. It was not the mouse-king who uttered those soft words, but his wife beside him, her milk jug clutched against her side.

'No.' *This much I know. This much is sure.*

'But you are not sure,' said the mouse-king, as if she had spoken the thought aloud. 'You are weak here. You know you are.'

'Stop.' *Let me think. Let me find myself again. There's too much stone and I need air. I need the sky. I need the warmth and the wind and to hunt. I am so hungry . . .*

'Why?' He spread his hands again. 'I am a liar, a thief and a spy. Why fear any words of mine?' He stalked towards her, moving with the lithe grace of a wild thing. Around her the brown people watched with their black eyes, staring, hungry, waiting. Behind her, she heard the squeals of the mice, sharp and piercing, creeping shadow-dwellers, waiting, watching for the thing that was left unguarded. Waiting to snatch it up, to bite it through, to run away and bury it in the darkness between the stones, never to let in the light of day again, to gnaw and crack and nibble at it until there was nothing left at all.

'We are so many,' whispered one voice.

'Hush. There is enough for all.'

They would do this if she did not strike. Strike, break, tear, feed.

She lunged. She could not have stopped herself any more than she could have turned the tide. Arms outstretched, fingers curled into claws, she lunged for the mouse-king, crashing through the ewers, heedless of anything but her prey.

He dissolved, melting away until there were only mice around her, filthy, skittering mice everywhere, moving too fast for her clumsy body, her useless hands. She screamed in frustration as they swarmed around her, quick as insects, never there no matter how fast she charged and lunged. They laughed at their game, and they would turn soon and attack. She must strike. She was so hungry. She must strike.

Her hand came down on fur and living warmth and something squirmed and squealed against her palm. Elen screamed in her delight and snatched the creature up. The little brown mouse bulged about its hips and belly. It was great with child, and that had slowed it down, made it clumsy, made it prey.

Elen grinned, barely aware that the mouse-king was before her again. All her attention was on the thing in her hands.

'Please,' he said hoarsely. 'Don't hurt her.'

But she wanted the little thing dead. She wanted this squirming, unnatural creature with its monstrous young wrapped tight within it, dead. Its heart beat faster than a bird's in flight. Why did such a thing have heart and mind when she had none? Why did such a thing have life and

love when she was lost in a world so far away from her
home that not even the gods or the dead could hear her?

'Whatever you want you will have. Please.'

The beat of its heart fluttered against her thumb, spurring
the pain of her madness with desire for that beating to fill
her. The other mice milled around, chittering frantically. They
clawed at her skirt, they scrabbled at her feet. She didn't
care. She would tear the thing apart with her teeth. She
would rip out that beating heart and swallow it whole.

And she thought of the Grey Men and their horses
devouring the green wheat.

And she thought of the first babe she ever delivered, warm
and red and wriggling, already struggling to reach its mother.

And she thought of Geraint's eyes as he spoke of madness,
and how it swallowed the good man who was his father
whole.

And she thought of the one they had ordered to lead them
to this cursed place and how the hills had echoed with his
laughter. *You are his. You are his.*

No, said a voice, hard and stern within her. She did not
recognize it at first, and then, a long, slow moment later, she
knew it to be her own. *No. Any doom but that one.* She bared
her teeth. *Gwiffert, I deny you. I refuse you.*

But she could not make her hand open. It trembled inde-
pendent of her will. Her body was starved, starved of food,
starved of vengeance, and her fingers were strong, strong
enough to crush the little thing she held, to stop the vile,
unfair beating of its tiny, tremulous heart.

'Take her,' whispered Elen. 'Take her, quickly.'

The man, the mouse-husband, snatched his wife from her
hand. As soon as the heartbeat was gone from her touch,
Elen collapsed to the floor, curling around the pain that filled
her hollowness. It was eating her from the inside out. The
darkness was smothering her. She squeezed her eyes shut

and she was alone in the blackness, cold, a corpse who had yet to lie still, already dead and buried down here. The stones of the floor cut and scraped her, and there was no rest, no respite. She was dying, and all her last sane thoughts were swallowed up by the pain and it hurt, it hurt, it hurt . . .

Hands caught her and their touch grated against her skin, and the heartbeats they brought smothered her. They prised at her jaws and she screamed. The hearts and the heat pounded at her with a force like cudgels falling.

And then, something cool poured down her throat. She choked and spat, and swallowed. It was rich, it was sweet, it went straight to the ravening pain inside her and stilled it. She swallowed gulp after gulp of it and never had anything tasted so good. This was the food of the gods. This was the first and last blessing. She drank and drank, blind as a newborn babe. For it was milk, she realized, pure, fresh and full of cream. She did not know how long she drank. She only knew that the pain eased and ebbed, and though the hearts beat too near and too strong, the sensation of their pounding became bearable.

Gradually, she was able to put up one shaking hand and pull away from the vessel.

The mouse-king towered over her, but in front of her knelt the woman. Her brown hair fell almost to her feet. Her belly beneath her brown dress was high and round. *Not yet dropped,* thought Elen's midwife mind automatically. *But will soon.*

It was her jar Elen had been drinking from. She held it in both hands. White liquid filmed its rim, and yet more foamed inside. Where did it all come from? Where were the cows that replenished that vessel? Elen did not ponder on that. Madness still nibbled at the back of her mind. It would come fast, like a summer flood, if she provoked it.

Now that she could see again, she noticed that the mouse-king was gaping at his bride. His people surrounded him,

men and women once more, all of them hanging back as far
as the room would allow. The ewers were tipped on their
sides, some cracked in two like eggs, lakes of white milk
puddled between the uneven stones, and the king and queen,
god and goddess maybe, before Gwiffert imprisoned them
here, stood in the middle of this domestic chaos and stared
at each other.

'Why would you do this?' he demanded. 'She is his thing.'

'No, she is not,' replied the woman. 'If she were his, she
would never have touched me. For if I am dead and our
child is dead, what hold does he have over you?'

The mouse-king stared at her and she met his gaze with
her own cool stare in reply. 'I know what I am, my husband.
I have thought many times of taking my life to free you.'
She turned on her heels to face Elen. 'What do you need
from us?'

'Your pitcher,' Elen whispered, panting. The pitcher that
could not be emptied. She had seen that it was so, seen it
before when she had first stumbled across the mouse-queen,
and when she had made her desperate plans, she had counted
on there being enough milk in that pitcher to drown even
a fire that had burned for a thousand years, if only she could
get it into her hands.

She had to breathe, breathe, breathe, just to remind
herself that there was air enough, that she was not smothering under stones and madness. She was a mess of sweat
and spittle and milk. Her dress was soaked. Her hair hung
lank and sticky on either side of her face. None of that
mattered. All that mattered was that she keep hold of her
thoughts, that she keep breathing, despite the cold, despite
everything.

'It is our last blessing,' said the mouse-queen. 'We fill his
storehouses with the milk that once fed our children to keep
him amused. It allows him to force us into the fields of those

who have even less than us to steal their grain when they've displeased him. What will you do with it?'

'I will call the smith.'

The mouse-king laughed, high and sharp. 'You may not be his, but you are a fool. You cannot call the smith. None can, save the king.'

'I can.' She climbed unsteadily to her feet. Her body felt wrong. It was too heavy, too huge. Her eyesight was too sharp. She could see everything around her, despite the fact that the brazier was long dead. 'Blood may call to blood and blood must hear. And more than that,' she grinned at the mouse-king – mouse-god? – fierce and mad, 'I know his name.'

The mouse-queen required nothing more. Without another word, she passed the jar to Elen, who took it in equal silence. She turned and walked into the hall, her heavy skirt dragging across the puddled floor as if it meant to drag her down to drown. She clutched the rough clay jar for dear life, as her passport from all the eyes and hungry teeth at her back.

In the corridor there was no light to see by, no way to tell which direction she should turn. It didn't matter. She had the lodestone she needed within her.

'Maius,' she said softly. 'Maius the Smith. I call you. I am your daughter Elen, and I call you from the darkness.'

And Elen waited for the darkness to answer.

'So,' said King Gwiffert. 'Fast as we were, we were not fast enough.'

Geraint and the king stood at the edge of a rough patch of bracken and spindling trees that provided them some little cover. With three nervous boys to attend them, they looked out across the valley floor. A shallow stream cut across the way in front of them, filling the air with its chatter. The birds

had all gone silent, except for one wise crow croaking dili-
gently above, letting its comrades know that here were men
dressed for slaughter.

The ragged column of the army was still arriving behind
them, waiting in the deeper wood for orders.

Had Geraint been asked to describe a dangerous position
to be in for the start of a battle, it would have been very
close to the situation before them. The Great King's army
had arrayed themselves at the top of the hill that stood across
the narrow valley. Scrubby woods stood sentry between their
army and the other. Geraint shaded his eyes against the sun
and tried to see. They were, at least, no better armed. It was
hard to count the spears at this distance, but there did not
seem to be more than Gwiffert had brought. He saw only a
handful of men on horseback, and there was one in a chariot.

This was the Great King. The chariot put him head and
shoulders above even the men on horseback. Geraint wished
he was closer. He wished to look into the man's eyes and
see with what mind he faced the coming battle. What
unnerved Geraint more than knowing nothing of the men
at his back was that he also knew nothing about the men
he faced.

One thing he could see clearly. There were no grey horses
or grey cloaks among Rhyddid's company.

'Where are the Grey Men?' Geraint asked, to hear what
Gwiffert would say.

'I don't know,' frowned the Little King. 'Could they be
circling behind us?'

A good tale. Geraint nodded. 'We should send to the
outriders and bid them be vigilant.' *And hopefully keep that
many more men out of this madness.*

The Little King repeated the order to one of the boys who
ran at once to see it done. Geraint wondered if the Grey Men
might indeed be behind Gwiffert's army, waiting for the word

of their master, waiting to see, perhaps, if anyone tried to flee.

It did not matter immediately whether the Grey Men were there or not. They had a more formidable foe to deal with, and that was the land itself. The Great King had picked his place well. The top of the hill, the screen of trees – it was good ground, and it would be foolish to try to fight their way up to them. Worse still, the valley was small and rocky. Their armies would meet on rough and ragged ground without room enough for all their numbers. They would be forced to fight in and out of the trees and up and down the slopes.

Geraint's warrior instincts grew grim and cold at all he saw about him. It occurred to him that the Great King might be hoping that they would become discouraged enough by the lay of the land to parley. A vain hope, given what he surely knew about Gwiffert's nature, but better than trying to stand off a siege in his poor hall.

With an effort, Geraint reminded himself that however bad this was, it played well into his own hand.

Now is the time. Remembering form, Geraint climbed down from Donatus. One of the remaining boys took the horse's bridle. Geraint knelt before the Little King.

'Sire, I would beg a boon.'

'What boon, Sir Geraint?' A hint of genuine surprise coloured the question.

Geraint lifted his head. Gwiffert's face was impassive, but his eyes had narrowed slightly. The hand holding the spear twisted it uneasily. The Little King did not know what was happening and he did not like it. Best to speak quickly. 'There is a way to end this before it begins. Let me challenge the Great King to single combat.'

In an honest war, this was commonly done. It was a custom left from the most ancient times. The two champions would meet on the ground between the assembled armies and fight, one against the other, to the death. Once, when chief had fought chief, the grievance would then be considered settled. In more recent wars, the armies still clashed, but the side whose champion lost was disheartened, and that much could sometimes turn the tide.

Today, there were other things it might also accomplish.

Above him, the Little King was frowning. Good. He had not considered this possibility, but he was not dismissing it lightly. *You trust your hold over me.* 'I do not like it, Sir Geraint. We know his fortifications to be far weaker than we thought, but I have seen him fight, as you have not. He is formidable in ways other than his size.' *And you know you need me. This is good, but what if you will not risk me?*

'Sire, the men are tired. They are frightened by the enemy they must face, and I think the absence of the Grey Men will work upon their nerves almost more than their presence would have. It is the enemy you do not see that is the most on your mind.' He paused, letting that sink into the Little King's thoughts. 'They need a good omen,' he went on. 'Let me give them one.'

That sparked a smile in the Little King's pale eyes. 'Warrior's pride, Geraint?'

'Nonetheless.' *Yes, look at me. Do you see your chance to be rid of me? If he takes my life, you will have a clean shot at him, and I will have spared you the trouble of murdering me yourself.*

For he was fairly certain that once this enemy was defeated, Gwiffert would have little use for a trained knight among his company. Such men were apt to become bored and discontent when they were not given active employment, and once discontent, they tended to turn on their masters.

'We are in a bad place, Majesty,' said Geraint bluntly. Beside him, the boy holding Donatus looked nervously up the hill. Geraint longed to reassure the lad, but it would not do now to show concern for any but Gwiffert. 'If we cannot get them down the hill, they will have the advantage over us. If I can kill their leader, they may rush us, and we will meet them on level ground.' *There, a truth for you to chew over while you consider my pride.* 'It will also give us time to get our men arrayed on the opposing slope. If they can be goaded into giving away their advantage, we gain in every way.' Gwiffert nodded, his lips pursed in judicious consideration. Geraint wondered if he truly cared, if there was the smallest chance that these rebellious men aligned against him would pose any threat after their king was dead. 'Even if they do not, they will be without their leader, and that alone would make the risk worth taking.'

At last, the king said, 'Very well.'

'Thank you, Majesty,' replied Geraint fervently. *One victory,* he told himself. *One only. You will need many more before this day is through.*

Geraint swung himself back into the saddle. He tried to give the boy an encouraging glance, but the child was looking down at the ground. Geraint touched up Donatus. If the horse the Lady had bestowed on him possessed any special properties, he had yet to note them, but it was a steady mount, and it walked him unafraid into the open ground and splashed without hesitation across the fresh, silver stream.

How to do this? How to call down the one king in this land who might be a king by heart and blood as well as fist and fear?

How to do it in a manner that did not give him away to the king who waited behind him?

Geraint reined Donatus up short and squared his shoulders. The whole of Rhyddid's army looked down on him. It would not do to seem afraid.

'I call for the one who styles himself the Great King!' he shouted up the hill. 'I, Sir Geraint, son of Lot Luwddoc, nephew to Arthur the High King at Camelot, knight of the Round Table, I call you here!'

There was silence, and then a confused ripple of men's voices as in their hundreds they murmured to each other, perhaps cursing him, perhaps wondering what fresh gambit this was.

A man shouted down at him. 'What would you of the Great King, Sir Geraint?' Probably that was not the king himself. Probably it was some trusted captain. That was one of the dangers. If the Great King would only fight king to king, the remainder of the plan might not work. It was only Gwiffert's rage which would bring the carelessness Geraint needed.

'A challenge, Great King! Your skill against mine. Let us stand before God and let Him judge which of us has the right cause!'

'And why should the Great King fight any such as you?'

Here it was. 'Because word of his fame has reached the High King at Caerleon. They say he is such a grand coward he will not risk one hair of his beard in honest battle, but needs must lead his armies from behind! The High King would not stoop to come before such a one himself, so he sent me to find if the tales were true!' *There now, if you are a man that will bring you. And may my uncle forgive me should he ever hear this tale.* He took another deep breath. 'Refuse me now and I will know what answer to take him!'

The ripple of voices rose up again. He could hear nothing of what was going on behind him. His hands itched at the uncertainty of it. Were Rhys and Taggart arranging the men as they should be, or were they just hiding in the woods, crouching frozen between their fears of their king and the Grey Men?

I must not let this come to a battle.

On the slope in front of him, the mass of men began to shift ponderously. They parted, making a wide lane, like the Red Sea readying itself for Moses and his people. The Great King's chariot rolled forward. His driver was a slip of a youth, perhaps even a boy still.

'You stand there for your king, Sir Geraint?' called the giant.

'Yes!' *Let the ones who hear this think what they will. It is for my king I stand here. My king, my wife, myself.*

'It is as Gwiffert's man you stand here?'

'Yes!' *For that is the part I must play.*

'I am sorry for you. He is no master for a brave man!'

Be sorry if you will, but not so reasoned, man. 'Would you speak against my king? Come down here and speak with me as warriors do, or are you great only in the size of your boasts?' *Come down, come down. I am a true man, not like the other you challenge. You cannot allow your men to see you afraid before me.*

The Great King's silence stretched out. Geraint's heart beat heavy in his chest. The cawing crow had been joined by one of its fellows, and together they gossiped, perhaps laying wagers on the fight to come. Donatus stamped and snorted, impatient with all this standing about.

Then, the Great King touched his charioteer's shoulder, and the boy in turn touched up the great brown horses, and slowly, carefully walked them down the hill.

The effect was of a god descending. Geraint had seen the Great King from a distance, and he had seen another giant up close once, a little more than a year ago. He had thought himself ready for the one named Rhyddid ap Carchar. But what came to him now was nothing like the phantom that had come seeking Gawain. The Great King was a man of flesh and bone: that could be seen in his eyes and his skin

and the war-hardened hands. But he was of a stature such
as Geraint had never before seen in mortal man. Had he
lifted his arm out straight, Geraint could have walked under
it without bowing his head. Despite his enormous size, it was
easy to see that the Great King was still a young man, perhaps
even younger than Geraint. Thick, brown hair fell to his
waist, bound in a leather thong. His beard was scanty yet,
and his pale green eyes were wide and unlined as they looked
out from under the battered Roman-style helmet. He wore
armour of boiled leather over his chest, leather trousers on
his legs and leather guards on his wrists. In place of sword
or spear, he held a great, thick club, knobbed with bronze
and scarred and stained from use. His shield matched it, a
relic from the Roman times like his helm, great and square,
such as a man might hide his whole body behind, even when
the body was the size of the giant before him.

The Great King climbed down from his chariot and planted
his feet on the ground. Even on horseback, Geraint felt puny
before him.

'Will you meet me on foot, Sir Geraint?' inquired Rhyddid,
his voice filled with exaggerated courtesy. 'Or are Arthur's
men only brave when they're mounted?' Geraint ignored
the crude joke, but his heart quailed at the challenge. On
horseback, he could manoeuvre more quickly than the
chariot. No doubt the Great King knew that and so made
this choice. Young he might be, but he was not unseasoned.

Geraint dismounted. He wished he'd brought one of the
boys to take Donatus away with him. Well, the horse was a
smart beast and would save itself should the need arise.
Rhyddid reached out without taking his eyes from Geraint
and tapped the chariot's side. The boy whistled to the team
and turned them around, moving back to the base of the
hill, but going no further. He would not desert his king.

Now that they faced each other on level ground, Geraint

felt he had indeed shrunk back to a stripling boy. Had they
stood side by side, the Great King would have been head
and shoulders above Sir Kai, who was called the Tall by the
bards. The club might at first seem a crude weapon, but its
master carried it as easily as Geraint carried his spear, and
probably he knew as much of its use. Geraint's own arms
seemed suddenly flimsy in comparison. Even his shield felt
thin as parchment.

'Come then.' Rhyddid swung his club back and forth, and
Geraint thought he heard regret in his voice.

In answer, Geraint stepped back and let the Great King
come forward.

Slowly, they began to circle one another, the first steps of
the dance that might end with life for all, or might end only
in death.

TWENTY-THREE

Elen waited in the darkness. Behind her, she felt the others rather than heard them. The vibrations of their many hearts woke again the hunting hunger within her.

Where was Calonnau? Where was Geraint? Had the battle been joined yet? Did he even still live? She did not dare take her mind and will from what was before her.

Angry now, she called out again. 'Maius! Maius Smith! Your daughter Elen calls you!'

I cannot have been wrong.

'It would seem your tryst will not happen,' came the mocking voice of the mouse-king. 'Will you go in search of the smith now, bitter willow bound about your brow?'

But even as he spoke, the darkness around them changed. The red light of the forge seeped across the floor, turning the pools of milk to pools of blood. Ahead on her left, Elen could make out a doorway limned in the fierce glow. Heat crept across her skin, prickling the fine hairs on her arms and cheeks.

Ching-ching. Ching-ching. The smith's hammer rang out from behind the door.

Behind Elen, all was still.

Elen walked forward, the precious jug held close against her, as if it might shield her from what was to come. At her approach, the door fell open, and beyond it, she saw the forge. It did not matter that this was not where she had seen this chamber before. Nothing mattered, save that the crucible heat of the forge poured out to envelop her. And there was the smith, twisted and bent under the disfiguring scars, standing behind his silver anvil, forging yet another link for the golden chain that bound him as tightly as it bound all the others in this cursed place.

It was not the fae you displeased. Oh, father, I am sorry.

Pity drove out fear, and Elen was able to stand at the threshold of the forge. The heat beat down on her in wave after wave. She welcomed its first touch, as one welcomes the dawn after the winter's night, but soon she felt its claws sinking into her skin, seeking the flesh underneath. She could not imagine what it was like for the smith with his many burns still so raw.

'Maius,' she whispered. She had no doubt he heard her. He lifted his ravaged face, turning the swollen and ragged slits that had once held eyes towards her.

'Daughter?' The word was thick and heavy, for his lips were so twisted by their scars they could scarcely move to shape the words.

'Yes.' She stepped across the threshold. Heat seared her skin. Perspiration sprang out against her brow, and was gone in a moment. 'I am the daughter of your daughters.'

'Ah, gods all!' Maius raised his face as a man might when praying to heaven. To her surprise, Elen saw the tracks of tears running from his burned and ruined eyes sockets. 'I did not think there was more he could do to me. Why came you here?' Even as he wailed aloud his hands worked. The hammer fell, again and again, his fingers turned the gold chain.

Ching-ching.

'I am come to free you, father,' said Elen. 'I have come to put out the fire.'

'You cannot,' he said with the conviction of a man speaking of destiny. 'There is not water enough in the world.'

But Elen strode forward. The heat worked down her throat into her lungs. She stood in a stone oven. The coals glowed so brightly her eyes squinted and her vision blurred, but there were no tears for her. The heat had dried them up before they could fall. The stench of burning surrounded her. It filled her mouth and lungs. It was the smell of death, the smell of the ravaged village as she ran through it trying to reach her mother's corpse. It was the smell that came when she fell onto the ground and saw Beven, his hand stretched out towards his broken harp.

'Stop, daughter, stop,' lisped the smith, his hammer beating frantically at the gold. He was trying to drop the tool, trying to move, she saw his muscles bunch and strain beneath his skin. 'Go back before he finds you. He'll know.'

His words made her shudder, but all he could do was plead. He must stay where he was, forging the golden chain. It lay snaked across the cracked flagstones. It was piled in loops and heaps, impossibly precious and delicate, infinite and endless, both contained within this one strange chamber, and stretching out beyond it. Elen picked her way over it. The chain caught at her skirt as if it had thorns, and all at once she felt the weight of the walls over her. She was buried. She was bound to the fire, to the stone and the earth. In her mind's eye she saw the mountains, the narrow valleys, the streams, and the forests spread out before her. She saw the teeming inhabitants, the humans and the beasts, and those who were neither, and around them she saw the shimmering walls of gold. She saw them beating wings and hearts against them. She saw them kneel in prayer with wailing voices that could not reach past the shining walls. She felt the weight of the incorruptible gold pressing down on her until she could no longer breathe and the fear glided through her that she would smother.

I cannot smother. I cannot die. She stretched out will and mind, and she found Calonnau. She felt the rush of the fresh air, and saw the green and brown of the country spread beneath her. Her heart soared safe. She could only be hurt, she could not be killed, and hurt she could endure. She could still walk forward, and she did, one staggering step at a time, until she stood before the forge.

'No!' the smith cried.

It was a rough-walled crucible, a curved and open oven with its wide bed of coals burning orange and red. A blue-hearted flame leapt up as if startled by her footfalls. Elen dragged in a deep breath of the searing air and raised the red clay jug.

She poured out the milk. Steam, smoke and ash rose up in a great, choking cloud. She could not breathe. She could not see. Her eyes burned as if the fire were in them. Sparks landed on her scalp and skin, pin-pricks of bright pain. She smelled the horrible stench of burning hair, and knew it was her own. She forced her hands to clamp tightly to the cool, curving sides of the clay jug, and she held it high that the blessed liquid might flow out freely and she held herself strong against the pain.

It was poison, this smoke. No living creature could breathe so much, she knew that as she knew the rush and rasp of it filling her raw throat and lungs. But Elen did not live. It was only pain, and she endured.

Little by little, the heat began to fail. The smoke began to clear. Elen's ravaged throat felt the touch of clean air. Little by little, the ash grew heavy and fell to the floor. One by one the red coals of the forge died and turned black. One coal at a time, darkness fell.

Elen's arms shook and her grip at last failed. The jug slipped from her fingers and crashed to the floor, broken into a hundred red shards.

Filthy, burned, char-covered, ash-choked, wheezing and filled with pain, Elen lifted her grit-caked eyes to see Maius Smith, surrounded by his chain, standing beside his silver anvil. His great arms hung loose at his side. For a long moment, they stood together, and there was only silence.

'It is done,' he breathed. 'Done!'

The delicate hammer slipped from his fingers, falling to ring sweet and clear against the stones. It was the sound of triumph. Maius stretched out his thick misshapen hands to her. Elen, moving slowly on her trembling legs, stumbled forward to take them. In their grasp, she felt again her mother's hands, swollen and wracked with their disease, and she wondered at it.

She tried to speak, but only coughed hard. The smith's strong grip steadied her as she shook. 'A boon, father,' she rasped. 'Before you go from here.'

'Anything, daughter.' His voice was gentle now, as if he had already begun to heal from his labours. She looked at him, blinking her own burning eyes, and for a moment, she saw the man beneath the ravaged slave. She saw how his eyes had once been clear and brown, and his hands strong with clean labour. She saw the pride, the strong, honest, pride that had led him astray to this place.

'Give me the chain,' she said.

Trembling now, those hands reached for the chain they had forged over a hundred lifetimes. They lifted it up, stretching a length of the golden lace between them, and held it out to her.

'It's yours now. I give it you, daughter mine. *I* give it.'

Her hand closed around that precious, unfinished link,

enclosing the weight and the warmth of the soft metal. 'Be
at peace, Maius Smith.'

'I am free,' was all Maius said, and as he did, Elen felt his
heart begin to beat.

Then it ceased, and he was gone and Elen stood alone,
gripping the golden chain in her burned hand.

It occurred to her slowly that she should have been in the
dark. But a golden glow shone before her eyes. It came from
the chain. It shimmered and pulsed as it coiled through the
chamber, like a snake's skin beneath the sunlight. It was
alive, this thing, alive with all the power Maius Smith had
poured into it. It was impossibly fine. It might have been a
chain of silken ribbon, it was so light. It might have been
the stones that made the mountains, it was so terribly heavy.
It was so long she could not find its end and it lay in shin-
high heaps about the floor. It was so short she could have
coiled it up once and held it in the palm of her hand.

It didn't matter, the mystery of the thing. What mattered
was she had been given it by its maker. It was hers now, to
do with as she would.

She wasted no more time. The light of the Little King's
fetter showed her the door. All around her, the room seemed
to be falling into shadow, as if it was melting back into the
darkness that had made it. Dragging the terrible weight of
the chain behind her, Elen waded towards the door. She did
not look back. She did not want to see the chain stretching
out into nothing but darkness.

Ahead of her stood the mouse-king and his wife and all
their people. They surrounded her with their pounding
hearts. They watched her with their black eyes. She felt weary
beyond all measure. She said not one word to the god or
goddess that Gwiffert's art had made so small. She only turned
her face towards where the air was lighter and began to
trudge forward.

They gathered behind her. They hoisted the great chain onto their shoulders, raising it up, taking what of the burden each of them could. In silent procession, they followed Elen as she led them out to the open air.

The great club swung down yet again, catching the edge of Geraint's shield, jarring his arm up to his shoulder. Geraint backed away again, circling. Rhyddid's reach was beyond any Geraint had ever known. With each step, each feint, he cursed the loss of his spear. Some time ago, Rhyddid had caught it with his great club and snapped the shaft in two. Now it lay useless on the ground somewhere. With only his sword left to him, Geraint's only hope was to keep his distance from his opponent. But Rhyddid knew his size and he knew himself. He had seen this tactic before, and he moved sparingly, letting Geraint wear himself out with his hopping around. Geraint would tire, he would slow down, and Rhyddid would be ready for him.

Another enemy might have grinned, might even have taunted, but the young king did his work in grim silence, watching Geraint, turning to keep his face always towards his foe, swinging at the nearest feints, but holding back otherwise. He would not be rushed. He saw that time was his friend, not Geraint's. The day was growing hot, and sweat poured down Geraint's face and made his hands slick. His throat was dry, his legs aching. The Great King saw all this, and he waited.

There was one thing he did not know. Geraint dodged left, then right. He took another blow, and his shield shivered, and he heard its wooden frame crack. It would break on the next blow. He backed away, circling again. Rhyddid turned, remorseless, fresh as if they had just begun, balanced lightly on his huge feet.

He did not know that Arthur had learned sword craft

against his tall foster brother before Sir Kai was lamed. Rhyddid did not know that Arthur insisted all the squires he took to train for the Round Table learn well at least one trick to even unequal heights.

But there would be one chance and one chance only. Geraint forced himself to breathe evenly. He blinked hard, clearing the stinging sweat from his eyes. If he failed here, with his shield set to break, he would die.

Geraint let his breath heave, shuddering his shoulders, making his jaw slack. He watched the Great King's eyes narrow.

Geraint screamed, high, sharp and wild, the scream of the blue-stained men who hurled themselves at the sides of Din Eityn when he was a boy. He ran in, his sword raised as high as his arm could take it, already sweeping down to cut at the Great King's jaw.

Rhyddid ducked his head, and brought up his club to block the blow. But Geraint saw the curved path of the weapon, and jerked his sword away, bringing it down behind while he swung up his shield. The shield took the blow, and failed, shattering, driving a sharp splinter into Geraint's arm. But while he cried aloud with the pain, his sword stroke did not falter, and he sliced down on Rhyddid's leg behind the knee. The Great King screamed and fell, and Geraint slammed forward with all his weight, bearing the giant down to the ground. They landed together, but Geraint recovered first, and he scrambled to his feet, kicking away the club. In the next breath, Geraint brought his sword up against Rhyddid's neck.

They stayed like that for a long moment, Geraint panting, blood pouring down his shield arm, almost unable to believe the feint had worked; the Great King lying on his back, his own blood spilling onto the ground, feeling the edge of Geraint's sword at his throat, knowing he was beaten, and knowing that beyond them, the Little King watched.

'Quickly,' he said in a thick and angry whisper. 'Kill me. Condemn me not to his slavery.'

'You are a great knight. Knight to knight, slave to slave, trust me now.'

The green eyes looked into his. Geraint stepped back and held out his bloody hand. 'Trust me,' he said again. 'I beg you.'

Rhyddid's eyes flickered back and forth, seeing what?

Whatever it was it caused the Great King to reach up and take Geraint's hand. Geraint braced his feet, leaning back, and in so doing, he helped his fallen enemy to stand.

From behind there came a furious scream and the sudden thunder of hoofbeats. Geraint turned, sword arm up high.

His blade knocked aside the spear of Manawyddan which rushed straight for his breast and sent it clattering to earth.

King Gwiffert's scream of fury changed to one of anguish. He reined his horse up, both his hands empty for the first time since Geraint had seen him. It was as if the Little King had lost a limb. He leaned down to lunge for the spear, and Geraint, breathing hard from the fight and the fear, stepped into his path.

Even as his eyes met Gwiffert's, the Little King began to change. His outstretched arm shrank and shrivelled. His skin turned brown and cracked like ancient parchment, pulling itself tight over his bones. Gold hair faded to white, his broad shoulders hunched up and his long neck drew in. So this was the ultimate power of the spear. As long as Gwiffert held it, he held all the long years of his life at bay.

Staggering, Geraint walked over to the fallen spear. His hand closed around it, and he lifted it up. He felt its power sing through him, and suddenly it was as if he had not fought at all. He was strong and straight, and whole and well. The blood was wet on his skin, but there was no wound beneath it. He raised the spear and levelled the tip of it at the Little King.

Gwiffert screamed again in wordless outrage, the shriek of a wild animal. He stood up in the stirrups as high as his bowed legs would let him. He flung out his arms and he screeched to the heavens. Geraint threw the spear, straight and true, but he was too late. The Little King was gone, and his horse, the innocent beast, lay on the ground, bleeding from the great wound in its back, screaming in its bestial pain.

Then the spear was again in Geraint's hand.

'Where!' roared Geraint. 'Where are you!'

'There is only one place,' murmured the Great King. Geraint stared. He had forgotten the giant. Without another word, he ran for Donatus and flung himself up into the saddle. He dug his heels into the horse's side and sent it leaping forward. He left an army of slaves, he left another of free men, he left an enemy standing behind him. He abandoned all command and all sense. There was only speed now. Only a mad dash as fast as this elvish horse could run.

For the Little King had gone to ground, and Elen was down there with him.

The way back to the great hall was long. They had gone so deep, the burden they carried was so heavy, Elen's body was crying out for rest. Her feet ached, her knees ached, her hands burned from the heat of the forge and from the press of the golden chain she cradled in them now. But she did not falter. She could not. She did not know what spells lay in the earth beneath the fortress, but she would not risk them smothering what was to come. She would break this chain, this vile enchantment, in the clean and open air.

But her strength was ebbing, even as they grew closer. The folk behind her bore the burden bravely, dragging the bright chain with them, but their hearts were failing. She could feel it.

Around them, the paintings grew clear again, the monsters fought their battles, the cattle lowed and grazed, the orchards blossomed. Elen staggered, and staggered again. Her hollow breast was falling in on itself. Her lungs strained against the ribs that caged them. She was too cold and she was too hot. She had nothing to hang onto, nothing but the chain, and the chain was dragging her to the ground.

Calonnau, she thought, casting her will out. *Calonnau. Come to me. I need my heart. I need you.*

She felt the hawk take wing. She felt the anger and the hunger, but also she felt her catch the wind that would bear her near. Elen found the strength to walk on.

The world around Gwiffert blurred, as if he flew more than rode through it. The land was still his to command. Distance and time knew his will yet, if not as well as they once had. Gwiffert could feel the power ebbing from him, running from his body like blood from a mortal wound. He would not have his enchantment for much longer.

It was as well he would not need it. There had always been the danger that either Geraint or Elen would attempt deception. He had prepared for it, for Morgaine's warnings might be double-edged, but they were seldom wrong

He had left the gate open behind the army as they left. He did not want Geraint to see the way it was opened. More, he did not want to be denied entry to his own hall should his hold on the spear fail. His feeble hands pulled at the reins and his horse came to a halt in the middle of the yard. The remaining slaves stopped and marvelled to see the arrival of such a tiny, wizened man. He did not hesitate as he dismounted, but hobbled into the foyer and from there to the great hall. All he passed stood and stared, but only for a moment. The lessons of their lifetime had been well learned. They had no orders for such a situation, so they turned their faces away, lest they do something to anger their master. Oh no, not one of them would risk the wrath of the Little King and stop this strange old man.

Panting hard from his exertions, Gwiffert mounted the stairs to the mews, half pulling himself up by the rail. His own gasps nearly choked him, but he could not give himself any rest. He had felt the smith's absence the moment he entered the hall, felt it like a knife in his belly. So, Geraint and Elen had together worked their deception. She had the chain now and struggled to reach the open air. It was perceptive of her to take the chain beyond the protections woven so deep into the foundations of his fortress. It would avail her nothing, though. He knew her weakness, hers and her man's, and he would use it now. After that, they would have much leisure to repent what they had done in his service.

With shaking, withered hands, Gwiffert pulled the key ring out from under his shirt. He selected the golden key and unlocked the door. The lock had never felt so stiff in his fingers before; never had it taken so much strength to pull the portal open.

It does not matter. It does not matter.

The familiar confines of the mews surrounded him, and he inhaled the scents of straw and fresh wind, gaining strength. On her perch, Blodwen looked at him and hooted, first in anger and then in querulous confusion.

'Yes, Blodwen, it is your master,' he said as he shuffled across the room. 'Do not attend to my form now.' He lifted the owl from her perch. She hooted anxiously again, but seemed to recognize something in his touch and his voice as he stroked her feathers, murmuring to her. 'Yes, it is I. It is your king. All will soon be right, with your help, Blodwen. I need you now.'

He carried her gently to the windows, speaking to her all the while, reminding her who he was.

'There is a hawk, Blodwen. She comes here to her mistress. Bring her to me, Blodwen. Bring her to me.'

The owl hooted once more then raised her dusky wings and launched herself into the sky.

Gwiffert watched her through his rheumy eyes until she disappeared, her shadow merging with the forest. Now there was only one thing to do.

He ached. The weight of his years sat heavily across his shoulders. He'd had no time to accustom himself to it, and its wrongness distracted his mind and sent twitches and palsies down his muscles.

Soon, all will be right again, he told himself. *Show them your strength. Show them it is not just your father's gift that they should fear.*

He rested his hands on the stone lintel. He reached out, feeling his way downward through the stones to the earth in which they were rooted, the strong earth that was both tool and traitor, the earth that like Blodwen still knew his touch, but unlike her was already restless in its obedience, for it too well remembered its other shape.

Not yet. Not yet. First, you will bring me Sir Geraint. Let him come, and let him come fast.

Gwiffert felt the earth obey and he lifted his hands away from the stones. He did not care how they shook with their weakness. He still smiled, and so smiling he returned to the stairs. Elen was going to the yard. It would be rude of him as host not to meet her there.

Elen emerged at last into the fortress yard, her burden cradled close to her breast. The yard was full of people, but they all cowered in shadows and corners, unable or unwilling, perhaps, to understand that their master's power had truly begun to break. The only one who stood before her was an ancient man. His pale skin was spotted brown with age and hanging loosely from his fine bones. His jaw stuck out past the tip of his nose. His lips shrivelled against his toothless gums. His eyes were all but white with cataracts. He hunched there in a leather corselet that was far too large for him. He had a gauntlet on one hand and he smiled up at her, a cheerful, black-gummed, mischievous smile.

'Elen,' he said. 'And what pretty present is this you bring me?'

She froze, suddenly understanding who stood before her. Then she noticed the spear was missing, and she felt victory ring through her.

'Well you may be surprised,' chuckled Gwiffert as if it were all an excellent joke. 'But it is good of you to bring me back what has been stolen.' He held out his skinny claw of a hand. 'You will give that to me now.'

Elen rallied her wits. 'You are no more king here, Gwiffert pen Lleied.'

The smile did not falter. 'You think not? You think it was the spear that made me king? You see my empty hands,' he turned them up, 'and you ask yourself, "Where is the spear?" Better you ask yourself, "Where is my heart?"'

As he spoke those words Elen's mind skittered away. She saw the world where Calonnau was, the trees below, the sky heavy with clouds above. She saw the undulations of the valleys and hills, and she saw the fortress walls. The hawk beat her wings and spread them, soaring on the gathered wind.

Pain struck. It slammed against the back of her neck, knocking Elen from her feet. Calonnau cried out in pure panic and Elen screamed. She was on fire, she was torn apart. She fought, she flailed her arms, wings, talons, hands, but it did no good, the pain only got worse, and she was borne down by a great weight until her breast pressed hard against the cruel ground. Blood poured down her back and head: Calonnau's blood, her blood, Calonnau's. Talons gouged her flesh.

'No, Blodwen. Bring her to me,' said Gwiffert.

The world tipped and spun, flesh separated from bone as the claws dug in deeper. Elen screamed until her back arched and the fingers of her left hand raked the sky. Her right still clutched the chain, but barely. Then she went limp able only to feel the pain that would not end.

Through the haze and horror, she saw Gwiffert turn to the ones who had followed her. 'Well, brave ones? Will you not run to help her? Will you not stand and fight me? Come! I am an old man!' He flung out his arms. 'Which of you will be the first!'

'I will!'

Elen cried out again. Hoofbeats thundered through the gate. She could see nothing clearly. She saw Geraint through a mist of green and brown and red. Geraint, tall on horse-back, reined Donatus up short. He held the spear of Manawyddan in his hand. Through her pain he seemed a hundred miles away, but he was there. She pushed herself up onto her knees. Her right hand still held the chain. She must not let go. She must not lose that.

'Kill me if you will, Sir Geraint,' the wizened king said calmly. 'But hear me first. My owl, my Blodwen, holds the hawk you so prettily call Calonnau. It is by my word she returns with the living bird. If I die, she will have no master. Her hunger is great, Sir Knight. When I am dead, what will keep her from tearing the hawk to pieces and feeding that hunger?'

Horror drew Geraint back. Elen saw the stones of the courtyard. The world turned and rushed forward. The Little King lifted his hand. The dull thud as she, Calonnau, she, hit the stones at his feet was almost unfelt under the blaze of the other pain tearing down her back. She collapsed onto the ground, and saw the hawk, broken and bloody, saw herself seeing the hawk, and Calonnau cried weakly.

Geraint drew his arm back to throw the spear, but Gwiffert was on his knees, neatly scooping up the hawk in his hand.

'Now then.' Gwiffert grinned, clutching the hawk to him. 'Now then, she is mine, she is in my hand. My word shall heal her, and then what else is mine, eh? Give me the chain now, and give me the spear, and perhaps I will give her back to you. Give me the spear, Sir Geraint. Do not make me order your lovely wife to take it from you.'

Elen looked to Geraint, fear in her eyes and pain burning through her. *Remember your promise,* she said across all that separated them. *I love you. Remember that too.*

'Elen, stand up,' said Gwiffert.

Elen felt the geas descend, and, mute with need and fascination, she stood. The pain was beyond comprehension, but it did not matter. Her shaking hands clutched the chain, but she could not remember why. Only standing was important. Only standing.

Geraint.

Geraint hesitated no longer. He did not look at her. The blue-eyed knight cast out his spear, and the spear flew true. It split the breast of the hawk, and the pain split Elen in two. She screamed, and the dying hawk screamed, and she held up her arms in wordless horrified prayer, for heart and breast, and all her unhealed wounds were torn open.

She saw Morgaine standing over her, and she saw her heart in the sorceress's hand, and she saw the wound in her breast, and she felt . . .

She felt the wound close. She felt her heart slamming hard against her ribs, driving her lungs to draw great gouts of air and sending her burning blood coursing through her body.

Her wounded throat closed, her wounded wrist closed. She felt it. She felt her skin grow whole and sound, but most of all she felt her heart, her own heart within her. She felt its beat driving the river of her living blood in the rhythm that had its echo in every living thing. The whole world lived, and she in its embrace was whole and strong and alive. Alive!

She staggered to her feet. Wild-eyed and wild-hearted she shouted a wordless and ecstatic cry to the heavens. All at once, Geraint was in her arms, crushing her to him with the strength of his one-armed embrace. She kissed him hard for joy, for love, for life itself.

When at last they parted, and she could bear to look away from Geraint's shining face, she saw what he had done. On the ground of the yard lay the Little King, Calonnau held before him like a shield. The spear was already back in Geraint's hand. On the ground there was only the blood and the broken bodies of the Little King and the hawk.

Elen swallowed hard at the pathetic sight of Calonnau. She could not move for a time. Geraint's arm curled around her shoulders.

Then, someone she had forgotten about, the mouse-queen, walked silently forward. She held out the golden chain to Elen.

'Please,' she said softly. 'Please. Let it be done now.'

Elen took the chain from her. She turned her gaze to Calonnau broken upon the breast of her enemy. She called up the memory of the hunts, the strength, the wild delight, the feel of breaking bones beneath strong talons.

With all the strength of Calonnau's savagery, Elen snapped the golden chain in two.

Everything fell still for a single instant. Then, the air shuddered. The fortress walls melted into the ground, and beyond them the narrow gorges broadened into green valleys. Stands of trees spread out to become whole forests. Streams turned to rivers, pools to silver lakes. It was as if all the world was a fist clenched too tightly that now fell open before their eyes.

All around them, the people, huddled where the shadows had been, so long prisoners, stared at each other in reverent wonder like people who see a holy thing. They lifted their hands, reaching out to the land, each of them seeing some familiar shape or place. And then they were gone, Elen was sure, to those homes which had been gathered up so tightly in the Little King's fist and were now turned loose to resume their proper places.

A warm wind blew, and Elen knew there was more to come. She heard a sound, a shiver, the sharp bark of wood hitting stone. Doors. Doors opening – a hundred, a thousand, and a great column of half-formed shapes rising into the sky. She saw dragons there, she saw the fae, she saw eagles and stags, great boars and white stallions galloping on the wind. All the monsters and beauties painted on the Little King's walls. Then they too were gone, and the great labyrinth that had trapped them for so long was no more than a ring of standing stones.

It was all so like a dream, Elen could feel no fear, only profound wonder. Beside her, Geraint was bright eyed and staring in awe.

But they were not alone. The mouse-king and his queen still stood beside them, but they too were changed. The hunched, brown, wild people were no more. These two shone, even more brightly than the Lady and the Lord. Husband and wife they were, and so much more. They brimmed with life, like a forest, like a mountain, like the earth itself. God and goddess, they were all they had been, and they stood with their hands clasped before Elen and Geraint. Elen went down on her knees at once. Geraint's hand moved to cross himself, but he cut short the gesture, and he too knelt.

So many husbands, so many wives in all this long strange time, thought Elen, bemused, thinking of Morgaine and Urien, the Lady and Lord, even Eynon and Gwin. So much power shared between them all. Was it odd that it was only Gwiffert who did not have someone beside him, and Gwiffert was the one who fell?

'Thank you,' said the god, and his voice was warm and green, and flowed like water beneath the summer sky. 'We will not forget.'

The goddess did not speak. She went to Calonnau and lifted the bird up gently.

Elen licked her lip. 'Can you . . .' she stopped, feeling suddenly like a greedy child.

The goddess shook her head. 'It would not be wise to reverse the order of things at this time, child. But she will be buried with reverence, and blessings will come from the place where she lies.'

Elen bowed her head. 'Thank you.'

'What of him?' asked Geraint, nodding towards the body of the Little King.

A light sparked in the god's eye and Elen felt colder than she ever had while her heart was gone from her. 'His doom comes.'

She heard the hoofbeats, and she raised her head. They rode up the hillside on their grey horses, eleven of them, their naked skulls bare to the broad light of day. As they came closer, she saw that the brands that marked them were gone. Elen drew back and Geraint wrapped his arm around her. But the god and goddess made no move. The Grey Men gave no sign that they saw the living beings before them. Two of them dismounted and hoisted the Little King's body onto the twelfth horse. In silence, they remounted, and in silence they led the twelfth horse away down the hill, vanishing into the tangled forest.

'Now comes your last deed in this place,' said the god to them. 'Turn towards the east and walk. You will soon find yourself at your home.'

Elen bowed her head. Geraint did the same. The warm wind blew, smelling of spring and summer together. When they raised their eyes, they were alone on the high hill beside the standing stones.

They stood, shaking a little with fear and awe. Elen turned to Geraint. Whole for the first time in so long, she looked into his eyes and she felt how her heart beat heavy beneath its burden of joy to see him before her, to feel him take her hands and pull her close so that she might kiss him with all the warmth, all the life that they between them had won.

'Come now, my husband,' she said at last. 'Let us go and finish our task.'

TWENTY-FOUR

They travelled down the Roman way out of the Black
Mountains by the light of the waning moon. Geraint led the
way on Donatus, and Elen rode behind on the little brown,
holding Manawyddan's spear in her right hand. They had
found the horses grazing beside a swift-running river below
the hill of stones. They did not ask questions but accepted
their presence and rode away.

Torches shone on both sides of the river, and the hushed
sounds of men's voices rippled like the moonlit water. Elen
looked across the Usk and up towards her home. The sparks
of torches burned at the high house as well. Urien was on
the watch tonight. Did he know they were come?

'Halt!' A stern-voiced shadow stepped out onto the road
and brought three friends with him. 'Who's that?'

Geraint reined Donatus to a halt. 'Sir Geraint of Camelot
and the Round Table,' he said loud enough to be heard by
half the world. 'With him the Lady Elen, Adara's daughter
and rightful holder of Pont Cymryd!'

The first man's face went slack with shock. In the next
moment he gave out a jubilant whoop. 'Sir Geraint!' He
ran forward to clasp the knight's hand. 'God's legs! We

thought you were dead! Cyril!' He slapped one of his mates on the shoulder. 'Run for Sir Agravain! Sir Geraint's returned!'

Cyril pelted away towards the camp, shouting out at the top of his lungs, 'Sir Geraint's returned! Sir Geraint is here!' The three men around them were cheering. Soon, the whole world was cheering and running towards them. The men pulled Geraint down off Donatus's back so they could clasp his hands and beat upon his shoulders and embrace him in brotherhood. Geraint bore all this with a great grin on his face, laughing and calling out the names of those he recognized.

'What the merry hell is all this?' bellowed a new voice. All instantly fell silent. The crowd of grinning men parted, suddenly looking like children who know they have been caught in mischief. Down the lane they made in their ranks stalked the lean, angry man who had been at Geraint's side when he came in disguise to stand before Urien. Now, he was clean-shaven and dressed like a city man in boots, breeches and a blue tunic, but there was no mistaking his eyes, nor his voice. 'Does the enemy need to know all our business? Are you barbarians or are you soldiers and king's men? Get away!'

The bravest bore Sir Agravain's glower for ten heartbeats or so, and then scurried meekly after their companions, all save the sentries who took up their posts again, leaning on their spears and grinning at the show.

Agravain ignored them. He turned to face Geraint.

'God be with you too, brother,' said Geraint mildly.

Agravain looked him up and down, but Elen could not tell whether or not he was satisfied with what he saw. 'We thought Urien had dropped you into the river.' Elen's command of the eastern tongue was not fluent, but she understood enough to follow Agravain's drawling words.

Geraint raised his brows, as if a bit surprised at this news. 'No, that he failed to do.'

'Gawain will be pleased.'

'How does our brother?'

Agravain sighed, clearly put out by either the question or the answer he must give. 'The High King sent him on some business among the Saxons, so I am left to deal with the mess you left behind here.' Agravain folded his arms and turned his glower on Elen. 'I see you have retrieved the lady.'

'Mind your tongue, brother,' Geraint's words took on a warning tone. 'We are man and wife.'

Shock silenced Agravain for the space of three breaths. 'You are not,' he announced flatly.

'Yes,' replied Geraint. 'We are.'

'Geraint . . .'

But Geraint cut his older brother off. 'This is not a subject for debate, brother. Nor will our uncle find it so when he hears the full tale.'

Even in the torchlight, Elen could see Agravain's face flush red with anger. 'Upon my life, Geraint,' he said softly, hoarsely. 'This is not even worthy of Gawain. I thought you had some sense.'

Geraint's face remained quiet and unperturbed. 'Odd, I thought the same of you.'

Elen dipped her head to hide her smile. Agravain did not miss this, and his eyes smouldered.

'Geraint . . .'

Geraint ignored his brother. Instead of answering Agravain, he took Elen's hand. 'Forgive me, my wife. The fond greeting of my brother makes me forget we have serious business still. Let us gather the captains and tell them what has happened.'

Elen's smile fell away. She pressed Geraint's hand. 'No. I will go to the bridge.'

Donatus stirred, responding to his rider's uneasiness. Agravain was looking from Geraint to Elen, his mouth pinched into a thin line. 'Elen, we can do nothing until morning,' said Geraint.

'No,' she said again. 'I know what I must do, and I must do it now.'

Geraint sighed. 'Very well. I will take you.'

Which was too much for Agravain. 'Geraint, what is this?'

Geraint gathered up Donatus's reins. 'Step back, brother, and trust for once. There are matters here more suited to Merlin's ways than ours.'

At that, Agravain did step back, and Elen rode at Geraint's side through the maze of pavilions, fires and men, down the slope to the riverside. She dismounted and he took the reins from her. The whole camp seemed gathered in their wake to watch whatever was about to happen. She heard the men's questions to each other, both soft and loud, and the orders of their commanders, and Geraint's voice making answers and giving yet more orders, but she was beyond understanding any of it. Before her waited the bridge, where this long and tortured quest had begun and where it must now end.

Elen mounted the steps slowly. The night air was cool against her skin and smelled of river water and coming rain. The Usk murmured and chuckled as it flowed around the supporting stones and hearing it was like hearing the voices of her family.

Across the way, she saw Urien's men, made white, black and orange by torchlight. She saw them fingering their knives and their staffs and wondering what they should do.

She let them wonder. She stood on the bridge and raised the spear high. 'Urien!' she cried out and her voice rang in the darkness. 'Urien y Tarw! Adara's ghost calls you to the bridge! Urien! Yestin's ghost calls you to the bridge! The dead of Pont Cymryd murdered by your word rise up this night and call you forth!'

He would hear. If he were a hundred miles away, he would hear that call. Torches flared higher. The guards on the far side of the bridge gathered together, murmuring and pointing, trying to decide what to do. The night wind caught her cloak and sent it billowing behind her like wings.

She waited. Be it a short time or a long time, it didn't matter. She could wait by her own will now. She was free and alive and no one would ever bind her again. She had all the time there was.

She saw eyes and armour shine amid the dark mass of men beyond the torchlight, and through them walked Urien.

'What is this? The little girl's returned?' He sounded lazy, and annoyed, as if by a busy fly.

'Yes, she's returned, safe and whole to her home, as was promised,' replied Elen. 'Safe and whole, Urien.' She spoke those words slowly, letting the import of them sink into him.

Urien stepped into the torchlight. He was much as she had seen him last when he gloated over her as his prize to dispose of at his whim. 'Right glad I am to hear it.' He folded his arms. He wore a dark cloak, pinned with a silver brooch. 'Where's that husband I gave you to?' His gaze drifted past Elen, searching the riverbank behind her. 'I have a word or two to say to him.'

Elen gripped the spear all the more tightly. It was a calculated insult. *Let it go.* 'His business with you will wait on mine.'

Urien barked out a rough laugh. 'You think you have some business with me, little girl?'

They had stood like this before, at the beginning, when she had held a sword she did not know how to use, and had not understood the nature of her enemy. He must brag, he must shout his prowess for all his men to hear. He would not appear afraid to them, but she had learned the ways of watching close since she had been away. He knew that she had changed. She saw the glitter of his eyes as they narrowed, she saw the way his weight came forward onto his toes, and how hard his fingers dug into the flesh of his own arms.

'I've come for my home, my land and my people, Urien.' She called it out loudly. Let Urien's men hear. Let all the world hear.

Urien snorted and climbed the stairs of the bridge. 'You'd have done better to wait for the army behind you to mount up.'

He came to stand before her, his hands loose at his side. The Usk swirled and chattered beneath them, suddenly sounding very loud. 'This matter is first between you and me,' said Elen.

Without another word, Urien lunged, knocking Elen onto her back, but she was ready for that, and she tucked her chin to keep her head from banging against the stone. She thrust the spear cross-wise before her, shoving him back to land awkwardly on his buttocks. He laughed and rolled and came up faster than she would have guessed. He grabbed for the spear. Elen thrust it between his legs, tripping him. He slammed down, cracking his head on the stone while she scrambled to her feet. Urien came up, teeth bared, knife in hand, and Elen with all the power of her rage and vengeance, cast the spear out.

It pierced the silver brooch at his throat. It pierced flesh and sinew and bone. It sent Urien staggering backward, blood pouring from him, until his body, dead already, fell from the bridge and splashed into the river. The waters swirled with blood for a moment and then closed over him, and Urien the Bull was gone.

The spear was back in Elen's hand. She scarcely noticed. She was looking at the place in the river where her enemy had fallen. She realized she was not breathing, and she took in a gulp of air, and another, and another. Her heart, which had stopped, beat wildly again, and Elen's whole body shook. She leaned against the spear for support, but she could not seem to look up from the river.

Then she heard footsteps and felt Geraint's familiar touch on her shoulders, but she still could not move. It was done. After all the fear and pain and awe, it was done, and all she could do now was stand and shake.

'Elen,' whispered Geraint.

Elen jerked her head up. Geraint was pointing towards the eastern riverbank. But the camp was not there, neither was the bank it had stood upon. There was only the swirling whiteness of a mist, and within it stood a single figure, so pale it was difficult to pick him out from the fog around him. His green eyes shone brightly, and he stretched out one long hand.

Elen nodded, and she cast the spear again. The Lord caught it neatly in his outstretched hand. It shimmered onyx and silver for a moment, and then the mist spread out and was gone, taking them both with it.

The world came back in a rush. Pandemonium had broken out on the western bank with men screaming and shouting and vowing vengeance. A mass of men from Agravain's camp swirled forward, dragging Elen and Geraint off the bridge. Orders were shouted. Swords rasped as they were freed from sheaths. But none of Urien's men actually charged the bridge. A few spears were thrown, but they fell harmlessly into the river.

Geraint held Elen tight, while the crowd of men around them dissipated, running to defences, for torches, for men to get themselves into ordered lines. As more lights sprang up, Elen was able to see that a lean man still stood between them and the bridge, his sword out and ready in his fist.

Agravain.

As it gradually became clear that the howling across the river would break into no immediate battle, Agravain fell back to stand beside his brother. He shouted to a youth who came panting out of the darkness to stare at Geraint with a boy's delight plain all over his face.

'Donal, wake the herald,' ordered Agravain. 'Mayhap Urien's lieutenant will be better minded to bargain now.'

The boy bowed hastily and sprinted off into the teeming camp. Agravain sheathed his sword, and unafraid turned his back on the river.

'What tale is this, brother?' he asked.

Geraint chuckled. 'A long one. Will you hear it?'

Agravain's gaze slid from Geraint to Elen and back again. 'I had better. Come then.' He began trudging back towards the tents and the brightening camp fires. 'Bring your wife.'

'Thank you, brother,' said Geraint to his back.

He got no answer, so Geraint smiling, took Elen's hand, and she walked with her husband and his brother towards the morning that was to come.

EPILOGUE

The River Usk flowed black and silver beneath the moon. A woman, clad in a black cloak and a black dress, raised her tin lantern high as she picked her careful way down the bank to stand beside a drooping willow tree. Behind her, two men followed, grave and quiet. She pointed to a still shadow in the rippling water. Without hesitation, they waded into the ice-cold shallows, freed the shadow from the entangling roots, turning it so that the dead man's white face could be clearly seen. Straining, they lifted it from the river. Water sluiced off, a chittering silver cascade. The two men laid the corpse on the bank, straightening it as best they could and then they stepped back, their heads bowed in respect so that the black-clad woman could stand beside the dead man.

Morgaine knelt. The blow that had taken his life had driven her brooch into the flesh of his throat. She laid her hand there, feeling how terribly cold it was. She looked a moment into his eyes gone white and grey, all their colour washed away by the river's tears.

'You were not hers to take,' she said, the fury in her words as cold as the death beneath her hand. 'Never hers. Nor yet was it Geraint's place to bring you down. You were mine.

Mine!' She lifted her head, her face white as the moon. 'Listen to me, sister. Hear me well where you have gone. I might have spared them. I might have at the last remembered they were yours and remembered they share blood with my own son. But your son has killed my love. Your son, all your sons, will pay at the last, no matter what mercy they may beg for themselves or theirs.'

She stood then, and turned without glancing back. With her pale lantern to light the way, she led her men, the living and the dead, away into darkness.